Radical Research

Is it still possible, or even advisable, to ask why it is that so much research contributes so little to democratic questioning of the powerful? Has research become just a tool for the powerful, the complacent, the satisfied?

Radical Research explores the view that research is not a neutral tool to be employed without bias in the search for truth. The overall motivation of radical research is to drive democracy further down to individuals engaging with each other, drawing upon their *power* to create community as a facilitator of each others' talents and thus to enrich each other as individuals. Radical research in social contexts implies a radical politics because it raises questions that make the powerful feel uncomfortable, even threatened. This multidisciplinary book, of relevance for those in the social sciences, cultural studies and media studies, draws upon data gathered from a diversity of funded projects in health, education, police training, youth and community, schools, business and the use of information technology. Wide-ranging in appeal and example, data is drawn from observations, interviews, texts, the media and the Internet.

The book presents a radical view of research in a way that enables both beginner and the experienced professional researcher to explore its approaches in the formation of their own views and practices. It progressively leads the reader from discussions of concrete illustrations or cases to critical explorations of the philosophical and methodological concepts, theories and arguments that are central to contemporary debates. In essence, this book shows how to design, develop and write radical research under conditions where 'normal' research rules apply and it offers a ground-breaking and proven alternative to traditional research techniques.

John Schostak is Professor of Education in the Education and Social Research Institute at Manchester Metropolitan University, UK.

Jill Schostak is Visiting Fellow at the University of East Anglia, UK; and currently contract researcher with the College of Emergency Medicine, UK.

Radical Research

Designing, developing and writing
research to make a difference

John Schostak
and Jill Schostak

Routledge
Taylor & Francis Group

LONDON AND NEW YORK

First published 2008
by Routledge
2 Park Square, Milton Park, Abingdon, Oxon, OX14 4RN

Simultaneously published in the USA and Canada
by Routledge
711 Third Ave, New York NY 10017

Routledge is an imprint of the Taylor & Francis Group, an informa business

Transferred to Digital Printing 2009

© 2008 John Schostak and Jill Schostak

Typeset in Times New Roman
by Keystroke, 28 High Street, Tettenhall, Wolverhampton

British Library Cataloguing in Publication Data
A catalogue record for this book is available from the British Library

Library of Congress Cataloging in Publication Data
Schostak, John F.
   Radical research : how to design, develop and write emancipatory research
under "normal" research rules / John Schostak and Jill Schostak.
       p. cm.
   ISBN 978-0-415-39927-2 (hardback) – ISBN 978-0-415 39928-9 (pbk).
1. Social sciences–Research–Methodology–. 2. Power (social sciences) 3. Social control.
4. Democracy. 5. Social change. I. Schostak, Jill. II. Title.
   H62.S3397 2007
   001.4–dc22   2007007853

ISBN10: 0–415–39927–0 (hbk)
ISBN10: 0–415–39928–9 (pbk)
ISBN10: 0–203–93992–1 (ebk)

ISBN13: 978–0–415–39927–2 (hbk)
ISBN13: 978–0–415–39928–9 (pbk)
ISBN13: 978–0–203–93992–5 (ebk)

Contents

List of figures   vi

Introduction   1

1 Bodies in chains   14

2 Unchaining, deconstruction and the intertextual   39

3 Fragmenting and reframing bodies   67

4 Incarnating/incorporating data as understanding and
   explanation   91

5 Events of transposition   113

6 Power, rights and the real   139

7 (Il)legitimate knowledge(s) – wrongs and injuries   159

8 Provocative identities, radical edges: difference, diversity
   and the same   184

9 Universalising the singular: designing the radical game   211

10 W/ri(gh)ting fashions   243

Conclusion   269

References   273
Name Index   286
Subject Index   290

Figures

1.1	The God's-eye view and the wandering-eye view	17
1.2	Producing the good society	31
2.1	Communities and total coverage	54
2.2	From power to power	55
2.3	Signifier and signified	58
2.4	The cut of the signifier	58
2.5	The synchronic and diachronic axis	61
3.1	Many signifiers but one signified	83
3.2	Framing the paranoid	84
3.3	Intentional network as multidimensional space	88
4.1	The visible and the invisible	108
5.1	How to join the dots?	122
5.2	Texts and codes	124
6.1	Humanity and division	148
7.1	Mirror groups	172
7.2	Architectures of the social	180
8.1	Power and contested spaces	193
8.2	Cut of the signifier and liminal spaces	196
9.1	Historic chains of communication	213
9.2	Sign repetition	222
9.3	Representing universal truths	225
9.4	Reconfiguring the field of the visible: friend/enemy	227
9.5	Including all except one	228
9.6	Totality	229
9.7	Always one more . . .	232
9.8	Individual, game and taking sides	233
10.1	The play of design and de-sign	253
10.2	Extract from contents list for TYDE report	267

Introduction

Is it still possible, or even advisable, to ask why it is that so much research contributes so little to democratic questioning of the powerful? Has research become just a tool for the powerful, the complacent, the satisfied? Radical research in social contexts implies a radical politics because it raises questions that make the powerful feel uncomfortable, even threatened. What makes research radical is this political dimension, it suggests the possible overthrow of a previously stable or at least dominant order of ways of knowing, thinking, believing, acting. But if there is an overthrow, won't the resultant circumstances be just another orthodoxy secured through power and thus just as open to radical challenge, starting the whole process over again? Radical research, we argue, thrives in this apparent paradox. It has its counterpart in radical democracy, that project which as Mouffe (1993) writes is forever an 'unfinished revolution'. It is unfinished because every individual is capable of asking questions like:

- Why do things have to be like this?
- Why am I considered to be inferior to them?
- Why do they have more than me?
- So, what is actually going on here? Who benefits from these circumstances and who loses?
- Why can't I do just whatever I want?
- How do I stop them from doing whatever they like and in the process hurting me?
- Why can't we all just get on with each other?

It's in asking such questions that there is a demand for change and action. It is at the point of making this demand that research takes on a radical edge. There are those who want to organise the world around to fit in with their desires, and those who want to be organised, and those who want to be left alone. Some like to compete, others to cooperate. Whether this is said to be 'natural' or 'learnt', it matters little when face to face with the demands of the other. When the powerful make radical demands, it depends on the extent of their power, the force they can bring to bear, the extent to which people are subject to their power, whether or not they succeed in getting what they want. So what can be done to counter the demands of others when they are felt to be excessive? What can be done simply to be fair in the context of some who have so much and many who have so little?

Look around and see how space is used. Who is able to take up space and who has to get out of the way? Who is rich in space, having the freedom to spread around. Who has to confine themselves to little corners, the edges – and why? Some young people aged about ten years old involved in a project with creative practitioners and teachers in a school were asked to walk around the neighbourhood of their school and reimagine their community. One particular focus for the project was racism and how people's attitudes towards others might be changed. The question, then was, can people change?

Boy: Well some people do but some people don't cos like I said you've got people of 30 running round smashing bottles and burning cars but I can't really see well, maybe I can. I can't really see 50 year olds doing it but then I saw that programme with the antisocial old people.

Girl: And um like on TV there's racist people and bullies that are going around and they're so bad that the people, people take their own lives. So then they learn and they send out messages to like other people on the TV not to bully because um that's what will happen, having a conscience on your life for ever like you've killed someone.

Girl2: And my mum said um that if somebody like hung themselves just because of getting bullied um in circle time they said um don't keep it all bottled up inside just tell someone like a friend or teacher or a grown up.

JFS: So circle time is something that came from the project?
[*more than one voice*]Yeah, they done more of it.

Boy: We did it before but since the project I've realised we're doing a lot more of it.

JFS: So that's a good thing.

Girl: Yeah.

Girl: So like you said before 'do you think people will change' I think they would cos they would know what other people will feel like.

Girl2: And they're realising that maybe like one day they might decide to kill their selves just because they're getting bullied in a fight. If I bullied someone and then they killed theirself it'd just make me f' (think?), you might as well have just killed them. Could be they killed theirselves cos of you. I wouldn't like to think of myself as a murderer.

(CAPE 2005)

In this sense of responsibility for the other, the recognition of becoming someone disvalued, blameworthy, reprehensible in the eyes of another and of oneself for an action imagines the possibility of radically alternative selves. That moment of insight begins when an individual looks around at the people passing by and realises that no matter how strong, each individual is vulnerable to the actions of another.

No one is immortal. And ultimately, each, simply as individuals, stripped of their money, their security guards, are equal in the face of death. If we are all equally vulnerable in this sense, then how should we behave towards each other? How is security to be assured? Should we all have equal security? What does having security involve? Does it mean sheltering with the strongest groups, following the orders of the one who commands most respect, or fear? Do I have to give up something to join with them? If enough of us join together can we get more security under better conditions? How do I know what's best? It is in asking such questions that current conditions become open to challenge by alternative propositions. However, those who have a stake in current arrangements have to convince the rest, that is, the greatest number, that there is no alternative or that the alternatives are worse, or that they are powerless to make changes. It is here that research plays a role in public decision-making about what is or is not possible and realisable through action. But how is research to be conceived? What counts as 'real' research, for who and for what purposes and with what consequences?

What is 'normal research'?

Everyone has an image of the 'scientist' drawn by popular culture, modelled a bit on the wild crazy hair of an Einstein figure or the eccentric gadget-maker of spy films or the absent-minded professor lost in thought. Perhaps, more seriously, research is popularly identified with a sense of discovery as when the bewhiskered scientist and *his* robot buggy stuffed with instruments is sent on its way to sniff out the secrets of the planet Mars. Then there is the researcher as 'hero', who engages in medical science and delivers wondrous drugs to cure killer diseases. Or maybe it is the research scientist presenting or being interviewed on television documentaries warning of global warming or the extinction of various species. Whether in the cosmos or on Earth, the scientists boldly go, fearless, intrepid, hot on the trail of undiscovered knowledge treasures. But there are other, more prosaic, images of the researcher. In marketplaces, on street corners and hanging around in pedestrianised areas, market researchers stand clipboard in hand scanning the passers-by for a likely 'fit' – or 'suspect' even, if one were to be cynical for a moment – for their category of the day. Matching their quarry with their target criteria for the day they fire pointed questions, tick the appropriate response boxes thereby fulfilling the quota required by the particular commissioning agency. Less visible by far are the social scientists of academic institutions or government policy researchers. Less visible, less romantic in nature, their work may often be regarded as useless, or as trivia, or even as annoying, perhaps even as an outrage – a waste of public money. Unless there is a patent that someone can make money out of, what is the use of research? Particularly when it is in those useless subjects like sociology or, even worse, cultural studies.

In the UK, in the 1980s, social science came under sustained attack by politicians in the Conservative Party then led by Prime Minister Margaret Thatcher. These were not sciences, it was argued. And, indeed, the name of the body that funded academic research had to change its name from the Social Science Research Council to the much less grand Economic and Social Research Council. What's in a name, or more particularly, the change of a name? The privileging of 'economics' as the first term of the new name picks up on the then and still continuing belief by UK politicians that somehow research should be useful and provide a service to the economy. Second, the loss of the term 'science' symbolically reduces the status of the disciplines involved in researching social phenomena. The status of science is to be reserved for those disciplines able to subject or master their fields of study through the application of mathematically precise models through which the world can be manipulated and outcomes predicted. Science, in short, is equated with precision and mastery.

None of the disciplines composing what had been called the 'social sciences', however, were able to research society and social processes or predict outcomes with comparable precision. Hence they were not worthy to be baptised with such a prestigious name as 'science'. Normal scientific practice thus came to be socially identified with the technical successes of a particular *paradigm* as Kuhn (1970) called it. A paradigm is defined by the key texts in a given scientific discipline that provide the models for doing research. In a sense, they provide the normal recipes for practice. Kuhn also uses the term 'paradigm' to indicate a particular way of seeing the world that results from engaging in the normal practices defining a scientific discipline. If the world of science is to be conceived as composed of measurable entities whose essential identity can be specified in ways that do not change over time, then terms like 'soul', 'mind', 'love' that cannot be measured and whose definitions seem able to change according to whoever does the defining must be excluded. The more like 'normal science' a given discipline becomes, then the higher its prestige and the more likely it can claim the name 'science'. Normal science sees no alternative, only puzzles to solve in order to complete the whole picture of what can be known.

Normal research, in social and cultural forms of inquiry and critique is employed to echo Kuhn's characterisation of normal science as puzzle-solving, that form of practice that does not question the rules of the game, that accepts accepted approaches to doing research and the questions or puzzles that are framed by those who define what counts as problems to be solved. There is great comfort in this. And to be a professional, it is necessary:

> And [in the] antenatal clinic [there] was like, there were anywhere between four and six people around to see all these women, so, um, if there was a really complicated case you just didn't take it anyway. If it was a case that was interesting you might have taken the case and had a quick chat with the woman and see what it's about, and then discuss it with the Registrar or with the Consultant. So this was actually really quite good. Um, you could choose just seeing somebody who was routine for whatever reason just being there because being very young or a little bit older, but no problems in the sense of a real problem and so by seeing them more often, feeling the tummies, you

got an idea of what is normal and what not. So, by doing things, yes, you got experience of. So it progressed and probably, patients you at the beginning you would just briefly talk about, 'These and these findings, to me it looks normal. Is that alright? Can I send her off or shall I organise that?' By the end of the six months you didn't discuss these cases, you did your writing, signed it, and the patient was sent off without being seen by somebody else, or the case even discussed. Um, so, in that sense, it made, we made progress. Yeah, first, even so-called backwards looking where normal things you discussed, and in the end you knew what was normal, what was expected, and you could send these patients off without anybody asking you any more, 'Are you sure what you are doing there?' It was expected that you knew what you were doing and that was quite alright.

(Interview extract from a trainee: Schostak et al. 1999)

Learning to become a medical practitioner demands competencies and confidence that is informed by the best evidence available. It involves being recognised that one has become an 'expert'. Science underpins professional action. But science is not enough:

Yeah, and I hope they take a slimmed-down version of what I have said with them in their career, because it is actually very healthy, even if they go into surgery later on, or whatever, to realise that whatever, that our medical rational way of thinking is a structure, that we impose upon things. Um, and it doesn't necessarily mean that that structure reflects reality, fully. And accidents and difficulties always arise when that mix-up occurs, when someone thinks that our way of thinking is all there is to it. Um, in that case, um, you know, clinicians becomes less effective, I think. But that's a personal, that a very personal opinion. So that's what I try to imbue to them as a personal opinion of what medical science is, what medicine is all about.

(Interview extract from a consultant: Schostak et al. 1999)

Learning that science does not cover everything opens the way for alternative possibilities, for being alert to other ways of seeing. It also creates the conditions for anxieties and uncertainties:

I: I guess if you feel that hospital, certainly in some posts, is about survival, you must develop a sense you can survive anything?

T: Yes, that's what I think now.

I: Oh right.

T: That's what I think now.

I: [Laughs] So that the preparation isn't just 'Wow!' what a wonderful clinical preparation, it's I can take what's thrown at me.

T: Yes. I mean it's dealing with uncertainties, it's dealing with your non-existing knowledge, knowing what to do, dealing with that situation, dealing with, er,

yeah, getting your own adrenalin levels down again, and just being quiet if
there's a volcano erupting next to you, just give confidence to other people in
a situation where you're maybe not that confident but that's what you need
at the moment, doing things that you've never ever done before, but they are
life-saving so you just do it.

> (Interview extract from the consultant with responsibility for trainee
> education in a hospital: Schostak et al. 1999)

The normal is, in a sense, a buffer against the unpredictable framework for dealing
with the unpleasant but necessary. Normal research is employed to include the
application of scientific evidence in everyday settings where informed judgement
is required. Whether it is children thinking about their everyday lives or medical
practitioners facing a client with a problem, the normal research process is initiated.
It begins in a question that is then resolved through thinking processes that are
accepted as 'normal', being aware, of course, that science should not be mindlessly
applied, that there is room for individual judgement.

What is 'radical research'?

Just as there are popular images of the 'normal scientist', there are popular images
of the 'radical'. Radical tends to be associated with revolutionaries, subversives,
rebels, extremism of all sorts – in short, people on the margin of, or who in some
way challenge or oppose, the mainstream. However, there are also positive associations to the term 'radical'. A radical treatment of a life-threatening condition
may save a life. Radical, in its meaning of 'root', also implies a focus on the
essential assumptions, foundations or values of some view, way of life, way of
thinking. It can be evoked in demands for a return to conservative principles just
as much as a way of replacing such principles by others. Such radical returns
to first principles, values, definitions of identity can be used to raise issues of purity,
faithfulness, truth and ethics. It is at the centre of debates and disputes about
cultural identity, race, class, gender, religion and politics. How should one actually
behave, what values should be expressed and who should I identify with as a
'class', 'community', 'people', 'culture', 'faith'? The question of the radical
emerges in conflict, where fundamental approaches to life, to ways of thinking, to
ways of seeing the world are in dispute.

Take, for example, a medical trainee who was for the first time experiencing
working in a gynaecology and obstetrics department of a hospital and had not fully
realised the implications of agreeing to perform terminations of pregnancy. She
had not sorted it out in her own mind and, at the time of interview, was no longer
'keen' on this subject area. One termination in particular, at twenty-one weeks,
continued to cause her distress:

T: [A]nd the other thing is like, you're in a big machinery, you have, you have to
function well, so you and your personal needs, they sometimes, um, yeah, put
apart, put aside, or I don't know how to say that.

I: Suppressed?

T: Yeah, they're suppressed. But they build up and build up and you have to get rid of, of them somehow. But with the, I mean, with the Thursday release course, and, you, you know you get a feeling and you do your exercising and you know that you have to do a kind of a house-cleaning, a house-keeping in your self, so you know, so you get a bit of an inside of yourself and you know what to do. You get an idea of how to handle the problem and how to go with it.

(Interview extract from a trainee: Schostak et al. 1999)

Reflecting back on her six-month experience in Obstetrics and Gynaecology, although still psychologically 'traumatised', she felt it was a worthwhile experience because, as a result, she 'has a feeling for it', which she otherwise would not have. The conflict here is between personal sensibilities and the 'big machinery'. The demand to 'function' no matter what leads to a repression of feelings that actually cannot just be ignored. There is a build-up of feelings until a 'house-cleaning' has to take place. Feelings are ready to erupt through the machinery unless some further action takes place. The question concerns the nature of the action – is it about dealing with the problems in a way that leaves the circumstances that gave rise to them in place; or is it about changing the circumstances? In a similar case, another trainee had a clearer conception that it was against her faith to perform terminations. She was allowed, of course, to follow her conscience in this matter. However, someone had to do the terminations. The fundamental problem of rightness or wrongness was not resolved as such. And nor could it be to the satisfaction of all, where there are a plurality of viewpoints, many of which are in radical opposition to each other. For any individual meeting what seem to be impossible demands, the question is how to position themselves in relation to the alternatives. Is it just a matter of 'house-cleaning', or is there something else at stake? Continually defusing the inner tensions never attends to the underlying issues. It leaves the 'big machinery' in place. Similarly, opting out by calling on conscience also leaves the underlying tensions in place and may stimulate resentment from those who take on the burden. Research that undertakes to explore such underlying issues raises questions that go to the roots of what is at stake for those who are committed to particular solutions. Since different individuals and groups in society have different levels of power to act according to and enforce their commitments, the less power-ful will have to resort to different kinds of strategies to undertake research that challenges the status quo.

One familiar example can be seen in the strategy of the investigative journalist, uncovering the hidden and denouncing wrongdoing. It may involve 'outing', that is, revealing the otherwise hidden or disguised identities of individuals, groups, organisations. It includes asserting publicly the critical, radical and fiercely inde-pendent role of the journalist as researcher – it is in a sense an 'heroic stance'. Many experience threats; others may lose their jobs; some have gone to prison and, indeed, some have been killed (cf., Muhlmann 2004). Much investigative journalism may initially be carried out covertly in order to get to the 'truth' that would not otherwise be told. Similarly, sociologists researching dangerous gangs, for example, might also research covertly and also publish without employing real names of people and places (Patrick 1973). Here the aim is to raise awareness of conditions rather than to blame individuals and organisations. Raising awareness of poverty, violence, unemployment does not, of course, necessarily succeed in stimulating an ethical and political concern amongst those who acting together could make changes. Bringing change needs further strategies. Rather like covert-observation research strategies, a more proactive approach might be adopted that involves 'smuggling' practices, values and courses of action into a project, that is, operating by stealth. The researcher operates under the mantle of 'normal' research, hiding or infiltrating the radical research agenda that enables the collection and interpretation of data in ways that ultimately deconstruct and transform the project. However, this may progressively lead to conflict within the project as the implications of the smuggled agenda are gradually experienced. The conflict might lead either to a breakdown or a modification of the project. A similar but less problematic approach builds in mechanisms of open negotiation into the project. It is the stance of the facilitator, the broker of interests. It is an approach that recognises different interests and seeks ways of including and managing differences in an open and fair manner. At its best, such an approach can lead to radical change within groups, communities, organisations, systems. At its worst, it produces compromises enforced through an alliance of the most powerful. This is where negotiation can lead to a process of making deals or trade-offs between interest groups and thus carries all the shady connotations of the word 'dealing'. A deal is, in a sense, a settlement with power. Striking a deal already implies that some interests are sacrificed whether to the 'greater good' or to the good of the desired 'cause', or 'interest'.

The purpose of radical research, however, is to suggest an alternative to the preceding strategies. It is an approach that maintains a radical openness to difference while seeking to build communities of support for difference. To maintain such an approach means that there is a sense in which radical research is 'post-disciplinary' in that it refuses to be reduced to the confines of particular disciplines and refuses to keep the boundaries of disciplines intact in their combination as multidisciplinary or integrated approaches to a given study of the social world. Rather it seeks a more encompassing approach, a kind of critical philosophical refocusing of research and action on the political, the cultural and the social without splitting them into separate disciplines: economy, sociology, psychology . . . and so on. What this means will be progressively explored through each of the chapters. What it does not mean is that there is any straightforward recipe that can be culled from a textbook and applied mechanistically. To bring the kind of paradigmatic change described by Kuhn (1970) that impacts on the social world cannot be found in the textbooks of normal research. Rather, it is to be found in the questioning undertaken by people face to face with issues in their everyday lives.

Designing issues

What does a research design hope to achieve? Does it seek to settle a question, resolve an issue, promote a course of action, map the terrain of an unknown territory? Radicalness, in the sense employed in this book, is not about war, destruction, terror, but about constructing the cooperation necessary to engage with change, to keep up with the productions of difference and, thus, to be creative about developing ever-inclusive communities. How this is done involves getting into the ways that we think about social conditions, the conceptual tools we employ, how evidence is formed and what counts as 'proof' or 'sufficient reason' or sufficient 'warrant' for decision-making and action at intimate, personal, local and global levels. There is a sense in which social-research methodologies have always been radical cultural practices, having to do with drawing out the opportunities for freedom of action in relation with otherness. However, research, like any other social practice, can become routinised and compromised by the powerful. Hence, design has to be undertaken to counter routinisation and compromise. How?

A key demand of radical research is that any discussions of 'findings' are in the context of what is at stake in adopting particular perspective-shaping methodologies. Where power is located – the Heavens, Nature, the Leader, the People or Reason – shapes the way the world is seen and the extent to which action to change the world about can be undertaken. How the world is configured in terms of who has access to what, who can do what and where is an exercise of power. This has implications for what is seen as data, how it is to be processed and what sense can be made of it. Each chapter explores power, its location and its limits. Implicit is the theme of design and de-sign. Where design structures, de-sign loosens and opens the possibilities for a play of alternatives to inform judgement and action ethically, politically. Chapter 1 begins the exploration of those enchaining processes through which bodies of individuals are controlled and incorporated into political, rational or faith 'bodies', each of which provide a vision of the 'good' society.

Radical research, it is argued, takes place at the points of irresolvable tension between world views. Chapter 1 sets into tension the relation between power as that dominating force of the state, the king, the god or nature with the powers of the individual as one who seeks freedom. The central theme of the equation of rights and powers is introduced based on a discussion of Spinoza's conception of *potestas* (centralised power) and *potentia* (power of the individual). By focusing on the near equality of people's natural powers so that no one individual is so strong and powerful to be immune to a fatal attack from another, the strategy of forming communities of mutual interest based on the desire for protection is elaborated through successive chapters. But community – no matter how secure and comfortable – does not absolutely resolve the conflicts between what people want and what they consider to be right so that, as in Chapter 2, there is the tension between 'keeping it together' and 'blowing apart'. It is here in the tensions that radical research explores the ranges of viewpoints through which culture is potentially enriched and finds that loosening of the chains is at once liberating and threatening. Where Chapter 1 raised the issue of the politics of methodology, Chapter 2 introduces deconstructive approaches exploiting the structure of language itself through which worlds as systems of interpretation are both constructed and deconstructed. This provides the basis for radical research to explore the conditions and potentials of change in the organisation of power. However, Chapter 2 focuses on the pervasive experience of an 'unchaining' of the bonds of community leading to the fragmentation that is the subject of Chapter 3. But in fragmentation of the social order there is the potential of the multitude, the crowd, the rabble as alternative expressions of power. The multitude thus has many forms of expression, each capable of enlarging the fault lines of power. Just as the multitude overflows the boundaries of power, so language slips from its bonds with content and opens up the possibilities for reconfiguring the visible, the audible, the real according to desires, interests, needs. Each individual of the multitude can form a multiplicity of relationships to satisfy their interests. The patterns of their relationships provide a means of focusing on the fluidity and complexity of lived experience as a precondition to designing action.

Data, then, is not given as fixed but is open to reconfiguration and, thus, alternative ways of seeing. The production of ways of seeing, ways of configuring the world about depends as much upon the power of states to enforce as on the potentials of individuals to deconstruct and reframe the possibilities. Chapter 4 explores data in terms of the visible and the invisible, who controls 'seeing' and thus what can be seen and known. Where Descartes based what could be known on the power of individuals to reason, knowledge is today so complex, so vast that no one individual can know more than a minute fraction through their own resources. The problem, then, for radical research is how to design approaches to knowing and thus engaging in action that do not blindly trust those who claim to be experts. What is the ground of the valid? If there are multiple ways of seeing, multiple forms of community, multiple worlds that can be aesthetically, ethically, politically constructed, what is the basis for action?

Events become significant by and large after the event, as explored in Chapter 5. How can one know that the event currently taking place is momentous or trivial? Only after the French or the American Revolution or the fall of the Soviet Bloc can the event be named as a fundamental change and not a minor hiccough. For Rancière, politics has two meanings. The first has its roots in the concept of the police, the process through which each part of society conforms to the whole. The second is a rare occurrence, as in the Fall of Ceauşescu or the American War of Independence where there is an eruption that has the potential to overthrow the previous social order. How does this begin? Are there implications for the design of radical research in ordinary everyday circumstances?

The problem of radical research centres very much on power, rights and the way in which the real is constructed. Following a revolution, there is a redistribution of rights and powers. But how should people be treated and represented in public arenas of decision and policy-making? Chapter 6 goes more deeply into the relationship between how people talk about the world, how they can make their accounts heard and the forms of political power that most readily realises the different needs and interests of people. In short, how may radical research design forms of action that includes the rights of all?

In the police order, as Rancière calls it, alternative viewpoints are excluded. How then is any sense of injustice or wrong felt by the excluded to be made known other than through violent eruptions? Chapter 7 explores how the sense of wrong is raised and managed as well as how there is a need to include the repressed, the forbidden, the invisible in order to underpin freedom of expression as a basis for political stability. The crowd provides what may be called a levelling experience, where each individual is no more than any other individual. It is in such a sense of equality that the haughty can be humbled and the powerful brought down. As progressively elaborated in the preceding chapters, language itself provides the means for the destabilisation necessary for a reframing that includes the excluded.

Every telling is a way of writing particular agendas into the more general agendas of people who want freedom, security and a sense of fulfilment. In order to make change identities become provocative, that is, in its Latin meaning 'call forth' the complexities of experience to escape the restricting definitions that engineer their thinking, confine their actions. Through provocations, the edges of boundaries are contested, and ambiguous, liminal spaces emerge. Chapter 8 explores the kinds of identity that emerge, split between Power as the controlling order and the powers of the individual in conjunction with others negotiating new forms of order. The promiscuity, as it were, of language in conjunction with the new globalising technologies are provoking the conditions for change by enabling a reach across boundaries, action and a play of identities that erode the containing powers of individual states. The emphasis falls back upon how communities emerge in everyday practices both in their local and global dimensions. Radical research contributes to the rethinking of individuals and their communities by building into radical designs the means through which the voices of all are able through 'oratory', through making accounts, making appeals and framing demands in dialogue with others be effective in the public arenas of communities.

In particular, provocation brings about the radical game through calling forth the voice, a voice that demands a listening, a recognition and, thus, a witnessing. It is in this process that difference is validly incorporated into the designs of the radical. Chapter 9 explores the design of the radical game that is founded upon the conflicts, the disagreements that emerge when two or more individuals and groups engage with each other to universalise their demands. The issue for the radical is not what is generalisable or what is universal but how to construct, deconstruct and transform the 'general' and the 'universal'. If radical research has the goal of bringing about the desired state of affairs of including all people with all their differences, then the spaces for the inclusion of difference has to be designed into each project with each discovery of an otherwise excluded difference. Is this possible, or even desirable? Since there is always another difference with every new-born individual, every calling forth of a voice, where a new configuration of the way the world can be seen and talked about, then what is desirable is difference itself as cultural, personal and community enrichment.

Writing difference into the ways in which the world becomes meaningful is itself a radical act. It is the place where rights are accountable and the defining, shaping, restricting rites of passage are transformed into rights of transposition, trans-formation. Writing the project is not a summary act to be undertaken after a project has been completed. Writing goes on all the time from the first ideas for a proposal through the processes of negotiation with people in the chosen field sites, the formation of data, its analysis and interpretation, through to the final acts of creating a project report and disseminating it. Radical research is itself a writing project at every stage. With every interpretation of what the research 'really means', a new writing of it emerges. Through the process of writing, the radical becomes embedded in ways of seeing and acting. Chapter 10 explores how writing fashions the sense of the project as an event, its beginnings, middles and ends.

Radical research is all about the case that can be made for the inclusion of difference. It starts from the multiple perspectives of individuals voicing their demands whether in particularistic or universalistic forms. It begins, therefore, in the recognition of dis-agreement, that is to say, heterogeneity. Each chapter therefore returns to the core design themes of describing what is going on from the viewpoints of people – that is, ethnography as a writing of and about peoples – and thus identifying the case composed of differences as a basis for identifying what kinds of actions can be developed to bring change, which in turn can be evaluated for their capacity to include the different voices and demands made by individuals. Without making a difference desired by people the radical is pointless. In brief, there are what may be called four moments to radical research:

1. *Description*: what's going on? What are the material and symbolic structures, processes, identities, cultural practices, events and narratives that together comprise an experience of the everyday realities of peoples?
2. *Analysis*: deconstruction – reframing. How have controlling and binding categories been constructed? What is the basis for their persistence? Are there repressed, hidden, excluded ranges of meaning, associations, conflicts, disagreements that once revealed can unsettle the constraining structures and thus mobilise forces for change?
3. *Action*: action research, implementation of innovations, education. What kinds of action are possible through which transformations may be made? What kinds of actions or mechanisms and procedures need to be incorporated into project designs in order to mobilise the expression of demands from all viewpoints? Can action research, as a process of combining research and action into a cyclical process of refining actions towards desired outcomes, be disseminated throughout a community of action? How are innovative actions to be implemented and what kinds of education can provide the support for transformation through action?

4. *Evaluation*: setting in train a further cycle of description, analysis, action and evaluation. Was the original description appropriate? What was lacking? What has emerged through the disturbances caused by action? What needs to be incorporated in order to be inclusive of excluded differences? How can the original design for research and action be modified, redesigned to ensure inclusion?

Each dimension is explored in the particular themes of each chapter. Radical methodologies begin at the point where individuals associate with others in order to organise their needs, interests, ambitions, desires and so on. Where the interests of one set of associations conflicts with another, then there needs to be some sort of political organisation that can manage those conflicts outside of war. Radical research is essential to the promotion of creative, supportive relations between individuals and the communities they compose. The game plans of both normal science and radical research revolve around a kernel question: why is anything intelligible at all? The answers in each case both differ and haunt each other. Where normal research begins with a schooling in instructions to solve puzzles, radical research begins with a drawing out, that is, an education, a calling forth of questions that dis-solve the puzzles. The overall motivation of radical research is to drive democracy further down to individuals engaging with each other, drawing upon their *power* to create community as a facilitator of each others' talents and thus to enrich each other as individuals.

Chapter 1

Bodies in chains

Wanting to do something, to make a change, to see things as they really are, not as they seem, not as *They* want you see them? Is it possible? Is it really possible to see radically? Being radical implies some counter-stance to the world as it is, a stance that is active, engaged and committed to bringing about change. But this demands some conception of the world as it is, as it 'should' be and where 'I' am in it. Being committed and engaged means that any such conceptions of a 'world' and an 'I' are embodied in material realities where everything is in some way connected as in some sort of either mechanical or organic whole. Can you just ask someone what they do, who they are and this whole shape of connected entities making up 'reality' will just pop up? Will a world where people are located in places caught up in some combination of plans, actions and contexts of circumstances begin to be mapped out?

JFS: In order to start can you just sort of give me a sense of your role a' as you see it in relationship to this area?
Andy: To the project, or to this area?
JFS: To this area generally so I can get some sort of context.

(Transcript extracts, 2006)

It begins with 'this area', the defining moment, the setting of boundaries, the framing of context, giving it the sense of a place. This shaping, controlling the field that will be talked about, the field within which things, people and actions and organisations become visible, nameable, addressable. For Andy, once the question of 'area' has been settled, responsibilities, identities, purposes, causes, relationships, histories and spheres of action can be named, made known, assigned:

Andy: OK, well, um, I'm responsible for the youth service for X and Y. And I also have a borough wide brief for Millennium Volunteers and for young carers as well. And another part of me remit is uh trainin' young people and adults in youth work. And that's how this came about because whereas I was initially asked to get involved in the parenting course it was very much about what we could do for these children of the parents who were having problems.
JFS: Right.

There is a sense of narrative, of a story ongoing, one thing leading to another, purposefulness, being involved in something with people, for people. As he talks, Andy adds detail upon detail, trying to give an accurate nuanced description of 'how it started', its 'origins', and why it 'fitted' the then purpose:

Andy: So that's how it transpired and it just so happened that we had a course already off the peg that we were doing which was called 'Youth Work and the Transfer of Local Skills' which was based between eight and ten weeks – it depends sometimes on the group – but we aim to end it after eight weeks but sometimes it lasts longer which this one just has. And it's very much about . . . it started out as a senior members course. In other words it was for, originally, for young people who expressed an interest in youth work but were too young. So that was how it started out, and then it turned into this transferable skills course cos we suddenly realised it actually fitted into key skills which is—

There is a sense of luck – 'it just so happened' – and of contingency – 'it depends sometimes on the group' – and of a discovery of connectedness, rather like the 'aha' experience of a sudden realisation that the 'transferable skills course' fits with 'key skills':

JFS: Key skills, do you mean in relationship?
Andy: Key skills in relationship to like every school and every college and the whole world is doing.

The image is of a totality, a unity of parts, each contributing to and fitting within a whole, a single purpose, a nameable body or mechanical system of action. It is the realisation, the 'aha' not of radical difference, but of being a member of a group one hadn't quite realised before as in Denzin's (1989) alcoholics who realise that they *really are* alcoholics. In the social worker's case, all is subsumed under a directing policy or body (whether this 'body' is organic or 'mechanical' in nature) of policies within the body politic – he recognises that what he is meant to be doing is fitting in, being the same. And yet, there's a hint of resistance in the tone of the voice which leaps from every school and college to the 'whole world' with its grand universal categories that leads to a further realisation:

JFS: Yeah yeah yeah.
Andy: And the xxxx based citizenship.
JFS: Yeah.
Andy: And all that sort of stuff I won't bore you with that but we suddenly realised that the course wasn't so much about young people wanting to become youth workers but young people who needed support in terms of self-esteem you know, stuff like that. So we messed around a bit with the course,

took bits of key skills out. So, as you're probably aware you know with key skills you have to look at sort of literacy and numeracy and stuff like that.

The realisation that a universal concept or general purpose like the 'citizenship course' had to be interpreted, interrupted, shaped to be appropriate to particular needs in a particular place and time with specific individuals on a 'course', initiates a warping, a twisting of the structure:

JFS: Mmm.

Andy: So we twisted that a bit cos a lot of the young people um we work with are not good with those sort of things and in eight weeks you couldn't do a great deal in that way but what we thought is well if we do a lot of group work skills at least um they'll feel a bit more confident. And then maybe we can think of other courses later so that was the sort of aim really. So, it was very much around confidence building, equal opportunities – we obviously have to get in because we're an equal opportunities service you know – and also uh have fun. So a lot of things we do, sort of group work games to get them to sort of um communicate because a lot of the young people we find who are coming are very quiet, weren't used to being in a group, weren't very happy being in a group, so the first four weeks to be honest is very much the emphasis on having fun but obviously learning something from it.

The narrative ends with a resolution of the tension between the whole and the parts. It is a resolution which seems to privilege the needs of the young people. Yet not entirely. What the young people 'need' is defined in terms of some image of what they ought to need in order to rectify a lack: they're 'not good with those sort of things', they need 'confidence', they're 'not used to being in a group'. It is too early to say from these transcript extracts whether the image of the 'whole' that is figured here by the social worker is 'organic' or 'mechanistic'. However, there is a sense of dynamism, of pliability, of evolution rather than rigidity and stasis which seems to suggest an organic rather than a mechanistic conception. Whatever is the case, there seems to be a tension between the individual and the whole which, on the face of it, seems resolvable by making the young people fit for social life by constructing a course of activities to help them learn through fun. To become a part, they have to be schooled to fit into the 'serious order' of demands, duties and responsibilities. Fun, of course, has the potential to subvert as well as lure. Young people want to have fun, have a laugh (Willis 1977). But the adult of the 'serious order' wants fun to be kept within bounds. Already it is tempting to see here the emergence of a 'universalising case', something that binds, something that encompasses, within which Andy works in relation to the others who are the actors within 'the universalising case'. He is a bearer of some universal values that not only allow but also professionally demand that he engages with people at the basic levels of families and the ways people associate with each other in the streets. He 'incarnates' those socially or governmentally universalising values, that is, he is the concrete, particular, historical instance through which professional work is undertaken in this particular place with these particular people.

So what are the opportunities for radical research? How does it begin? One beginning is to explore the processes by which complexity is captured by the simplifying categories of normal everyday practices. The opportunity to engage in research radically involves identifying what is at stake for people in engaging in 'normal' everyday practices, those practices of 'fitting in' and getting others to 'fit in' or engaging in strategies in response to their refusal to fit in.

Normal research: what's at stake?

Normal research, rather in the sense that Kuhn (1970) employed his descriptions of normal science, refers to how research is conducted in the context of prevailing, compelling ways of seeing the world as a brute reality, a reality that stands 'out there' as something to be encountered, described, understood, mastered. Its features can be seen in any textbook. Its ultimate purpose is to master a view of reality in such a way that all can be explained, all can be subsumed under the general, the universal vision or the covering law of positivistic science (Hempel 1942), with no loose ends, nothing that is not a part of the body of scientific knowledge. It requires some sort of ultimate vantage point as in Figure 1.1, an 'X' where all can be surveyed, like looking out from the top-floor windows of the world's largest most encompassing skyscraper and seeing the scurrying people below, watching their antics, mapping their behaviour, manipulating their comings and goings in what can only seem at street level to be a complex, mystifying labyrinth where everyday events always have the potential for the unexpected, the accidental.

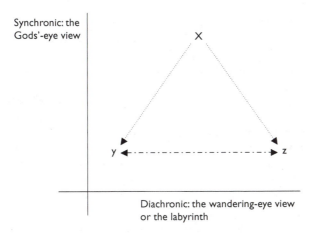

Figure 1.1 The God's-eye view and the wandering-eye view

The Enlightenment philosophers led the way in contesting the position ('X' in Figure 1.1) from which the possession and the legitimation of all knowledge could be claimed. It is a strategy where the radical subjectivity of the individual thinker could suspend all prior thoughts about, beliefs in and dogma concerning the world and how it came to be created. As such, radical subjectivity was in a position to contest the position of God as creator, the one who fashions and sees the 'whole picture' – a position that could, and often did, bring the wrath of vested interests to bear on the one making the claims. As in any picture, whether the religious, the mythical or the scientific world views of Enlightenment thinkers, everything has its place, both the shadow and the light. Radical subjectivity, while not yet mastering everything, seeks to master all and subject all to the will whether under Reason, as in Descartes, or under Desire as in Sade. Effectively, one founding myth is substituted by another: Reason or Desire takes the place of God – or they are in complicity with each other. Of course, such challenges in Western cultures can be traced back to other periods of philosophical activity such as Ancient Greece, where Socrates, Plato and Aristotle debated with others about the nature of the world. And around the world, whether in Egypt, India, China or elsewhere, there was the search for knowledge based on human reasoning, observation and skill. It is in these acts that the position of the 'X' is made the focus of disagreement, contest, conflict – especially war. It is the place of power and, as such, a highly desirable place to occupy. And from the position of power, all can be commanded through chains of control, reasoning or belief. This is what is at stake for individuals and, in particular, individuals who see themselves as members of a people subjected to the needs, interests, desires of the people.

That 'knowledge is power' is a cliché, but, more threateningly, knowledge is political. The control of knowledge and, in particular, the control over what is to count as knowledge is power. For Adorno, O'Connor (2005) argues, every philosophy of knowledge, or epistemology

> is determined by a normative commitment to how the world *ought to be*. Epistemologies thus work within rationalities that defend particular pictures of the subject–object relation, of relations in the world. The description of the subject–object relation is therefore never a neutral report of purely natural responses.
>
> (O'Connor 2005: 1)

Each normative commitment constructs a position 'X' from which a god or a godlike being can look down from and map out the entire world according to Reason or Desire as a single fully connected, organic body or structural unity composed of mutually related, functional parts. Of course, there was, and for many still is, only one view concerning how the world ought to be, and that is the one ordained by God, Reason, Science, Tradition or the Leader. There have been, and still are, dangers in being seen to challenge such orthodoxies. Socrates was put to death for having corrupted the morals of the youth; Galileo was imprisoned for the sacrilege of challenging the church's views on cosmology (1633). The influence of such thinkers as Descartes had personal consequences. A friend of Spinoza, Adriaan Koerbagh 'was convicted of impiety and sentenced in 1668', and this friend's death in prison was probably the reason he (Spinoza) decided to publish one of his major works anonymously (Balibar 1998: 23). In contemporary times, the consequences of challenging orthodoxies can be equally dangerous – either life-threatening, as in the case of Salman Rushdie (1989) for publishing his novel the *Satanic Verses*, or career-threatening, as in the case of being pro- or anti- some prevailing political view, or being made the object of scorn and ridicule, such as the Picard–Barthes controversy in France (Barthes 1987; Rabaté 2002; Davis 2004) or the more recent diatribes against 'postmodernists' as exemplified by Sokal and Bricmont (1997, 1998). While courting controversy may often be a good career move in itself, 'leaking' research that damages powerful interests or attempting to undertake research into powerful interests remains a risky enterprise whether for life or career or reputation. Research that radically upsets the status quo is troubling. What it does is assert that freedom to explore the roots of 'ways of seeing', 'ways of thinking' and their associated social, economic, political and cultural practices is absolute.

The Enlightenment names a philosophical, social, cultural and political project focused upon rationality and freedom challenging the received opinions, beliefs and knowledge about the world as well as having implications for forms of government. Allied to scientific and industrial advance as well as creative experimentation in the arts, it sets apart and establishes the sense of the modern mind and 'modernity' from all that had gone before. The march of the enlightenment impulse and modernity has been, it seems, unstoppable. Through it, people came to see the world differently. From the position of the 'X' in Figure 1.1, God/Tradition/Faith was ousted by 'Reason'. The rule of reason could be applied to anything. As applied to education, Locke (1989) considered that reason should rule passion, even to the extent of training children to go to the toilet only at set times in order to bring the bodily functions under the rule of the rational will. It was the mastery of reason over nature, the flesh. Indeed, a German educationalist, Schreber (Schatzman 1973) wrote many influential educational tracts describing in detail the ways in which children should be trained from birth, focusing upon the rational control of behaviour, a precursor, perhaps, to Skinner's (1953) behaviourism. In such a view, human beings are not constrained to whatever 'is', not reduced to being a bundle of instincts, a product solely of 'nature', like animals, but are able to construct culture, generate civilisations and have control over their destiny, employing reason in the creation of that freely chosen destiny – a power previously attributable only to the Divine. In short, nature and, in particular, the body, was to be enchained by reason. If people could be educated according to reason, and reason was subject only to the will, then people could be moulded and fashioned to fit any rationally produced vision.

Transitions and revolutions are rarely smooth. Adherents to world views tend not to let go without a struggle. How could rule by reason fit with the traditional forms of society, with the vision of a world created by and ruled by God? What would happen if, through the application of reason, it could be demonstrated that the Earth was not made in six days,[1] that it was more than its biblically defined age, that human beings were not made but evolved from the apes, that indeed, the Earth was not the centre of the universe but circled around a sun that itself was lost at the edge of one of millions of galaxies . . . What then?

One solution is to recast God in terms of Reason. If God is perfect, then He is hardly likely to be irrational. Even more usefully, Descartes used the existence of God to solve the problem of other subjectivities. As a rational subject, I can only prove my own existence through the formula, 'I think, therefore, I am'. I can prove that 'I am', but can I found the *independent* existence of others, the Other (the 'X', the whatever it is that's outside of 'me'), on 'me', my individual 'ego'? The existence of God as a locus of Absolute Reason transcends all individual rational egos, hence, it could be argued, assuring their existence and the existence of the world and providing a unifying centre for everything. This, of course, is fine if one believes in the existence of God in the first place. But suppose we do. In this case, there is a powerful alliance, hegemony one might say, between religion and reason. But in the process the ways in which people think about themselves and about God undergoes an alteration; that is to say, their identities change. This in itself, of course, is problematic, making a split as it were, between a prior conception and a modern conception. Those who are uncomfortable with such a transformation may want to cling to 'fundamental' beliefs, values, ways of thinking and ordering society; preferring to keep the location of authority with the 'word of God' as revealed through sacred texts and interpreted by an authorised priesthood; that is, preferring to exclude reason as a basis of action in order to rely on faith in the revealed words of a divine being. Each is radical to the other; each are subversive of the other. As well as the split between a prior revealed truth and truth discovered through reason, there is a split inherent between mind and body, the ideal and the material. If the individual *sovereignly* decides to doubt all previous knowledge and suspend belief in the everyday realities, then any *thing* that appears to consciousness is just that: appearance. The solidity of the world is just what appears, the phenomena of consciousness – hence, there is a split between what appears (Kant's phenomenon) and reality as it is in-itself (Kant's noumenon). The mind and body split continues, in a sense, the spirit–body split of Christianity – hence paving the way for an accommodation between the two. Where the mind/spirit is set above the body, then there is potential conflict if what the mind/spirit considers to

1 As one instance of a resurgence of creationism. 'Dozens of schools are using creationist teaching materials condemned by the government as "not appropriate to support the science curriculum", the *Guardian* has learned. The packs promote the creationist alternative to Darwinian evolution called intelligent design and the group behind them said 59 schools are using the information as "a useful classroom resource"'. The *Guardian*, James Randerson, science correspondent, Monday, 27 November 2006.

be right does not accord with the passions, the urges, the instincts, the weaknesses of the body. Constructing the chains of discipline, control, surveillance become paramount in order to overcome, free oneself from nature. Given that Descartes and others saw geometry as the paradigmatic method that is both exact and practical in terms of defining and manipulating objects in the world, the implication for research strategies is that the object is split away from the subject, the subject seeking to master the object by isolating it, quantifying it, measuring it in order to manipulate it. This is as true of one's own body as of the world about. Can the split be resolved in some other way?

Spinoza took a different strategy while adhering to Cartesian principles. It was one that did not involve an essential split as between nature and mind/spirit/God. Rather, the 'fixed and unchangeable order of nature or the chain of natural events' is due to God and thus 'the universal laws of nature, according to which all things exist and are determined, are only another name for the eternal decrees of God, which always involve truth and necessity' (Spinoza 2004: 44):

> Now since the power in nature is identical with the power of God, by which alone all things happen and are determined, it follows that whatever man, as a part of nature, provides himself with to aid and preserve his existence, or whatsoever nature affords him without his help is given him solely by the Divine power, acting either through human nature or through external circum- stance. So whatever human nature can furnish itself with by its own efforts to preserve its existence, may be fitly called the inward aid of God, whereas whatever else accrues to man's profit from outward causes may be called the external aid of God.
>
> (Spinoza 2004: 45)

This opens out a radically different project, one where the body and the objects of the world are not seen as 'corrupt' (through original sin), not split apart from the 'nature' of the mind, nor set into an inferior relation under the control of the mind and reason. This strategy enables Spinoza to analyse nature, reason, power and rights in a way that has important implications for radical research method- ologies. Given that 'the power in nature is identical with the power of God' then what is 'right' is also identical with that power:

> it is certain that nature, taken in the abstract, has sovereign right to do anything she can; in other words, her right is co-extensive with her power. The power of nature is the power of God, which has sovereign right over all things; and inasmuch as the power of nature is simply the aggregate of the powers of all her individual components, it follows that every individual has sovereign right to do all that he can; in other words the rights of an individual extend to the utmost limits of his power as it has been conditioned. Now it is the sovereign law and right of nature that each individual should endeavour to

preserve itself as it is, without regard to anything but itself; therefore this sovereign law and right belongs to every individual, namely to exist and act according to its natural conditions. We do not here acknowledge any difference between mankind and other individual natural entities, nor between men endowed with reason and those to whom reason is unknown; nor between fools, madmen, and sane people.

(Spinoza 2004: 45)

Thus Spinoza does not accept any position privileging reason above non-reason, wisdom above foolishness, sanity above madness. It is what may be called an ultra-Cartesianism (cf. Balibar 1998) which pushes the whole method of doubting everything to its furthest extremes essentially recasting reason as simply another aspect of nature having no more rights to a privileged position than any other natural power. This has important consequences for democratic projects as will be discussed in a later section. At this point, what is at stake for the individual is that the 'X' in Figure 1.1 is equivalent to the power of nature (which, for the religious minded, in turn is identical to the decrees of God) and each and every individual has the natural and *sovereign* (or God-given) right to survey, pursue his or her interests and protect his or her own position in the world. This is prior to any revelation that may be provided through the prophets and scriptures. It is this that is most threatening to the vested interests of any institutionalised religion or other power that seeks to overrule the sovereignty of the natural rights of individuals that are equivalent to the powers given by nature. In his own project, Spinoza was trying to make a distinction between philosophy and religion, on the one hand, and, on the other, distinguish true religion from the interpretations of the various churches. The radicality of his approach made him, for many, a hated figure.

There are three key approaches implicit in this discussion so far, that can now be drawn out in terms of their implications for research design. There are those that:

1. frame research to be consistent with orthodoxies;
2. challenge or suspend these orthodoxies in ways that create a split between mind and material realities;
3. challenge or suspend orthodoxies without splitting mind from material realities.

Orthodoxies have their religious, political, cultural, economic and social dimensions. All would be easy if each dimension fitted the other like gloves, each moulding to the other. Each, however, is typically at odds with the others. Religions claim that knowledge and laws are revealed by a god. The sphere of rule of a god may be localised to a particular 'people', and their territory or it may be claimed to be universal and thus global for all peoples. It is, of course, useful for powerful people if they can claim to be appointed by God, or indeed, be a living god. However, there is potential for conflict between priests who claim authority over scriptural interpretation and monarchs, and between monarchs and the aristocracy, and between the aristocracy and the business elites, and between these and the 'people'. How do you get all these different interest groups to fit harmoniously? This, it may be recalled, was the central conflict explored through the words of the social worker attempting to design a course that would shape the minds, attitudes and behaviours of young people to 'fit in'.

There are stark choices: either fit people into the system or, failing that, exclude them; or change the system. Each choice involves the use of power in some way. For Hobbes writing at the same time as Spinoza and Descartes, the question of how to resolve conflicts between individuals and interest groups is to be resolved under the agency of a powerful leader that all fear. Knowledge is not enough without the power to enforce it. Where does that power come from?

> The Power of a man, to take it universally, is his present means to obtain some future apparent good, and is either original or instrumental.
>
> Natural power is the eminence of the faculties of body, or mind; as extraordinary strength, form, prudence, arts, eloquence, liberality, nobility. Instrumental are those powers which, acquired by these, or by fortune, are means and instruments to acquire more; as riches, reputation, friends, and the secret working of God, which men call good luck. For the nature of power is, in this point, like to fame, increasing as it proceeds; or like the motion of heavy bodies, which, the further they go, make still the more haste.
>
> The greatest of human powers is that which is compounded of the powers of most men, united by consent, in one person, natural or civil, that has the use of all their powers depending on his will; such as is the power of a Commonwealth: or depending on the wills of each particular; such as is the power of a faction, or of diverse. factions leagued. Therefore to have servants is power; to have friends is power: for they are strengths united.
>
> (Hobbes 1914: Chapter 10)

There is in this passage an arithmetic at work, a summing of powers. For Hobbes, as for Descartes and Spinoza, geometry is the model for reasoning because it is both accurate (as in arthimetic) and practical because it can be directly applied to the material world, which, of course, in politics translates into both individual bodies and their powers and the body politic, which is a summation of the powers of its individual members. It led to what Husserl (1970) referred to as the mathematisation of the world. Hobbes clearly expresses it thus:

> When man reasoneth, he does nothing else but conceive a sum total, from addition of parcels; or conceive a remainder, from subtraction of one sum from another: which, if it be done by words, is conceiving of the consequence of the names of all the parts, to the name of the whole; or from the names of

the whole and one part, to the name of the other part. And though in some things, as in numbers, besides adding and subtracting, men name other operations, as multiplying and dividing; yet they are the same: for multiplication is but adding together of things equal; and division, but subtracting of one thing, as often as we can. These operations are not incident to numbers only, but to all manner of things that can be added together, and taken one out of another. For as arithmeticians teach to add and subtract in numbers, so the geometricians teach the same in lines, figures (solid and superficial), angles, proportions, times, degrees of swiftness, force, power, and the like; the logicians teach the same in consequences of words, adding together two names to make an affirmation, and two affirmations to make a syllogism, and many syllogisms to make a demonstration; and from the sum, or conclusion of a syllogism, they subtract one proposition to find the other. Writers of politics add together pactions to find men's duties; and lawyers, laws and facts to find what is right and wrong in the actions of private men. In sum, in what matter soever there is place for addition and subtraction, there also is place for reason; and where these have no place, there reason has nothing at all to do.

Out of all which we may define (that is to say determine) what that is which is meant by this word reason when we reckon it amongst the faculties of the mind. For reason, in this sense, is nothing but reckoning (that is, adding and subtracting) of the consequences of general names agreed upon for the marking and signifying of our thoughts; I say marking them, when we reckon by ourselves; and signifying, when we demonstrate or approve our reckonings to other men.

(Hobbes 1914: Chapter 5)

It is, as can be seen, a recipe for the production of chains of reasoning allied to powers starting from the inaugurating role of names and their definitions in the way that geometry does. This mathematisation or geometrisation is of fundamental importance to the exercise of power in the 'natural' and 'social' worlds and 'in the first place, I put for a general inclination of all mankind a perpetual and restless desire of power after power, that ceaseth only in death' (Hobbes 1914: ch 11). There is a ruthless logic in Hobbes that may be disliked but cannot be ignored. Through it he sets out what is most fundamentally at stake for people:

Nature hath made men so equal in the faculties of body and mind as that, though there be found one man sometimes manifestly stronger in body or of quicker mind than another, yet when all is reckoned together the difference between man and man is not so considerable as that one man can thereupon claim to himself any benefit to which another may not pretend as well as he. For as to the strength of body, the weakest has strength enough to kill the strongest, either by secret machination or by confederacy with others that are in the same danger with himself.

(Hobbes 1914: Chapter 13)

Thus:

> From this equality of ability ariseth equality of hope in the attaining of our ends. And therefore if any two men desire the same thing, which nevertheless they cannot both enjoy, they become enemies; and in the way to their end (which is principally their own conservation, and sometimes their delectation only) endeavour to destroy or subdue one another. And from hence it comes to pass that where an invader hath no more to fear than another man's single power, if one plant, sow, build, or possess a convenient seat, others may probably be expected to come prepared with forces united to dispossess and deprive him, not only of the fruit of his labour, but also of his life or liberty. And the invader again is in the like danger of another.
>
> (Hobbes 1914: Chapter 13)

The solution to this for Hobbes is the construction of the Leviathan (Hobbes 1914: Chapter 17). This refers to the aggregation of the powers of individuals and their subsumption under the state, nation, commonwealth in the person of the sovereign. What does this mean for 'normal' research and for 'radical' research?

Recall Andy, the social worker. He is located in a system of powers. Think of it as a kind of Hobbesian Leviathan. There may not be a single individual who incarnates the sovereignty of the Leviathan, but there is the sense of a them who rule us, or at least create powerful Leviathan-like conditions of control and surveillance.

Living with or subverting Leviathan?

The question then is to what extent individuals as researchers see themselves as adherents of this structure, desiring to make it work better – say for the general improvement of the quality of life of the people; or, to what extent they see themselves as wanting to change the system – equally, say for the general improvement of the quality of life of the people. What counts as data and how it is used as evidence will in each case differ – radically. What counts as data depends on who controls the definitions by which data is made visible. How the social worker defines the people, the area, the nature of the problems and the appropriate solutions may well be very different from the way the residents, the gangs, the police, the politicians and so on make their definitions. What is data for a social worker may not be 'seen' as data by a police officer or a gang member. Whose definitions should be taken as fundamental? In the Hobbesian world of Leviathan, of course, the answer is clear, the fundamental categories are those defined by the highest power. As in the geometrical sense of measuring and manipulating the world about, all individuals are then but controllable parts of a system, pulled by the chains of command, reason or belief.

The research itself will be the object of political concern. Is our social worker the agent of Leviathan or the facilitator of subversion? The 'data' could be used to support either. On the Leviathan 'side', the social worker is trying to shape young people to 'fit in'; on the subversion side, the social worker is manipulating the courses available to provide opportunities for young people to assert themselves confidently in groups. This assertion provides just the opportunity for individuals to express their needs, interests, wants, and these may in turn open the way for freedom of expression and action to meet their needs, interests and wants – and these, of course, may be quite different than those required by the system. It is here that a fuzziness enters on scene paving the way for the next chapter where the chains of power keeping all in place begin to dissolve. Human beings are not stable elements in a system of controls. It is always possible for them to 'think and act otherwise'. The extent to which they can assert their interests, needs and wants without fear indicates the degree to which they feel 'at home' in the community. How at home can one feel in a Leviathan? What range of difference or variation can a Leviathan accommodate without either collapsing into another political form or chaos (see later discussions in Chapters 2, 4 and 9)? The professional service of the social worker could be argued as being directed towards bringing those who are defined as problematic, as acting outside the law, back under the law and in conformity with 'normal' society.

Spinoza, although influenced by Hobbes, offers an alternative solution, one that leads to a change in the social order rather than a change in the individual to fit in or be expelled (or, indeed, killed). In this context, the strategy of the social worker could alternatively be argued to be the manipulation of conditions and the nego-tiation of changes in both system and the young people to prevent their expulsion by recognising and responding to their individual needs. In Spinoza's terms it is a process that begins, as for Descartes, with the methods of geometry (Negri 1991) that is, a process of systematic thinking by the sovereign individual subjecting all to critical reasoning and thus taking nothing for granted in identifying a firm foundation upon which to build knowledge, decision-making and action. It is this that allows him to undermine the orthodox interpretations of the scriptures by churches and in the process frame the possibilities for the development of democracy by the multitude of sovereign individuals rather than a monarchy or tyranny that subjects the multitude. Again, like Hobbes, he begins with the powers of the individual that are not so great that he or she cannot be harmed by another or a gang of others acting together. In the context of the social worker and the young people growing up in an impoverished and difficult, even dangerous, community, it makes sense for them to find mutual safety and to augment their powers to get what they want in gangs. Such a gang operates an elementary social contract, where for Hobbes a contract essentially consists in 'The mutual trans-ferring of right' (Hobbes 1914: Chapter 14). In the gang, each member cedes some portion of their individual rights to the gang and gang leader in order to gain mutual protection. For Hobbes, the process naturally leads to power being vested in a single individual – monarch or Leviathan (which could be a collection of powerful people acting as one under the name of the state). Rights and the transfer of rights in the formation of such forms of association for some common purpose provide a focus for social analysis, critique and political action. Hence, the process through which the gang assimilates power is essentially the same as that of the state.

Spinoza makes no founding judgement about the rightness or wrongness of what people want and what they try to obtain through the use of their power. He founds his approach on a conception of *natural right* whereby every individual is 'conditioned by nature, so as to live and act in a certain way' (Spinoza 2004: 200). However:

> The power of nature is the power of God, which has sovereign right over all things; and, inasmuch as the power of nature is simply the aggregate of the powers of all her individual components, it follows that every individual has sovereign right to do all that he can; in other words, the rights of an individual extend to the utmost limits of his power as it has been conditioned.
>
> (Spinoza 2004: 200)

This move is not cognitive as such, as in Descartes, who establishes the individual ego, the cogito, the I-think as the starting point for methodological certainty. It is ontological. It is grounded in the positive existence of being, on power that reveals itself to the intellect because it is prior to the thinking, doubting subject. This may be hard to accept. Yet it could be argued as the way of nature, as simply a given: 'Existence, as such, does not demand definition. It is the spontaneity of being. Philosophy affirms, is a system of affirmations, inasmuch as it expresses directly and immediately the interlaced networks of existence' (Negri 1991: 45). Rights are of the order of existence. This concept of natural right includes all creatures as well as humans who are not necessarily rational, or sane: 'as the wise man has sovereign right to do all that reason dictates, or to live according to the laws of reason, so also the ignorant or foolish man has sovereign right to do all that desire dictates, or to live according to the laws of desire' (Spinoza 2004: 201). This seems a very harsh statement. It basically says that those individuals who use their individual strength or the combined strength of gangs to impose their wills upon others have the 'natural right' to do so. This means that the

> natural right of the individual man is thus determined, not by sound reason, but by desire and power. All are not naturally conditioned so as to act according to the laws and rules of reason; nay, on the contrary, all men are born ignorant, and before they can learn the right way of life and acquire the habit of virtue, the greater part of their life, even if they have been well brought up, has passed away. Nevertheless, they are in the meanwhile bound to live and preserve themselves as far as they can by the unaided impulses of desire. Nature has given them no other guide, and has denied them the present power of living according to sound reason; so that they are no more bound to live by the dictates of an enlightened mind, than a cat is bound to live by the laws of the nature of a lion.
>
> (Spinoza 2004: 201)

The radicality of this position is such that it undermines any externally imposed or decreed hierarchy that sets some behaviours as being good over those considered to be bad or evil. Thus for each individual creature, since in nature their rights are coextensive with their powers, they have the right to preserve their existence and to fulfil their desires in so far as their power allows. The individual is sovereign to the extent that they can impose their sovereignty. In Spinoza's view they will choose whatever they consider to be good and reject or flee or destroy whatever they consider to be bad or fear. If they are faced with a choice between two evils, they will choose whatever they consider to be the lesser evil. For example, if a promise has been made to do something, but it is later considered that doing it will lead to an experience that is worse than keeping the promise, then one has the right/power to break the promise. Thus, like Hobbes, Spinoza argues that, 'Everyone has by nature a right to act deceitfully, and to break his compacts, unless he be restrained by the hope of some greater good, or the fear of some greater evil' (Spinoza 2004: 204). The kind of promise or 'covenant' that is being considered here is that of individuals joining with others whether they come together for mutual defence against others or to increase their wealth and pleasure. In the case of one person wanting the protection of another, some part of that individual's power/right is given over to the other. In the case where each individual voluntarily gives up some part of their power/right in relation to the whole so that through the unity of the whole they are mutually supported and protected, then what has been created is the body politic:

> The possessor of sovereign power, whether he be one or many, or the whole body politic, has the sovereign right of imposing any commands he pleases: and he who has either voluntarily, or under compulsion, transferred the right to defend him to another, has, in so doing, renounced his natural right and is therefore bound to obey, in all things, the commands of the sovereign power; and will be bound so to do so long as the king, or nobles, or the people preserve the sovereign power which formed the basis of the original transfer.
>
> (Spinoza 2004: 207)

The transference of right is at the heart of the construction of the chains that bind people, producing a single body politic from the bodies of the multitude. It is here in the multitude that there are the seeds for a dissolution of the chains of reason, power, cause and effect that produce what may even be called the Great Chain of Being (Lovejoy 1936), but that's for Chapter 3. At this point, the focus is on keeping it all together. The project is essentially Hegel's social, cultural and political project of reconciliation to reason (Hardimon 1994), the radical-research implications of which will be discussed in Chapter 2. At this point, research explores what is at stake for individuals and for social organisations in either expressing fully one's natural rights or in giving up some part of those rights for a degree of protection or for pleasures that could not otherwise be achieved. Since most cannot live as absolute masters of their fate, there is necessarily a tension, an irreconcilable conflict at the heart of social order. To be a member, each has to give up some essential part of who they are by suppressing some part of their 'natural rights'. How do you live with that?

Reconciling and managing lives

The social worker, in trying to manage the lives of others, is involved in a process of reconciliation. But in a Spinozan-like framework, this process cannot be one-sided. If young people on disadvantaged estates are to be successfully reconciled to social order, then social structures must also modify to address, at least in part, their needs. Otherwise, there can only be either sufficient force or fear to ensure compliance or the containment, expulsion or eradication of those who will not comply. All of this raises the question of the purpose of society and what counts as a society that is 'good' for its members. That in itself is a key question of radical research.

Perhaps the most influential image of managing people's lives in order to produce the 'good society' is that offered by Plato in his *Republic*. Plato was an enemy of democracy, seeing it as a system that was bound to collapse into chaos. If each individual could choose according to their whims and desires, there could only be conflict, unhappiness (1994: 303). Hence, it was necessary to build a society according to the rules of reason for only in that way could happiness, peace and well-being be assured. Waterfield in the introduction to his translation of Plato's *Republic* (Plato 1994) commented on the republic being a metaphor of the good life and psychic harmony. This depends on seeing society as essentially cooperative in nature and ensuring therefore that no individual gets more than their fair share. For Plato, a 'moral person is one with psychic harmony under the rule of reason' (1994: xli). But:

> This formula must, however, be spelt out somewhat differently in the case of different kinds of people. It applies with full force only to those few with inherent philosophic characteristics who survive the further-education pro-gramme of chapter ten and attain the vision of goodness. They are moral experts because they know what is good, and because they are best equipped to educate others in morality (412a, 500d, 540b).
>
> (Waterfield in Plato 1994: xli)

What is important here is the notion of different kinds of people. Who are the dramatis personae, the cast of characters, in Plato's world? It is a society composed of three classes: the guardians (the rulers), the auxiliaries (these are guardians who remain as soldiers) and the commoners (artisans, merchants, the rest of the people – excluding slaves, of course). To get people to accept this framework, they are to be told a noble lie (cf. Strauss 1952a, 1988): that people, like the metals gold, silver and bronze, possess different qualities. In possessing different qualities they should not go against their nature but use them to fulfil the different specialist functions of society. This principle of specialisation founded on the noble lie of the different qualities of people is essential to social order. It echoes Plato's vision of unity and harmony not only for society but also for the individual. The ruler guardians are the head, rationality, goodness. The auxilliary guardians are the soldiers who are courageous, protecting society. The commoners do the work, they follow their appetites and have to learn to keep them in check. And, of course, there are those who are largely invisible: the slaves and those who are outside, the barbarians. In this imaginary world we see all the elements that recur throughout discussions of social order, social classes, gender and racial differences. 'Education'[2] plays a vital role in maintaining this imaginary order. Each classification of individual has their particular form of 'education'. For the workers it is to specialise on the one skill that they must perform. What is produced is a sense of totality, unity:

> Plato's contention that dissension, or even any kind of pluralism, must be ruled out in a community worthy of the name leads to all his most notorious political provisions. The common possession of wives and children is a direct result of the desire for unity (462aff.). The philosophers are to rule because only they have the kind of overview which enables them to regulate the unity. The community will only remain a unity if every member of it sticks to PS [the Principle of Specialisation] (423d.). – that is, keeps to his or her natural class. In short (in the case of the guardians, at any rate), individuality of thought is to be excluded by the education, and individuality of expression thereafter. Education and politics are mutually maintaining: both exist to keep the other stable, unified, and unchanging (423c–427a); legislative reform without a proper programme of social engineering is like an invalid trying out various remedies.
>
> (Waterfield in Plato 1994: xxviii–xxix)

The role of reason, truth, unity and stability in Plato's Republic is to be assimilated with god (Waterfield in Plato 1994: xxxi). It is the perfect image of being in chains. It is what Rancière (1995) calls the 'police' order of the state. Here police refers not to the uniformed police officers but to the force of law that unifies the parts under the whole. Plato's is a radical solution. To put it into practice would transform society. But is it desirable? It is founded on a deceit, the noble lie of essential differences between people that legitimises hierarchy and thus inequality. The 'educational' task is to instil belief in the naturalness of this inequality, whether, say, through the historical legitimacy of 'good breeding' and

---

2 Although the term 'education' is commonly employed to mean many things, we later want to make a distinction between 'schooling' and 'education'. Following from that later distinction, the term 'education' as employed above is equivalent to 'schooling' which we employ to mean the process of moulding and fashioning minds and behaviours (cf. Schostak 1983).

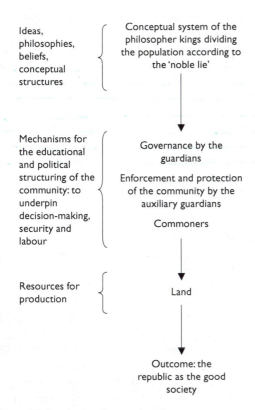

Figure 1.2 Producing the good society

inherited wealth, or through the winning talents of competitors in the marketplace. The design of the Platonic project is crudely shown in Figure 1.2.

There is, in this outline of Plato's Republic, a structure, expressed in Figure 1.2, that is designed to realise ideas through their enactment by key mechanisms employing appropriate resources to bring about desired outcomes. It is essentially a stealth structure that presents and realises one set of ideas – the 'noble lie' – while denying others (Schostak 1999, 2002, 2006).

Of course, Plato's Republic is an ideal case, a utopia, it never has and perhaps it never will exist. However, it is an example of what may be called a 'normative rationality' (cf. Adorno 1973; O'Connor 2005), a framework which grounds a way of viewing a world, of constructing it and of working or functioning within it as expressed in Figure 1.2. This normative rationality – whether or not based upon a noble lie – opens out a space for alternative ways of organising societies in terms of the extent to which it amplifies people's fear that others may desire what they have and seek to take it; or the hope for freedom from a social order that has grown restrictive and no longer, if it ever did, feel like a home. For Plato's utopia, or the sense of living at home in an ideal community, was to be developed not by a sovereign or God, but by the philosopher kings (Plato 1994: Chapter 8): it is the rule of philosophy over a rationally organised population, each part rationally and functionally related to each other part. This contrasts with Hobbes where it is the rule of awe over a fearful multitude. In both cases, the best political organisation is effectively totalitarian: for Plato the reconciliation of the individual to social order is through a combination of reason and the noble lie; for Hobbes it is through overwhelming force that compels compliance. For Spinoza, the best political organisation is democratic, through which the multitude rules itself under a principle of equality so that no one individual has greater power than another and thus cannot distort the social organisation and distribution of benefits and social goods to individuals and groups. What is at stake for individuals thus differs according to which approach is adopted as the desired form of society; or, the extent to which the dimensions of power, reason and equality uneasily combine in the construction of social order. Radical research takes place at the points of irresolvable tension in order to explore what is at stake for individuals and the ways in which they engage with others to realise or defend their interests. It may begin simply as in the following illustration from research undertaken for a major nationwide community-regeneration programme:

> There were five of us, three people from the bank and two researchers. We were discussing which fieldsites to go to in order to build up a preliminary picture of the current state of the programme. [. . .] At one point a discussion centred around one potential site which had failed to get funded.
>
> When I said it would be very interesting to go and interview some people at the field site, the co-ordinator of the programme was adamant that there was no point in interviewing anyone there. Moreover, it was politically sensitive. The co-ordinator explained that the whole programme was intended to be the bank's way of 'giving something back' to the community. It did not want to be seen to be imposing its decisions upon the community. I responded that it would be interesting to see whether the community saw the bank's withdrawal from backing the proposal as a positive reflection on the bank's intentions. Of course, the bank was interested in having a positive image. It wanted people to know it was doing good things socially. It was a part of corporate social responsibility.
>
> 'Actually, it's interesting that when you ask people who complain to the bank what their level of satisfaction with the bank is, it is of course, rock bottom', said Mark, the person responsible for Marketing. 'But if the bank acts positively in relation to the complaint then their satisfaction rating goes up. So, I wonder whether the community's satisfaction rating with the bank has gone up because we listened and didn't go ahead.'
>
> 'But we'd never know', Martha the Coordinator responded.
>
> 'There is a way', said Maggie, an accounts manager, 'through changes in the activity of current account transactions and so on'.
>
> (John Schostak: notes on meeting November 2005)

There is an image here of how communities are recognised in relation to the interests of powerful institutions. It seems an irresolvable conflict of views as to what constitutes a community and what it is for. For the company, a community is made visible through accounts transactions. Those who do not have accounts, of course, quite literally cannot be counted. Accountants, as 'philosopher kings', rule transactions between corporate bodies, communities and individuals. What now if we drive further into the community to make visible those people and forms of organisation not registered in the accounting systems?

In the interview extract that opened this chapter, Andy, the social worker, described a strategy that was in response to the perceived problem of young people with nothing to do, hanging around on the streets and causing trouble. The gang, whether as a loose association of friends or more sinister, as a criminal organisa-tion, is one expression of people coming together for protection or for friendship. Thrasher (1927) provided an early study of gangs, 1,313 of them in Chicago, ranging from very young children playing to criminal gangs. He saw them arising in the 'interstices' of communities, in the margins, the in-between, where 'normal' or official social control and the rule of law fails to reach. The existence of the gang thus already generates a sense of threat to the normal spaces of social order. It was the existence of such 'interstices' and the formation of gangs hanging about and causing trouble that led to the project Andy described, as well as to the nation-wide programme funded by the bank. A bank, of course, has a different interest to a charitable housing trust. However, each is in the position of being a powerful organisation engaged in interventions in the lives of people in its target community. To be seen doing good, for whatever altruistic or commercial reasons, involves responding to perceived problems, needs, interests, in ways that can be justified. For example, Joan was the Estate Manager of a housing trust in the UK that managed the houses in the estate where Andy was working. She was asked to explain why the parenting project described by Andy was started, how it related to her work in the Trust:

Joan: I think when we came here the perception of the estate was that it's a very rough area with a lot of social problems and it was difficult to manage the estate. There were a lot of empty properties here, I think, I can't remember the numbers cos I wasn't here. But you know, over forty odd empty properties boarded up, some tower blocks, nine tower blocks which were definitely associated with a lot of anti-social behaviour. They're very typical of um young transient single people who've not got much consideration for community. And uh, the stock was run down, needed a lot of repair work which, I think one of the reasons for the stock transfer process because it's a way of bringing uh investment for stock improve-ment into an area. Over the six years that we've been here we've done a lot to improve the physical condition of the properties. We've pulled down the tower blocks and the general perception 'n feedback that I get from tenants and people coming up here who've not been for a while is that that process has made a considerable difference to this estate. This project started, I think, in response that there was still a lot of teenage, perceptions of teenage nuisance. Uh, this particular patch of the estate with the shops here um lots of kids hanging around in the evenings being a general nuisance, graffiti, vandalism. And the, the statistical information about the area, the surveys that we've had say that people get bugged by criminal damage. And if you ask them about it it's things like damage to cars, you know people passing by and—

JFS: Mm, scraping.

Joan: Having a quick scratch and a scrape and loitering round the shops. It's improved a lot on this parade recently because the off-licence closed, so the little, the magnet's gone.

JFS: Yeah.

Joan: There's another magnet at the top of the estate. But generally, it has calmed down a lot. And that's what people tell us.

(Transcript extract from interview, 2005)

As Joan speaks, a range of issues emerge that address concerns at three levels: the state, the institutions of society and the residents of the community. The interests of powerful institutions organise questions for particular purposes. They want research to be undertaken to address those questions. These, clearly, can be seen to fit in with (or counter) the policy agendas of states just as most people in the community may also desire the development of strategies that reduce violence and increase opportunities for employment. And, indeed, the residents of the community are said to want strategies that reduce the degrees of violence, and the parents want a way to control their wayward children. However, as the social worker pointed out later in his interview, the community also needs employment opportunities. The young people have few prospects. Those who do find employment eventually leave the estate rather than contribute to its regeneration. What then are the real research questions at stake for this community and for the wider society and its policy-making?

Framing questions

Research that explores the interests of different individuals and groups equally will be called radical research in this book. Such research asks different questions, or at least, poses the same questions differently, adopts a view that frees itself radically from any single dominating position. It is a view that recognises essential conflicts due to diversity of viewpoints and differences in interests at play in personal and social organisation.

So, the question may be asked: should research be designed to address and reinforce the aims and interests of a dominating group in order to bring the rest into harmony; or should it be designed to be inclusive of all the viewpoints of the multitude of individuals and thus accept diversity, difference, disagreements and conflict? The question is essentially about the good of the state versus the good of the individual. Satisfying the one is necessarily in conflict with the other. States require individuals to give up some part of what they want since no state can accommodate every difference stemming from the particular, unique viewpoint of every individual. Radical research involves exploring what is at stake in adopting particular viewpoints concerning the organisation of individuals and collectivities of various kinds. The fundamental tension is between the enchaining of individuals under the laws of a state versus the freedom of individuals to express and act according to their desires, interests, needs – that is, according to what Spinoza defines as their natural rights. A collectivity essentially incarnates the powers of the individuals that compose it, creating a 'body' that can be named, identified, defined, bounded of which the individuals are parts. This then generates the problem of keeping each 'free' individual within the body of the collectivity – whether through awe of the power of the Leviathan, through the Platonic 'noble lie', or through ensuring that the collectivity is sensitive to and representative of the needs, interests and desires of the overwhelming majority; or, of course, through some combination of all. Research defines itself in the way that it explores and engages with this problem of the freedom of the individual and the aggregated powers of individuals to incarnate nameable, definable associations of individuals from gangs and friendship groups to organised workforces, militaries and states with their towns, cities and villages. Under the Leviathan, research is normal if it contributes to the stable functioning of the state; it is radical if it defines problems in such a way that the state is undermined. Hence, normal research focuses upon issues of control, improvement and problem-solving. Radical research focuses upon what is at stake for the freedoms of individuals when they are constrained by awe, noble (and not so noble) lies and the dominant views of majorities. What is at stake involves a problem structure that, on the basis of the discussions of this chapter, can be sketched as follows:

1. How to do and get what one wants.
2. How to protect one's self and one's loved ones and friends from others.
3. How to develop and make use of one's natural talents, interests.
4. How to create the ruling laws by which to govern a collectivity. What is at stake in seeking to govern, whether by guardianship, philosopher kings, monarchs, tyrants or, indeed, the people through some variant of democratic organisation? Under what conditions do individuals transfer their 'natural rights' to others? How are the chains of transfer maintained or undermined?
5. How to carry out education appropriate to members of the society according to their roles, functions and positions in society.
6. How to define what is permissible.
7. How to define who 'belongs' and who does not. How to distinguish one's self, one's 'community', one's people, from the others.
8. How to define the public citizens whose voices must be heard in policy-making. How to define the masses whose opinions and power must be

LEVIATHAN

manipulated. How to define the 'people' in whose name the state exists and is judged. Who are the dramatis personae?

9. How to define how individuals are to be represented. What are they to be told about who they are, their nature, their purpose/mission/destiny?
10. Where are the points of irresolvable tension? Where are the interstices?

Such questions contribute to posing the problem structure of a project. Identifying the problem structure of a research project is the strategic step to take. It never emerges straight away but has to be painstakingly revealed, rather like an archaeologist stripping away the layers of mud and stone in an archaeological site. It emerges from the voices of the people as they engage with each other – cooperatively or conflictually – defining their territories, their roles, their sense of identity, their friends, their enemies, their obstacles, their values, their hopes, their frustrations, their successes, their tragedies. The questions raised from different viewpoints frames the case to be answered.

Towards designing the radical

It is in the recognition of cases to be answered that the design of radical research is shaped. Through the resistances that each different viewpoint makes towards the other, boundaries emerge, separating sides who are in conflict over a disputed 'territory' or scene of debate and action. What is at stake in a case can be explored, therefore, by addressing the problems posed by each viewpoint and the arguments made for their preferred solutions. In this sense, a case is not designed to explore a bounded system of parts in harmony with a whole but is a design for the exploration of conflictual relations and conflictual views of how representation should be organised. If this is so, then a major design task is the elaboration of the case through a descriptive mapping of the range of voices who claim a stake in what happens within some contested terrain. Terrain, here, is about symbolic as well as physical space.

If ethnography is a writing about peoples (cf., Schostak 2006), and peoples are defined through their identifications with symbolic and/or physical territories, then the radical case emerges from descriptions of how each viewpoint defines a people and what is the normal for this people and the circumstances that are considered to disturb the normal and have to be put right. Recalling Figure 1.2, this equates to the dimension of 'ideas' that are available for realisation. This then raises the question of how peoples manage disagreements, what mechanisms, procedures or cultural practices they use between themselves as individuals, as groups and as more formal organisations in ways that are considered appropriate, just, right; as well as how problems are managed between peoples. Essentially, it is a mapping of the multiple ways – whether conflictual or cooperative – in which the symbolic and physical terrains are organised for individual and social purposes. The mapping identifies physical and conceptual structures, processes, disagreements, identities grounding a sense of everyday life as a multiply constructed 'reality'. The features of this 'ethnographic reality' are further explored in the following chapters. As a reality, experienced as hard, brute, raw, it provides a ground for people's actions, conditioning them, creating a sense of no alternative. For alternatives to be found, then 'reality' itself may need to be questioned, perhaps through a Cartesian method of doubt or phenomenological suspension or some other process of critical reasoning.

Description is not enough. How can a design for action be formulated to address conflicting views between coexisting peoples who together compose the 'multitude' within some territory locally or across territories globally? Is it a design for action to reconcile people to the status quo, to some 'noble lie', or one that seeks reform or even revolutionary change? Is there an ideal political framework for the production of social order? Can a political framework built on a lie, however noble, really persist? And already it can be seen that even the Leviathan has its weakness: without the support of the multitude, it falls. If the multitude no longer feel the awe, or suddenly see through the noble lie, then there is nothing to keep the state unified – witness the collapse of the Soviet Union. Within the framework of the unified whole, individuals and the data concerning their lives neither has any existence nor any meaning unless it is lawfully produced. All else is chaos, criminality, illusion, error or evil. Replacing awe by Enlightenment reason may seem to promise democracy where all members can be rationally satisfied. But if the Enlightenment had its impulse to freedom, and if its expression in the industrialised marketplaces of modernity is the great design to ensure the welfare and progressive development of individuals, it has its dark side as is to be the focus of the next chapters. Generating a design for action is fraught with political issues that need to be carefully explored. Action research, in its most general definition, is undertaken by actors in given social settings in order to improve the quality of action in relation to some set of values and desired goals. It is increasingly employed as a form of local action across professional groups from the business setting to the public sector. To what extent is its radical potential tamed by drawing it under the demands of the powerful? To what extent can it contest power in order to be inclusive of the views of all the peoples described through the ethnographic process? Such questions address the potential impacts of action research, and, in addressing them, they are opened to evaluation.

Evaluation can either be framed according the 'god's-eye view' of how the world should be; or it can be framed to address the multiple views of people formed from the street level of the confusing labyrinth of everyday life. MacDonald (1987) described what he saw as three kinds of evaluation stance: the bureaucratic, which effectively provides a service to implement the goals of policy-makers; the autocratic, which stands apart from both policy-makers and those who are targets of policy giving their judgements imperiously; and, finally, the democratic, which seeks to provide the means for all stakeholders to be represented equally and form their own judgements as to the success or otherwise of actions. In complex social circumstances, it may be argued, it is the democratic that provides the best basis for the development of judgements, decisions and actions that will be accepted by the widest range of people and thus provide the most stable basis for change.

Radical design involves the three dimensions of ethnography, action and evaluation. But it is not limited to them. Since radical design involves critical reflection on the 'normal' from whatever viewpoint the normal is defined, it questions the apparent seamlessness of the normal, paving the way for the loosening of the seams that may enable new possibilities to be seen and courses of action undertaken.

Chapter 2

Unchaining, deconstruction and the intertextual

Often there is the feeling of holding it together despite some sense of pressure to blow apart. Where Plato, Hobbes and Spinoza helped think about keeping it together under the rule, power and authority of, for example, some incarnating body such as the king, the divine being, the people, state or reason, the sheer act of an individual employing reason to challenge taken-for-granted, traditional orthodoxies concerning religion and the natural and social worlds has the power to disturb. In the different stories that can be told about keeping it together or blowing it apart, a dramatis personae and the imaginary, symbolic and physical structures that hold them together becomes a fundamental research issue. In a rapidly globalising world inaugurated by industrialisation, communications technologies and multinational corporations exploiting global marketplaces, an 'outside' becomes increasingly difficult to maintain. The stakes are increased. What is undesirable, dangerous, dirty cannot just be excluded to another scene. As professionals, as managers, as workers, as citizens, as individuals, there is the need to know that something can be done to improve things, that a good way of life is achievable. But how?

Rather than blind faith or accepting authority without question, the radicalising seed of doubt always asks, but what do I know for certain? And am I doing the right thing? In particular, what are the discourses employed in professional action? For example, recall the concerns of the social worker described in the previous chapter. He had been asked by the manager of the housing trust that was managing the estate to work with them in resolving some problems caused by teenagers. This was an estate where the houses were in poor condition and the residents had few employment prospects. The social worker was asked by the researcher about the availability of jobs in the area, and he pointed to the massive warehouses on the business park and said it's all automated and the few jobs that there are in the local supermarket were all low-paid 'shit jobs'. Yet at the same time as this sense of the reality of the conditions of people's lives, there is the aim of managing their lives. The estate is to be managed, the relation between parents and children are to be managed and their time to be filled with extra-curricular activities. His role was to create courses for the young people that would be complementary to the parenting course. Joan, the manager of the housing trust, described her reasons for developing a parenting course:

Joan: But this te' this course was put in place in response to what residents were telling us about that anti-social behaviour. And I think the, set up by a predecessor and she was working with the project at the Community High School the Estate Parent Partnership Project. They were really trying to get parents involved in school activities and involved in the children's um development and do lots of extra-curricular activities, coach trips and all sorts of uh real wide range of um I suppose non-vocational classes, coffee mornings and craft classes. And the person who design who developed this particular package um was doing a lot of work in parenting skills in [a nearby town]. So I think the combination was a course to actually help parents to have more and better communication with the young people and maybe then help them to sort of you know stop the kids going out every night and being a nuisance. I think the general feedback was that they were being criticised for being bad parents and letting the kids run around and not caring. In actual fact they were quite responsible parents who were just at the end of their tether.

JFS: Right.

Joan: I suppose it's re', it's re' in the last couple of years there's been television programmes which have—

JFS: These parenting things.

Joan: Have you know flagged, just that up you know the people are not happy with it, don't condone it but are really at their wits end about how to change. And the courses that we've put on we're looking at working with parents and young people at the same time to try and improve the communication on both sides and see if that has a sort of an add on benefit to parenting courses.

(Transcript extracts, 2006)

Just as houses can be designed and estates managed, so too there is the desire to manage or 'design' the lives of people. In the course of interviewing people involved with the parenting course, the range of organisations and professionals involved in overseeing, managing and intervening in the lives of the people on the estate was mapped. Besides the professionals in the trust, those most closely involved were the police, social workers, schoolteachers, vocational teachers and leaders of non-vocational classes. More widely, there are the law courts and justice system involved in dealing with offenders, the local council and regional development agency involved in social and economic planning. And still more generally, there are the institutions of government through which resources are allocated and laws formulated. As in Figure 1.2, there is a design structured to enact ideas or philosophies of how communities and peoples should be, through mechanisms and the allocation of resources to bring about desired outcomes. It is easy to imagine a single system seen as a single body of which the estate is a part. In defining the estate as a case to be studied, it can only be studied as a part in the bigger case that is the state. But the state too is subsumed under something that can only be intimated as being the 'global', that emerging space within which all states are subsumed in processes of competition, conflict and negotiation, but also in uneasy relationships with other nameable entities that organise people under multinational corporations as employees/labour and other entities that define peoples, such as faiths, cultures, races.

The metaphor of the body, the unifying whole – whether it is through awe or through reason under God, monarch, dictator, president, heads of corporations or philosopher kings – involves total mastery over each element, each part of the whole to produce a police order (cf., Rancière 1995) that none can escape unless they are to be seen as mad, bad or enemies of the state, corporation, faith or race. This body of the state again mimics the structure outlined in Figure 1.2: the head refers to the conceptual structure and the mechanisms of reason that masters the body through which work is undertaken transforming the material world according to the master plans of the head. Under such a rule, education can only be limited to training individuals – has 'hands' governed by, or enchained by, employers, politicians, capitalists and so on – to fulfil the needs of the police order. Research, in this case, has as its proper goal the engineering of the individuals and organisations that compose the dominant entity to fulfil its needs. Yet the underlying goal of individuals is freedom as soon as the weight of control becomes unbearable. Of course, control is not always felt as unbearable.

A harmonious, well-ordered society gives a kind of freedom. If the alternative were a Hobbesian vision of war of all against all, then the peace and stability offered by the Leviathan provides a freedom to live under the rule of the sovereign. Plato offers a freedom to live under the wise rule of the philosopher kings, and Spinoza offers a step towards the freedom of democracy under the rule of the people. The impulse to freedom is what is at the back of the Enlightenment. And it is this impulse that is the subversive seed in all forms of social organisation. It is revealed just as much in simple everyday settings as in the great dramatic moments of historical crisis. When the sense of expected order is somehow disturbed – unexpectedly, dramatically or indeed trivially – then the fragility of the binding chains of everyday order is felt and the world, however slightly, feels out of joint.

Being out of joint

It is almost felt like an interruption to the rhythm of walking, its unconscious heart-beat of footfalls manifesting themselves:

It is a bright spring, late morning; my lunch guest has arrived, and we walk along the narrow path in the university grounds towards the building housing the dining room. Early daffodils and late snowdrops attract the eye, bunches of colours amidst the winter-wet grass either side of the path. My guest is a consultant psychiatrist, someone I have met through an earlier project researching the learning experiences of junior doctors. One of the topics we intend to discuss over lunch is future further research possibilities. We chat as we walk. A young man is coming towards us. If I gave it any thought, which I don't until now as I write up this event, I would think he is most likely to be a student. The path is narrow, too narrow to accommodate three people. Deep in conversation I start to take evasive action, aiming not to step off the path unless I strictly have to. I am on the outside edge of the path and so I step to my right, thinking that the approaching stranger can simply keep to a straight line and we will avoid each other. However, the stranger steps to his left and once again we are on a collision course. I have to concentrate. I am now completely unaware of N's location as all my awareness is focused on how to extricate myself from impending collision. I step to my left in the hope that this is an appropriate response. I look attentively at the stranger's face – a sea-change in public body conduct where familiarity is kept to the minimum – attempting to read the facial gestures to get some clues as to how to extricate myself from this strange 'dance'. His face is expressionless, his eyes far-away and unseeing of here and now. No information is to be found by me there. What to do? Often if such an entanglement happens you look at the other and see laughter perhaps, or frustration, even anger. But not here. The move to my left fails to work either as the stranger moves to his right. This rhythm of my move initiative followed by his seemingly counter-move occurs for several more minutes. The lack of emotions in his face puzzles me and I wonder how we will end this. My inability to extricate myself also begins to cause me some degree of embarrassment inasmuch as N and I have only begun to get to know each other both on a professional level and on a personal level, and, thus, I begin to worry as to what N might be thinking here. Time to step away, I decide, and so I step right off the path and walk away into the grassy area, putting a significant distance between myself and the stranger. The ploy works. N joins me from his witness position on the far side of the path. I apologise, chuckling at myself and saying how I couldn't figure out where the stranger was going to go next. Yes, says N, I saw him walking towards us, noted his 'robotic' gait and his body language and thought aha he's on drug X and will not respond to an other but just keep on walking, so I need to step right away.

(Jill Schostak, a recalled incident, 2006)

How things ought ordinarily to be are somehow out of joint with how things are expected to be. Anticipation is essential to the ordinariness of order – it underpins how to read a situation. It is like reading a passage from a book and knowing that what you're reading fits with other readings from other books; that is, one text relates in some way to another text, thus giving a feeling of being grounded in what is known, or typical. The process of texts referring to other texts, or a sign in one sign system being imported into another sign system, may be called more generally, 'intertextuality'. More complexly:

The term *inter-textuality* denotes this transposition of one (or several) sign system(s) into another; but since this term has often been understood in the banal sense of "study of sources," we prefer the term *transposition* because it specifies that the passage of one signifying system to another demands a new articulation of the thetic – of enunciative and denotative positionality. If one grants that every signifying practice is a field of transpositions of various signifying systems (an inter-textuality), one then understands that its "place" of enunciation and its denoted "object" are never single, complete and identical to themselves, but always plural, shattered, capable of being tabulated. In this way polysemy [multiple levels or kinds of meaning] can also be seen as the result of a semiotic polyvalence – an adherence to different sign systems.

(Kristeva 1984: 59–60)

It is this sense of intertextuality as 'transposition' that is most marked in the story of the incident of meeting and feeling 'out of joint'. It is in this very banality of meeting another that we find our deepest, most ingrained, commitments. But it's not just a commitment like when someone says 'I'm committed to environ-mentalism' or to 'going on a diet', or 'giving up smoking'. There is a force in the ordinariness of order, of a sequence to be completed, a direction to be pursued, something that compels but compels without thinking, without submitting, with-out decision. It is essential to the performance of everyday life and work. It is what Dennett calls an intentional system, 'that is, entities whose behavior can be predicted by the method of attributing beliefs, desires, and rational acumen' (Dennett 1989: 49). It is essential to 'expertise' to be able to make and justify such attributions. This is as much about the 'expertise' involved in being a member of a given everyday community as it is about the expertise of a professional. Yet the everyday has no sense without access to some code, some common frame-work of understanding, some trust in the witnessing of the other. There is a certain knowledge that has to be drawn upon to be a competent member of society – it is not given logically as such, it is given, or constituted thetically, contingently, characteristics of what makes up everyday 'ordinariness' being built up, often accidentally, over time and becoming formed into typical patterns of association. The 'dance' above began because the expected cues and responses were not forthcoming. The psychiatrist, however, employing a different code, a different signifying system, saw different signs, the symptoms of some 'real' condition drawn from experiences derived from medical contexts that led him to take a particular course of action. The walk of the other was thus the object of two – or more – signifying systems. Transposing the signs of walking from one to the other gave different interpretations. But which signifying system pro-vides the 'best' interpretation of 'what is going on here'? There is always a danger, even if the explanation seems plausible. Why should any layperson believe some expert; or why should one interpretation be considered 'true', or the 'real' explanation?

The issue at stake here is whether I, as an individual, can only accept as actionable information the evidence that I have reduced to my own resources for testing evidence; or whether I can trust the judgement of another who claims to be an 'expert' and, indeed, has supporting evidence – in terms of qualifications, years undertaken in a professional role – of being an 'expert' in a particular area of practice. If, following a Cartesian approach, I need to cast doubt upon the world about in order to achieve certainty, then I can only rest upon my own abilities – my 'on board resources', as it were – in terms of reasoning. However:

> Suppose now that my trusted doctor of many years tells me that I have a rare medical condition in my foot. Let us imagine that she has good evidence for her claims: given her years of training and experience on the job, she is able to form a reliable judgement by studying X-rays on my foot, and by observing how I walk. Assuming finally that I feel no pain, do not observe any irregularity in my walk, and find nothing surprising in the X-rays (medical layman that I am). In the imagined situation, my doctor then has good reasons to believe that I have the condition. Moreover, since I trust her, I have good reasons to believe that she has good reasons to believe that I have the condition. But do my good reasons constitute evidence for the truth of the claim that I have the condition? On an individualistic understanding of the evidence, the answer must be negative.
>
> (Kusch 2002: 46)

Kusch argues for a 'communitarian' epistemology, that is, that our knowledge is not derived exclusively by our own resources for examining evidence but is dependent on there being a community resource. What is at issue here is the extent to which under contemporary circumstances where it is no longer possible – if it ever were – to be entirely self-reliant in terms of determining 'knowledge', 'certainty', 'truth', the word of an 'expert' can be trusted. There is thus an essential split between what I know and what I have to accept even if it mystifies me because, if nothing else, I have come to accept the authority of the other as expert to make a judgement as to the 'real' conditions that I can only mistake for something else.

The question of the 'real that can be grasped' is central to any methodology that seeks to base action upon knowledge. And radical research typically seeks action through some form of changed practices in order to bring about desired outcomes *for real*. But to what extent does this *real*, in some radical way, always seem to slip away from the grasp? And when that happens and the real is no longer a firm foundation, how can a reliable chain of reasoning from first principles to conclusion be constructed? How can the sense of being split, divided, multiple, fragmented and hazy, fuzzy, blurred, impure be addressed? In the absence of fully being able to affirm 'reality' by employing my own resources, the slippage can only be kept in place if I make the step of placing my trust in another. It is here where there is a reliance on the role of the expert and trust in the 'system', the 'state', the 'nation', the 'people'. Yet, there is something disturbing too about 'expertise', state and system and the consequent submissiveness that can take place in relation to 'expert' judgement and actions legitimised on the basis of this.

Disturbing the picture

Kusch (2002: 47) explores the proposition that:

> Believing the experts is not only an epistemic right; in many cases it might even be a duty. If my child suffers from a serious illness, I have *ceteris paribus*, the duty to believe the doctors regarding what would be the best treatment. At least this is what we would all naturally assume. This is not to deny that the rational layperson is entitled to engage the experts in argument. She is also entitled to reject scientists' claims once there are grounds to suspect the distorting influence of political biases and interests. In the absence of reasons for doubt, however, she is ultimately obliged to admit to her 'rational inferiority'.

Professional expertise, moreover, is hard to contest even though there are 'reasons for doubt' when it is interconnected with legal requirements. In 1991 there was a nationwide panic concerning satanic abuse of children. It came to light through the evidence of social workers in an Orkney community, an island just off the coast of Great Britain. Indeed,

> It was quite the season for sex cult spotting: in the late 80s and early 90s, more than 100 children were removed from their families in Cleveland, Nottinghamshire, Rochdale, Bishop Auckland and Ayrshire, by social workers citing allegations of ritualistic abuse. In the most extreme cases, these included accounts of children forced to eat faeces, drink blood and have sex with hooded adults.
>
> (Esther Addley, the *Guardian* 21 October 2006)

A full apology was given to the four families involved, and compensation given to all but one in 1996. One of the children of that family who had been taken away by social workers, the subject of the 2006 *Guardian* story, sixteen years later, as a result of her experiences, decided to sue social services. Children, of course, have to be protected. If parents are deemed to have failed, then professionals are able to stand in and 'act in the best interests' of the children. The Convention on the Rights of the Child agreed in 1989 recognised for the first time that children needed special care in ways that adults may not. However, in practice, if their rights are mediated by appointed adults, do they have 'rights' in the way that an adult has? There are difficult issues here whether under the law (cf., Freeman 1983; Fortin 2003) in education (cf., Holt 1974; Harber 2004) and in philosophy (Wringe 1981; Archard 2003). This story is an example of 'expertise' gone wrong, but it is one amongst many that could be told across a wide range of professions, institutions and locations. Thus, to it can be added stories of politicians abusing their power by covering up evidence or giving data the 'right spin' and corporations manipulating research findings in their favour. Does this mean the system itself is wrong or that only the wrongdoers need to be dealt with? Such scandals have the function of highlighting what is wrong but also what should be considered right. The problems can be reduced to the 'few bad apples' theory of social order that effectively says: the final political form has triumphed, it's just a matter of ridding the system of the few bad apples and sorting out the little local difficulties (cf. Fukuyama 1992). What is needed is proper monitoring, auditing and assessment procedures. Research takes on a utilitarian purpose providing evaluation and developmental services to identify problems, issues and opportunities to improve the practices, processes and procedures through which the system can be perfected. This is where action research and evaluation strategies can be subsumed under or compromised by the system, being reduced to mere tools for the 'improvement' of a dominant system whether or not it actually improves life for people.

However, the stakes are raised when the issue moves from being about a few bad apples who abuse power and position to being about 'enemies without' and 'enemies within'. Here there is the spectre of alternative, incompatible, ways of life, the one negating the other with adherents of the one calling the other evil. Even here a resolution may be sought where good and evil, positive and negative are all necessary parts of the whole. For example, Jullien (2004: 9) introduces his discussion of the relation between evil and negativity by saying that there is a shadow in the picture of the world that we have constructed, it is 'death, illness, war, injustice' and so on. But without such 'shadows' it could be argued that we would not know 'good', peace', 'happiness'. It is this setting into contrast that brings into focus the notion of society that prevails in the minds of people. Society is the 'picture', the way of grasping a sense of the whole of which each individual is a part and how the 'shadows' – perceived as necessary and internal to the whole picture – are to be managed and rationalised. Thatcher famously said that society does not exist, yet:

> Ask yourselves, rather: Which is the part of all your thinking and all your ways of looking at things and doing things that *is not* to a decisive degree conditioned and codetermined by the structure and the meanings of the English language, the organisation of the world it carries with it, your first family environment, school, all the "do"s and "don't"s to which you have been constantly exposed, the friends you have, the opinions in circulation, the ways forced on you by the innumerable artefacts that surround you, and so on? If you can in all sincerity truly answer, "About 1 per cent," you are certainly the most original thinker ever to have lived. It is certainly not our merit (or demerit) if we do not "see" a nymph inhabiting every tree or every fountain. We are all, in the first place, walking and complementary fragments of the institution of our society – its "total parts," as a mathematician would say.

The institution produces, in conformity with its norms, individuals that by construction are not only able but bound to reproduce the institution. The "law" produces "elements" in such a way that their very functioning embodies, reproduces and perpetuates the "law".

(Castoriadis 1997: 7)

This unity that Castoriadis talks about is held together by what he calls 'the "magma" of social imaginary significations' (1997: 7). This magma seems to have a mediating function as well as implying a materiality – that is, it mediates between the social and the real, a theme to be developed further in Chapters 8 and 9. It is through this mediation that individuals are radically the products of their society, their imaginary forms of seeing. Each society is a 'system of interpretation' (Castoriadis 1997: 9), creating its world, enclosing it cognitively within what it defines as seeable, knowable, actionable.

If a 'society' is a system of interpretation, then it is productive of texts, readings, writings. In pre-modern societies, the question of the natural order of the world could be settled through appeal to creation stories or myths. In modernity, post-Enlightenment, the old stories were displaced from the centre if not from memory and cultural practices by stories of scientific and social progress based upon reason. If there is a system to replace the old certainties and verities, then it would simply be a matter of educating people to accept the new stories of rational progression. Rather than faith, there is methodology. And in the wake of 'progress' as well as the immense creation of wealth, the stunning advances in technology, medicine and understanding the universe, there has been poverty, social unrest and mass destruction through warfare and environmental destruction through pollution. It could be argued that the story of progress has failed, or its influence should be limited to particular areas of social and cultural interest. Equally, it could be argued that the story of progress has not yet been perfected nor fully learnt and accepted. If this is so, then it could be said the real function of social science is to underpin social progress in the interests of individual society members.

In the pre-modern story, knowledge is revealed through faith and/or imposed through fear, transmitted, interpreted and enforced by authorised sources; and in the story of modernity, it is discovered through individual free acts of reasoning applied to experience. In each case, there is an underlying discoverable/revealable enchaining structure, each structure disturbing the other. Is some sort of reconciliation like that of the picture composed of light and dark possible? A kind of reconciliation can be seen at play in Hobbes' *Leviathan*, which is a vision of reason applied to individuals 'chained' into order by fear of the sovereign. However, Spinoza offers more hope through his conception that God equals Nature and hence all individuals partake of natural rights and that these natural rights are held equally. This equality means that it becomes rational for individuals to ensure that as many diverse views and interests are drawn into public debate and decision-making to reduce the sense of injustice accumulating to the point where social order is threatened. That is to say, an open democracy is the best guarantee of public and, hence, individual safety and well-being. However, the democratic inclusion of difference has the effect of disturbing the well-ordered picture. The chains loosen as each new demand is taken into account. This will be discussed more fully starting from Chapter 4. However, the issue that remains is the fragility of social order, the necessity of continually addressing the problems, the tensions, the disagreements, the disturbances that can cumulatively wreck the system. It is through addressing the relationship between individuals and the big policy issues that research plays both the 'normal' and the 'radical' game. It is here that wrongs experienced by individuals can be raised, wrongs that unsettle, unchain, deconstruct and open out onto alternative configurations of the social. Participation in the research of all the viewpoints of those who have a stake creates the dynamic through which alternative theorisations of the social as a basis for alternative actions and alternative, more inclusive, formations of the state becomes possible. These viewpoints include the rights of all who complain of a wrong to be resolved and desire a benefit to be achieved. In essence, this evokes Hegel's project to reconcile his contemporaries to what he saw as the fundamental revolution in society that had occurred. The task was to learn to feel at home in the newly emerging world, a world in which it was possible to conceive of the reconciliation of all opposites under reason. As such, it is a pedagogical issue.

Learning to be at home

The ancient world did not have to actualise individuality for people to feel at home in it, according to Hegel, but in the modern world as he understood it: 'the social world is a home if and only if it makes possible for people to actualise themselves as individuals and as social members' (Hardimon 1994: 99). This is an important condition, the radical implications of which are essential to thinking through the nature of community and of democracy. For Hegel, what distinguishes modern society from previous societies is the emergence of individuality, the desire for individuals to be free to express themselves. This ties neatly with Spinoza's privileging of nature and thus of the natural powers of individuals that derive from nature. However, to express themselves, they need to feel the support of a community, not just for safety needs but as an effective nurturing resource. What does such a community look like? Who composes it? The concept of community can be articulated in policy terms in many forms: as citizenship courses in schools; as the management and control of immigration; as community regeneration schemes; as community policing; as commissions addressing issues of racism, sexism and poverty. However, the essential dimension in Hegel's formulation of what it means to feel at home in a community is the support that is felt to develop one's sense of individuality. This implies that each individual does not want to lose what is distinctive or positive about him or herself under the more inclusive category that unifies and identifies individuals as being members of a named community. But individuals being essentially different, it implies also the possibility of conflicts that have to be managed under the unifying name of community.

The name of the community, in a sense, has the potential to homogenise due to its reputation to colour anyone from such and such a community with particular characteristics. The function of community is to mobilise a process of identification – that is, 'I identify myself with these people in this community'. This can be illustrated in the following extracts from a project involving children of about ten years old working with creative practitioners in a school. They were asked to explore their own community and to imagine their ideal community. When asked to describe their community one girl said:

Girl 2:   You got to see like different cultures like ehh, black people and white people. And people like Indian people, you got to see what their life is like. [. . .]

JFS: Are there different sorts of communities around here because I don't know the area?

G2:   Yeah there's like, like . . . if you go out in a car like a 15 minute drive there's like [place name] which is really clean. And if you go like down, this way out the school, that's clean, but when you come onto my street, that's real mucky. Our mum hates it there.

JFS: Why's that then?

G2:   Because there's teens that are always like cause fights and the police are always round. And I've got like you know them porches outside me 'ouse, everyone's wrote their names on it. And me mum's like phoned the council and the police and everythin'.

(Transcript extracts, 2006)

There are separate communities defined by their dominant characteristics. Then there are distinctions to be made within 'communities' in terms of this street and that street. The sense of underlying conflict is expressed in the complaints about noise and aggression and the litter and graffiti. Their frustration, their sense of powerlessness to affect the conditions of their lives is expressed simply as 'And me mum's like phoned the council and the police and everythin''. None of them liked living in the area: *Boy*: 'Cos sometimes you just can't get to sleep at night, cos like shouts 'n you can hear bottles smashing'. Next they described their ideal community 'where we worked in pairs and then we wrote like a script and we done like models [. . .] and there's loads of stuff in it like banks' and 'stuff that we needed like hospitals, doctors, banks, ambulance, fire brigade, police station, gyms' and [Boy] added 'and we had different churches and different' and

Boy: And we wrote a script where there was a family who came from Jamaica [. . .] there was a racist person who was in the scrapyard [. . .] the police warned him and he continued being racist and he tried to capture the children and then at the end the police just arrested him, then he felt lonely at the end. But near the end it said what they had in the perfect city.

The other group did a story about a gang that came from another city called the rotten rebel gang. They burnt down the museum to steal things. A group called the cool gang informed the police.

The listings of institutions required to meet the needs and the narratives of conflicts and their resolutions provide a sense of a demand for a rule of law whether by police or by gangs. And then they reflected on the comparison between the ideal and the actual by means of a video where 'we went on a community walk around [name of place] and we had like what we needed and what improvements we could make. We saw like the library and bakers, hairdressers, like loadsa stuff like [. . .] and we all walked round and they video camerad us'. And so:

Boy: They videoed all the bad parts of [name] like old derelict streets. Then afterwards I thought it was alright.
JFS: Did it actually seem like the place you lived in?
All: No.
Boy: [I]f you didn't think how [place name] was and took your mind off what we were doing, if you looked at the surroundings they were like, you know 'oh I wouldn't like to live there'. Cos if you looked at all the houses they were all boarded up and, all the graffiti and smashed bottles [. . .].
JFS: So would you have done a different story, you know for (place name)?
Boy: Yeah.
JFS: What would you have shown?
Boy: Well I'd have shown the good bits, like the park and . . . [*laugh*] hmmm, there's a point.
Girl: The good parks, the local parks are all trashed up so we don't get anywhere to play.

To feel at home, there are institutions, public spaces and a certain kind of ethos that are necessary to nurture the sense of self, identity and being in community with others. There is a sense of frustration, of complaint, of wrong being committed in the voices of the children. The transcript extract from an interview carried out during research evaluating the impact of a very small amount of money given to the school by a charity to enable two teachers and two creative practitioners to work with each other on a project with the children provides insights but not concrete solutions to these pressing problems that dominate the lives of the children. It brought some benefits to the children and the school in terms of the children finding out more about each other and in terms of the teachers listening more to the children. These were considered by the teachers and the children to be significant. But the external conditions remain. The research by the teachers and creative practitioners, although designed as 'action research', arrived at an impasse. Its brief was not, as such, to be radical. The evaluation of their work could only show them meeting this impasse which, in a real sense, made the research 'out of joint' with the experienced realities of people's lives in the community.

What more needed to be done? This is a question that went beyond the life of the school but included it. It went to the heart of 'community' as more than a concept and problematised the role of institutions, professionals and policy-makers in communities. To take it seriously ups the stakes of research.

If a community is to exist as something recognisable and desirable by individuals, there needs to be a particular way of being with each other that is felt to be a belonging, something that Hegel called *Sittlichkeit* and Hardimon refers to as ethical life:

> Hegel holds that the members of ancient *Sittlichkeit* identified wholly and completely with their particular community. They enjoyed the satisfactions of community without the pain of alienation. Hegel characterises this relation as a "happy state" (*Glück*) (PhG, 266/214) and holds that its "happiness" consists precisely in that absence of separation and division between community members and their community. It is the happiness of "being in the substance" – the happiness of "unity."
>
> (Hardimon 1994: 34)

However, such a unity is not sufficient for the modern age and the modern individual. What is missing is the sense of individuality that requires also a sense of freedom. This sense of freedom can be expressed in many ways making demands upon the definition of 'unity', of 'belonging' to a community of communities. It can, for example, be expressed by people of different faiths wearing symbols and signs of their faith. The expression of faith, however, can clash with policies, policies that can be formed for many reasons apart from faith: rationally, according to the rules of evidence; covetously, according to desire; fearfully, according to a sense of awe of some dangerous power. For whatever reason the freedom to express an opinion, a judgement, a belief, a feeling, a 'truth' is asserted, it presupposes a principle concerning the freedom of expression. However, such principles may be hard to enact. Feeling that no one is listening, or that what is being said is devalued leads to a sense of alienation, of not being at home in one's 'community' (see Chapter 8 for a further development of this issue).

As in the case of the children, there is a desire for community but also a sense of separation from their actual community, a nostalgia for an ideal that is forever distant. As they constructed their ideal community, they filled it with the kinds of buildings and spaces they desired along with the kinds of stories they wanted to tell in those spaces. How do people 'own spaces' in the realities of everyday life? The spaces into which children are born are not of their making, made for purposes not of their design. But built environments do not fully determine the stories that take place within their configured spaces. There may be a disjunction – or out-of-jointness – between what is intended and what actually takes place, further reinforcing a sense of alienation and a desire for change.

For the architect Tschumi (1996: 113–14), 'an architectural programme is a list of required utilities; it indicates their relations, but suggests neither their combination nor their proportion'. The relation between space and action shades between ritual and spontaneity, where 'ritual implies a near-frozen relationship between action and space' (Tschumi 1996: 127). And spontaneity thus implies a freedom of interpretation as between space and action. But:

> Few regimes would survive if architects were to programme every single movement of individual and society in a kind of ballet mécanique of architecture, a permanent Nuremberg Rally of everyday life, a puppet theatre of spatial intimacy. Nor would they survive if every spontaneous movement were immediately frozen into a solid corridor. The relationship is more subtle and moves beyond the question of power, beyond the question of whether architecture dominates events or vice versa. The relationship, then, is as symmetrical as the ineluctable one between guard and prisoner, hunter and hunted. But both the hunter and the hunted also have basic needs to consider, which may not relate to the hunt: sustenance, food, shelter and so forth. Hunter and hunted enjoy these needs independent of the fact that they are engaged in a deadly game.
>
> (Tschumi 1996: 127–8)

For Tschumi, architecture is not just about 'plans, sections, or elevations' but also 'dynamic movements that take place in time' (interview, in Damianni 2003: 22). Thus, for him, architecture includes the social, movement, people, the dramas that can unfold as summed up in one of his 'Advertisements for Architecture'. On a poster headed 'To really appreciate architecture, you may even need to commit murder' showing a woman who seems to have pushed a man out of a window is written:

> Architecture is defined by the action it witnesses
> as much as by the enclosure of its walls. Murder
> in the Street differs from Murder in the Cathedral
> in the same way as love in the street differs from
>   the Street of Love. Radically.
>   (Damianni 2003: 29)

So, the function of an off-licence or 'liquor store' is just that: to sell alcoholic drinks. But when young teenagers with little to do hang around outside, it takes on other meanings for residents who worry inside their homes. It incites dramas other than the peaceful exchange of goods and services.

In a project involved in regenerating sites for sports in disadvantaged communities, the object was to explore the impact of site development on the local communities. To this end, interviews were undertaken with a range of participants and case studies of the experiences of developing sites selected. This enabled a broad mapping of 'who, what, why, how, when'. In one area, the site was a large open area of rough land used as a dumping ground in the midst of a large economically depressed estate owned by the local council. The project manager described how every day fire engines were called to put out fires on the land and how it was a meeting place for gangs, drug users and was a very dangerous place day or night. Funds had been obtained to clean up the area and to begin to develop facilities of interest to the local teenagers. In about three years, money from different organisations had been obtained to construct a rough-rider BMX track, heavy-duty outdoor exercise machines and structures, a multi-user games court and a skate park. At the time of the interview with the project leader, two foot-ball pitches were also nearly ready for use. He talked about the changes already visible in the community: the fire engines were no longer called out, the gangs had moved elsewhere. Although still dark, and therefore dangerous, at night, during the day the site was now used by local people, and, in his view most importantly, there was the development of a neighbourhood structure. What this meant was that community policing had been introduced, a variety of community support services had moved to a building adjacent to the site which also acted as a community centre. In Thrasher's (1927) terms, this meant that the interstices in which, in his view, gangs thrive were being sewn up. Interstices only emerge at the points where the reach of the law is seen to be weak. Hence, one impact of creating the new developments was the need to ensure the proper use of the site and to avoid vandalism, graffiti and bad behaviour. Thus, in another site, the role of CCTV was mentioned. 'It's not everywhere', the project manager said, 'but they don't know that.' In yet another bigger site involving a million-pound multi-games area with several courts and games pitches, there was the same concern about vandalism, with CCTV where possible but with an additional solution. The coach engaged with the young people, saying, 'This is your site, look after it, make sure people don't mess it up. Tell me if they do.' And he offered rewards like free seats to the league games of the local football team. At another level, since the programme of regenerating sites was national and funded by a major financial institution, staff in the local branches who had volunteered to help in the com-munity were also asked to look out for instances of graffiti and damage. Thus, areas that were outside of surveillance and control were now being brought back under 'community' observation and control. What counts as community, of course, is open to debate and will be discussed in further detail in Chapters 3, 4, 6 and 7. For present purposes, it simply names an area and the people who live and work in that area. In this way, it can be argued that the community is a part of a greater whole, a whole that organises communities so that each part can be regulated for some overall purpose. See Figure 2.1. It's a simple, crude picture of a sovereign state which has power over its executive levels, which in turn have power over all in the community.

> Observation tells us that every state is an association, and that every asso-ciation is formed with a view to some good purpose. I say 'good', because in all their actions all men do in fact aim at what they think good. Clearly then, as all associations aim at some good, that association which is the most

sovereign among them all and embraces all others will aim highest, i.e., at the most sovereign of all goods. This is the association which we call the state, the association which is 'political'.

(Aristotle 1992: I i, 54)

Aristotle goes on to describe the evolution of this state from the 'natural couple' that is, first, man and woman and, second, master and slave. The natural desire for procreation brings man and woman together as the natural ability of the master who thinks ahead and the ability of the slave to do the real physical work are brought together. Rather than master and slave, one could more easily today think about the rise of a meritocracy: the leaders and 'captains of industry' are those who have the greater ability to think and plan while the rest are, in varying degrees, the workers, the governed. From the families of the couples are formed the village and the collection of villages becomes the state. Thus: 'For all practical purposes the process is now complete; self sufficiency has been reached, and while the state came about as a means of securing life itself, it continues in being to secure the *good* life. Therefore every state exists by nature, as the earlier associations too were natural' (Aristotle 1992: I ii, 59).

And 'the state has a natural priority over the household and over any individual among us. For the whole must be prior to the part' (Aristotle 1992: 60). The broad dramatis personae and their relationships to each other in the state has thus been defined resting on some notion of the 'natural'. In Chapter 1, three approaches for developing a methodology to transform the social were sketched: the revelatory (as in religion); the cognitive (as in Plato, Descartes, Hobbes); and the ontological, as in Spinoza. Each define who and how the real is imagined and thus how power

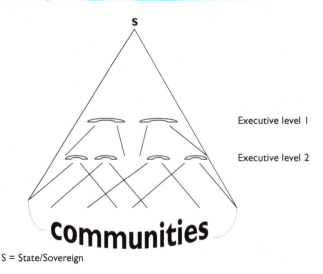

S = State/Sovereign

Figure 2.1 Communities and total coverage

is organised. Spinoza distinguishes two kinds of power: *potestas* or power as a top-down organisation of the whole; and, *potentia*, the local organisation of power. That is to say, the state can be conceived in two ways. In Hobbesian terms, there is the awesome power of the sovereign expressed as the Leviathan through which absolute power is expressed. The power of the sovereign could be that of the tyrant who controls through sheer terror, or it could be the monarch whose power is legitimated by God, or it could be a ruling group as in the Platonic guardians or philosopher kings, or an aristocracy that supports a monarchy or some other form of elite grouping, an oligarchy whose only commonality is the protection of their private wealth and power from the multitude, the poor. In Spinozian terms, the power that rests with the King or oligarchy is imaginary. This is the power of domination and mastery from the point of view of the subject at the top of the pyramid. The real power is the power that rests with the multitude at ground level. It is only by individual members of the multitude giving up some part of their rights in return for security and participation in a wider richer cultural world than can be obtained alone that the power of the leader is produced. The leader is the symbolic focus for the satisfaction of the multitude's needs and hopes. However, unless the state acts in such a way to recognise and meet the diversity of needs of its members, it will become unstable. Žižek (1991) describes the fall of Ceauçescu as a stripping away of the illusions held by the mass of people that had kept the tyrant in power. MacGregor (1998: 20) describes the sudden falling away of the apparent solidity of the Soviet state in 1991. The implications of this for radical methodology will be discussed more fully from Chapter 6. For now, what is important is the inherent instability of any social organisation that does not organise power around the sovereignty of the 'people'. The forms of organisation so far sketched can be diagrammatically represented as in Figure 2.2.

Potentia belongs to the labyrinth, the level of residents in communities; *potestas* belongs to the level of policy-makers in governments and corporations (see Figure 2.1). How can *potestas* – or the power of individuals and its aggregation as the 'multitude' – be employed to put people in the place of power? This is a question of research allied to action engaging political structures through which people organise their lives with each other.

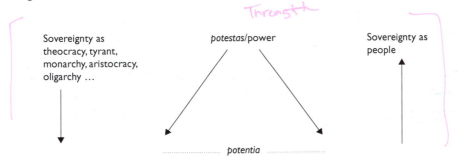

Figure 2.2 From power to power

Structuring lives and communities

If all is working like clockwork, then action of a certain kind is not taking place. These are acts without consciousness, will and judgement – perhaps better called 'behaviour' engineered so that each definable unit of behaviour is linked to the next in a specified sequence to produce predictable outcomes. But what if the chains slip? What happens then to the sense of predictability? What happens to multiple structures of power that frame and order sequences of behaviour in a given context?

If, like Spinoza, individuals are thought of as possessing natural powers to preserve their being, and that being as nature precedes reason, then it seems natural to suppose that if it is in their power to form ideas about what will satisfy a need or desire, and if it is within their physical and mental powers to engage in action to manipulate the resources around them to achieve outcomes that will satisfy their needs and desires, then they will do so. This conforms with a broadly critical realist conception of the relationship between ideas and the material, social and cultural conditions appropriate for the production of desirable outcomes (cf., Sayer 1993; Schostak 2002, 2006). This sense of natural power – in Derrida's terms, perhaps a 'force' (1992a), or in Lacan (1977) as an 'insistence' – to effect something in the world co-produces a sense of self, agency, identity: someone who is an actor not just an element that behaves. Actors structure their engagements with the world about through language and the processes of decision-making, debate, negotiation, as well as through feelings of pleasure or fear within an agonistic, even antagonistic context leading to victory over another, cooperation with others, distancing from others or submission. Actors engage in struggles about the use of power to organise the world according to their needs, interests, desires. Each individual tries to bring the different aspects of the world under their control. Groups of individuals working with each other have the aim of organising as much as possible of the world about in their interests. The sense of community is a sense of oneness, a bringing-together under one name, the name of 'our community' – or, in much wider terms, one under God and our nation, or people. This sense, or indeed 'force', creating the unity of individuals under a name also distinguishes it from others. Theoretically, these others may be far away, and each may never come into conflict with each other's interests. In a globalised world, communities, faiths, corporations, nations, peoples, cannot distance themselves from each other: the global creates a single playing field on which to contest or cooperate, but not stand outside. Each defines in their own terms 'the good', that is, what is good for individuals, communities, corporations, states, peoples and, finally, humanity, that all encompassing category that sets 'us' apart from animals, defining what is civilised as opposed to what is merely natural or uncultured.

Take for example, a now (in)famous statement, by President Bush in his State of the Union Address four months after the tragic and world-changing events of the World Trade Center destroyed by terrorists crashing hijacked planes into it on 11 September 2001. Of the presumed states supporting terrorism, he said:

Whose lives?

States like these, and their terrorist allies, constitute an axis of evil, arming to threaten the peace of the world. By seeking weapons of mass destruction, these regimes pose a grave and growing danger. They could provide these arms to terrorists, giving them the means to match their hatred. They could attack our allies or attempt to blackmail the United States. In any of these cases, the price of indifference would be catastrophic.

> (President Bush, 29 January 2002, see *Washington Post*, <http://www.washingtonpost.com/wp-srv/onpolitics/transcripts/sou012902.htm>)

Apparently simple and straightforward, this is a complex statement that turns on the phrase the 'axis of evil'. It divides the world into two radically opposed camps. The phrase does not come out of the air, newborn. It has a history:

> We need to probe the mentality that neatly divides the world into forces of evil and the forces of good, to understand its sources and its appeal. For this is an outlook that is currently widespread in American culture, from Hollywood to Washington, although it has a much longer history, reaching back to ancient forms of Gnosticism and Manichaeism.
>
> (Bernstein 2005: 12)

The phrase was carefully chosen to fit contemporary circumstances:

> Frum has given an account of how Bush came to use the phrase "axis of evil" to refer to Iraq, Iran, and North Korea. In his initial draft, he compared America's enemies today with those in World War II, and referred to them as the "axis of hatred," but Michael Gerson, who had the overall responsibility for it and is an evangelical Christian, changed "hatred" to "evil" because he "wanted to use the theological language that Bush had made his own since September 11."
>
> (Singer 2004: 207–8)

It seems common sense that people can distinguish between good and evil. However, the boundaries can soon muddy as real acts begin to flesh out the contents that are placed under the category of good or evil. As Machiavelli argued in his political writings, what is good for the state is not necessarily good for the individual (and vice versa). And what is good for one state and one individual is not necessarily good for others. The content of the categories thus differs according to whoever is making the judgement. In order to explore in more detail how language may be used to construct and maintain divisions, the approach to the analysis of language developed by Saussure (1966, 2005) will be introduced. In this approach, a sign which associates a category with a content is divided into two entities: a signifier and a signified. A signifier is the material side of the sign: the mark, the sound waves, the electrical flickering of nerve impulses. Its function

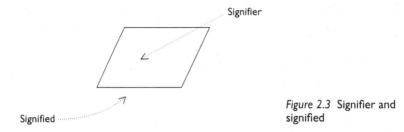

Signifier

Signified

Figure 2.3 Signifier and signified

is to call out a distinction in the world marking a difference between a 'this' and a 'that'. Figuratively, it makes a cut in the undifferentiated flux of experience, separating out something. For Saussure (2005: 157), language is comparable to a piece of paper – imagine the top side is the signifier and the underside the signified (see Figure 2.3).

Now imagine that a pair of scissors cuts through the paper. Suddenly, a 'this' and 'that' emerges: that is, content 'a' and 'b' falls out due to the act of cutting (see Figure 2.4).

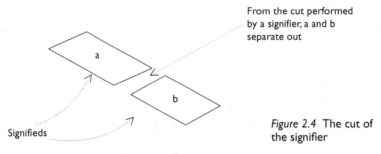

From the cut performed by a signifier, a and b separate out

a

b

Signifieds

Figure 2.4 The cut of the signifier

There is a sense in which something cannot be perceived to exist without the originary cut, the mark of the signifier. While Saussure described the signified as dominating the signifier, Lacan turned it upside down. Rather than taking for granted Cartesian-style clear and distinct real entities in the world – dog, house, tree, love – to which signifiers can be matched, Lacan's inversion has the effect of recognising the indistinctness, the fuzziness, the otherness of the real which cannot adequately be captured in a category, hence making the call that cuts out a distinction the primary act from which content – the signified – is, as it were, called into being. The signified then, is a simplifying act. The French word 'agrume' is a good way of illustrating this. Typically translated as 'citrus fruit', it refers very roughly to fruit that largely include citrus fruit but which also include non-citrus fruit. Hence, asking someone to put citrus fruit in one bowl in English would lead to a different set of contents in the French context – which is 'right'? It depends on context. It is this relation between a signifier and the signified that becomes critical when there are two universalising signifiers – good and evil – which are politically employed to carve up the world into opposing camps. As already indicated, there is a long history at the back of such a political move. It is a history that is intensified further in the wake of political philosophers who constructed political methodologies on the necessity of identifying 'friends' and 'enemies' in order to reinforce political power within a given state or, indeed, alliance of states (Schmitt 1996; Strauss 1988; Norton 2004). This will be discussed in more detail in Chapter 6. Terms like good and evil, friend and enemy act like hinterlands between particular current circumstances and more general stories. Depending on one's cultural heritage, different stories telling of who are good and who are enemies haunt these terms. They make it possible to inscribe the political agendas of the day into the ready-made imagery and dramatis personae defining identities, roles, values, sequences of action, duty and historic destiny that frame the cultural resources of a People.

At its simplest, then, the sign is comprised of the association of two distinct elements that have no necessary relationship between them: the signifier and the signified. Building upon these concepts, Saussure constructed a model of the structure of language which seemed to offer those who wanted to research society a way of doing science that was as objective as for those using mathematical theories to study chemistry and physics – the approach has been broadly labelled 'structuralism'. Language could be seen as providing the mechanisms through which ideas and things in the world could be coordinated to produce desired outcomes. It was a way of engaging with the promise of the Enlightenment thinkers in being able to master the world about by the use of formal systems of analysis. If language could be seen as a system where each element, was simply defined and took its value from being different from each other element then this would provide a logical abstract structure against which to mark out and map the social world: that is, the signifying structure would correspond to the perceived worlds of the people marking out their practices and providing insight into their mental conceptions. It was thus a matter of listening to how people talked about the world in order to analyse the key relationships or structures of that world. For Saussure, 'One could call language (la langue) the domain of articulations – taking this word in the sense defined on p. 26: each linguistic term is a little member, an *articulus* where an idea becomes fixed into a sound and the sound becomes the sign of an idea' (Saussure 2005: 156 [my translation, John Schostak]).

On page 26, Saussure says what he means by the term 'articulation' by referring to the Latin origins meaning 'member, part, subdivision of a sequence of things'. Thus, in terms of language, articulation refers to the subdivision of the chains of meanings into signifying units. As an example, take the idea of the 'yard' as a length of measurement. What exactly is a 'yard'? The story is told that a yard was to be measured along King Henry's outstretched arm from the tip of his finger to his nose. In the context of the English language, this provides an amusing image of the 'ruler' and the nature of a 'rule'. A monarch's reach was made to extend throughout the country. Everything comes under his 'rule'.

The term 'yard' is composed of sounds when spoken, or marks of ink, graphite, chalk, scratches on rock or some other way of making a mark. However, a 'yard' also designates an area at the back of a building. The sound and the marks of the two distinct meanings are indistinguishable from each other. Nevertheless, there is a difference which can be established by saying what the 'yard' is not: by yard as standard of measurement, I don't mean yard as the area at the back of a building. There are thus two meanings – or signifieds – at play here which give alternative values for the sign (as composition of signifier and signified) to designate either the standard of measurement or the space at the back of the building. There is a kind of shuffling going on here as one signifier in relationship to other signifiers (house, measurement) and signifieds (meaning content, thoughts, concepts associated with signifiers) are passed around like cards from an indefinitely numerous deck of cards until a settling out occurs: 'Ah, that's what you mean, you mean unit of measurement not backyard'. So one card is chosen in relation to the intended thought or concept and in a relation of difference to all the other cards – none of the others are appropriate. How does that settling out point take place?

Returning to the length of the King's outstretched arm from tip of finger to nose, some courtier could say to the quantity surveyor, see, that's what I mean by a yard. There is a physical, real but arbitrary something that can be pointed to as what should be marked out in the real world as designating a 'yard' in terms of measurement when someone says, cut me a yard of cloth. That act of outstretching the arm seems to get us out of the system of words defining words and signifiers indicating their difference from other signifiers. Kripke (1981: 76) used this very example to indicate what he meant when he said a name was a rigid designator; that is, in English, 'yard' as a standard of measurement in no matter what context or what 'possible world' will always designate the distance between tip of finger and nose of the outstretched arm of King Henry. The length of the arm is in one sense an arbitrary reference point. It could have been anyone's arm, or the King could have had an accident that shortened the length of his arm or, indeed, have had his entire arm cut off. Or it could have been some other physical object, like the length of a branch cut from a tree. However, in another sense, it is not arbitrary. It was this king's arm, and a king has the power to command throughout the realm. In this ruleful formulation of the power of the king, the fixing process of language appears as both intimate and external and necessary and arbitrary. In this way, a world may be said to be articulated, that is, subdivided into measurable or identifiable parts that together constitute a whole, a whole that can therefore be mapped according to its parts. Saussure (2005: 124–5) provides another image by which to analyse this. First, the naming of the yard can be seen as a historical accident. There was no way of fixing the length of a yard using some process of logical reasoning. There had to be a whole sequence of historical events that led to a particular king proclaiming that the length from the tip of his finger to his nose would from this time forward be known as a yard. This is a *diachronic* process, a process unfolding over time: first, this event, then this one, then this one, . . . , until the moment when a king says, this shall be the length of a yard. Once fixed, however, the term 'yard' passes over into the repository of the English language and, as an element of language, it is available like all other elements of language

Concerned w/ something, especially a language as it exists at one point in time.

Unchaining, deconstruction and the intertextual   61

at a given state of the language, independently of time, that is, *synchronically*. It is like a still photograph of the body of language providing a picture of all the elements all at once. Saussure describes this being like the cross-section of a plant stem. On the horizontal cut surface of the plant can be noticed a complicated pattern. This pattern is then revealed to be the result of the vertical fibres that run the length of the stem: 'the longitudinal section shows the fibres that constitute the plant. The transversal section shows their particular plan by which they group together. But this second is distinct from the first because it reveals certain relations between the fibres that would never be grasped longitudinally' (Saussure 2005: 125 [my translation, John Schostak]).

In language, the diachronic relations between things and people that unfold over time are represented as the horizontal axis; the overall plan of the body of language, the synchronic dimension, is represented on the vertical axis (see Figure 2.5).

Categories of words are stacked in piles like the cards in a deck of cards, each according to their suits. The hand dealt is the contingent, or accidental, or random falling out of the act of dealing. Of course, in speaking, selection takes place: I baptise the length . . . Nevertheless, the selection is historically determined, not pre-given, just as the randomly dealt hand of cards is not pre-given. Thus, there are fixed rules of a game for it to be recognised as a game, just as people employ their terms in ways that can be recognised by others. That is to say, in any game, cards or language, there has to be a degree of fixity between signifier and signified as between a sign and the referent or object it designates in the 'real' material or symbolic worlds of people's lives. When a text is composed and written down or when a discourse is heard and recorded (in memory or by tape or digitally) again there is a kind of fixity so that the text can be referred to by other texts. Therefore, the texts can be held up for analysis, the vocabularies classified and the rules of combination identified in terms of the stocks of key terms they use and the patterned

Synchronic

I	baptise	the	length
you	name	this	measure
she	call	that	extent
he	dub	it	outstretch
it	define	·	·
we	·	·	·
they	·	·	·
(etc)	(etc)	(etc)	(etc)

| I | baptise | the | length . . . . etc | Diachronic |

Figure 2.5 The synchronic and diachronic axis

ways in which they articulate or put together these terms. In Lyotard's words (cited in Bennington 1988: 66): 'A text is what does not allow itself to be moved. The intervals which separate its elements, letters, words, sentences, which punctuate them are the projection onto the sensory support, the page, the stone, of the intervals which separate the distinctive and significant terms in the table of *langue*.' Although the text begins as a place of fixity, the 'thing' that 'does not allow itself to be moved', movement takes place. Language is not just about matching signs with real objects. There is also creative play, imagination through which works of fiction arise and also through which a piecing-together of the world arises; the world is not just read name by name but imaginatively grasped, thus:

> language is also a deep thing, it must be possible to make it the object of operations of fiction; and the proof can be found in the very work of estab-lishing the language; that proof is that the linguist, at the very moment of establishing the place of terms in the plane of structure, which has no thickness, makes use of a procedure, commutation, which nonetheless demands depth. But there are other pieces of evidence which bear witness to the fact that a text must not only be able to be read according to its signification, which comes under linguistic space, but *seen* according to its configuration, which is supported by the sensory-imaginary space in which it is inscribed. Fiction, which is what makes figure out of text, consists entirely in a play on intervals; the figure is a deformation which imposes a different form onto the disposition of the linguistic unities. This form is not reducible to the constraints of structure.
>
> (Lyotard 1971: 61, cited in Bennington 1988: 66)

Lyotard unsettles the apparently simple opposition of the relation between seeing and reading. It is perhaps the difference between *reading* the cards held in the hand and *seeing* the unfolding drama of a game of poker – a sensory-imaginary space of moves, sweat, poker faces, nerves, strategies, winners and losers. This drama is both real and fictional, prosaic and poetic.

The text, any text, provides a fixed place of reference. Yet, to 'see' and to 'read' requires work. Experiencing a given text, even if it is felt to be barely understood, or not at all understandable or experienced as 'meaningless' is valid experience. But this 'validity' only gets to be made socially useful, culturally enriching and transformed through dialogue with others. These 'others' may be other texts, other people or, indeed, one's own readings at different times. Every text, therefore, is related to other texts. And this is what gives interpretation its sense of shiftiness and livingness.

However, as soon as a sign fixes the relation between a signifier and a signified so that something real, physical, alive is captured in the sign, it 'dies'. The word on the page is a representation, an *alias*, not a reality. In that sense, then, the words on the page are 'dead'. In other words, the sign is a threshold between the world of sensible objects that can be felt, that live, and the intelligible worlds of the mind playing with symbolic representations of the real, that evoke the real, making it, as it were, live. This work of dialogue with others, is poetic work where the 'animated signifier, is a monument both of life in death, a death in life' (Llewelyn 1986: 2). This life/death dynamic is a space of hauntings, 'the space of *alias* and so the object falls away, as does the subject yet without being denied' (Derrida 1981: 88). That is to say, the object as real cannot be held within the grasp of the sign and thus 'falls away'. Moreover, since the signifier does not stand in a one-to-one relationship to a particular signified, there is the '*travail*' (work, labour) that employs an anonymous middle-voiced process that is always 'going on': '*il s'agit, il se passe*, it travels' (Llewelyn 1986: 63). The work is to bring elements that have no necessary relationship into relationship, travelling or being vehiculed, as it were, along chains of signifiers, which threaten at any moment to derail. This derailing is, in many ways, quite natural. It can occur, for example, through ambiguities in the sounds of utterances. Saussure's (2005: 146) example is the sound that can either be heard as *si je la prends* (if I take it) or as *si je l'apprends* (if I learn it). The familiar 'Freudian slip' provides another way of thinking about the derailing process in terms of a covert, hidden or unconscious reason for the 'hearing' or saying of one word rather than another. Is rail, then, the tracks of a rail system or the railing of someone who is angry? Context normally provides the criteria through which decisions about the 'real meaning' or 'real intention' or 'real reading' are made. However, when the sense of a natural 'fixing point' becomes unhinged, and the sense of certainty falls away so that meanings get thrown off track, what happens to the sense of coherence of the world – what then?

Design shifts

The unfolding dramas of people's experiences of change, disturbance, feeling unsettled or out of joint provide a focus for ethnographic accounts that reveal something of the fault lines, the broken tracks, the derailments of sense that can disrupt or put out of joint the structured relationships between ideas and the mechanisms and cultural practices through which outcomes are realised. What are the courses of action, the strategies adopted by people to hold onto sense, to refix and re-turn to the sense of a traditional order through which the production of desired outcomes can be assured? And what are the alternative strategies to unchain and shift towards alternative social designs for alternative outcomes? The ethnographic task, then, involves mapping these fault lines, identifying the alternative designs and the process and experience of shift. Many questions could be asked following on from the discussions of this chapter, such as:

•   What accounts do people make of the alternative views of how the world should be? How are these different accounts judged?

- How is the world carved up? In opposing binaries?
- What social structures, processes, beliefs, actions do people call 'natural'?
- Under what circumstances do people feel at home or not at home?
- What do people mean by community, their 'ethical life'?
- What is the relationship between individual and community? Do they experience it as supportive, antagonist, repressive, stifling . . . ?
- How is identity determined? Is it with other particular people, or *the* people as an ethnic group, a specific culture or faith or nation and so on? Is it with territories and places?
- What counts as power? Who has it?
- Who counts as trusted witnesses as the sources of legitimation, validity, reliability concerning accounts of the world?
- Do individuals have an individual sense of power? Is that sense restrained in some way? If so, how, by what?

Detailed analysis of the accounts they make can be carried out by identifying the paradigmatic categories they employ to fix the structures of their sense of identity, rights, powers, community, social order and the world. What are the rigid designators employed through which their everyday life is pinned down, or how they would wish it to be structured? Are they organised into binary relationships of this *and* that, or this *or* that. And are these structured into antagonistic poles as in friend and enemy, us and them? Or are they cooperative poles that mutually respect and find complementarity in each other? What are the threats they experience to their sense of a world? How do they try and defend against these experienced threats?

The resulting ethnographic descriptions and analyses thus provide some insights into the world whose moorings are being experienced as shifting. Whether it is a design of the great chain of being (Lovejoy 1936) or of reason or some form of traditional order, the focus of this chapter has been upon those who feel that the chains of order are being dismantled or are under threat. What now are the implications for research-based actions?

Action research, as described in the literature, typically involves a cycle starting from an interest or problem(s) that requires action followed by a sequence of mechanisms or practices: the collection of data, analysis and/or the generation of hypotheses, planning action steps, implementing the steps, the collection of data about the impacts of the action steps, which are then analysed and generate further more focused problems or interests requiring action (McBride and Schostak 1995; see also Elliott 1991, Somekh and Lewin 2005). As pointed out by Schostak (1999), there are different ways of thinking about action and how action is to be formulated to bring about specified outcomes. In the context of the discussion in this chapter, action is not a simple process of seeing a problem and taking steps as a consequence of that seeing. What counts as a problem is already politically structured. For example:

- Action may be illusory. How much change can we really bring about? Is action just delusion? Often there is a sense of talk and talk, but the action that results leaves everything much the same as it was. Power demands to leave itself in power.
- Global and local speed tracks – some changes are too slow to notice. Some people, organisations, institutions, communities can change faster than others. Even within one institution, change made at one level, or in one section, can be noticeably much faster than in another. The structures are different. Some cultural practices and values are conducive to particular changes; others are not. Hence, action that does not take into account these different speed tracks will generate further problems.
- Action may be undertaken with the object of curing or repairing the system. Both imply something wrong that is put right. Basically the system is OK, just get rid of the rotten apples, repair the leaky tap. This again keeps power in position due to the action undertaken. If the problems are worse than the original state, then it may be considered preferable to return.
- Some forms of action are designed to eat away at structures that are too solid or powerful or inert to tackle all at once. These are like 'experimental border skirmishes'. It can be argued that they are just playing at the edges, never tackling the real/deeper concerns; or, alternatively, it could be argued that there is some latent subversive/viral action that follows as a consequence gradually working away to bring change.
- Action, its possibility or its impossibility is typically embedded in narratives about how the world works. Narratively, statements can be made that there is no alternative to the present course of action because 'that's the way the world is'; or, others may draw upon narratives by which they can claim 'there is always an alternative'. In each case, alternative courses of action that counter the dominant views will require some form of narrative deconstruction, that is to say, an unchaining of the sequences of action 'glued' or fixed into their sequences by the key rigid designators, the categories and names of things through which prevailing sense of the reality of a world is constructed. Again, such narrative deconstruction can be viral in effect, spreading throughout networks.
- Stealth architecture is a term that can be employed to indicate that there's always more going on behind the scenes. Action may present one impression on the surface, while behind the curtains other kinds of action may be going on (see also theoretical developments of this in Schostak 2002 and 2006). For example, an organisation may publicly proclaim that certain policies are being implemented – and indeed, publicly available audit results may even confirm what is said. However, many complexities and outcomes that are in contradiction to the expressed policies may not be addressed by the audit. Furthermore, mechanisms and procedures that are advocated publicly may have unintended deleterious consequences that are not recorded by the approved forms of monitoring and evaluation. In that sense, there are structures

and processes 'behind the scenes' producing outcomes. A stealth architecture presents a minimal front, but, behind it unseen, is a greater set of structures and processes at work.

Depending upon one's viewpoint, action can be seen as ineffective, complicit in maintaining the status quo or as subversive and radical. The same act may be evaluated positively or negatively depending upon whether it is or is not experienced as contributing to maintaining in being or bringing into being the desired form of society. However, the multiplicities of demands and competing actions may instead contribute to a widespread feeling of fragmentation. The robustness of designs to implement action sequences are continually under threat when the chains between ideas and desired outcomes progressively loosen and fragment. At the point of fragmentation, what are the implications for radical research?

Chapter 3

Fragmenting and reframing bodies

The feeling of falling apart, of no longer being able to hold together a once-comfortable unity with others, crumbling or the predictable order of everyday life dissolving is the experience of modernity described by such writers as Bauman (2001) and Berman (1982). However, this 'liquidation' of what had seemed solid also provides the conditions for innovation, reordering, reframing, and is thus essential to radical research. Whether this reframing is motivated by fears or by the lure of opportunities and profits, the scene is set for conflicts and contests in figuring forth alternative pictures of how the world should be. Central to the emergence of alternative possibilities is the role of the 'multitude(s)' in a world criss-crossed by the globalising technologies that dissolve boundaries, places, identities and time (Virilio 1996). It is here in exploring the notion of the multitude and its role in political thought that radical research finds its subject.

What is the multitude? It may be the locus of the Freudian-like seething cauldron of 'drives', 'desires'; it may be the bland mass of anonymous humanity; it may be the fascinated crowds at football matches or pop concerts; it may be the passionate, angry mass of protesters at a political rally. Or is it the confused, frightened mass at an airport under threat of terrorist attack? Or, maybe, is it the desperate queues of families fleeing a war zone? Or, perhaps even, the dead, the dispossessed after the floods have subsided from a tsunami or hurricane? Or the dots of humanity seen from the top of a skyscraper. The multitude are those who are the objects of fear, desire and control by the few who have or seek power. And: '*Multitude* is the term Spinoza uses to describe the collective social subject that is unified inasmuch as it manifests common desires through common social behaviour. Through the passion and intelligence of the multitude, power is constantly engaged in inventing new social relations' (Hardt, translator's foreword in Negri 1991: xv).

It is the multitude, in this sense, that is the ground of democracy because it is here that no one person is 'greater' than another, it is here that each individual finds they are cut down to size. And the central power has power only to the extent that the multitude grounds that power. Hence, for a bureaucracy, the multitude represents that possibility of a radical decontextualisation, a radical unfixing of the points of reference for meaning, a radical reframing of possibilities for social order. But the fear for states is that from the multitude as rabble comes insurrection and revolution. Multitude becomes rabble, chaos, melting the mechanisms that keep society in check. The fall of the Soviet Union and the Eastern Bloc states is a clear example of the speed with which political order can be transformed when the multitude makes its presence felt in the streets as the 'voice' of the people in that moment of radical disjunction between the fall of one political order and the emergence of another. This disjunction and the move towards the multitude performs or enacts a radical decontextualisation. In the terminology of rhetoric, a radical decontextualisation is involved in *catachresis* – a bringing together of elements into a unity that otherwise do not fit, as it were, all the ruling texts in which the laws of the land are inscribed are displaced. The context within which they take their sense no longer obtains. At that moment, when it is undecided whether the state will fall or the multitude will be dispersed and the tensions diffused or repressed, there is fear, anxiety, panic on one side and, perhaps, hope and joy on the other. At this point both politics and research methodologies engage with the extreme, the place where 'data', 'evidence', 'judgement', 'the law', 'decision-making' and 'action' are ambiguous as well as clear and distinct. It is a place where change, transition, melting and solidification are all possible but not yet fully actualised. It is a place where shadows dance but figures do not settle. For Descartes, there was the one certitude that emerged from this place where all is in doubt, the existence of the thinking being. But in this radical place of schizophrenic-like flux, there is not even that certitude. With every thought there is the possibility of a new identity that thinks and claims existence – a multitude of selves.

During a time of riots, in the early 1980s, a young man who had been involved described the smashing of shop windows and how it was 'only natural' to steal. Another described how they had learnt from doing the riots and would be ready next time (Schostak 1986, 1993). Next time never really came. During a time of love and peace – or 'sex, drugs and rock 'n' roll' – that time of hippy revolution when the Vietnam war was still drafting young Americans to fight against the communist threat, in 1970, four protesting students at Kent State University, USA, were shot and killed and many wounded by those who upheld law and order. Protest in the form of the multitude is frightening. When the miners were on strike in the 1980s, at Orgreave in the UK, police charged on horseback. Speaking about the incidents at Orgreave, Margaret Thatcher, the then Prime Minister, commented: 'You saw the scenes that went on in television last night. I must tell you that what we have got is an attempt to substitute the rule of the mob for the rule of law, and it must not succeed. It must not succeed' (30 May 1984, <http://www.margaretthatcher.org/speeches/displaydocument.asp?docid=105691>). It was, in effect, a war: 'We had to fight the enemy without in the Falklands. We always have to be aware of the enemy within, which is much more difficult to fight and more dangerous to liberty' (Margaret Thatcher, Parliament, 19 July 1984).

In the view of the miners' leader Arthur Scargill, on 29 May 1984: 'We've had riot shields, we've had riot gear, we've had police on horseback charging into our people, we've had people hit with truncheons and people kicked to the ground ... The intimidation and the brutality that has been displayed are something reminiscent of a Latin American state' (<http://news.bbc.co.uk/onthisday/hi/dates/stories/may/29/newsid_2494000/2494793.stm>).

The miners lost. Pits were closed. The key words 'liberty' and 'law' were employed to justify the actions against the miners. However, they were equally employed to justify the actions of the miners who were, in their own terms, legitimately seeking to save their livelihoods while standing up against 'intimidation and brutality'. The words 'liberty' and 'law' as well as the words 'intimidation' and 'brutality' are open to interpretation by the opposing sides as each point to the acts of the other. There is then an essential 'emptiness' to these words (cf., Laclau 1996, 2005). That is to say, their defining contents are open to dispute by opposing camps as each tries to control the key words. Žižek (1991) provides an account of the melting away of the authority of Ceaușescu in December 1989. It is like a momentous gestalt shift; instead of seeing a unifying vase, two opposing faces are seen. When the army shifted sides on 22 December, Ceaușescu's fate was sealed, and he was executed on 24 December with his wife, and their bodies were exhibited on television the following day.

In such events, radical methodologies need to be alert to the essential tensions, contents, the particulars, the individual lives and the strategies employed by protagonists in order to marshal individuals and particular groups, organisations, institutions under the great universalising categories of law and order. Recalling Figure 1.2, what are the mechanisms through which the tiny insignificant steps made by individuals in their everyday lives combine into some real or imaginary common voice, some shared symbol focusing the attention, framing intentions and mobilising the will to produce the acts of institutions, corporations, nations on the one hand and revolutions on the other?

On 9 November 1989 the Berlin Wall, a major symbol of the Cold War came down. During that year there were a wave of revolutions across the former Eastern Bloc of the Soviet Union. On 26 December 1991 the Soviet Union itself officially no longer existed. In the West, it seemed as if the 'liberal democracies' had won – the world could be reframed. George Bush Senr. proclaimed a New World Order. The idea of there being a single world order had long been the obsession of conspiracy theorists. Gorbachev had talked about developing a new world order as a reframing strategy following his liberalisation of the Soviet Union. But it was Bush Senr. who took it over to justify the role of the alliance leading to the Gulf War of January 1991, saying

Today that new world is struggling to be born, a world quite different from the one we've known. A world where the rule of law supplants the rule of the jungle. A world in which nations recognize the shared responsibility for freedom and justice. A world where the strong respect the rights of the weak. This is the vision that I shared with President Gorbachev in Helsinki. He and other leaders from Europe, the Gulf, and around the world understand that how we manage this crisis today could shape the future for generations to come.

(President Bush's speech, 11 September 1990, 'Toward a New World Order', <http://www.sweetliberty.org/issues/war/bushsr.htm>; see also <http://video.google.com/videoplay?docid=8259800846851144110>)

The imagery is of a world response unified under a rule of law against the invasion of Kuwait by Iraq in 1990. The fall of the Soviet Bloc and the success of the alliance of nations in the Iraq war seemed to confirm, in the title of a book by Fukuyama (1992), the end of history. If Western democracies had won the battle of ideas, then history as a narrative of that battle was indeed over.

Yet, not quite. In the same year as the fall of the Eastern Bloc countries, there were peaceful demonstrations by Chinese students held in Tiananmen Square called to coincide with a visit by Mikhail Gorbachev in 1989. There was the poignant symbol of a young man standing before a tank, preventing it from advancing. There was also the ruthless repression of the democracy movement.[1] Nevertheless, it could be believed that slowly, inevitably, China too would transform itself through its liberalisation of the marketplace. But there was yet another source of disquiet. In 1993, Samuel Huntington wrote a paper called 'The Clash of Civilizations' (see also, Huntington 1996).

It is my hypothesis that the fundamental source of conflict in this new world will not be primarily ideological or primarily economic. The great divisions among humankind and the dominating source of conflict will be cultural. Nation states will remain the most powerful actors in world affairs, but the principal conflicts of global politics will occur between nations and groups of different civilizations. The clash of civilizations will dominate global politics. The fault lines between civilizations will be the battle lines of the future.

<http:///www.whitehouse.gov/news/releases/2002/01/20020129–11.html>

Following the tragic events of 11 September 2001, when hijacked planes were crashed into the World Trade Center, the hypothesis was seen by some to be prophetic. In his State of the Union Address, 29 January 2002, Present Bush Jnr. linked the attack to Iraq saying:

Iraq continues to flaunt its hostility toward America and to support terror. The Iraqi regime has plotted to develop anthrax, and nerve gas, and nuclear weapons for over a decade. This is a regime that has already used poison gas to murder thousands of its own citizens – leaving the bodies of mothers

---

1 See for example, <http://news.bbc.co.uk/onthisday/hi/dates/stories/june/4/newsid_2496000/2496277.stm>.

huddled over their dead children. This is a regime that agreed to international inspections – then kicked out the inspectors. This is a regime that has something to hide from the civilized world.

States like these, and their terrorist allies, constitute an axis of evil, arming to threaten the peace of the world.

(Huntington 1993)

Since most of the countries identified as members of the axis of evil are Islamic – apart from Communist North Korea – the clash of civilisations and the axis of evil rhetorically merges, a rhetorical catechresis, reframing complex peoples, faiths and nations under simplifying and unifying names. Events have to be named, a kind of baptism (Kripke 1981), before they can become symbols of protest, resistance, freedom and humanity, on the one hand, and symbols of threat, terror, inhumanity and the need for repression, on the other.

In theorising, just as in politicising, there are temptations to 'see' conspiracy theories, to call on a notion of humanity and the people in the justification of wars against 'evil', as well as to see only fragmentation, a series of monads with events just happening. Yet there is another way of appealing to the power that can be wielded under these great sounding signifiers. They can be used to break down the enemy camps by appealing to a more encompassing unity, a unity that does not blow apart when recognising particular differences, by accepting that individuals and situations are irreducible in their complexity to any simplifying judgement:

'Take a boy like my son, who was 12 years old. He was born between two intifadas. What does he know but tanks and soldiers and jet fighters? He only meets Israelis who are soldiers. He thinks all Israelis are soldiers. This does not help us. Seeing each other as human beings helps us,' says Ismail.

(the *Guardian*, 11 November 2005)

Ismail wanted the organs of his son killed by Israeli bullets to be available for transplants and gave his consent for them to be used for Israeli patients – an act that made world headlines. Such humanity seemed to have the potential to reframe by radically decontextualising the confrontational acts of enemies. What is at work here is a glimpse into the radical significance of equality as a method for deconstructing power and hierarchy. If we are all 'the same' in terms of being equally human, equally individuals, equally unique, then a way opens up to remake and keep on remaking our relations one with another under the name of difference and each new difference that emerges rather than freezing differences into those of oppositions. In effect this is a radical destructuration. How might that work as a methodological process?

From structure to deconstruction

As introduced in Chapter 2, Ferdinand de Saussure provided a way of thinking about language as a structured system that in turn became a model for social theorists thinking about social relations in general. To recap, language can be described as a system of differences where each element has no necessary relation to any other element. Yet, it is a system having the power to coordinate images, concepts and things in the world. As Saussure describes it, when someone speaks, there are, on the one hand, the sounds that are made and thus heard and, on the other, there is the act of signifying which produces a chain of signifiers, an enchaining that produces a sense of order. It is like pointing to indicate something, but what do you look at? Do you look at the finger pointing or trace out a mental path towards the thing presumed to be pointed at? So, in this system, there are distinct elements, none of which have a necessary relation to another: the sounds made which relate arbitrarily to the act of pointing or signifying and each such signifier then relates arbitrarily to the mental act that produces the thought of the thing being pointed at. In Saussure's words, do the sounds made when speaking make 'language'?

> No, it is only the instrument of thought and doesn't exist for itself. A new correspondence arises at that point: the sound, a complex acoustic-vocal unity, in its turn forms a complex unity, physiological and mental, with the idea. And that is not quite all:
> Language has an individual and a social side and you cannot conceive of one without the other. Moreover:
> At each instant, it implies at once an established and an evolving system; at each moment it is a current institution and a product of the past. At first sight it seems very simple to distinguish between this system and its past, between what it is and what it has been; in reality, the relation uniting these two things is so close you can hardly separate them.
> (de Saussure 2005: 24 [my translation, John Schostak])

Saussure is pointing to a unity that is composed of quite different things. These different things do not merge into each other, so becoming indistinguishable in their unity. It is a synthesis of heterogeneous things, where each element keeps its own identity as an essential condition for producing meaning or significations. This mechanism of meshing or knotting or cementing together quite disparate things into a supposed unity has affinities with, as pointed out earlier in this chapter, what in classical rhetoric is called a catachresis. This is a figure of speech that intentionally misuses and thus violates what a given language community considers to be the normal use of particular words. In short, the terms should not go together, but when they do they actually express a unity of thought that could not be represented any other way. Over time, such 'misuses' may well become acceptable usages and thus a 'norm'. Examples include 'I will speak daggers to her' (*Hamlet*).

There is no 'proper' relation between the act of speaking and a dagger. Uniting the two is an act that in a sense comes from nowhere. There is no external reference point that says that they can or should be brought together to produce a meaning. In that sense, bringing them together is a violence to the norms of a given community's social use of language. Derrida, in particular, has drawn attention to the sense of violence underlying catachreses and their relevance to understanding philosophical issues:

> I have always tried to expose the way in which philosophy is literary, not so much because it is *metaphor* but because it is *catachresis*. The term metaphor implies a relation to an original "property" of meaning, a "proper" sense to which it indirectly or equivocally refers, whereas *catachresis* is a violent production of meaning, an abuse which refers to no exterior or proper norm.
>
> (Derrida, in Kearney 1995: 172)

Where Derrida sees in the core categories of philosophy a violence in the production of meaning, so Laclau sees in the unities of political alliances or communities only temporary resolutions to essential conflicts of viewpoint and demands – a hegemony, which, in that sense, is a catachresis. Hence, inherent in the apparent stability underlying the structures of philosophical thought or political action are the points of tension that threaten collapse at any moment. Deconstruction is possible only because of such forced stabilities. Structures, however, may be built upon the foundations of these forced stabilities as modelled on language itself, where de Saussure analysed language in terms of the idea as a complex unity of the physiological and the mental. There is a kind of 'edgework' (cf., Schostak 2002) involved at every moment where a distinction is being called into being between one 'thing' and another 'thing'. Each such 'thing' only exists in the act of making a distinction that can be made recognisable in acts of meaning making with another. When someone wants to point something out to another, a play of coordination takes place: no, not that, I mean this . . . no, not quite that, I mean this . . . ; a play that goes on until it can be said: yes, that's right. The structure of 'this' distinguished from 'that' is essential to the production of identity. An identity is defined in terms of its 'outside'. In a world where everything is white, no single object can be discerned until, say a black background is painted, leaving only a circular white disk. The white disk becomes defined and discernable only when it can be distinguished from an 'other', the black background. Identity is defined in relation to its other. However, if the production of the other is essentially arbitrary, then, so too is identity. Any structures that are founded upon such arbitrary productions of identity are also vulnerable to deconstruction. If an identity is always only defined in terms of its structural context, then it has the sense of being necessary. If the structural context, however, is challenged by pointing to the essential arbitrariness of its construction, then each identity becomes decontextualised, that is, it no longer has the protective context of the structure to assure its being. In a world of colour, white is no longer defined exclusively in terms of being not-black. The world of differences has become much more complex, nuanced. New meaning-making and thus identity-making opportunities emerge as the world of differences is enlarged. Identity in this sense is not stable but always at the threshold to new possibilities. A system that is defined by the binary relation between 'black' and 'white' shifts its centre when a range of colours are added to the system. Black takes on a new sense in relation, say, to red. The identity of black is changed in that it now has to include a relationship to a colour. Black is not found on the colour spectrum. Nor, as such, is white. White light may be thought of as the unrefracted state of light. But, in a sense, light in itself is not seen but is the means of seeing the objects that refract light. We struggle to make sense of what we see and experience by trying out distinctions with each other.

For Derrida, catachreses, as the name for radical acts of decontextualisation, are located on the *marge de sens*, that is, the threshold of sense (Derrida 1981). However, in a politics structured in terms of 'friend and enemy', there is no room for manoeuvre – decontextualisation is to become invisible or mad since there are no categories other than 'friend' or 'enemy'. For political philosophers such as Carl Schmitt and Leo Strauss, the friend–enemy distinction is the very essence of politics. A community or a nation is defined by its friends and its enemies. Every individual takes their political identity in relation to their position in the structure as 'friend' or 'enemy' of a given community or state. As in the naming of the axis of evil by Bush Jnr., the process of travelling between the pole of 'good' and that of 'evil' reveals the oppositional point between one term and all others within the linguistic system. The term 'evil' only has a value in relation to its opposite 'good' and, thus, confers meaning. Hence, in addition each term acts as a crossing point – rhetorically, a *chiasmus* – each site dependent on other sites for their existence, para-sites, no less. If each term is essentially a crossing point, then each term is also ambiguous and, as parasite, not essential. Derrida explores this in terms of the *pharmakon* whose very ambivalence as both remedy and poison can constitute the setting, or milieu – *mi* (middle) *lieu* (place) – in which opposites are opposed (Derrida 1981), where the milieu itself is 'both centre and circumference, text and context' (Llewelyn 1986: 87). The 'axis of evil' in this sense signifies a milieu, a setting for thinking about particular states of affairs, a way of thinking about there being a circumference around disparate states, placing them in the same bag so that: 'The lieu of the milieu is not a position or a proposition. It is instead in stead, in lieu, of a position, at most a pro-position' (Llewelyn 1986: 88).

The 'axis of evil' – and indeed, the civilisations that are supposed to 'clash' – stands in place of, in stead of, the different places, the particularities of the specific states, peoples and individuals that are lumped together. This use of 'in stead of', 'in place of' signifies a shifting, a displacement that in turn effects a radical decon-textualisation. The breaking of the word pro-position is itself an act of breaking up, making a gap appear in order to try and point to some nuance missed by an over-easy use of words. As such, the terms point to a semantic void to signify a spacing and articulation of some difference, some slippage, some reduction of complexity that otherwise would go unnoticed (Derrida 1981). There is a spacing between the states that align under the two terms 'good' and 'evil' that articulates the global framework that structures a struggle that can only end in the death or absolute submission of one side. There is in this formulation no longer an outside where the 'evil' can be banished. In the new world order of the emergent globalised market democracies, the enemy can only ever be the enemy within, the terrorist threat that is everywhere and nowhere.

> One is a taxi-driver, another delivers pizzas, one group buys and sells used cars. They earn their livings in unremarkable ways.
>
> They are family types, with young children and pregnant wives. They live in typical suburbs and ordinary towns. To relax, they watch cricket and football, meet their friends and pray at the local mosque. On the surface, their lives are unexceptional.
>
> But in the early hours of Thursday morning, 23 young men and one woman were arrested in a series of raids in connection with an alleged plot to bring down five airliners packed with passengers.
>
> (Jonathan Brown, Geneviève Roberts and Cahal Milmo,
> *The Independent* 12 August 2006)

The article was titled 'The Enemy Within? The Ordinary Men in the Midst of an Extraordinary Plot'. There is a sense of no hiding place and no way of telling who the enemy is. Unless, of course, they belong to communities that represent the clash of civilisations, wearing the symbols of that alternative 'civilisation', symbols that can be interpreted as a desire not to integrate as was the case in the UK when the then Foreign Secretary Jack Straw made a public statement: 'Mr Straw said that wearing the full veil was bound to make "better, positive relations" between communities more difficult, as it could be seen "as a visible statement of separation and difference". He had felt "uncomfortable" whenever a woman had worn one in his Blackburn constituency office.' (Nigel Bunyan and Graeme Wilson, *The Daily Telegraph*, 6 October 2006; <http://www.telegraph.co.uk/news/main.jhtml?xml=/news/2006/10/06/nveils06.xml>). In France, a ban was imposed by the Government on the wearing of Muslim headscarves as well as other religious symbols in 2004.[2] This led to many protests.[3] What is at stake are issues concerning whether different individuals and communities of whatever faith, political allegiance, social class, sexual orientation and so on feel they 'belong' and that their interests are valued. What is at stake also are the universalising principles under which a state defines what is to count as a political 'community'

---

2 See the BBC report, <http://news.bbc.co.uk/1/hi/world/europe/3619988.stm>.
3 See, for example, the *USA Today* report, <http://www.usatoday.com/news/world/2004-02-03-head-scarves_x.htm>.

that encompasses the particular communities of faith, political allegiance and so on and identifies those who are 'enemies'. The issue of wearing the religious symbol in a secular state thus becomes a point of tension. It acts like a crossroads – rhetorically, a chiasmus – a place where 'civilisations' or communities can either cross peacefully and take the opportunity to communicate and enrich each others' experience of life and practice or clash and perhaps spiral into conflict and war. The crossroads or chiasmus is the intertext described in Chapter 2. It is that place which opens up to a range of possible directions or communications with other (con)textual sites. At the crossroads there is the otherwise impossible conjunction of the secular demand for not wearing religious symbols in public places like schools as well as the demand by faiths for the wearing of such symbols. The crossroads is internal to the system itself and thus the impossible conjunction is also internal and necessary. How can it be dealt with?

One way is to try to banish the other into places that are out of sight. In this connection, for example, there is an irony in the lieu of the *banlieue*, commonly translated as 'suburbs' but composed of *ban* as in punishment (*bannir* – to banish) and *lieu* as in place. It is in the 'places of banishment' that large numbers of poor and immigrants in France live. It is in the *banlieues* that riots erupt. However, the *banlieues* are not outside but internal to the state and to everyday life, the problems cannot be simply exported:

> November 10 2005: The situation in France appears finally to be calming after the country's worst urban violence in 40 years. Riots in Paris escalated over 12 days, spreading to other parts of the country, with hundreds of youths arrested and thousands of vehicles and buildings torched.
>
> The rioting began when two teenagers of African origin were accidentally electrocuted while hiding from police in Clichy-sous-Bois, north of Paris.
> (the *Guardian*, <http://www.guardian.co.uk/gall/0,,1636268,00.html>)

These were riots waiting to happen. Many news reports on the riots referred to the 1995 film *La Haine* by Kassovitz that had described a day in the life of a group of friends following riots in the *banlieue*. In the real-life riots:

> On Oct. 25, French Interior Minister Nicolas Sarkozy visited Argenteuil, a low-income suburb west of Paris. "Sarko" is a controversial figure in France. Last summer, he infamously vowed to "Karcherize" – i.e. sandblast – *la banlieue*'s criminal elements. At Argenteuil, he was greeted by a hailstorm of stones and bottles. The minister dismissed his attackers as "*rapaille*," [*sic, racaille*] a word that's often translated to English as "scum," though "rabble" comes closer. Either way, the fuse was lit.
>
> Two days later in Clichy-sous-Bois, another Parisian *banlieue*, three teenagers were electrocuted as they tried to evade police. (The cops were searching for break-in suspects, and had wanted to inspect their identification. The boys, who'd been playing soccer at the time, fled inside a power substation

to avoid questioning. Police have denied chasing after them.) Two of the boys died, the third was hospitalized. "[Clichy-sous-Bois] has three principal communities, the Arabs, the Turks and the blacks," one of their friends told reporters. "The three victims each represented one community."

(Mathew McKinnon, 8 February 2006, <http://www.cbc.ca/arts/music/hangthemcday3.html#content>)

There were other reports that referred to the prophetic lyrics of French Rap songs:

'What is it, what is it you're waiting for to start the fire? / The years go by, but everything is still the same / which makes me ask, how much longer can it last?'

The words are from the 1995 song They Don't Understand, by one of France's best known rap singers, Joey Starr of the group NTM.

He was far from alone in providing a grim prophecy of the events of the last three weeks.

Take these lines from the song In Front Of The Police, by the group 113:

'There had better not be a police blunder, or the town will go up / The city's a time-bomb / From the police chief to the guy on the street – they're all hated.'

Or this from Don't Try To Understand, by Fonky Family:

'The state is screwing us / Well you know, we are going to defend ourselves / Don't try to understand.'

Or this – uncannily accurate – from Alpha 5.20: *'Clichy-sous-Bois, it's gangsta gangsta / And Aulnay-sous-Bois, it's gangsta gangsta.'*

(Hugh Schofield for BBC News, 15 November 2005; <http://news.bbc.co.uk/1/hi/world/europe/4440422.stm>)

The *banlieues* house the poor, the immigrants, the *sans papiers*, illegal immigrants. As capital flows freely around the world, people have become the subject of strict controls and leaky frontiers (cf., Legrain 2006). The crumbling walls between nations are continually being shored up as new realities, some might say a 'new world order', emerges:

Chicago/Los Angeles/New York; May 2, 2006 – More than a million immigrants and allies took to the streets in cities across America yesterday in the latest of escalating demonstrations for recognition. The outpouring was an expression of immigrants' power and importance to the US economy as many skipped work to attend mass rallies and marches and refrained from spending money.

Protesters made their biggest showings in Chicago, New York and Los Angeles, but smaller events – in some cases tens of thousands strong – took place in dozens of cities nationwide.

In Chicago, where even the police estimated that at least 400,000 marchers turned out in the streets, participants demanded legalization and workers' rights for immigrants. In the morning, feeder marches from various parts of the city converged in Union Park, near the headquarters of many labor unions. The crowd erupted into chants of "Sí se puede" (Yes we can) and "El pueblo unido jamás sera vencido" (The people united will never be defeated).

(Kari Lydersen, Jessica Hoffmann, Michelle Chen, Jessica Azulay,
The New Standard 2 May 2006
<http://newstandardnews.net/content/index.cfm/items/3114>)

In the name of the people, demands for a reframing of identities are made by people taking to the streets, whether peacefully or violently. The multitude, as rabble or as revolutionaries, or as protestors, represent the possibility of the fragmentation, melting down and transformation of the political body – the condition of both its possibility and impossibility as well as being the condition for the survival of people as individuals, communities and globalised societies. It is at the crossroads between places, between communities, between alternative 'ends' that language provides the threshold to creative possibilities for living.

Language at the threshold

The threshold is a place of potentials, half-glimpsed openings, half-glimpsed closings. It is a place of tension 'between'. Each word is a threshold word, promiscuously open to intercourse with other words, yet also rulefully – indeed, ruefully – closable, shutting the door on liaisons. Language thus frames the battleground where all is possible or impossible. The threshold is a place of work. To be on the threshold is to be not yet 'there', 'not yet departed', 'not yet arrived'. Work has to be done in order to 'return', 'stay' or 'leave' and thus 'arrive'. In rhetoric, this place of work is the place of the 'parergon' and thus goes alongside the previous discussions of the role of catachresis and the chiasmus. It signifies the place between possible worlds, a spacing where nothing is yet in formation and thus creating as yet no information that can be framed by the codes that would allow a clear reading or readings. It is here that all radical moves begin whether 'back to fundamentals, traditions, revealed truths' or 'on to the new utopia' or indeed, 'radically grasping reality'. This is a place of play, a play of tensions whether these are the forces a bridge is subjected to, or the vibrations of the strings of a guitar or the changing probabilities of having the winning hand in a game of poker as each card is shown. Play is as deadly serious as it is fun.

Similarly with multitudes . . . It is with the multitude – its act of crying out, making a noise, demanding attention – that language takes on its power to disturb the fixities of law and order, the state, the system, through a play of tensions which at times transforms the multitude into a crowd, a mob, a rabble instead of an audience, a congregation, a mass of consumers. For Rancière as for Spinoza, the political emerges from the multitude. It is there where *potentia* is seen to be grounded in the aggregated powers of the individuals who compose the multitude and through that power name, or in Kripke's (1981) terms, baptise the event in which they participate as 'protest', 'strike', 'revolution', or 'celebration', 'mourning', 'devotion' and so on. The power of the multitude to name and thus either reinforce or undermine the status quo, the 'fixed' is feared by the elite who are few in number and whose power is dependent on the support of the multitude. But the multitude is unpredictable and there is always the fear of desires let loose from controls, from managed environments, from the policing of desire. Desire running amok is the fear of sex and sexuality, the permissiveness that runs riot, that grows like a plague, that leads to a panic.

Returning to the theme of the *banlieue*, there is in its imagery a grimy sexual allure as well as the fear of violence that forms the basis of much commercial popular entertainment. In, for example, the video that accompanies a French rap song by Disiz la Peste,[4] a white bourgeois family goes on a visit to the *jeunes de banlieue* (slum youths, or young people of the housing projects – neither of the possible translations into English, however, picks up the sense of youth in the places of banishment that is visible in the original French phraseology). They take a ride on the *train de banlieue*, a kind of fairground show. There they see images of Muslim youth in headscarves confronting police in riot gear followed by a young man and two young women dancing sexily. The white woman watches the male, the white man watches the women. There is a moment of sexual jealousy between the wife and her husband. The evening's entertainment finishes with watching a simulation of a car-burning. But it is not really burning, it is only streamers that fly out to look like flames. After the white family leave, the workers at the *train de banlieue* show clock out. One of the workers who had provided the entertainment of *banlieue* life has ambitions to take a job in the world of the white family. His CV lands on the desk of the father who cursorily glances at it, sees it is a young black man and screws up the CV to throw it in the bin. As rap, as entertainment, as something outside mainstream 'normal' society, the *banlieues*, the slums, the housing projects can be sold for consumption: the setting and the material for a thousand Hollywood films and the commuter or holiday reading of millions. However, as the product of immigration, globalisation and the search for employment, safety and a better future, they are a reality that cannot simply be assimilated. What is created is a 'halfway house' described by Homi K. Bhabha (1994) commenting on Gordimer's *My Son's Story*, the story of a South African who is neither white nor black but 'coloured':

4 See the French television channel, <http://www.tv5.org/TV5Site/musique/clips-3128-jeune_ de_banlieue.htm>.

This halfway house of racial and cultural origins bridges the 'in-between' diasporic origins of the coloured South African and turns it into the symbol for the disjunctive, displaced everyday life of the liberation struggle: 'like so many others of this kind, whose families are fragmented in the diaspora of exile, code names, underground activity, people for whom a real home and attachments are something for others who will come after [Gordimer 1990: 21].'

Private and public, past and present, the psyche and the social develop an interstitial intimacy. It is an intimacy that questions binary divisions through which such spheres of social experience are often spatially opposed.

(Bhabha 1994: 13)

Neither white nor black, or as a second- or third-generation member of an identifiable 'immigrant' community experiencing discrimination the result is 'a hybridity, a difference "within", a subject that inhabits the rim of an "in-between" reality' (Bhabha 1994: 13). It may lead to a search for origins, the true identity on the one hand, or its abandonment on the other. In each case, there is the question of 'fitting in', or creating a society that enables people with their different sense of origins, their different communities or their sense of 'in-betweenness' to 'fit in'. For each to hang onto their sense of their own difference, something must be given up in order to achieve community. But in a compromise community can anyone feel at home?

Is anyone at home?

At the back of 'normal' society is a scandal. It is one that Nordmann (2006) sets at the centre of her study of the issues that separate Bourdieu and Rancière: why don't people revolt?

Bourdieu's whole work is worked through, animated, tormented, by a scandal: the fact that injustice at the level of the social order is not recognised by the very ones who are subjected to it, that domination seems to them, for the main part, natural and, more exactly, that the dominated recognise in themselves only those capacities the dominating order wants them to recognise.

(Nordmann 2006: 9 [my translation, John Schostak])

Feeling at home under domination is less to be explained than feeling a sense of injustice and a need to revolt. If nothing else, as Hobbes argued for his Leviathan, domination gives a sense of security, of knowing one's place in a clearly ordered society that therefore gives a sense of predictability. It is the enormity of the task of dealing with the multitude that gives a kind of relief to know that every one of the multitude is subjected to the same overwhelming order.

The normal is that which has no need of being contested, no need to being rethought anew with every moment. The 'normal', by its very definition, implies an overriding sense of sameness, whether in space or time. This overwhelming pervasive ubiquity about identity reaches far into our ways of thinking and of acting. The 'normal' eschews difference, it forgoes the fluidity and movement of change and it forecloses on a concept of the other. Through its very inflexibility, it fosters the privileging of the uniform. There is no room for the other. Indeed, that other to the normal cannot be seen or heard as s/he has no place and no voice with which to emerge from its mass, nor any distinguishing features with which to make a difference and stake a claim towards being an individual. This is why the multitude holds and casts forth such terror when it appears to claim a unity of voice, as people, a unity that is both one and many – the many counting as one – as Badiou (2004) refers to it. Or if that is too mystical, then at least it is something like a temporary hegemony that has not solidified into some form of strategic alliance that can reproduce the conditions of its survival over time, taking on a sense of 'normality'.

The normal is treasured like the pot of gold at the end of the rainbow. Under contemporary notions of 'normal research', its searchers being those followers who steadfastly believe that research findings only count under (quasi-)laboratory conditions whereby all variables but one are controlled by the researcher when conducting scientific experiments. The model for scientific experiments is located within a binary modality whereby the 'test' and the 'control' constitute the elements, or subjects, by which to put a hypothesis on trial. The trial of these elements or subjects is repeated x times, where x constitutes whatever the figure is for the number of repetitions that is agreeable (i.e., the norm) to all the professionals involved. Only out of such rigorous conditions, so the story goes, comes 'truth'. If all variables but the one being tested are controlled, and, if the results are infinitely, or at least indefinitely, repeatable, then the test results can only mean one thing, namely, what is true or credible for all cases, at least until proven otherwise. And here the slippage begins. It is, in Lyotard's terms, a story, a figure made of text. Thus, the normal comes to mean what is seen and/or heard for all cases. But is that a mirage, a delusion, a 'con' in such cases that essentially stripped of individuality and can only appear as 'mass', 'crowd', 'sample' and so on? What then is the research task in terms of the 'mass', the 'multitude', the 'many', the few, the particular and the singular? What is being seen, or not seen in each case? And does this sense of the 'normal' mean the same as feeling 'at home'? In Bourdieu's terms, 'Domination cannot be perpetuated if it is not "interiorised" or incorporated by each one, if, in particular, the dominated do not think of themselves via the categories produced by domination, if their desires are not fundamentally in conformity with what the social order demands of them' (Nordmann 2006: 9 [my translation, John Schostak]).

Hence, it could be argued that feeling at home is a process of interiorising domination and subjection. Yet, there is something more. This very interiorisation is itself an unsettling process leading to a sense of what Royle (2003) has explored as the 'uncanny', a sense of being at home and not being at home. A limit is being set between what is possible to do, and what is not possible; what is comfortable, and what is uncomfortable; what can be done freely, and what is constrained. It is this limit that operates between the dominated and the subjected, thus framing the limits to feeling at home, between what can be made visible and what can be actionable and articulated. Being at home connotes something intimate, something hidden from the public gaze as well as feeling safe, at ease and in place in the public sphere. However, the relation between the private and the public involves a tension that finds no rest. In it, Bhabha sees the unhomely, the uncanny drawing on Arendt and Freud:

> Arendt's description between the public and private realms is a profoundly unhomely one: 'it is the distinction between things that should be hidden and things that should be shown,' she writes, which through their inversion in the modern age 'discovers how rich and manifold the hidden can be under conditions of intimacy' [Arendt 1998: 72].
>
> (Bhabha 1994: 10)

It is in this unhomely relation that the impossible condition of modernity resides, the condition described by Hegel as the tension between the desire for full and free individual expression in the context of a richly supportive community. However, if there is neither a sense of being able to express one's self in freedom nor the experience of a community that encourages and promotes individuality, there are the conditions for alienation, disappointment, anomie and so on, leading to a kind of oscillation between a paranoia of the borderlands between the intimate and the public and a collapse of borders where nothing is fixed. Berman (1982) describes, in his terms, the experience of modernity as a sense of all that had been solid as having melted.

Losing the threads

If 'tree' as a signifier is just a sound, or just a set of marks on a surface that has the capacity only of making distinctions, then distinctions can be drawn anywhere and distinctions can arise within what may be singled out as a signifier. The collection of marks – 'tree' can be decomposed in the search of alternative configurations that still make some sort of sense in English – t(r)ee as in tree tee – or may be heard in other signifiers like 'entreaty', which could be heard as 'n tree tee' which may then set in train a movement of sense-making in search of sense at this thresholding of sense: where is that nth point or place of sense-making where tree and tee – or tea – meet? Without some sort of fixing point, the process of decomposing and recomposing, deconstructing and reconstructing into alternative configurations seeming to allude to sense without actually seeming to make sense, can continue indefinitely, perhaps producing a 'schizophrenic-like' experience: 'For the schizophrenic, all signifiers can be made to designate a single concept or signified. In other words, the signified or concept is not bound to anyone signifier in a stable manner, and numerous permutations of signifiers designating that signified is possible' (Lemaire 1977: 236).

There is an unchaining, as it were, from the way in which signifiers interlace and fuse or fix with signifieds to map out a world of a multiplicity of independent things, concepts or signifieds. In Figure 3.1, signifiers 'a', 'b' to 'n' are made to designate one signified. If a series of signifiers are made to refer to one signified, then metonymically, each signifier is made to refer to a conceptual whole. There is a loosening, an unchaining of the signifier–signified relationship to produce a symbolic world that floats away from the referents to which concepts refer as the material and symbolic world of others intersubjectively defined. The schizophrenic, as characterised by Lemaire's Lacanian analysis lives 'in a world of symbols'. But 'For the delirious subject, on the contrary, a single signifier may designate any signified. The signifier is not bound to one definite concept. The persecutor, for example, will be interchangeable' (Lemaire 1977: 236).

In the paranoid framework, the relationships in Figure 3.2 are reversed.

For example, say there is an unyielding bureaucracy that is materially designed to keep control of everything. Everything, or every signified, then is an object for control. Such a bureaucratic framework rigidly designates every referent back to the central or master signifier, the bureaucracy that adopts the place of Power in Figure 2.1. Anything is potentially out of place and thus dangerous to the bureaucracy, a conspiracy, perhaps emanating from 'below' in the place of the people conceived as persecutors, those signifieds who are to be dominated, those whose powers (as *potentia*) have to be kept in check, moulded, ordered, exploited for fear they might occupy the place of power. Similarly, any individual could see in every act of the state a persecuting intent. Whether schizophrenic or paranoid,

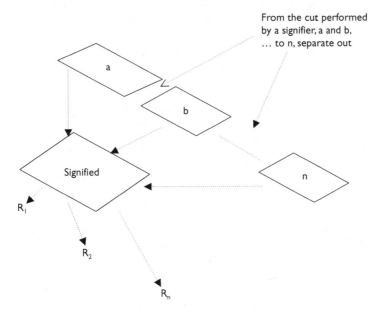

Figure 3.1 Many signifiers but one signified

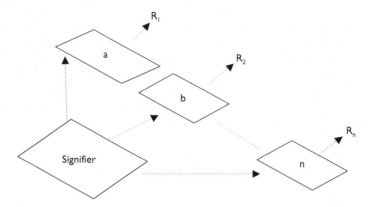

Figure 3.2 Framing the paranoid

an unchaining between signifiers and signifieds takes place that threatens the stability of the relation between a subject, the everyday worlds of others and the world of things. From a point of view outside of the 'schizophrenic' and 'delusive' readings, all seems as if it is fragmenting or melting.

Tying the knots: reframing the subject

A human life, it might be said, is full of events, which, ultimately in some form or another, can be told to another as a story, a biography, in a sense, in a process of becoming a subject, an embodiment. Within this life story are embodied – as a single signifier – many stories depending on how the individual draws the different threads together and on how these different threads become interpreted by the other. In other words, action incorporates narration and narration embodies action, thereby enmeshing a life story, a narrative and a politics through which events are subjected to provide some 'meaning'. For a recountable narrative, therefore, there needs to be fixing points that synthesise signifiers and signifieds to enable meanings giving value – a value? – to life. But, for Arendt, life is not a 'value' as it is for some humanistic ideologies. Rather life is 'realized only if it constantly *questions* meaning as well as action' (Kristeva 2001: 42). Such questioning is achievable, Arendt suggests, through thinking, willing and judgement, which all together comprise the 'life of the mind'. Life is not life without life and meaning. By questioning meaning, the narrative, the life story, the event comes under threat as points of fixity are problematised, hystericised as Lacan might say, as continual questioning challenges the fixed or programmed relation between a concept and its signifier, thus throwing out of skew, or out of joint, the programmatic order.

So, for example, a consultant surgeon recounted the habit of walking into the consultation room and intentionally saying to the patient 'Hello, you are Mr or Mrs X, aren't you?' so as to avoid any patient mix-up. There are good reasons to do so, not just bureaucratic reasons, but reasons of due care for another.

[T]he nurses are forever checking. I sent a lady for a mammogram, a Mary Smith, date of birth 1st of January 1923. When she went to the mammogram unit the nurse had called out 'Mary Smith' and two ladies got up.

She [the nurse] said 'Okay, who are you?' 'Mary Smith'. 'Who are you?' 'Mary Smith.' 'What's your date of birth?' They had got the same date of birth.

And I had sent one for a mammogram, having seen her in clinic, and Breast-Screening Unit had sent for the other one purely by chance, on the same day.

It happens.

(Taped CasE core team meeting transcript, 14 January 2002)

One Mary Smith had attended this consultant's breast clinic on a Tuesday morning in early January. The lump in her breast revealed by the physical examination required a further investigation, so Mary Smith made her way from the outpatient clinic to the mammogram unit. But on the exact same morning, another Mary Smith had attended the breast-screening unit, called by a routine screening programme that aimed to catch breast cancers early. It seemed astounding – what are the odds? And yet, as the anecdote is told, it sets in train other accounts where a 'signifier' – say, Mrs Smith – has many potential candidates as content of the signifier, each potentially 'replaceable' by the other. A consultant rheumatologist described how in the department there were two female patients, both with rheumatoid arthritis, and both were 'roughly the same age, but they've actually got very different severity and they've been confused in notes. And because they're roughly the same age and they answer yes to the same name the wrong notes have been written on the wrong patient and that's extremely dangerous' (Taped CasE core team meeting transcript, 14 January 2002).

It was clear from the discussions with the CasE consultants that unless due care and attention is paid to individuals as individuals, the professional may too easily just rely on blind bureaucratic procedures that are not necessarily attuned to differences. As in the following story told by the consultant psychiatrist, expecting something to be true, in effect deceptively constructs that reality, that is, the symbolic order of concepts loosens from the material signifier the physical human being in the room. A GP in a market town had referred a seventy-six-year old man to psychiatry with possible dementia. As usual, the consultant's secretary telephoned beforehand to ensure that the prospective patient will be at home and not out shopping when the consultant arrives. The consultant continues:

So I arrive at this address where there's a little Close – where there's Something Close and Something Road and Something Lane. Number 2. I go to number 2. An aged 76 little old gentleman opens the door, looks a bit flummoxed and perplexed and I said 'Good morning, Mr So & So, I'm Dr Z.' 'Oh, do come in.' We have a chat. [. . .] I diagnose vascular dementia, moderately severe, and write a letter to the GP.

(Taped CasE core team meeting transcript, 14 January 2002)

Later that week, the social worker telephoned the consultant to ask, 'Who on Earth did you see? I was waiting to see you.' With the same name for the Close, Road and Lane, the address given to the consultant had become muddled; arriving at the wrong address was the consequence. The referred patient was not seen on that occasion, another visit was thus arranged, whilst another individual altogether, who up until this mis-take, was outside the system and not included in the set of patients referred, was deemed in need of some psychiatric help. The single signifier, Mr So & So, could in the right circumstances, it would seem, be applied to any content.

A system of addresses cannot work without some way of making distinctions that are universal in application tying a signifier to a particular signified. In practical terms, with an address, you're always in contact. Indeed, you identify yourself with an address. This naming of an abode justifies you in a myriad of social and cultural ways. For instance, you can vote, sign up to financial and business transactions, make purchases, partake of the legal system, borrow library books – in short, it grants validity and substance to being. In other words, it secures an abiding citizenship, a privilege from which the homeless are for ever barred. The phone number, the postal-code address, the IP address, the vehicle number plate . . . it's all about location, location, location and keeping tabs. And most properly of all: are you in the right location? Of course, one pays even more to live in the most favoured location, whatever the criteria for that particular spot might be. Are you in the right catchment area for the school of your choice for your children? If not, will you have to move? Is your area a rough neighbourhood? Can you afford to move to a better one? The parents of the children in Chapter 2, who designed their own ideal community environment, certainly could not do so. Do you have a view of the sea or the lake or the mountain? And so the list of criteria continues. Thinking and acting towards a totality – the system of addresses – culminates in an identification of subject/object, such that reason and rationality will prevail in the end, surely? A lot rides not only on having the right address but also on that address being stable, inasmuch as it functions as a unique identifier. However, as in the above case, there is always the possibility of slippage, confusion, ambiguity.

The CasE consultants' accounts thus, illustrate the ease with which mistakes could and do arise and the importance they give to taking this into consideration. The very fact that each patient's full name and date of birth is recorded on medical records, it could be argued, should confer an individuality-through-medical-record that is water-tight. This is the programmed intention underlying the system:

> a system whose behavior can be at least sometimes-explained and predicted by relying on ascriptions to the system of beliefs and desires (and hopes, fears, intentions, hunches, . . .). I will call such systems *intentional systems*, and such explanations and predictions intentional explanations and predictions, in virtue of the intentionality of the idioms of belief and desire (and hope, fear, intention, hunch, . . .).
>
> (Dennett 1976: 179)

An intentional system can be thought of as a chain of intentions. However, in this sense, intentionality is not being used in the everyday sense but in a technical phenomenological sense deriving from Brentano and employed by Husserl in his analysis of the structure of consciousness. In Husserl's phenomenology, consciousness is always directed towards something for someone. This 'directedness', that is, being about something, some object, some one, is the essential structure of consciousness and defines 'intentionality' as a mental state that is always about something in the world. Any mental act, like seeing a house, involves an act of consciousness which directs attention towards the object, the house. If the house is in a line of houses, then consciousness is directed towards that line, that is, the street. The street involves a chain of acts whereby conscious acts are directed not only towards each house, but towards the idea (mental object) of the street as being composed of the line of houses. Very simply and crudely, this sequence of acts can be seen as composing an intentional system, with each act being linked in a chain to each other act. The whole is named 'the street'. But the street itself relates to other streets, composing a 'neighbourhood', a 'community'. And each neighbourhood and each community relates to others composing a village, a town, a city. And so on. In very general terms, this can be conceived as a system of addresses, each location has its own identity, its own location in the system so that precise directions can be given for any person to orient themselves within the system and locate any particular place or address. It doesn't stop there. To be of cultural, social, political, economic, that is, of human significance, it all depends on language, the process through which addressing systems are constructed for human purposes. In this process, the objects (and subjects, and subjective states) of consciousness are named and the names organised through the application of rules of combination (codes, grammar) to produce meaningful outputs (utterances, texts, signals) that anyone who shares the codes and the names can decode and use in some way. At its most general, as discussed in the previous chapter, developing from the work of Saussure, language has been used as a model for analysing signs of any sort. Combining this with concepts of intentionality and intentional systems, the subject is subjected, rendered object to the system as in the paranoid/ delusional system described above. However, through questioning, by hystericising the system, the subject re-emerges not as object but as the 'gap' between systems, between, above, below the cuts made by signifiers. That is, the unrepresentable, the instance of change, the minimal something of existence that is always outside systems but is that which is directed towards objects and produces associations, or in phenomenological terms, intentional networks of varying degrees of predictability where particular individuals are directed towards each other, held/knotted/bound together whether as friends, or as enemies or as colleagues in real or imaginary ways (Schostak 1985, 2002, 2006). Through the intentional networks by which individuals, families, gangs, communities, organisations, states are directed towards each other internally and externally, the givens, the data, of everyday life are produced defining who is in step with who and who is out of joint.

Intentional designs

An intentional network, because it describes the ways in which people act towards each other and the world about, provides a useful analytic framework that maps over the Saussurean synchronic and diachronic axes. At any one moment, as if taking a global snapshot, all individuals are intentionally connected, perhaps not directly, but indirectly, at some level. Perhaps like a half-serious joke that starts, 'I once shook the hand of the person who shook the hand of the person who shook the hand . . . of Elvis Presley'. This network of handshakes can be described graphically as points connected to each other from start point (I once shook . . .) to end point (the hand of Elvis Presley). It is a one directional path. However, more complex networks can be described in terms of multiple connections (see Figure 3.3).

Suppose Figure 3.3 describes a relatively small and simple intentional network of people directed towards each other in some way. The most highly connected people are A and B. Both A and B have four people who are directed towards them. But A and B are not directly in touch with each other. Their relations are mediated by C and D. Suppose now that A and B are rival gang leaders. That could mean that C and D play critical roles – are they spies? Or what if A is a gang leader and B is the chief of police? Say, C is a 'bent' police officer providing information to A; and D is an undercover agent. Who knows what about who?

The network in Atkin's (1981) terms describes a multidimensional space where B is connected in terms of four dimensions and D in three dimensions and C in two. Of course, in reality, people are connected much more complexly than this. Nevertheless, the network, if desired, can be mathematically described and analysed in terms of particular kinds of relationship each hold with another. Each connection can be given an orientation like A loves C, but C does not reciprocate. How information flows through the network and where it is inhibited can be described. Interviews can be carried out with each member of the network to find out what they know about each other. Alternatively, an ethnographer can start anywhere in the network, even at one of the one-dimensional outer limbs of the network and gradually map the key dramatis personae until they get to more highly

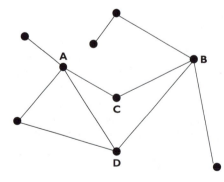

Figure 3.3 Intentional network as multidimensional space

connected individuals who can get them closer to A and B. By close description of the intentional relationships each holds towards the other, the nature and intensity of those relationships that bind cooperatively can be distinguished from those that bind in enmity and those where the binding is tenuous or more apparent than real. An ethnographic case study of intentional networks can thus be explored in order to describe the multidimensional spaces in which given individuals operate. From the discussions in this chapter, a step towards describing the dynamics of these spaces may be made in terms of:

- the patterns of the transferral of rights from particular individuals and groups to others and the extent to which this is done willingly or unwillingly in the production of power over the actions of people;
- chains of reference following from an act of naming, of witnessing;
- chains of identification with a group, community, organisation, culture, people, leader, faith . . . and so on;
- the sense of a loss of connection with desired others: group, community, organisation, culture, people, leader, faith . . . and so on; leading to
- the sense of a loss of addresses, that is, actions towards some goal are initiated but always seem to end up going nowhere, there is no recognisable home address for them; leading to a
- sense of a loss of being at home.

The structures of intentional networks are like architectures. And, like architectures, there are designed relationships between the conceptual structures brought into play and their realisation through key mechanisms like doorways or hinges that have designated functions either opening up or closing off spaces – planning rooms, meeting rooms, office spaces, factory spaces and so on – shielding groups from each other, concealing their agendas.

The notion of a stealth architecture (Schostak 1999, 2002, 2006) can be used to explore what happens when intentional systems in effect go undercover, thus concealing what is at stake and what is happening from one or more groups and individuals. Such structural relationships can, of course, be used deliberately and with duplicity as when glimpses are revealed in order to arouse desire and thus lure or to protect from attack or to undermine and make surprise attacks. The idea of a stealth architecture was inspired by reading Mical's (1992) concept of the stealth landscape which he introduces as follows:

> The stealth landscape operates around us, unseen. As objects, incidents, and spaces within the city are lost or disappear, the question of their duration and destination are raised. If they are reconfigured or recede into the mottled and weathered back ground textures of multiple (formal, conceptual, electro-mechanical) landscapes, clearly any space, city, or landscape can be defined by its negations rather than its institutions. The spaces of modernism are the scene of disappearances or theaters of negation. These alternate readings, in their entirety, comprise the stealth landscape.

Mapping intentional networks as stealth architectures over the physical spaces of built environments together with the notion of a stealth landscape gives something of the bewildering complexities that compose everyday life. From observations, the accounts of people and reflections on experience employing a dialogue between viewpoints, this intricacy of interaction that seems to defy analysis can be explored. A dialogue between viewpoints takes place on the condition that there are differences to explore; otherwise, no matter how many voices, it would be a speaking as one, a monologue – singing from the same hymn sheet, as politicians like to say. The complexity ensures that no one has a complete grasp of the whole picture. Indeed, given the dynamism of everyday life, there is no whole picture. However, there are the struggles that people experience. Even if all seems to be falling apart, fragmenting, there are the attempts – successful or otherwise – to grasp and to organise a sense of the whole, a sense of their part in some greater whole whether that is their personal life with those close to them or their involvement in wider social projects and faith communities. What are the attempts to forge meaning that people make as they walk the labyrinths of their lives with others?

Chapter 4

Incarnating/incorporating data as understanding and explanation

Data is a matter of seeing. And seeing is a matter of perspective. Without the senses or the tools that augment the senses, nothing can be seen. Without subjects expressing viewpoints from their perspectives to each other, data cannot be made publicly visible. Without public recognition, there is no data that can be evidence as a basis for understanding and explanation. But how is recognition organised? In Chapter 2, the God's-eye and street-level views were described in relation to Spinoza's concepts of power. This gives the possibilities of recognition by some all-defining master subject or by the contest of views dispersed in the multitude. In the egality of the multitude is the birthplace of politics, that is, the emergence of associations to lift individual interests into the combined efforts of cooperatives, gangs or other kinds of organisations. It is here too that there is the birthplace of the hatred of democracy, the plurality of views, that Rancière (2005) sees as an ever-present danger. Democracy is an object of hate for those who see it as undermining their claims to universality, their belief in some notion of the 'good' or their desire for privilege and wealth. For the poor, it is an object of hope. It is the place where old evidences of an uncontestable reality melt and explanations and understandings no longer hold. If in the multitude there is necessarily a plurality of perspectives, there can only be a unity, a society, a world, if there is some kind of reconciliation with the multiplicity of differences, or at least a sufficient range of differences. Even where a majority of viewpoints claim universality, as in the claim for equality, they do so in the face of and conflict with those who benefit from inequality. Each 'side' may seek knowledge to realise their interests, and they may seek a certain body of knowledge so that they never lose power over those objects that satisfy their interests. But: 'No object is wholly known; knowledge is not supposed to prepare the phantasm of the whole. Thus the goal of a philosophical interpretation of works of art cannot be their identification with the concept; it is through such interpretation that the truth of the work unfolds' (Adorno 1973: 14).

The whole, in which each part takes its meaning, is not simply the summation of the elements through which a painting is composed. From the analysis of colour, brushstrokes, lines, proportions, no sense of the 'truth' of the 'painting' emerges (cf., Derrida 1987; Carroll 1987). Something more is required for understanding.

It is in that 'more' that creative, sense-making acts incarnate the 'elements', form them into a body of thought, a knowledge, a theory to explain and understand the 'world'. In a world with a single vision, however, all is brought under the rule of that single order, that single way of seeing, that master view.

Radically seeing and not seeing

> 'Do you see?'
> 'Oh, yes, I see.'

On one level, (a) there is a subject who 'sees'; (b) there is an object that is 'seen'; (c) there is a relation between 'seeing' subject and 'seen' object; (d) there is a call to another to gain some confirmation of recognition; and, (e) there is affirmation of recognition by the other. It could of course continue indefinitely, as in a hall of mirrors: I recognise you recognising that I recognise that you. . . . But what is the nature of, and, of what matter is this 'subject', this 'object', this 'relation' this 'reflection' and reflexivity of recognising that reflecting is going on for a self and the self of another? Who controls these 'seeings' is a fundamental political question governing the difference between what is 'normal' and what is aberrant, what is visible and what is invisible, and, thus, about the production of subjects or the manner in which they are made to be subjects within a field of experience who see, recognise, act, speak:

> Politics is about subjects, or rather modes of subjectification. By '*subjectifica-tion*' is understood, the production, through a series of acts, of an instance and capacity for enunciation which is not experienceable in a given field of experience. The identification of this is coupled with the reconfiguration of the field of experience.
>
> (Rancière 1995:59 [my translation, John Schostak])

With each mode of subjectification and each field of experience, data is incarnated differently. If it were not, there could only be one way of seeing and no foundation for the contest and dispute through which knowledge is produced. For Kuhn (1970), such knowledge does not progress uninterruptedly in terms of an accumulation of 'known facts' and 'true theories', each piling up to produce a clearer and clear and more fully articulated map of everything. Rather, knowledge 'advances' as a series of revolutions. Each new revolution has as its body of knowledge para-digmatic texts as to how to do science 'normally'. It has its normal way of seeing. To move from one way of seeing 'normally' to another involves a 'reconfiguration of the field of experience' that Kuhn calls a paradigm change, involving a revolution in the way in which the world is perceived to be.

This suggests, perhaps in line with Popper (1963), that truth cannot be attained in any final way. Rather, for Popper, the strategy is to produce hypotheses or conjectures that can be tested and at least proven to be false if they cannot be proven to be true. However, this still appears to suggest that there is a particular method that, while not attaining the truth of something, can at least prove the falsity of some *proposition* or *conjecture* about 'the world'. Knowledge then becomes any proposition, conjecture, theory that offers the best explanation until proven false or replaced by an explanation that explains things better. This still gives a way of talking about an accumulation of knowledge, that is, an accumulation of explanations that currently survive in relation to a knowable world, albeit too complex to be known in its entirety. He described his reasoning as follows:

1. It is easy to obtain confirmations, or verifications, for nearly every theory – if we look for confirmations.
2. Confirmations should count only if they are the result of *risky predictions*; that is to say, if, unenlightened by the theory in question, we should have expected an event which was incompatible with the theory – an event which would have refuted the theory.
3. Every "good" scientific theory is a prohibition: it forbids certain things to happen. The more a theory forbids, the better it is.
4. A theory which is not refutable by any conceivable event is non-scientific. Irrefutability is not a virtue of a theory (as people often think) but a vice.
5. Every genuine *test* of a theory is an attempt to falsify it, or to refute it. Testability is falsifiability; but there are degrees of testability: some theories are more testable, more exposed to refutation, than others; they take, as it were, greater risks.
6. Confirming evidence should not count *except when it is the result of a genuine test of the theory*; and this means that it can be presented as a serious but unsuccessful attempt to falsify the theory. (I now speak in such cases of "corroborating evidence.")
7. Some genuinely testable theories, when found to be false, are still upheld by their admirers – for example by introducing *ad hoc* some auxiliary assumption, or by reinterpreting the theory *ad hoc* in such a way that it escapes refutation. Such a procedure is always possible, but it rescues the theory from refutation only at the price of destroying, or at least lowering, its scientific status. (I later described such a rescuing operation as a "*conventionalist twist*" or a "*conventionalist stratagem*.")

One can sum up all this by saying that the criterion of *the scientific status of a theory is its falsifiability, or refutability, or testability*.

(Popper 1963: 33–9)

For Kuhn (1970), however, there is not much evidence that scientists actually follow such a method in their work, quoting cases such as Kepler who placed the sun at the centre of the solar system simply because for him the sun god was the centre of all life. Feyerabend (1975) went as far as to say that 'anything goes'. Although Feyerabend admitted later that not quite anything goes, the point remains:

scientists do not just follow the limited rationale of forming hypotheses that are then tested and rejected once having found to be 'false'. Does 'falseness' persist over time? Does the 'conjecture' fit well with a broader set of ideas or theories?

> A major problem in considering a refuting observation is that a theory consists of a *complex* of refutable universal statements, rather than a *single* refutable statement like, "All crows are black." Furthermore, to permit testing, more statements than those of the tested theory are involved – the theory must be augmented by auxiliary assumptions, such as laws and theories governing measurement and the use of instruments. Initial conditions, such as description of the experimental set-up, must also be added. If a prediction that follows from these joint premises turns out to be false, then all that can be logically concluded is that at least one of the premises is false and, hence, no individual hypothesis or theory is conclusively falsifiable. This problem of the jointness of testing, is referred to as the Duhem problem (see Duhem [1954])
>
> In accounting research, for example, market efficiency research has generated many anomalies [. . .], but researchers in the area have not viewed the efficient markets hypothesis as falsified, because of, *inter alia*, the impossibility of locating the source of the "falsification" within the maze of premises which is effectively tested by a capital market efficiency test [. . .]. A capital market efficiency test jointly tests premises concerning data quality; assumptions relating to transaction cost estimation; whether information is good/ bad; the timing of events and information release; a specific asset pricing model; measurement theories, instruments and procedures, and so on. Indeed, Foster [1984, p. 169] and Lev and Ohlson [1982, p. 274] prefer to call efficient markets hypothesis counter observations "research puzzles" and "surprise results" respectively, rather than "anomalies" or "falsifications".
>
> (Hines 1988: 660)

Ariew (1984) specified that for Duhem '"To seek to separate each of the hypotheses of theoretical physics from the other assumptions upon which this science rests, in order to subject it in isolation to observational tests, is to pursue a chimera" (Duhem [1954], pp. 199–200 and elsewhere)'. As Ariew goes on to explain:

> According to Duhem, physics as a science has reached a stage in which the observational consequences of its theoretical hypotheses need to be interpreted by another chunk of theory; as a result, no theoretical hypothesis by itself has any observational consequences: 'a physics experiment is not simply the observation of a phenomenon . . . It is the precise observation of a group of phenomena, accompanied by the *interpretation* of these phenomena; this interpretation substitutes for the concrete given, actually gathered by observation, some abstract and symbolic representations which correspond to the given by virtue of the physical theories admitted by the observer'

(Duhem [1917], p. 153; *cf.* also [1954], p. 147). This is the separability thesis. Duhem's reason for it rests on his empirical thesis about a peculiar feature of experiments in physics. A physics experiment might require the measurement of the electrical resistance of a coil; another might require the measurement of the volume and temperature of a gas. These measurements cannot be observed directly; they require sophisticated instruments that rely upon other theories for their construction and operation, and for the interpretation of their results ([1894] and [1954], pt. II, chap. iv).

(Ariew 1984: 320)

Ariew argues against reducing Duhem's formulations to what is called the Duhem–Quine thesis, which is that 'our statements about the external world face the tribunal of sense experience not individually, but only as a corporate body' (Quine 1953: 41). Duhem's approach was more complex having an appeal to the body or whole as distinct solely to mechanics – it's a matter of relevance:

The watchmaker to whom one gives a watch that does not function separates all the wheels and examines them one by one until he finds the one which is defective or broken. The doctor to whom a patient appears cannot dissect him in order to establish his diagnosis; he has to guess at the seat and cause of the ailment solely by inspecting disorders affecting the whole body. The physicist concerned with remedying a defective theory resembles the doctor and not the watchmaker.

(Duhem 1954: 187–8)

Rather than an analytic bit-by-bit testing of small hypotheses to accumulate into a greater theory, the idea of the theory of everything remains a guiding motivation for many scientists. As Tragesser (1977) pointed out, mathematicians may have an incomplete grasp of the whole to which they are directed in trying to solve a problem. And the problem may remain insoluble for centuries but still attract mathematicians to try and solve it because they feel in some way that it can be solved. This feeling is based upon a non-arbitrary but incomplete grasp, a *prehension*, rather than apprehension of what is at issue. There is a prehension based upon experience that a solution is possible or indeed, impossible. It is this prehension that determines whether or not work is carried out. Individual failures do not necessarily contradict the prehension, merely indicating which approaches seem less fruitful. The prehension has more to do with Adorno's appeal to the truth of a painting than to the painstaking stacking-up of tested hypotheses or the analytic approach of Duhem's watchmaker. If one wishes to mend a watch, then the analytic approach is advisable. However, if one wishes to intervene in the health of a living being, or create a new way of thinking about some aspect of the world, or formulate new political approaches to the issues of everyday life, then the approach of the watchmaker is no good. The watchmaker will never transform the watch being mended. The role is simply to make the given structure of mechanisms work as they were designed to work. However, what if the design and the purposes are to be changed? What will take the role of the guiding 'prehension'?

An intervention that unsettles the present order is essentially a singular act, a particular that sets in train change to a new order. As such, it is radical or revolutionary. There is a distinction to be made when talking about a radical intervention or a revolutionary intervention. The revolutionary adheres to an alternative set of values, beliefs and objectives which are desired to be put into practice and so supplant the current state of affairs. The radical may indeed be revolutionary, but it will lose its character as radical if its revolutionary import overturns the preceding state of affairs and so becomes the 'norm'. To remain radical is to be open to difference. To complete a revolution is to achieve mastery such that no further change is needed. It remains revolutionary and radical only historically with reference to the previous state.

To remain radical is never to settle, never to adhere to a single revolutionary framework – that is, to be always in disagreement with the present order. This means that reflexive and critical stances to such questions as subjugation, as objectivity and as relations between subject and object are essential *prehensions* for radical research methodologies. Subjugation, for example, imposes upon and possesses the object as property. The object is constrained, restricted and reduced to conform to whatever the norm (both socially and professionally constructed) in the researched context may be; what Cixous (1981; Cixous and Clément 1986) calls the 'Proper'. The relation between subject and object – under a given order – therefore, is both polar and totalising: the subject commands and demands imperialistically, whilst the object obeys automatically. The subject as master, controls, whilst the object, as slave, is subjugated, thereby being rendered (the) proper(ty). The reference here, of course, is to an aspect of Hegel's dialectics of history. As property, the slave is made into a 'thing' – a thing that exists only to follow the law of the master, thereby conforming to the name of the father (Lacan 1977) and also to the proper (Cixous 1981; Cixous and Clément 1986). In other words, in this relation, object is nothing but a thing, which can be used, exploited and disposed of. The radical is in dispute with any such order. Take, for example, the following story about an eighty-year-old female with severe dementia – a story unfolded during six months of shadowing a consultant in psychiatry (Consultant B):

Key: CasE team: R1 is Jill Schostak; C1 and C3 rheumatology consultants; C2 a consultant in general surgery

R1: And she has two children, a son and a daughter. The daughter is in Portugal and the son lives here, and he's been involved in a road-traffic accident and there's some question as to his ways of thinking, but that's all there is because he's a bit strange when you speak to him. Erm, anyway, the patient has now been assessed and it's time for her to move on and erm the medical staff and the nursing staff want to see her placed in a registered nursing home and for her son to visit her in the home as often as he can.

[. . .]

R1: And she often didn't have food in the cupboard although her son was meant to be visiting and keeping it, keeping her cupboards well stocked. And there was a case when the social worker went, in winter, and the windows of the conservatory were broken and er the house was freezing. So there is a history. However, the son does not wish his mother to go into a nursing home. He's visited a few and he says he doesn't like them. And we had the pre-discharge meeting last Tuesday, [. . .]. So erm the plan had been, there had been some strategy towards this because erm in order to try and persuade the son that his mother should go into a nursing home. And because of the history they wanted to get the erm, there's a care, a group that offers care, home care, and they wanted to get the manager from his home care to come to the pre-discharge meeting so that she would say, 'We really don't want to take this on' because actually, medically speaking, [Consultant B] is completely stuck, if the son says he wants to put, he wants to look after his mother there's nothing [Consultant B] can do. He has to go along with that. He can just recommend that she should go into a nursing home and they can put all this evidence on the table, and say, 'Look, this is why we suggest,' 'This is what happens.'

(Taped CasE core-team meeting transcript, 29 October 2001)

What is at stake here is a sense of humanity. In Chapter 3, the anger of those without a voice in the *banlieues*, the immigrants, the poor, was expressed in popular culture and through the violence that erupted. In this case, the individual has been dehumanised through a physical and social process. It is altogether more silencing, more excluding. Her visibility remains but uncannily, unhomely in that sense described by Royle (2003) as well as signifying a dispossession, a deprivation, a divesting (*dépossession*), which is a key term in Bourdieu's work as a basis for analysing domination and exploitation:

There is, . . . , a scandal Bourdieu calls "dépossession": inegality in the social order deprives the dominated of the potential. It despoils them, forbids them access to what is their Right, as for all people. It brings about the mono-polisation of 'universal goods' such as the ability of enjoying a work of art, developing a rational discourse or elaborating political analyses.

(Nordmann 2006: 9–10)

Humanity is a collective term, a universalising category. Outside it are only monsters, the mad, the uncivilised. The patient's rights are effectively stripped from her and become the contested possessions of others: experts, kin – while being capable of being seen as rational, legal and caringly supportive under the name of humanity. We are all equally human if we meet certain criteria defined by the powerful. In this case of the elderly patient, she becomes a focus for dispute only because her human rights are now shifted to those who are legally entitled to act upon her behalf, in her interests, in her place, in place of her – it is another kind of *banlieue*, or place of banishment. There is a sense too of the professionals being stymied by the circumstances where friends and foes are identified, and sides have been taken. The conflict between the two protagonists is under way. This conflict does not point so much to a breakdown in law and order as when riots take place but to the constraints under which social action is ordered, the functional incapacity of social actors to act any way they would wish, the inability to initiate solutions outside of the current, imposed framework(s) of mechanisms. This story transcribed from the CasE core-team meeting tape establishes a dramatis personae and positions each character in terms of powers, rights, lines of authority and lawful relations recognisable to the consultants as the plot of the story unfolds resembling a 'case-history' approach familiar to these professionals. Based upon a shared approach for the role of stories in presenting 'cases', points are made tying listeners, both medical (consultants) and non-medical (researchers), into a framework of interpretation. There is an implicit and lawful context of scene-setting, of judgements made and decisions taken. Under the law, the characters devise strategies to make something happen. However, there are different senses of law at play here: law as legal requirements and also law as some sort of foundational myth (Fitzpatrick 1992), and as 'police' in Rancière's (1995) sense:

> As the general law that determines the distribution of parts and roles in a community as well as its forms of exclusion, the **police** is first and foremost an organisation of 'bodies' based on a communal **distribution of the sensible**, i.e., a system of coordinates defining modes of being, doing, making, and communicating that establishes the borders between the visible and the invisible, the audible and the inaudible, the sayable and the unsayable.
>
> (from Rockhill's glossary in Rancière 2004: 89)

In the transcript describing the predicament of the patient, there is the contextual organisation of 'bodies' recognised by the community of experts in relation to the wider community that includes the communities of experts, the institution within which they work, the social world 'out there' and the family as mother and two children. However, this context is itself a dynamic of heterogeneous contexts. That is, there are as many contexts as the possible subject viewpoints that can be brought to bear upon people's experiences and their conceptions of a 'world'. What counts as *the* context or a 'relevant' context depends upon the circumstances and actors involved. Given several actors, then, how a context is established as the legitimate, authoritative context depends on their relative powers. This can be seen in the plot-like structure emerging around a disagreement over a conflict of interests between the different actors involved in determining what should happen to the elderly patient. It is here that a radical opening to other ways of conceiving relations, of configuring the social and the personal become both possible and impossible. The story continues:

R1: But the son still insists he is going to look after his mother. So the staff-nurse came in and she gave the whole nursing assessment – so, for instance, his mother has no idea of erm she's doubly incontinent, she has no idea what a toilet or bathroom is for, she can't pull down her trousers, he's going to have to do this. He still says he can. And that's what he's going to do. And he's asked for, he's asked for six-day care and on Sunday he will look after her for twenty-four hours. So he's framed it up that for most of six days his mother will be in a day-care centre and he will just have to look after her during the night-time. He knows that in the ward, on the ward, she's got a pressure pad so, when she gets out of bed, the staff know and the alarm goes off. And he's getting one. He's got lino on the floor he says because there'll be no spillages on the carpet but [of course] the lino will be absolutely freezing, but nobody mentioned that. But they did mention that, you know, if you're not there then it's really dangerous because she's going to slip up. And the floor on the ward is treated in such a way that although there's no, there is a sort of carpet but it's got plastic over it somehow but the staff are very careful about spillages. And of course they're only on for eight hours and then they can go away and recharge their batteries. And so he thinks he's just looking after his mum during the night and he doesn't sleep much at night anyway. And the social worker was there and she says, 'Well, (actually they know each other), I don't think I'm going to be able to get care in a day-care centre for six days, so you may find yourself looking after your mother for more than one day.'

(Taped CasE core-team meeting transcript, 29 October 2001)

Each character in the story draws on a different 'imaginary' by which to 'fill in' the missing elements according to their desires. The son's imaginary is that social services will deliver a six-day care package for his mother and that the hours his mother spends in day care will be long. The social worker's imaginary is the sheer inability of social services to deliver such care, and, hence, Mum should go into a suitable residential nursing home. The medical and nursing staff will hold similar imaginaries based on their experiences of delivering a health-care service in the community and of close working practice liaisons with social workers. All of this, in Bourdieu's terms, is incorporated in what he calls the *habitus*, the lived practical realities of people. This incorporation is revealed or ingrained in the way the body behaves:

> the manner of being corporal, postures, attitudes, ways of bearing the body that expresses interiorised social principles. Bourdieu defines it as a "permanent disposition, a persistent way of standing, speaking, walking, and by means of that, of feeling and thinking". Postures convey perceptual categories and social values that are anchored so deeply in individuals, with so much efficacity that, while not being explicitly formulated, they are relatively inaccessible to critique.

(Nordmann 2006: 22)

The situation is concretised in images of the house, the temperature, relations between actors and dialogue, the identities established:

R1: But he's absolutely adamant that this is what he's going to do because he thinks, well he's saying that this is what he thinks is best for his mother. And they go through the history, you know. 'You didn't keep, you didn't feed, you didn't make sure there was food in the house. It was often cold. She was malnourished.' [Consultant B] says, 'You know, we will have to monitor the situation because you're going against our recommendations and, as soon as we find that your mother is being neglected then we descend on you and we bring her' – well apparently she can't, I haven't been able to ask 'named Consultant' why she can't come back to the [Hospital X], but apparently she can't, erm so I don't know what will happen to her. But the interesting thing is that the mother has no, is clearly not of a sound mind in order to be able to say one way or the other whether she wants her son to look after her, and we are sort of crossing, you know, it's his mum, so it's not like a daughter, erm, and nobody, there's no legal, there's no law that says she has to have somebody who can represent her. So this scenario is going to happen. She is going out, to go out into her home, which, he says, he's moving into, but he hasn't yet sold his own house. She's going out, she's had one week, there's another week to go. And erm, the social worker hasn't yet got on to the business of finding six-day care [. . .]

(Taped CasE core-team meeting transcript 29 January 2001)

Significantly, it is at this point that the story engages the CasE core-team consultants in discussion with each other. Some sort of shared domain has emerged allowing them to get their bearings drawn from the narrated 'history' and to feel that they can participate in the action. That is, they have come to a mutually recognisable definition of the context within which events can be identified and interpreted. Their agendas and professional guesses and judgements are now called into play as they make visible what they believe to be at stake:

C2: He can only last one week until he realises that he can't practically.
C1: In fact there is, or I have, I mean I'm suspicious of what the motives are.
C3: Exactly.
C1: I'm very worried about.
C3: He's worried about his inheritance?
C1: Well, yeah.
R1: The grand-daughter's run off with the diamond ring.
C2: I suspect he doesn't realise how difficult it is.
C1: I think you're being kind [. . .]
C3: Well yeah.
C1: I am very suspicious, somebody who's doubly incontinent and got no, I can't remember anybody, there's no benefits in actually having them at home unless you've got, you've got.

C3: Ulterior motives, mmm.

C1: Ulterior motives. Well I don't think that even with full support you can.

C3: Has that come up in the sessions?

R1: Well you can't accuse him of.

C3: No.

C2: Well, he can think it.

R1: Yeah.

C1: He wants to move into his mother's home and sort out the inheritance for her, that would be my suspicions.

R1: Well they actually think that he's not going to sell his house, that he's pretending he's going to move in there and that things will go disastrously wrong and they think it is about inheritance. But there's nothing they can do.

C1: Well she might die and you're right there which is where you get the inheritance.

C2: Mmm, because he's occupying. Could be.

R1: She's put on weight whilst she's been in the [Hospital X]. But no, there's nothing.

C3: It's sad. [. . .]

C1: It just sounds illogical really.

(Taped CasE core-team meeting transcript, 29 October 2001)

Suffering from severe dementia, 'Mum' has no legal rights of her own. Nor is there a default to legal representation given her medical condition. In point of fact, she herself has no redress at all. Despite the fact that the right to legal representation is regarded as one of the fundamental tenets of being human in the Western world, 'Mum', or rather 'not-Mum', is thereby rendered a pawn in a life-and-death game between her son/would-be carer and the full range of health-care professionals. Both sides argue that what each recommends has 'Mum's' best interests at heart. But what each of them actually recommends is very much a world apart. As the battles of strategies and of wills play out, sadly, she has been reduced to a 'thing' to be used, in the views of the consultants, most probably, for 'ulterior motives' as the three non-psychiatric consultants listening to the patient's story put it. Deprived of legal rights, Mum is un-named in a Kripkean sense and rebaptised as being dependent on someone who 'stands in her place'. There is a forced transfer of rights. Mum, the central character, is absent in the *mise-en-scène* played out on the stage of her life, reduced to a mental illness in her declining years as represented in the transcript excerpts above. The complexity of who and what she was before dementia has been completely erased and entirely displaced by one singular identity, that of disposal. She can no longer remain an in-patient due to NHS policy; a place must be found for her. The health-care professionals will do their best for her, but their hands are tied. As far as the son is concerned, she is no longer a 'mother' to him, nor is she even 'a person' according to the consultants' viewpoints expressed above, rather she is an object of inheritance, where the problem of disposal is to be resolved according to his own desires. There is a sense of wrong:

> A wrong here is a specific form of **equality** that establishes the 'only universal' of **politics** as a polemical point of struggle by relating the manifestation of **political subjects** to the **police order**. Unlike juridical litigation, a wrong does not, therefore, occur between determined parties and cannot be resolved by juridical procedures. A wrong can only be treated by modes of political **subjectivisation** that reconfigure the field of experience.
>
> (from Rockhill's glossary in Rancière 2004a: 93)

This, of course, is an enormous job. Such a change would indeed be a revolutionary event.

Rendering the visible into bodies of knowledge

The field of the visible, in Rancière's sense, is the ground of what counts as data, and it is this ground that makes it possible to witness, record, represent and interpret and thus render bodies of knowledge. What is publicly visible is the ground of the valid, the reliable, since it is available for anyone to 'see' and verify. This is the kind of argument that sustains empirical science. For Kusch (2002) it is the community that is the vital factor, not the individual as Cartesian self-reliant thinker. From the Cartesian point of view, the individual tests everything for his or herself. However, Kusch (2002: 48) describes the scientific process quite differently. He refers to Hardwig's (1985) instance of a major scientific paper with ninety-nine authors who had contributed to the discovery. In the team, no single member had an overall knowledge of every detail in the production of 'knowledge'. Thus, it is the team that is the incarnating subject of knowledge, not the individual:

> Strict individualism insists that knowledge is the possession of the individual, and that knowledge presupposes evidence based on one's own 'on board resources'. A philosopher adopting this option would have to deny that *anyone* knows the results of the physicists' paper. Relaxed individualism allows that individuals know 'vicariously', that is 'without possessing the evidence for the truth of what [they] know.' Communitarianism sees the community as the primary knower ([Hardwig] 1985: 349). Thus it is the community of physicists, perhaps ninety-nine co-authors that is the epistemic subject of the knowledge reported in the paper.
>
> (Kusch 2002: 48–9)

In the communitarian sense, then, the visible is not reducible to the individual but exists only in a kind of public space. However, in Rancière's terms, what appears in public space is necessarily political, that is to say, conflictual, being subject to competing viewpoints, interests, demands. Communitarianism, in this broader sense, does not settle the truth of something. It does, however, provide the conditions under which thinking and contestation can take place. Under this logic, data becomes that which is open to such processes of contestation in public spaces, that is, object to contesting epistemic subjects, where each subject is incorporated as a community that frames the principles and procedures for the establishment of valid and reliable bodies of knowledge.

Objectivity is not object, but a function of the subject as community, inasmuch as the researcher intends that the 'seeing' (of object) that occurs during the research process will be bias-free and, thus, objective. Thus, in contemporary mainstream science, it is thought by a given community that the practice of setting up the appropriate controls to study only one variable at a time will deliver this bias-free data. In medical and social science, however, people are not the inanimate contents of test tubes in laboratories to be benchmarked and standardized. Having minds of their own, and possessing abilities and proclivities to make judgements and take decisions, the delivery of bias-free data is somewhat more problematic.

> Last month brought welcome news for nicotine junkies everywhere. According to press reports from an American conference, "new research" suggested that "smokers who've tried but failed to kick their habit may want to pop a daily aspirin, ibuprofen or naproxen (Aleve) to help cut their risk of mouth cancer". The reports, however, failed to mention the other side of the coin: that these painkillers cause more medical emergencies than any other pharmaceutical product. "Research", in fact, suggests that stomach bleeding triggered by these so-called "non-steroidal anti-inflammatories", or NSAIDs, leads to about 3,500 hospitalisations and 400 deaths among Britons over 60 each year.
>
> (Deer 2006: 13)

The work on mouth cancer to which Brian Deer is referring here is that of Dr Jon Sudbo, and the article lists Sudbo's impeccable credentials. The work on the risks of painkillers and bleeding is that of Prof. Michael Langman, whose impressive credentials are likewise printed in this News Review article. Clearly a health-related significant dilemma exists for anyone who regularly (a) smokes and/or (b) takes painkillers. A closer examination of the adversaries might help in the resolution: 'Reporting last October in *The Lancet*, once the flagship of British medical publishing, Sudbo and a team of 13 other doctors laid out an impressive nine pages of text, tables and statistics pointing to the painkillers' benefits' (Deer, 2006: 13). So, in fact, this dilemma continues to exist despite the view that one can overcome this barrier by carrying out surveys of large randomised populations and by correcting statistically for biases due to gender, ethnicity, class and so on. No help apparently resides there. The relation between subject and object still remains both polar and totalising, however, granting, as it does, supremacy to the norm and homogeneity of values – a supremacy that is quite literally life-threatening. Data is the focus of conflicting evidences and rhetorical strategies. It does not by itself resolve anything. Rather, recalling Duhem, what becomes important is the intertextual, mutually reinforcing framework of theories. What matters in the public domain is what is socially, economically, ethically, personally at stake in reporting scientific discoveries, breakthroughs, advances in 'knowledge'. Are people freed, enriched, or mastered, manipulated by such knowledge?

> Amazingly, two months before the press reports announcing his dramatic "new research" for smokers, *The Lancet* had published a worrying 52-word statement buried on a left-hand page.
> "We have received confirmation", Dr Richard Horton, the journal's beleaguered editor, admitted, "that the paper published by Jon Sudbo and colleagues in *The Lancet* contains fabricated data . . . and we now retract this article in full".
> (Brian Deer, *The Sunday Times*, News Review, 21 May 2006, p. 13)

Thus, evidence is beginning to point to the fact that Sudbo's work is possibly unreliable in comparison to Langman's research reports. But we are not out of the woods yet. Langman, Deer explains, is 'no faker' but is, at times, a little over-enthusiastic (Deer, 21 May 2006, p. 13): an investigation by *The Sunday Times* 'last summer' revealed that he flew to America at Meck's (drug company) expense to 'lobby regulators in support of Vioxx' (Deer, 21 May 2006, p. 13). Vioxx was later withdrawn due to its connection with heart deaths. This is a far cry from the practice of working with test tubes and controlling all variables but one. Fundamentally, the issue is one of trust in a context of social and economic interests. Community vigilance seems to have worked. Scientific method, as such, is not threatened. However, in the public domain, scientific method without trust cannot alone provide the evidence upon which decisions are to be made. Few are experienced and competent enough in a given area of research to be able to verify at first hand the mathematical proofs, theoretical consistencies and the detailed procedures of processing raw data into categories that can be manipulated to produce findings. In an example from mathematics:

> Donald MacKenzie (1999) follows the history of attempts to prove the four colour theorem[1] and shows how only close cooperation between men of very different professional backgrounds (pure and applied mathematicians, computer scientists) was able to succeed. What is more, the 'successful' proof by Appel and Haken continues to be controversial since it involves the use of computers. If computers are needed for proving mathematical truths, then we have to give up a natural and traditional way of thinking about mathematical knowledge. According to this way of thinking, one fully knows

---

1 Kusch's note: The theorem states that every map on a plane or a sphere can be coloured with no more than four colours in such a way that neighbouring regions are never coloured alike.

a mathematical truth only if one is able to prove it on one's own (with one's on board resources). Standing within this tradition, Bernard Williams has argued that there is a clear distinction between knowing a mathematical truth on the basis of one's own proving, and knowing a mathematical proof on the basis of testimony (Williams 1972). If computers are essential to proving theorems, then Williams's boundary will dissolve.

(Kusch 2002: 51)

Relating this back to medical research, the illustration was not employed to suggest that all medical research is of poor quality and immediately suspect, nor even that medical research itself is the bad apple in the barrel of scientific research. Rather, it is provided as a graphic example of Barthesian doxa,[2] of Rancière's 'police' and of Lacan's name of the father, which is to say the law of a self-governing, mutually critiquing community that depends on a tension-filled process of suspicion and trust in the development of its institutions. The polarising and totalising moves through which bodies of knowledge are constructed are fundamental to living communally, since they pull together, unifying, however temporarily, what would otherwise be a fragmented world: it is in this way that the political of the public domain is defined in frameworks constructed historically and culturally by individuals seeking to live together. What is problematic is any unquestioning reliance and blind commitment that positions these sorts of moves as the holy grail of science and hence undermines the possibility for research that radically challenges founding assumptions. Thus: 'the most despotic master is the one who believes he has received a sacred mission to save those whom he dominates, and who sees himself as the humble servant of another Master, whose will cannot conceivably be resisted' (Balibar 1998: 15). That master may be science, just as much as religion.

If trust and community action are essential to the production and use of knowledge then they become the object of intense attention, the battlegrounds between those who seek to dominate and those who seek emancipation. Methods that produce bodies of knowledge that reinforce the power and privilege of those who exploit that knowledge are legitimated and defended; the alternatives are derided and condemned as nonsense. That is to say, the choices are as fundamentally political as epistemic. In the public domain, it is difficult to assess the competing merits of alternative paradigms. If people are asked to trust scientists as experts, there is also a requirement for trusting the processes through which the trustworthiness of scientists and their findings are investigated. There is then another order of investigation that takes place in terms of those people who report on science and the use of scientific knowledge for the public, making it available to them as people who are non-experts. Muhlmann writes of journalists who either

---

2 Barthes used the term 'doxa' to point to the fixity and rigidity of the status quo, bureaucratisation and conformism.

incarnate the wishes of the powerful elites or who incarnate the public, becoming heroes who liberate the public (2004: 36). The examples that are given include the case of Lowell Bergman, the producer of the CBS television programme *60 Minutes*, who in 1996 sought to broadcast the testimony of Jeffrey Wigand, a senior chemist in the tobacco company, Brown and Williamson. This documentary concerned the addition of ammonium-based additives to tobacco that accelerated the absorption of nicotine. These additives were harmful to the nervous system. The broadcast was cancelled, following legal threats by the tobacco company. Wigand was sacked and accused of having broken his contract of confidentiality.[3] Concerns about the power of big business have long found a parallel also in the concerns of researchers engaged in projects funded by government (e.g., in the context of UK research in education, Broadfoot 1988; Elliott 1990, or in medicine, Delaney 2006). In the context of research in education, O'Neill (2004), raised a number of questions that are relevant outside the confines of his home country New Zealand:

To what extent are the affective, nurturing and often tacit processes of socially progressive education amenable to 'scientific' research and policy-making that is all too often obsessed with measuring observable behaviours and outcomes in schooling? Are socially and politically committed teachers likely to want to undertake or accommodate within their complex, fluid classroom environments the kinds of sanitised, context-free research valued within the academy and the state policy-making apparatus? How can educational research make a tangible difference to young people's life chances? On which educational 'problems' should we focus our limited research resources? And, not least, how do we conduct and report educational research in ways that resonate with the lives and aspirations of real people in socially and economically diverse communities up and down the country? In short – how do we ensure that educational research makes a difference where it really matters?

As in most, if not all, states:

The Ministry of Education is a monopoly commissioner of educational research, thus to a great extent it alone decides what research will be conducted, how, and for how long. Well-regarded and credible educational field research is expensive: it takes place over several years, used multiple methods, gathers baseline data, includes control groups, monitors educational change

---

3 Some websites providing background information are: <http://www.berkeley.edu/news/berkeleyan/2000/06/07/bergman.html>, <http://www.pbs.org/wgbh/pages/frontline/smoke/cron. html>, <http://www.mcspotlight.org/beyond/cbstranscript.html>, and <http://www.jeffreywigand.com/insider/60minutes.html>.

over time, including the period following the withdrawal of research funding, and is undertaken by people who have no vested interest in the results. As far as I am aware, no current educational research projects in New Zealand meet these criteria.

Concern, of course, is not equivalent to action, not least because there may be no easy answers. On the one hand, globally, academic freedom can be seen to be under threat[4] and, on the other, ways of life, peace and security are open to violence by those who seek revolution. Much debate is about how to balance academic freedom and issues of security, particularly in the context of the use of scientific knowledge when as Jacobs (2005: 113) writes 'Breakthrough science can lead both to great good and to great evil. The September 11, 2001, terrorist attacks on the World Trade Center and the Pentagon and the anthrax letter attacks that followed highlight the fact that our enemies may use our own advanced science and technology against us.' The political function of the friend–enemy polarity has already been discussed in the context of the 'axis of evil'. Now it is employed to frame issues of secrecy, academic freedom and freedom of information generally. Making something visible and audible in the public domain meshes with the framing of good and evil in order to produce a 'balance'. Yet, the balance conceals the structure whereby the powerful make political pronouncements of policy which differentially affect those people who are visible to the system and those who are not. Those who are visible can make their interests heard legitimately, whereas those who are invisible cannot because they are 'inaudible' in the sense that whatever they say is just noise without real meaning (cf., Rancière 2004a).

As in Figure 4.1, the people who are visible to the system or community employ principles and procedures to make their views, discoveries, expertise known in ways that are considered 'trustable', whereas those who are invisible cannot. Considerable political and organisational effort, therefore, is put into managing access and knowledge not only by governments, business and the media but also by academics. Kuhn (1970) and Feyerabend (1975) have in their own terms discussed the paradigm battles that have taken place between scientists espousing different ways of seeing the world, concluding broadly that science does not progress linearly but by revolutions. Davis (2004), Rabaté (2002) and Barthes (1987) have similarly discussed the battles between those who locate normal forms of scholarship in terms of the Enlightenment project of reason and modernity and those who deconstruct or challenge. Sokal and Bricmont (1997, 1998) have criticised postmodernists – such as Derrida, Lacan and others – as writing incomprehensible nonsense. In 1996, Sokal wrote an article for *Social Text*, a prestigious journal, which was accepted (1996a) and which he later revealed, in *Lingua Franca* (1996b), to be a hoax. This was meant to prove that there were no

---

4 See, for example, such reports as the Human Rights Watch Report (2001) at <http://www.hrw. org/wr2k1/special/index.html>.

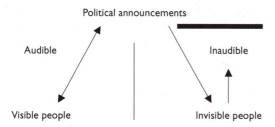

Figure 4.1 The visible and the invisible

rigorous criteria by which to judge the work of postmodernists. However, as Davis points out, the articles and the book have led to a series of explanations and counter-explanations where Sokal has tried to explain what he 'really' meant – an illustration of the postmodern process itself where 'truth' is continually deferred in a process of challenge and counter-challenge. Sokal and Bricmont are thus embroiled in the very process they claim to avoid through the 'normal' procedures of scholarship and scientific practices. The same process can be seen to be at work in debates concerning the merits of systematic review.

Systematic review in the form of the Cochrane Collaboration[5] seeks to provide an authoritative evidence base for health care. It developed in response to Archie Cochrane's 1972 book *Effectiveness and Efficiency*, where he emphasised the importance of randomised control trials (RCTs) in the evaluation of medical treatments. The most trustworthy evidence, it was argued, was framed within the procedures of the RCT. In brief, an RCT involves designing research that evaluates the effectiveness of an intervention by comparing two kinds of groups. First, there is the experimental group to whom the intervention is given or done. Second, there is what is often called a 'control' group which does not receive the particular intervention under investigation. In medical research, this second group would receive a placebo instead of the intervention. However, none of the members in each of the groups would be cognisant of whether they had been put in the experimental group or the control group. Both kinds of groups are composed in the same way: each member derives from the same population by the process of random selection. The groups are intended to represent the whole. Hence, if the results of the investigation reveal a difference between the two groups, then it can be argued that it is due to the intervention.

Medical decision-making should therefore be based upon evidence developed in this way. Systematic reviews of research employing RCTs, therefore, provide increased confidence for decision-making. However, RCTs cannot be employed in each and every circumstance, and suspicious professionals have to be brought on side; hence, in an editorial for the *British Medical Journal*, Sackett et al. (1996) made it clear that

5 See <http://www.cochrane.org/index.htm>.

Good doctors use both individual clinical expertise and the best available external evidence, and neither alone is enough. Without clinical expertise, practice risks becoming tyrannised by evidence, for even excellent external evidence may be inapplicable to or inappropriate for an individual patient. Without current best evidence, practice risks becoming rapidly out of date, to the detriment of patients.

Thus:

Evidence based medicine is not restricted to randomised trials and meta-analyses. It involves tracking down the best external evidence with which to answer our clinical questions. To find out about the accuracy of a diagnostic test, we need to find proper cross sectional studies of patients clinically suspected of harbouring the relevant disorder, not a randomised trial. For a question about prognosis, we need proper follow up studies of patients assembled at a uniform, early point in the clinical course of their disease. And sometimes the evidence we need will come from the basic sciences such as genetics or immunology. It is when asking questions about therapy that we should try to avoid the non-experimental approaches, since these routinely lead to false positive conclusions about efficacy. Because the randomised trial, and especially the systematic review of several randomised trials, is so much more likely to inform us and so much less likely to mislead us, it has become the "gold standard" for judging whether a treatment does more good than harm. However, some questions about therapy do not require randomised trials (successful interventions for otherwise fatal conditions) or cannot wait for the trials to be conducted. And if no randomised trial has been carried out for our patient's predicament, we must follow the trail to the next best external evidence and work from there.

(Sackett et al. 1996)

No one can deny the desire for best evidence to inform practice. However, what is a 'gold standard' in one context and its specific set of circumstances may be dangerous, even unethical practice, in another. As one surgeon in the CasE project commented during a discussion, that, based on his experience, and also citing a *BMJ* article (Howes et al. 1997), surgery is a case-by-case learning process.

When the context changes to the management of social behaviour rather than the cure of illness, the focus on control takes on different meanings. Controlling inanimate substances is different from the management of the behaviour of individuals. The engineering of behaviour by powerful individuals, groups and organisations involves additional political and ethical dimensions. Berman (1982) and Bauman (2001), amongst others, have described the social transformations that have taken place under the names of 'modernity', 'progress', 'reason', 'efficiency' and 'effectiveness'. Through reason people could act in the name of human rights founded on liberty, equality, community aspiring towards democracy rather than being subject to monarchy, religion; or, they could be engineered to perfection through the application of scientific methods leading to what Weber warned as the bureaucratic iron cage of reason (2001). Skinner's (1953) behaviourism or the time and motion studies of Taylor's (1911; cf. Taylor 1996) scientific management or contemporary management by objectives or performance indicators contribute to the bodies of knowledge through which social engineering can be attempted. Social engineering may be rationally supported for humanistic reasons to produce a 'better society' or for the purposes of making profit for the few. Welfare, health and education have been the focus of major national programmes to improve society. In relation to this, mass school systems and teacher education could be seen as critical to the aim of transforming societies by producing disciplined social bodies. Reynolds' (1996) concept of high-reliability schooling is a product of such a view. He models his view upon such organisations as those involved with air-traffic control or nuclear-power plants where high reliability is essential. Such organisations have the following features:

- They have a limited range of goals upon which total success is insisted. As an example, the air-traffic controller's job is to land the aeroplane, not to socially relate to the pilot.
- They recruit proactively and train extensively, both on a pre-service and in-service basis.
- They have formalised, logical decision-making based upon standard operating procedures.
- They have initiatives which identify flaws and which generate changes – an example of these are the simulations that test human and physical components within the nuclear-power industry.
- They pay considerable attention to the evaluation of their performance.
- They are alert to lapses: they take their stand on detail since they are concerned that any minor error may cascade into major system failure.
- They are highly coordinated and interdependent.
- They are, crucially, data-rich organisations which are continuously monitoring their functioning in order to improve the quality of their decision-making.

(High Reliability Schools website,
<http://www.highreliabilityschools.co.uk/home.asp?
Page_ID={57B4E83D-2AB9-410F-A107-372A502A6142>)

In the context of nuclear-power stations, such features are commendable. In the context of working with young people, there are real issues of what counts as being 'human' rather than being an element in a system. Being visible as a human being whose rights are based upon a principle of equality is quite different from being visible only as an element incorporated in a system that can be measured and manipulated according to principles of reason defined by those who are powerful enough to control research and policy agendas. The danger of systematisation is that it reduces and excludes competing views and thus erodes and stifles critical debate. Movement and change can only take place where there are alternatives and thus a milieu of conflictual debate.

Designing the visible

In the context of conflictual debate, what is to be made visible in the field of the perceptual depends on relative powers to control debate. In MacDonald's (1987) conception of the merits of democratic evaluation, control by power is subverted by including all voices as 'stakeholders' in the design of the project. However, since power cannot simply be wished away, its effects need to be mitigated by adopting principles that offer protection to the vulnerable. This is typically accomplished through agreeing 'ethical protocols'. In a sense, it is more like a process of bargaining that will govern what is or is not made visible, audible, accountable. A typical approach includes offering:

- Confidentiality. In so far as it's humanely possible, the researcher will not name particular individuals. The object is to protect the vulnerable; although, the powerful too can hide behind confidentiality.
- Anonymisation. This contributes to confidentiality by enabling things to be said under the guise of fictionalised names of people and places. Also, through processes of summarisation, where the specifics of people and places are subsumed under more general statements, particular individuals can 'deny' that they were the ones being described. Hence, confidentiality and anonymisation facilitate 'deniability'.
- The right to say no to participation at any time. Thus, the balance of power as between researcher and researched is raised. Those who are very powerful, of course, are more easily able to say no than those who are vulnerable. Is research itself an abusive act? And does the right to say no reinforce the imbalances of power to conceal what is going on?
- The right of reply. This offers the right of participants to respond to the accounts made of them by researchers. Sometimes, it may go so far as to include the right to 'correct' or modify transcriptions of interviews and written observations. The process can occasion the enriching of data through a dialogue of interpretations; or it can degenerate into forms of censorship.

In addition, of course, researchers may typically ask for:

- The right to approach people to participate;
- the right of access to documentation regarding the project's activities;
- the right of access to places.

These rights are included as a kind of pay-off for the rights granted to the participants being researched. Of course, such rights on each side may be continually renegotiated with each person, each time they are met 'in the field'. The negotiation of protocols is very much a political engagement with others about what can or cannot be seen, heard, recorded, interpreted and made known as a basis for understanding, explanation and action. These are key mechanisms to build into the design of projects that impact on real world, everyday practices. They are, in particular, a basis for building trust. Ethnographies, case studies, action research and evaluations that involve the multiple viewpoints of participants are more likely to identify the processes and the structures underlying everyday life and identify what is visible to one but not to another individual or group. In each case:

- What is the 'body', the incomplete grasp or 'prehension' of a 'whole', that is appealed to in framing what counts as 'understanding', 'interpretation'? What is visible to one but not to another?
- Who has power to rule in or rule out what counts as 'data', as 'knowledge'?
- What are the core disagreements between protagonists?
- What is the dynamic that creatively includes the voice(s) of disagreement?
- In framing action possibilities in relation to the multiplicities of voices, how can new/alternative prehensions be formulated as guides to action?
- What counts as a trusted public space as a repository of and a subject of knowledge that can guide action?
- How may the processes of negotiating ethical protocols concerning what can be seen or not seen, heard or not heard, represented or not represented contribute to the dynamics that creatively includes the voice(s) that otherwise would be excluded?

In asking such questions, and engaging in negotiations that increasingly include what otherwise would be excluded, research opens the way to a reconfiguration of the field of the perceptible and representable and, thus, challenges prevailing forms of power. However, the challenge to see differently is only part of the process. How can change actually be brought about through action? This is the point at which radical research engages with *the* political, that is, how the powerful control knowledge as a basis of action.

Chapter 5

Events of transposition

Events can be thought of as the small sequences of action composing everyday life or as something standing apart from the normal chains of action. In this latter notion resides the possibility of the radical and the revolutionary. How can it take place? In the model of contemporary schooling, young people are typically subjected to discipline, they undergo assessment and are subsequently sifted into classes based upon competitive performance in public examinations. Their examination results go a long way in determining their life chances. And the circumstances of their home and community backgrounds are highly correlated with their exam outcomes (Torrance 2006). There is a power, of course, when it makes sense, in just counting and comparing. But what then?

> there is something intolerable for Rancière in the idea that people's capacities are determined by their social position. All people are "speaking beings", all are equally susceptible "of being affected by political announcements or literary texts", of being torn by such encounters from "their natural destiny, which is to reproduce their life, leaving the care of governing to those who have the entitlement to govern."
>
> (Nordmann 2006: 13)

For Rancière, the principle of equality is essential to democratic processes, motivating challenges to hierarchy and privilege. But when does inequality become sufficiently intolerable for people to act?

Rancière believes that transformative political events are rare. In the French, a distinction is made between *le politique* and *la politique*:[1] *the political* (*le politique*) is that moment that erupts into the perceptual field when the marginal, the excluded make themselves visible and audible in such a way that there is a turning point; politics (as in *la politique*) is just that ordinary functioning of the 'police order', the administration and legal force involved in making and implementing policy.

---

1 In the French language, the term 'politics' has two nuances, and Rancière plays on this in order to argue his philosophy.

If the political is so rare that it can only be named in events like the American War of Independence, the French Revolution, the Russian Revolution, the Fall of the Berlin Wall and so on, what hope is there for making radical changes that progressively, continually include the excluded and bring about social justice for all? In this chapter, it is the event as an experience of the *possibility* of *the* political in everyday life that will be explored as the basis for radical research events.

Engaging with the political

Upon what basis should change take place? If one theory is better than another in the sense of explaining more, then, it *should* be chosen (Edgley 1976; Archer et al. 1998; Bhaskar 1991). For this reason, then, it could be argued, an approach like EPPI or the Cochrane Collaboration as described in the previous chapter should be undertaken as a basis for decision-making if it can be shown to provide the best possible means of evaluating research.

The logic of systematic reviews is that individual studies cannot always be counted on to provide the strength of evidence required for decision-making. Thus, by reviewing further relevant literature, it may be possible to come to firmer decisions. As Gough (2006) director of the EPPI centre comments:

> Before undertaking any policy, practice, research or any other decision it is sensible to know what is already known about the subject including evidence from research. This is particularly true for education which can have such an impact on individuals' lives. In health research there are many examples of well intentioned interventions believed to be effective yet are now known to cause more harm than good. There is no reason to suppose that the same is not true for some social interventions in education and child and family welfare. In addition, there is little point in investing heavily in primary research if the results are not synthesized together in a meaningful way to guide policy, practice and further research.

However, there are problems to be overcome:

> Firstly, there is a very large quantity of primary research produced and this is published in a wide range of different, usually academic, journals. Teachers are busy undertaking their normal professional roles so they do not have the time to access all this large diffuse research.
>
> Second, teachers' skills are in being teachers rather than in research so there are necessarily limits on what they can deduce from individual research studies.
>
> Third, individual research studies may be problematic in some way, so even if you can access them, they may not be trustworthy or relevant.

Hence, there needs to be an organisation – EPPI – which is trusted to do the sifting for the teachers or, indeed, other busy professional decision-makers who work with the public. It could be argued that the logic of systematic reviews fosters the notion of byte-sized packages of knowledge, panders to an individual's intolerance for self-reflection and critique and feeds an individual's insecurities that arise from having to deal with unfettered knowledge, presumably contaminated in its unfiltered state. Risk is thus both manipulated and managed. Such a practice fragments, pigeonholes and 'de-skills'. For Oakley (2002), doing a review systematically:

- involves a series of explicit, discrete and standard stages;
- means specifying a particular, answerable research question and criteria about what kinds of studies (by topic/population group/setting/research design, etc.) will be included and excluded in the domain of literature to be surveyed;
- requires clarity about which literatures will be searched for relevant studies, and how;
- includes making explicit, justifiable decisions about the methodological quality of studies regarded as generating reliable findings;
- needs some method of integrating the findings of individual, good-quality studies;
- is credible only if it has involved input from research users at all stages of the review process; and
- is a much more time- and resource-intensive activity than a traditional literature review.

Again, this seems thoroughly sensible. However, what actually is going on here? One rationale behind such a strategy is the notion of byte-sized knowledge packets as invaluable and essential to the smooth functioning of contemporary society, despite the fact that they fracture the individual's lived experience, however well-meaning the intent of instituting them. Do the discrete knowledge packets build an organic picture? That would depend upon whether or not the entire range of packets was accessed and assembled together to somehow fashion the complete story. Instead, offered as discrete and bounded entities, they pander to and enforce the individual's intolerance for self-reflection, critique and insecurities that arise from facing knowledge in all its bewildering excesses. The positive spin, of course, is the promise of reducing the risk of decision-making, and yet all the while that risk is being massaged, managed and manipulated; it cannot be removed. The strategic move here is to survey from a God's-eye point of view, or a bird's-eye perspective, perhaps, along the lines of a 'panorama and panoramagram' (Derrida 1978: 5). These topographical metaphors of a flat two-dimensional surface, and their preoccupations with the horizon, where it is possible to 'spread out' 'every element of signification [. . .] into the simultaneity of a form' (Derrida 1978: 25), indicate a structuralist approach to knowledge and decision-making. Structuralism, whatever its guise, lacks 'the richness implied by the volume', and 'is it by chance that the book is, first and foremost, volume?' (Derrida 1978: 25) – volume and richness, here, point beyond what can be captured through the systematising gaze. Decisions made in relation to such volume will differ in quality to those based on two-dimensional forms of rigour.

What is more, EPPI is defining itself as a source of reference for what counts as expert witnessing, becoming in turn an expert witness evaluating those who claim to be expert witnesses whose research evidence can be trusted. Thus, the issue of trust remains and cannot be removed: why should anyone trust the EPPI staff to make their decisions concerning trustworthy evidence for them? In Kusch's (2002) terms, there is no real choice other than to make decisions based upon 'knowledge' or 'evidence' that has been gained second-hand. It is sensible to trust the expert unless there is a reason not to.

Disquiet has been expressed by some researchers at Manchester Metropolitan University. For example, MacLure (2005) expressed concerns about the paucity of research activity that is selected to be included in a systematic review. Torrance (2004) likened the reviewing approach adopted to a 'call centre'. In 2004, when he wrote his article, Torrance carried out

> [a] few brief forays into search engines and websites certainly suggest that qualitative work is largely ignored at present. 'Systematic Reviews' brings up 1,600,000 hits on Google; 'Qualitative Research Reviews' brings up 644,000 hits; 'Synthesizing Qualitative Research' brings up 23,500; still a lot, but a lot less than 1.6M, and many, of course, irrelevant to the real topic of concern. Perhaps more surprisingly, searching for 'Systematic Reviews' on the ESRC/ TLRP [Economic and Social Research Council/Teaching and Learning Research Programme] website brings up '129 documents found', while searching for 'Qualitative Research Reviews' brings up 'no documents found', as does searching for 'Synthesising Qualitative Research'.

In 2006, a similar search brought up 900 reviews on the ESRC/TLRP website, many of which were actually a synthesis of research employing both qualitative and quantitative approaches. Interest seemed to have risen. However, a major issue remained. In their training for doing systematic reviews, there is an expressed concern for a democratisation of research which Torrance saw as implying that at present the 'use of research knowledge in society' is not democratic, something he called an 'extraordinary insinuation'. Referring to the EPPI-Reviewer,[2] he went on to say that 'the methods of systematic reviewing seem concerned to exclude expert knowledge from the process as much as possible, categorising and coding in immense detail the sorts of decisions on inclusion and exclusion that reviewers should make.' So much so that:

> just as bank managers and mortgage lenders are no longer trusted to reach face-to-face judgements about the credit worthiness of clients, and their professional knowledge and experience is codified into software programmes to be operated by clerks in call centres, so researchers are no longer trusted

2 At the time of writing login is at <http://eppi.ioe.ac.uk/eppireviewer/login.aspx>.

to carry out so-called 'narrative reviews'. Perfectly reasonable arguments about the transparency of research reviews and especially criteria for inclusion/ exclusion of studies, have been taken to absurd and counterproductive lengths such that, according to one article I recently refereed for a journal 'anyone interested in a review topic, can, with training in the use of systematic review tools, take part . . .'; no prior knowledge or expertise required, far less informed professional judgement. Systematic reviewing can thus be seen as part of a larger discourse of distrust, of professionals and of expertise, and the increasing procedurisation of decision making processes in risk-averse organizations.

The fundamental issue turns on trust. No matter how good a job such a centre as EPPI does, as a single centre of authoritative 'evidence', it is a politically bad idea. Its effect is to define 'normal science' and exclude the radical, that is, anything it cannot accommodate under its defining principles. By setting itself up as a mediation service between communities, it slips into reinforcing and legitimating hierarchies of 'knowing' and 'knowledge production'. Should it be closed down? Certainly not; it provides a service concerning what counts as normal research under conditions of mainstream policy. But what if you want to go outside the normal and produce that reconfiguration of the field that is *the* political event? There, it cannot help, because it is firmly structured within the police order, its implicit social function being to police 'knowledge' for the purposes of professional action within the given policy-making frames. In doing so, it reduces complexity, privileging certain forms of social and professional action in the production of policy (cf., Avis 2006). Here the danger is further embedded in procedures for conducting what is called in the UK, the Research Assessment Exercise (RAE) by which university research is rated. Stronach (2006) has pointed to this in a brief discussion of the word 'rigour' in relation to the key categories for defining research excellence employed by the RAE. Rigour, of course, is a key word in the definition of what counts as science. It is thus a political battleground defining what is 'seen' and 'audible' in research debates and policy-making. As Stronach asks of the RAE panels: 'is there a particular promotion of the notion of "rigour"? Is that promotion, if such it is, part of paradigmatic prejudice? Will "rigour" as a minimum competence be used to police the other two categories? Are covertly hegemonic moves being made in relation to RAE documentation?'.
The concern about paradigm wars and the policing of research was specifically instanced by Stronach in a footnote:

A natural riposte to such questions is to dismiss such possibilities as a slur on the integrity of reviewers. But our recent and highly analogous experience with an ESRC end-of-report review shows that such paradigm warfare does happen. The report and case study (Piper et al. [2006]) was reviewed. One reviewer said good things about the research. First, 'a qualitative approach is justified'. But 'with some reluctance I have rated this report "problematic" rather than "good".' Why? The reviewer's 'fairly strong reservations derive from my prejudices against qualitative research'. The other 3 reviewers rated the research 'outstanding', which was its overall grade. The example illustrates *both* the possibilities of bias and its correction. It highlights the need for careful moderation across reviewers and the need to take paradigmatic bias into account.

Nevertheless, such reviews are effectively being conducted not across a community of open debate but as a kind of quality-control procedure by a handful.

This perhaps would matter little if it were not the case that 'normal research' criteria and procedures are being established in relation to the control and allocation of research resources through which knowledge is legitimated and, thus, the work of researchers made visible and audible for public consumption. All else in this field of the visible becomes noise, nonsense at worst or, at best, at the margins, eccentric, excessive, barely tolerable and therefore not worth funding. Hence, in this case, the field of the visible is being defined in relation to what Anderson (1983) might call an imaginary community, that is, that community of busy professionals who do not have the time or the research training to make their own decisions concerning evidence. Knowledge is 'democratised' only to the extent that selected representatives from this community are included on boards and, in the case of EPPI, are able to undertake systematic reviews if they go through particular training procedures. However, such communities of professionals and lay people are much more complex, meaning that theoretical and practical knowledge, post-training, is systematically gained and tested by the realities of decision-making circumstances and their consequences. Research, if it is to be democratically representative of such experiences, focuses upon life situations as seen, felt, described by people. In this broader conception of the research field, the question is not how is evidence to be constructed but how is debate about what is to count as evidence for decision-making to be constructed in order to be fully inclusive of the multitude of viewpoints? And thus to do this, what should be involved in rendering research a democratic domain? More specifically, what, if any, is the relation between such a democratic domain and 'truth' as a basis for decision and action?

The fabulous event

At the back of research and practical decision-making is the question, 'What is the truth of a situation?' And what has to be dealt with in the immediacy of life situations is its 'volume' not its two-dimensionality.

C2:   I've got a bilateral breast cancer in a nurse who's fifty, and it's recurrent cos she's back and she's had chemo, and we admitted her in June and she was pretty well on the way out, and I got [Consultant P, consultant oncologist] to see her, and I talked to the family, had a long chat with her and her husband:

she's a nurse, she understands, she was having more chemo and that was it. She went off and the past few months I've been waiting for the letter from the Hospice saying 'Died in peace with her family surrounding her'. And last week I got a letter from [Consultant P] saying 'She's off on holiday in Tenerife and I'll see her in six months'. I thought what's he done to her?

C1: And that's what makes life fabulous, isn't it?

C2: Just comes out like that [*laughs*].

C1: A friend of mine who I had lunch with today, his Mum's got breast cancer, but she's eighty-three, no, she's got lung cancer, I think. Eighty-three, eighty-four, and you sometimes have a valid group, you can have people who live with their illness in symbiosis, with their cancer, and something else takes them five years later, and it can grow very slowly. It's very, very humbling.

C2: Unpredictable. [. . .] Totally amazing. I've had a twenty-six-year-old die within six months and the other thing is I've got a Grade 1 node negative, you know, all the best histology, died six months from multiple skin meta-[stase]s which you rarely get from breast cancer.

(Taped CasE core-team meeting transcript, 29 January 2001)

Truth, in the end, is about life, and what is at stake in life is its limit faced only in the figure of death. Truth in the context of life and death – made stark – in the above medical example is not reducible to propositional truth. But action requires the formation of testable propositions, otherwise 'anything goes'. This extract is taken from a discussion between medical consultants working in different specialties sharing and comparing their experiences. One recounts a story of a person who had been expected to die from her illness but who surprisingly recovered sufficiently to go for a holiday, thus changing her status from near-death to being 'well'. This led to other stories of unpredictable outcomes. What dominates the discussion is the sense of amazement, laughter and a feeling of humility before the realities of life. Truth, in this case, is outside of all logic. But logic is not thereby to be abandoned. Rather, it implies a particular attitude towards the 'real' and its 'truth' that should not be ruled out by logic and methodologies through which evidence is 'assured'. Logic provides a means of ensuring consistency in reasoning but does not in itself assure truth.

Thus, are the surprises identified by the medical consultants due to incompetence, lack of scientific knowledge or because science itself cannot hope to cover all? As consultants, they are assumed to be experts. As experts, they are assumed to have a command over available knowledge concerning medical conditions in their particular specialty. In particular, they are expected to make decisions based on best-available evidence. And this evidence is constructed through certain legitimated procedures – currently, RCTs. As such, the procedures conform to Kuhn's (1970) 'normal science', that is, the prevailing view of what constitutes science at a given time period. This science as has been discussed in Chapter 4 is founded in a particular conception of 'reason'.

These consultants are not talking about a gap in knowledge that can be filled, nor about incompetence that can be corrected. They are talking about something that is 'fabulous', in particular, something about the nature of life itself. Adorno gestures towards this something – this 'volume' as it were – that is outside of expert representation as follows: 'In truth, all concepts, even the philosophical ones, refer to nonconceptualities, because concepts on their part are moments of the reality that requires their formation, primarily for the control of nature' (Adorno 1973: 11). And more particularly: 'No object is wholly known; knowledge is not supposed to prepare the phantasm of the whole. Thus the goal of a philosophical interpretation of works of art cannot be their identification with the concept; it is through such interpretation that the truth of the work unfolds' (Adorno 1973: 14).

But, of course, this is art and not the highly skilled 'scientifically underpinned' act of the surgeon. Yet, as the surgeon and the other 'experts' speak, more of the art (or volume?) and less of the science appears at those critical moments of judgement and of surprise, those moments where lives are saved or lost. It is here that circumstances have to be grasped in judgement rather than deduced through a chain of logical reasoning operating on empirically collected 'facts'. It is here, too, that facts seem less solid, where the relation between concepts and the 'non-conceptualities' they are supposed to correspond with, slips, where the non-conceptualities offer a resistance to over-easy conceptualisations and theorisations. It is, thus, not a simple matter of making observations, gathering the facts and processing them in terms of 'evidence' that then informs judgement. The observations of what appears to consciousness themselves are in question. In commenting on Schelling's philosophy, Bowie (1994: 6) writes that for Schelling:

> The issue is Kant's question as to how synthetic *a priori* judgements are possible. They were possible for Kant because of the synthetic activity of the subject in judgements of the understanding. Schelling maintains, however, that there is a more fundamental problem, that of why there is a realm of judgement, a world of appearances at all. If judgement consists in syntheses of appearances, it must depend upon a prior separation of what is joined again in judgement, otherwise there would be nothing that required synthesising.

If all is just a mechanism where all things are conditioned by all other things in a chain, then, at least through rational procedure, it is possible to uncover the chains. But a being contained within this conditioned universe – flattened to the logic of a chain – would not be able to step outside this complex mechanism and ask how it all became possible (Bowie 1994: 9); nor, presumably, would it be free to speculate on and form judgements about how things are arranged or, indeed, be surprised by anything. A system of mechanical chains cannot produce consciousness, cannot produce the judgement that transcends how things are, nor make free decisions concerning how one should think about reality, what choices should be accepted and how to behave with others in the world. Thus, any system of thinking that suspends or excludes conscious freedoms in its search for causal chains is already inadequate. Yet, recalling discussions in earlier chapters, a narrow focus on Cartesian rationality does just this, leading to what Weber (2001) described as the 'iron cage'.

What these technologies seem to promise is the easy truth-machine or legitimised evidence-machine answers desired by paymasters and the iron cage bureaucrats of those agencies through which research is commissioned and constrained. Imprisoned in the 'iron cage' of bureaucratic reason, it is all about the big numbers through which populations are to be described and manipulated to produce desired outcomes. But, for critical judgement, however, thinking is paramount. Much of philosophy is about the depth of thought and critical assessment of the details of thinking, and a single instance can be the motive. For statistical surveys, it is all about large numbers of instances and the application of procedures without much further thought; indeed, the less thought the better for that just introduces human error and 'subjectivity'. Reason, in this view, is set over and against the world as a focus for mastery. As a way of mastering populations, as it were, schooling has been a key focus for debates concerning the extent to which children should be free to explore their interests and develop their talents or whether their learning should be managed in the interests of social elites. Normand describes the opposing approaches:

> In the USA, in the first half of XXth century, partisans of progressive education, following John Dewey, militated for a school more focused on children's needs and experience, and they claimed for the diversification of curriculum. But the conceptions of these educators were turned away by the main architects of educational reforms and by the partisans of "progress" in education which formed at that time a political elite named "administrative progressives". These reformers were a unified group sharing the same interests and values (Tyack & Hansot, 1982). Under their influence, the conduct of educational policies was held by an ideology of science and management which demanded the reinforcement of control on schools and teachers. For these administrators of education, an effective management had to accumulate rich and diversified information. This explains why they sought to develop school statistics and intelligence tests. As businessmen, they wished to master budgets in terms of cost-effectiveness and to implement industrial regulation in educational activities. These criteria of standardisation and assessment destroyed the progressive educators hope for the diversification of curriculum, at the same time they narrowed it through skills assessed by tests.
>
> (Normand 2006b)

An extreme example of such rational engineering applied to social organisations is what Reynolds[3] calls high reliability schooling (HRS), was discussed in

---

3 David Reynolds, <http://www.highreliabilityschools.co.uk>.

Chapter 4. However, schools are not nuclear-power stations, thus people adopt a very different attitude towards their purpose and functioning. Rightly, in dangerous environments, there is a concern for the strictest measures of control. Indeed, as pointed out in the conclusions to the web page:[4] 'Education for many practitioners of our generation has been mostly about transmitting values, not skills, and practitioners have been reluctant to take their stand on the detail implied in the HRS model, preferring instead a broad brush approach.' An early practitioner of HRS could be the father of Judge Schreber, a highly influential nineteenth-century German educationist who drove his children mad. Judge Schreber wrote a book on his mental illness that has been the subject of analysis by Freud and Lacan amongst others. It enabled Freud to develop his theory of paranoia (Schatzman 1973). The way in which the father systematically trained his children, monitoring their every move from birth, is the very model of a high-reliability system, producing what may be called the paranoid curriculum (Schostak 2000),[5] a curriculum dominated by the watchful eye of the expert as scientist.

In this world of what counts as contemporary or indeed bureaucratised 'normal' science (Kuhn 1970) involving quantification, randomised control trials and surveys, concepts are to be matched rigorously with the non-conceptualities they are to represent so that through manipulation desired outcomes can be produced. Perhaps rather like points that 'stand out' due to observation, the observable data of normal science can be crudely represented as follows:

Figure 5.1 How to join the dots?

4 <http://www.highreliabilityschools.co.uk/home.asp?Page_ID={57B4E83D-2AB9-410F-A107-372A502A6142}>.
5 See also an early schematic version of this at <http://www.enquirylearning.net/ELU/Issues/Education/PdOs%20curriculum.htm>.

When looking at Figure 5.1, what possible arrangements can be seen? Can the whole field of the visible be represented by just drawing a circle through each of the dots? That would then constitute the fabulous theory of everything. As such it would be the end of science in the way that Hegel described as the end of history and Fukuyama (1992) claimed to have occurred at the fall of the Soviet Bloc. Or can the dots only be joined by including the possibility of the 'fabulous' event? That is, always leaving open the possibility of some other explanation, of surprise? If this is so, then rather than the detail of HRS, there is an education of 'seeing' as an aesthetics of surprise and the fabulous that mobilises curiosity, the framing of questions, the formation of designs for research and action.

Data as events of transposition

As in the cases discussed by the medical consultants, it is through a mixture of observation, experience, exploration and judgement that the dots are sufficiently joined to engage in decision-making. That is, through scientific procedure, descriptions of clear and distinct entities are made as a basis for constructing theories (about how the entities are related in terms of cause and effect) in order to formulate treatments:

C2:   We've just operated, this is fascinating, we operated a week ago, on a fifty-year-old man, and I can show you the photographs, it will put you off your food, he had a cauliflower hanging out of here [*points to his lower abdomen*], a cauliflower hanging out of his belly. And we biopsied this thinking it was squamous. It was adenocarcinoma from his caecum, came right through the body wall. And literally, outside, I've got pictures there. And you sit back, think if it's got that big he's in symbiosis with it, he's living like ivy on a tree. So we operated on him, opened his belly, pulled all this out, did a right [*name of surgical procedure*] joined his bowels together, no bag, cored out a great big hole in his body wall, took out a chunk of meat that size [*gesticulates*], got the plastic boys in and moved his belly across and skin-grafted the defect, he went to ITU [intensive treatment unit], that's fifty-five, went to ITU that night and they took his tube out and he sits up the next morning and says, 'That's pretty good, doc. I feel better now'.
         [*Everybody (three consultants, two researchers) laughs*]
C2:   And the guy has left ITU and he's up on the ward. He made his will, he called in a lawyer and made his will on the day of his op. But liver was clear, lungs are clear, this thing's a huge cancer, and no spread. Now the opposite is you get a tiny little thing in the bowel and it's boom, lungs, liver, the lot.
                                        (Taped CasE core team meeting transcript, 29 October 2001)

In practice, the dots are never entirely joined up to complete the picture of the field of the visible, unless, of course, included in the field of the visible is 'the surprising', 'the fabulous'. These are points of transposition and not fixed dots. Thus,

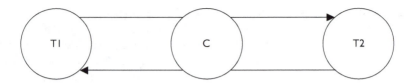

Figure 5.2 Texts and codes

the practical realm is perceived to be dynamic and not static. The existence of multiple contexts being brought to bear upon a given experienced situation creates the conditions for transposition. Suppose a given text, T1 that an individual wants to transmit to another individual, or even record for his or self as a reminder for a later date (see Figure 5.2, drawn from Lotman 1990).

Following an argument proposed by Lotman (1990), this text (T1) is then sent to the other person or picked up later by his- or herself. Upon reception, the text is decoded by employing Code C to produce a second text (T2). If the receiver uses the same code as the one used by the sender, then T1 and T2 will be identical. T1, in this case, stands for the master text that can only be decoded through C. However, given the dynamism of everyday life contexts, there are many competing codes which Lotman sees as a source of creativity rather than 'noise' or inter- ference. Applied to the medical discussion, Code C_1 might refer to the code employed by the psychiatrist, Code C_2 might refer to the code of the physiotherapist and Code C_3 to that of the client. Each will interpret texts – written, spoken, visual – according to their particular code and, thus, the resulting texts will be $T2_1$, $T2_2$ and $T2_3$. Which is 'right' and which is 'wrong'? In a context of mastery, or legiti- macy, then only one will prevail. In a context of creativity, then dialogue becomes possible where the differences are welcomed as enriching contributions to a debate about some cultural project(s). The debate itself introduces further coded exchanges resulting in further enriching texts. In such a dynamic of transposition, as between textual fields and codes, what is the effect on claims about what is real, true, good and so on? It could be argued that at the back of this dynamic is really a unity and that the only reason it cannot be seen as such is that the final theory of all, or the perfect code, has not yet been created. Alternatively, it could be argued that the reason it isn't is because there is an essential plurality and all we can do is act as if there is unity (Badiou 2004). In each case, what is real, true or good is a question still open to debate.

Thus, following on from the discussions between the medical consultants, no matter how experienced, nor how good a particular theory typically fits the facts, there is still the possibility of a surprise, something that seems to go beyond or defy the 'norm' as defined by theories and experimental research-based evidence concerning treatments and the course of illnesses. But life is not just about treating bodies, it is about living and, thus, about relations to others as conscious, feeling, experiencing beings. It is about making wills, dealing with lawyers, setting affairs in order. It is about values, what makes life worth living for a group of people who fear the circumstances in which their 'identity', their 'possessions', their 'way of life' are lost. In this domain of values defined by judgements made from a multiplicity of viewpoints, reason is the backdrop to desires, hopes, ambitions. The world is always more than what reason makes of it. In Lotman's terms, there are always a multiplicity of competing codes – composing a 'volume' in Derrida's terms – through which to make sense of the world. Reason may be in conflict with desire; there may even be the desire that reason rules desire and passions, but desire is always able to suspend reason through, say, seduction or fear and thus create the fantastic, the beautiful, the awesome, the horrific, the sublime.

For any community that makes claims about how to define the field of the visible, all must be reducible to accounts and explanations through which that field can be represented publicly. The question is whether that field can be conceptualised as being a unity or a plurality. If it is to be a unity, then at the back of any given account of some aspect of experience, there is a unifying text through which all individual accounts find their final meaning. This has a resemblance to what Riffaterre (1978) called the hypogram in his discussion of the difference between the mimetic and the poetic. The mimetic aspires to account for the real; it has, as its correlate, points of reference in the real. The real is complex and plural. The poetic is unified and has no referent outside the textual. In the poetic, the hypogram takes the place of the referent. As a text, it provides the final, authoritative meaning for other texts. Of the two, it could be argued that science is mimetic. However, science consists of its core texts. Each new text as an account of some aspect of reality makes sense only in relation to all other texts, thus progressively constructing a body of systematically accredited 'knowledge'. But all the texts make sense only if there is an agreed unifying text, even an as-yet incompletely realised ideal, a prehension, as it were. Hence, in Riffaterre's terms, it could be argued that the scientific ideal is poetic rather than mimetic. This would undermine scientific processes if it is necessary to maintain a clear distinction between the mimetic and the poetic. Recalling Rancière's (2004a) discussions of the political as an aesthetic that defines a field of the visible, then the mimetic process itself is governed not by a simple and unproblematic one-to-one empirical correspondence between concept and real referent but by a way of seeing, a way of synthesising under the unifying account, the explanatory theory of how one element relates to another element. There is in such a conception of the relation between the mimetic and aesthetic what may be called a transpositional event, a hinge like being towards the other where the other as real referent can be seen and accounted for only in the production of other as text. Such an event is fabulous in that it maintains its contact with the surprising, the excessive, the inexplicable, while drawing upon a language of accountability, evaluation, judgement. In science, data plays this role of transpositional event pointing towards an aspect of the visible while also pointing towards a dimension of the generalisable under a unifying, universalising concept. The relation between data as something observed and nameable and its transposition into 'category' and 'title' was discussed by Schostak (2006) in relation to trainees' accounts of experiencing real contexts of practice, that is, 'doing it for real' in classrooms or clinical environments. Listening to trainee professionals talking about 'doing it for real' led to this phrase becoming the title of a research report written by Phillips et al. (2000). Schostak discusses this further:

> Getting the title right can have a powerful impact not just for the fortunes of a research project but for the shaping of thought. Its power is poetic even if its phrasing seems literal, even banal. It gathers and condenses a prior range of texts (other interview transcripts, policy documents, and the various artefacts produced in the practices of everyday life) rather in the way that Riffaterre (1978: 25–6) describes the role of what he calls the hypogram. The hyopogram acts like a hidden text that provides the underlying sense of another text. That is to say, there is no relationship to a real referent outside the text (p.29). What happens is that a key word, a kernel word, provides a range of connotations or presuppositions or relations through puns with other words. Thus, 'A *flute*, for instance, presupposes a flutist, entails an audience, contains semes such as "melodiousness," but also "rusticity," since one kind of flute is Pan's, etc' (Riffaterre 1978: 26) and, of course, why not also the fluted stem of a champagne glass, which then might connote celebration? The possibilities expand but are all related in some way to the kernel word. This kernel may or may not be actually expressed overtly. Thus each of the other words, if they are used in a text refer covertly to the kernel, are organised in relation to it, each word a part that implies the whole, that is the whole semiotic space organised by the kernel. 'Doing it for real' thus refers to no single real instance but refers to accounts about an attitude, an approach, a set of experiences, the feelings, the pleasures, the anxieties that accompany the carrying out of action and dealing with the contingent, unexpected events that take place and give an experience the quality of 'real', not 'play', not 'simulation'.
>
> (Schostak 2006: 168)

Doing it for real contains a radical possibility. In the terms of the consultants described earlier, there is always the surprise, the fabulous or, indeed, the terrifying to be confronted in the realities of practice. In short, the data of practice always contains the possibility of a return from the textual unities of research theorisation to the exceptional, that fabulous moment demanding reconfiguration of the field of vision if it is to be counted as data capable of theorisation.

Whether it is the reading or writing of a research report, an academic article or a book, the radical is uncovered and figured out through the ways of addressing 'the demand that we return to a reading which is stripped of the illusion of mastery or exhaustiveness' (Readings 1991: xvi). The goal is to avoid 'possession' of the 'meaning' of the text whereby knowledge becomes an object to be possessed. As a possession, a commodity value is conferred on 'meaning'. Meaning as an object of mental representation is equivalent to content and to 'what happens'. The goal is rather to reveal and refigure the 'eventhood' of the event through the 'it happens' as a 'real'. The 'it happens' as a real, however, is not to be conflated with the *meaning* of 'it happens' because that is always in a meaning context. It is to be understood as radically heterogeneous to meaning and irreducible to content. In other words, 'attention to the event resists the reduction of reading to the extraction of meaning content (or its formal modifications)' (Readings 1991: xix). In Lyotard's words: 'we do not interpret, we read' (Readings 1991: xix). Lyotard views reading as a process during which phrases are linked in a way that is neither interpretation nor theorisation. Phrases here act more like a signifier. Acts of reading, judgements and phrase-linking offer sites of 'resistance to the rule of the concept' (Readings 1991: xix). Reading thus becomes a material practice involving listening out for an event as event, before it has been accounted for by the intervention of cognition to confer meaning and formulate concepts. Its status is as 'it happens', just as in that fabulous moment of patients recovering when all under theory seemed hopeless; or tragically dying, when all under theory seemed resolved. Where meaning resides in reference to the encompassing theory, then the event can only be read *as happening*; in terms of its eventhood, nameable first as a 'fabulous' figure emerging from the ground of experiences, it becomes a precondition to the emergence of alternative ways of doing theory and producing knowledge. Thus, as a radical act: 'reading as event [which] will raise up the figure against discourse, the libidinal skin against the organic body, a narrative pragmatics against the rule of "meta" or "grand" narratives; an aesthetics of the sublime against the sociology of art, an ethics against the totalitarianism of the political' (Readings 1991: xx).

The act of reading involves, for Lyotard, a philosophical stance, along the lines of *une explication du texte* (critical analysis or appreciation of text), paying careful attention to the minute but radical differences opened up in language. As described above, the production of data involves a naming that points to a happening, a happening that is not completely reducible to being an element in a greater theoretical whole or systematically synthesised body of knowledge. The act of naming, in Kripke's (1981) sense, discussed earlier, has the status of a baptism uniting the name with a referent. It is a performance that once carried out becomes a point of reference for a complex historical chain of references. As in the case of a marriage between two people, the performance of the marriage ceremony and the uttering of the words 'I do' is a real event that can be referred to by those who have become married and by others. The events of courtship can now be restoried in relation to the marriage event. What had seemed only a possibility amongst others can be storied as an inevitability – they were meant for each other – or as a catastrophe waiting to happen, a fatal attraction that can only lead to harm. From the moment of the baptism, a chain of references can be created that always leads back to the name. At one level, chaining has become personal, picking out the particular exactly. At another level, chaining is impersonal, abstract, bureaucratised for management control and surveillance. As already discussed, there is a politics of enchaining, addressing each individual from a complex of reference points. The foundation of this politics is the calling of a name, marking a distinction that can be remarked and made remarkable. Once named, the identity of an individual or element can be confirmed or disconfirmed by reference back to the historical chain that named something or someone as 'this' rather than 'that'. In research:

> One thing, however, that it will be most dangerous to do, and that we are very prone to do, is to take it that we somehow *know* that the primary or primitive use of sentences must be, because it ought to be, statemental or constative, in the philosopher's preferred sense of simply uttering something whose sole pretension is to be true or false and which is not liable to criticism in any other dimension. We certainly do not know that this is so, any more, for example, than that all utterances must have first begun as imperatives (as some argue) or as swear-words – and it seems much more likely that the "pure" statement is a goal, an ideal, towards which the gradual development of science has given the impetus, as it has likewise also towards the goal of precision. Language as such and in its primitive stages is not precise, and it is also not, in our sense, explicit: precision in language makes it clearer what is being said – its *meaning*: explicitness, in our sense, makes clearer the *force* of the utterances, or "how (in one sense . . .) it is to be taken."
>
> (Austin 1976: 72–3)

This danger opens up the possibility of engaging in some form of deconstruction.[6] A typical Lyotardian move is to pay particular attention to the performativity of a statement or phrase, 'precisely to the extent to which it problematizes its constative content' (Readings 1991: xxii). Performativity is not just about conveying a meaning, thereby putting something in context. Understanding the fuller signification of an enunciation entails more from its performativity in the form of its eventhood: '[t]o say something once, and then to repeat it, is to make two different statements' (Readings 1991: xxiii). Repetition is a figure of emphasis and temporality, capable of being rhetorically achieved in many ways. Whilst emphasis is added through repetition, the repeated statement does not mean exactly what it did before. The saying is a doing that calls forth a difference. It is this that gives a sense of volume – of there always being some further signification – to the event. Thus:

> the singular eventhood of the phrase stands as a *figure* which disbars the possibility of its ever claiming to be an entirely literal description, [and] displaces the rule of meaning. The discourse of logocentrism since Plato rests upon the identification of meaning with being: to tell the truth is to produce

6 The term 'deconstruction' is being used in its widest sense of presupposing a concept of 'construction' and, as such, has been used by Lyotard, Derrida and de Man amongst others.

a phrase whose meaning can state the being of a thing or phrase exhaustively. Lyotard's investigation of figurality moves toward a consideration of the temporality of the event as the site of a deconstructive resistance to logo-centrism.

(Readings 1991: xxiii)

If logocentrism is presumed to be no more than an exact representation or correlation between concept and thing, then it is the act of forgetting that is involved in the enchaining processes of naming, observing and stating that are composed as accounts, propositions, theories. It is the perfect, rational fit of real world and representation that deconstruction resists. Within this site of resistance, for Readings, 'the fact that phrases elude the order of literal description makes politics a matter of judgement rather than knowledge; an ethical rather than a social concern' (Readings 1991: xxiv). What is more, it could be argued, since each phrase is radically singular, the nature of the links made between phrases during enunciations can only now be posited as a matter of dispute. Neither a cognitive matter of mimetic representation, nor conceptual critique, but rather as a site of intervention, reading becomes an act, an event, a performance to be judged in practical, ethical or aesthetic terms. For instance, how do you know when someone, and, just as importantly, one's self, is good enough to be a judge and to act expertly? How many repetitions does it take to say 'yes', the event that signifies expertise has now occurred? How does one recognise during all the repetitions the build-up and becoming and succeeding in being expert? Take, for example, doctors in training, on the job, who feel frustrated but resigned to the practice they call 'going through hoops'. The consultants in the CasE study recalled their own experiences:

C1:   Yeah, you see, I think going through hoops is the fact you've actually become competent at the procedure and think you are but what you actually need to do is another ten, or another twenty, really to get properly accustomed to the odd, or something will go wrong. And that gets back to the ten hernia operating procedures and that somebody who has done thirty or forty hernias is probably a much better operator than the ten [person] but how you define at what stage between ten and forty they become competent is very difficult and I call the ten to forty 'going through hoops' because to the degree that it's a routine, just learning a bit more and a bit more and getting used to a procedure which probably the professional would think at ten they were completely competent at doing and the question is how you define what is necessary to go through those. And someone might say that you know that for one person they need to do three more and for another person it's 300 more.

My interpretation, and that's like medical procedures and seeing lots of patients, is actually accumulating knowledge that doesn't seem at face value to be of great educational value but is just accumulating knowledge and accumulating experience and that's one way. It's just it's not quite as negative as that [SHOs' viewpoints: cf., transcripts of recorded interviews, 1991; 2001, 2002–3, 2003]. It's just it's one way.

R2: Yeah, my one counter to it comes from another project – midwifery – and they also have a quantity and it's written in.

C1: Mmm, they've done so many deliveries. The wrong thing about that is there is a figure attached.

R2: Then there's the notion of catching babies – ooh, there's a baby being delivered over there, caught that one, snap!

C1: Yeah, tick the box, which is nothing to do with the actual follow-through. Yes, I accept that.

C4: A positive interpretation is very important because if you think back to the discussion about alarm bells because if you don't accumulate this whole host of normal events in medical practice then really you don't learn much from them because it's just one depressed patient after another.

C1: That's right.

C4: But it does provide you with a background against which alarm bells function and without that you don't pick up the alarm bells.

R1: Okay, that's quite interesting because my interpretation of 'going through hoops' is influenced highly by talking to trainees.

C1: Right.

C4: Mmm.

R1: Rather than talking to trainers.

C1: I wonder whether trainees at the end of 'going through hoops' might look at 'going through hoops' differently than when they are actually in the process of 'going through hoops'.

R1: They might.

C1: Why do I have to do another ten hernias, I want to learn something more interesting than doing a hernia operation? But actually it's still a bread-and-butter procedure, as a consultant you're going to have to do it and you've got to pick up the fat overweight difficult one where everything falls apart and the only way you're going to get that experience is having a few difficult ones that go wrong and go wrong at you because you were a bit complacent or whatever. That's how I look at it.

(Taped CasE core team meeting transcript, 14 January 2002)

Repetition, in some ways, is perceived as adding value, as creating the necessary conditions of spotting the abnormal, of getting the experience of 'alarm bells'. Data as transpositional event, or as phrasing, involves an implicit process of reading, a process through which data is constituted within a field of the visible as a precondition for being accountable, repeatable and real-isable. It is a matter of recognition, not just by the person performing but also by others and not just any others, but authoritative others who have already been baptised as those able to judge. There is the moment of the real when a 'hernia' has been accomplished or a baby 'caught'. There is the recognition that this has been done once, twice but not yet enough. There is the understanding that in repetition, no case is the same as another case. There is the further recognition that symbolically ticking boxes does not bring real competence. Consequently, data exists in a tension between the real (the non-conceptual), the imaginary (the field of the perceptual through which a witnessing subject can be constructed) and the symbolic (the lawful domains of language whether read under the orders of the theoretic or the mythical that provide the means for representing the realities of competence). It is in this tension that the fabulous is to be found as that exception that motivates further thought and revisions of the given. As discussed in Chapter 3, the constant crossover relation between thought and revisions of the given is rhetorically a chiasmus, a mechanism for transpositions. Thus, attention to the transpositional event as data escapes or goes beyond the limits imposed by a given theory and opens out the possibility of alternative explanations and theoretical creations.

Promoting the fabulous

How heterogeneous is a 'heterogeneous community'? Are there limits to what can be included? Can society be radically changed to be inclusive of all possible differences? In contemporary Westernised societies, there are few individuals who do not go through some socially approved form of schooling. It is here that many have seen the potential for systematic, progressive social reform or, indeed, revolutionary change. Apart from individual experiments with alternative forms of schooling, or indeed, Illich's (1971) vision of deschooling, what can be done within mainstream schooling? One possible way of answering this is looking at the impact of action research, an approach to research now increasingly common in the professions. In the UK, the movement was stimulated in the context of Stenhouse's (1975) Humanities Curriculum Project (HCP), which included the concept of the teacher as researcher and that there was no teacher professional development without curriculum development. HCP is famous for introducing the role of the neutral chair. Essentially, this subverted the role of the teacher as expert and thus changed relationships between teacher and students – placing them as equals within an arena of debate. As neutral chair, the teacher could no longer pronounce on the 'truth' but rather could only organise and, as it were, authorise rational debate around evidence. The role of evidence privileged both debate and research as essential features of a curriculum. The step towards action research was thus not too large to make within such a context, and John Elliott, who had been a member of HCP, took that step, becoming one of the founders of the action-research movement in the UK. Now, action research focuses on identifying and solving problems. As to what these problems are and how they are solved, for whose purposes, depends very much on the values underlying the process. For Elliott (1991), it is a process very much about values in action. Hence, the critical point is what values, whose values? Action research can be used as much for shoring up the prevailing social order as it can be about subverting it or transforming it (Schostak 1999).

Drawing upon his experience from HCP and action research during a project in Portugal (1990–2), Bev Labbett drew up some guidelines for the Portuguese coordinator that included the following:

- Action research is in the business of self-facilitation.
- A facilitator can best facilitate by taking on the role of quizzical enquirer. The most significant question a facilitator seeks to answer is, 'How do I go about working on my current practice so that what I investigate leads to surprises?' In the context of staff development, the question may be rephrased as, 'How do I go about working with others, so that what we investigate leads to surprises?'
- One way of bringing about surprises is if the facilitator focuses on trying to transform the taken for granted into the curious, the ordinary into the interesting.
- Action research ought to be about the careful scrutiny of the ordinary, the careful scrutiny of that which is taken for granted. Why bother with that? Because that which we take for granted, we do not bother to think about. The purpose of action research is not to take for granted such expressions as 'Well, it's so obvious that we don't need to talk about it'.
- Action research ought to be about the courteous challenging of assumptions.
- That is to say, if we are interested in the development of special-needs provision, and that interest carries with it the exclusive assumption that the only concern is the special needs of children, that assumption ought to be questioned.
- Action research is best characterised by its preference for the creation of evidence, which, when analysed, leads to the making of conjectural rather than assertive statements.
- When working with others, the need for procedures under the heading CONFIDENTIALITY exist because that which the researcher thinks may be reported to others should not be taken for granted.
- Action research is underpinned by the aspiration that everyone involved should survive the experience productively.

(Bev Labbett, unpublished notes, 1990)

Labbett was concerned that teachers should not interfere too much in the learning of children but rather, as facilitators, should learn the art of what he called 'skilful neglect' (1988; 1996). Within the context of the project, the purpose was to create the conditions under which the voices of the children and their communities could be heard and the arena of public debate redrawn for educational purposes. The task was to empower children by drawing upon what they felt to be important. In one very small school of twelve children aged between five and nine years old in the mountains, they were asked to work in groups with an adult to write down a list of their questions and wants. They had never worked this way before. A list was written on the board:

Gostava de ter quarto de banha (We want to have a bathroom).

Campo de jogos (Playing field).

Gostava de ter um cinema (We want to have a cinema).

Estrada bem arranjada (Good roads).

Gostava de ter casa da povo (We want to have a social meeting house).

Noa tamamos banho por que nao temo tempo (We don't bathe because we don't have time).

Gostava de ter frigorifico e televisao (We want to have a fridge and a television).

Por que Ragas nao temos uma casa do povo com medicos e enfermeira (Why doesn't Ragas have a people's house with doctors and nurses)?

Por que Ragas nao construiram casa de banho nas nossas cases (Why hasn't Ragas built bathrooms in our houses)?

O meu pai abandonou-nos a minha mae e a min (My father abandoned us, my mother and me).

Eu sou crianca porque tenho de trabalhas muito (I am a child, why have I to work so much)?

(Schostak 1990)

The teachers had wanted to develop a project with the children on health and hygiene. Their first thoughts had been to hose the children down because they were dirty and full of parasites. From this and other lists drawn up by the other groups, the teachers developed another way of working with the children. Rather than objects to be hosed down, they became individuals who had needs and could engage with them in discussing issues.[7] From it, a curriculum project began to be drawn up that involved exploring the fuller context of the community, its history, its culture and its current experiences. As in another community in the region, the children were asked to talk with local people to produce a map of their concerns, interests and experiences. In doing this, the curriculum was, in effect, a way of engaging with the voices of the community. The process transformed the typical hierarchical and distant teacher–pupil–community relations by including the voices that were normally silenced in school.

There is a similarity here with the views of Jacotot that Rancière drew upon as a way of thinking through the principles underlying democratic method. In Rancière's (1987) account, Jacotot had to flee France and sought refuge in Belgium, taking up a position at the University of Louvain in 1818. A group of students spoke no French, and he spoke no Flemish, but they wanted to hear what he had to say. There was only one book that was in both French and Flemish, thus they used this to communicate. What Jacotot learnt was that students could learn for

---

7 We expand upon this transposition from 'dirt' to 'withness' in our CESE paper, 'Violence – children's rights and educational challenges for an open world' by John Schostak, Concha Sáncez Blanco, Jill Schostak and Cathie Pearce.

themselves. They taught themselves to communicate in excellent French. Indeed, reflecting upon this, he came to the conclusion that hierarchical forms of teaching merely reinforce the gap between the expert and the non-expert, that indeed one can teach what one does not know. His core principles were that all people have equal intelligence, that from God all have received the faculty of being able to instruct themselves and that everything is in everything. In short, what this means is that:

> It is always a question of relating what one does not know to what one knows, to observe and to compare, to say and to verify. The pupil is always a searcher. And the master is first of all a human being who speaks to another, who tells stories, restoring authority to knowledge only on the poetic condition of every verbal transmission.
>
> (Rancière 2004b)

For Rancière, Jacotot provides a model of democratic engagement which accords well with his notion of politics founded upon disagreements and democracy as a process through which people can engage inclusively with each other as equals. For Laclau (2005) and Mouffe (2005), this, in turn, contributes to their vision of a radical democracy. There is a fundamental relation between education, schooling and politics. Schooling is the term, in this book, that is reserved for the process of expert domination and control of students that at the extreme levels of HRS engineers them to achieve expert prescribed goals. Schooling is fundamental to maintaining a given police order. Education is reserved for the processes of ever including new viewpoints, differences, disagreements and the consequent mapping and exploration of these through curricular action initiated by individuals in order to produce understandings that have been achieved by the students and teachers as equals. It is a risk, since including the new, the different and the voice of disagreement means undertaking action in the context of uncertainty. Like Jacotot, in such a context, all are 'ignorant masters'. That is what makes people equal, knowing that no one is able to master the situation. That is what makes it essential to search together in openness, taking the risk to engage with otherness. It is here where the fabulous is recognised in individuals as their essential point of difference and the recognition of individuality and community of inquiry.

Risking radical designs

Research is necessary to inform decision-making at all levels within societies. Stenhouse's HCP and action-research contribute to thinking about the role of research in engaging with everyday processes. However, if research and education are fundamental processes of freedom, then they are essentially political in that they challenge the status quo reinforced through schooling and the systemisation of knowledge. Education and research are radical in the sense that they continually question the given and are productive of designs for projects. They are restless, unfinishable and have parallels with the general project of radical democracy of Laclau and Mouffe where democracy is an unfinished and unfinishable project (Mouffe 2005). As Arendt saw the incompletability of politics in the ever-new viewpoints that are born into the world with every child, so too the education of these newborn viewpoints opens new possibilities, challenges and visions. What principles are required for including the otherness of other voices in the design of everyday projects? If research is risking otherness, risking drawing together the sense of a project, then risk itself is the necessary principle and, thus, a creative act in the formation of events. Where Beck (1992) speaks of a risk society, it is that risk that poses problems to be managed – the risks associated with the consequences of such hazards as pollution, side effects from medical advances – in short, those risks that are manufactured through the agency of human action. The risk of the radical is more like Derrida's (1992a: 26) madness of decision, a decision that is made in the knowledge that full knowledge is not possible. Although the two forms of risk are involved in any process of decision and action, the risk of the radical is not in managing hazardous consequences but in risking the new, including otherness, becoming something other. Risking designs in this latter sense involves an aesthetics, an ethics and a politics of judgement that is not reducible to the calculations of cost–benefit analysis in the management of hazards. Rather than calculation, there is a poetics through which the political and the ethical are embodied as expressions of the riskiness of living and engaging in projects that reconfigure the field of play through the inclusion of difference. There is a similarity with Kristeva's (1984) exploration of avant-garde poetry that 'calls up an aspect of the signifying process that destabilises the symbolic, logical, and orderly aspects of signifying' (McAfee 2004: 7).

It is at this point that the significance of Labbett's 'courteous challenging', the search for 'surprise' and the cultivation of 'skilful neglect', and Lyotard's notion of 'phrase-linking' weaves a texture that functions in the same way as Kristeva's explorations of avant-garde poetic language.[8] Rather than being constrained to a given master code, 'poetic language then forms a dynamic intersection of textual surfaces, a force for dialogue between several writings that would include those of the writer and of the addressee' where several meanings due to the application of several codes might turn on any given word thus opening up a multiplicity of possible interpretations (Schostak 2005). This poetics embodies the 'withness' of relating to the other not as someone who is like me but as someone different from me, thereby inhabiting the world (Ahmed 2005), filled with heterogeneous and plurivocal identities, all of whom are drawn together and incorporated, as it were, within a diverse community held in a bond of openness towards each other. A kind of unity through diversity is constructed through a desire born of a generous corporeality (Diprose 2002) that generates not homogeneity but difference, through a reflectively constructive critique of the strangeness of otherness. This kind of

---

8 Schostak and Schostak (2006c) expands this argument further.

desire is focused not on fixing one given kind of discourse but rather on observing and respecting the plurality of signifying practices constructing a multiplicity of discourses through which accounts may be made of experiences and worlds.

Risking the radical, in brief, is essentially about suspending the rule of the single code, the code that is legitimised and imposed through power. The issue then is not whether a research design should include a multiplicity of viewpoints, each with their different codes, but whether the research defines itself in terms of an overruling code and whether that overruling code sides with power. Designing difference into a project plays with the design structures of the normal and deconstructs a sense of what is to count as 'normal', 'objective' from the point of view of a given power.

How a world is talked about constructs that world in terms of its 'objectivity', and power is decisive in defining the paramount reality. Taking a Kristevan-like stance, 'All signification consists of the positing of the object through a linguistic proposition. This means that the constitution of an object will somehow always be present in the proposition' (Sjöholm 2005: 19).

Understanding that worlds are constructible means also understanding that they are deconstructible. That is to say, power, objectivity and what counts as the real in 'normal' terms already carry the seeds of their own deconstruction. As a strategic move, therefore, radical research, in this sense, takes the normal and reveals those seeds of deconstruction. In doing this, radical research explores both the constitution of objectivity and its instability through the normal processes of how meaning is produced in everyday life. But language involves more than communication and representation: it depends on the creative processes and energies through which there is the possibility of the dissolution and emergence of meanings, objects, subjects and worlds. For Kristeva, signification is dependant on pre-linguistic processes concerned with the predisposition of meaning. She attempts to show this, in part, through her concept of the *chora*. The *chora* stands outside of time, outside of matter as an element outside of any metaphysical principle. It is a space of energies, investments and drives. Thus, the *chora* does not give rise to a variety of representations or to a version of language, but, rather, it traverses representation and language, 'investing it with pleasure and displeasure, *jouissance* and abjection' (Sjöholm 2005: 20). With the experience of pleasure, displeasure, *jouissance* and abjection, the perceptual, experiential field is subjected to an aesthetics of enjoyment – an enjoyment that includes the 'pleasures' of horror whether as in the pleasure of a horror film or the Sadean sense (cf., Airaksinen 1991; Schostak 1996, 1998), or even the sense of the banality of evil as Arendt (1963) described the attitudes that underlay the crimes against humanity perpetrated in the Nazi concentration camps.

Returning to Labbett's approach, it could be described as a deconstruction of the prevailing legitimating codes to create the space and fluidity necessary for a creative reconfiguration of the visible, the thinkable, the communicable. Inasmuch as he fosters the imaginaries of change and of heterogeneity over those of homogeneity, his practices, as educator, affirm the flexible and open character of the subject and of a Kristevan-like speaking subject who, as subject, is always in the processes of being challenged, a *sujet-en-procès* (literally, a subject on trial, as well as in process, Kristeva 1984). Moreover, as Sjöholm argues, it is through such practices as these that 'the political domain is displaced from the public to the intimate and radicality is a negativity of movement and change, a heterogeneity of drive, body, language and meaning' (Sjöholm 2005: 2). Through his poetic language, Labbett engages in a politics of meaning, challenging, breaking down and reconstituting the imaginary field that defines a society. The existence of meaning depends upon postulating an existence of a relation: the desire of the subject is of necessity transferred onto something. Kristeva calls this something the 'Thing'. The Thing is not an object in the full sense of the word, rather it is the shadow of an object (Kristeva 1989). Metaphorical transference, as a result of the notion of 'skilful neglect', for instance, avoids the linguistic impoverishment that slavishly conforms to authority, the rule of the expert – as in the case of Reynolds's HRSs. As seen above, the feature, expressed as 'a limited range of goals', insists that 'the air traffic controller's job is to land the aeroplane, not to socially relate to the pilot' and thereby casts its shadowy Thing in very narrow and highly constrictive terms. Its very paucity affects the subject's ability to experience difference, distance and space. Labbett's 'skilful neglect', however, is quite different. The juxtaposition of 'skilful' and 'neglect' itself is an unusual one – a catechresis in rhetorical and poetic terms. It catches the eye and sparks the imagination as one begins to reflect on the range of possible potential meanings within this particular union of opposing terms. Its very mobility and flexibility opens up the mind to a very different order of experiencing otherness through difference, distance and space. Risk is essential to its process, risking challenge, risking surprise, opening to otherness, opening to judgement formed through aesthetics as much as through reason.

In avoiding risk, normal science produces the conditions for danger – the other as threat, as enemy – a kind of aesthetics of danger. Exploring alternatives, opening to the voices of others and otherness, creating new forms for a community of voices, constitutes a global educational and radical research project that draws upon the ways in which people create, interpret and communicate their worlds. In this context, evaluation cannot be about judging against predefined criteria, objectives, measuring performance – using the single code. Rather, it is a progressive incorporation that recognises the fabulous exception, the multiplicity of codes, the pre-linguistic creative spaces as a spur to reconfiguration and redesign. Evaluation, in this sense, explores the conditions under which programme designs can be redesigned throughout the process of undertaking the evaluation (i.e., *recherche-en-procès*, research on trial). A policy-defined programme designates its aims and outcomes and evaluates progress in relation to these. However, with the incorporation of new voices, new aims and outcomes, the prior fixity is challenged. What then? If the new is to be incorporated, how must evaluation projects be redesigned to meet changing ways of seeing and judging? How can evaluations then inform policies and reframe them? In this sense, evaluation is a precursor to action. And it is a precursor to a kind of creative ethnography – as the 'writings of peoples' – through which a sense of 'people' is continually rewritten, reframed. It is the process-*procès* through which individuals inscribe themselves onto the dynamic surfaces, or meaning structures and processes that constitute a 'people', a 'community of practice', a 'culture' and so on. If this is so, then such an evaluation is an emancipatory strategy. Can the voices of people, their rights and their judgements concerning 'reality' be progressively embedded into normal research designs in order to bring about real change? It depends on how power and rights are to be addressed and how the 'realities' of situations are thereby made visible. And this is the topic of the next chapter.

Chapter 6

Power, rights and the real

How should people be treated? How should they be represented on the public stage of decision- and policy-making?

C4: I remember one of the ward rounds you [*to R1*] sat in on, one of the things that is perhaps more difficult in psychiatry [*compared to rheumatology, general surgery and pain management*] is knowing, if you don't know someone very well on the staff, medical or not, what is their level of expertise? What can you assume they know and what they do not, and there was one ward round a few weeks ago when the physiotherapist was sitting there, who was, whom I've seen before, he was moving around a lot, and I had no idea actually how much of his physiotherapy training had actually been targeted to mental health as a discipline, so how aware he was of our jargon, our habits, our bad points, how we deal with things. And there was a place-ment that he had quite a few dealings with because of physical problems so I asked him, 'What do you think?' And he said, 'Well, she's very confused and she's very paranoid.' And this lady did not come in with paranoia.

C2: Yes, but he perceived her.

C4: But *he* [*italics indicate C4's emphasis*] thought she was paranoid, and so I said – well, because I didn't know him I actually was quite active with him, far more active than I would have done with someone else, but I hope that was [done] in a nice sort of constructive way, [. . .]. So I asked him what do you mean with 'confusion'? And he couldn't clarify that. And for me it was important to rule out dementia which she wasn't, had not come in with, either. So what he called confusion had a lot to do with agitation and walking around. That was his term for it and that was fine by me as long as I knew she wasn't dementing.

(Taped CasE core team meeting transcript, 14 January 2002)

The power to judge circumstances, the right to make an account of what is actually going on defines what is to count as reality. Power, rights and the real are coextensive. They define the perceptual field of a territory, how the territory is parcelled up, whether clinical area or community, who can act upon its various spaces and what kinds of acts can be carried out. Most importantly, they define who is a person, who is a subject and, thus, who can speak in order to represent their interests and who is an object and thus is to be managed, used, disposed of. The exercise of power in the representation of interests is nowhere more extreme than in the decision discriminating between sanity and mental illness. It is here that the perceptual field itself is at stake.

C2: Right.
C4: And then I asked him, 'You said she was paranoid, what was that about?' She kept saying that she didn't think she was going to get better. This lady had deep depression, and sort of either she was having ECT [electroconvulsive therapy] or close to it – I can't quite remember. But his term 'paranoia' had nothing to do with my term . . .
C2: Clinical term.
C4: 'Paranoia', and he threw me diagnostically. So I said, well, but when he described it and I said, 'Yeah, well we don't call that paranoia, what you described is what we call a negative, a nihilistic delusion – I am not going to get better'. And not being able to share that – so his semantics are completely non-psychiatric, but it took, I had to ask to find out, if I hadn't asked, I would have, well, I have, would have, there would have been an inclination to change the [. . .] diagnosis.
R2: So why did he use the notion 'paranoia'?
C4: I've no idea, really, we didn't.
R2: Is this a layperson's term?
C2: Yeah.
C4: I don't know where, because I've never heard it used that way by 'norm' technicians as it were. I've never heard someone call, you know, these are very dark beliefs that you see in depression, I've never heard them called paranoia. But come to think of it, the original term 'paranoia' in the old Greek word means nothing else but being outside your mind. It hasn't got anything to do with the persecutory flavour that we now attach to it either. So I had to tease out what he knew, what he was meaning because his term, in trying to turn it into psychiatric discourse he was failing, which was fine, you know, there's no problem, but I need to know.

(Taped CasE core team meeting transcript, 14 January 2002)

The search for the right term by which to represent the state of mind of a particular patient is critical. The psychiatrist and the physiotherapist employed different terms to describe their perception of the state of mind of the patient. The use of the term 'paranoia' by the physiotherapist problematised the psychiatrist's reading of the nature of the problem and, thus, of the possible diagnosis. Only by determining how the physiotherapist was using the term to signify certain behaviours was he able to judge that dementia was not the 'reality' of the case. Two different discourses were in play here, each parcelling up, naming and thus representing the perceptual field differently. The psychiatrist and the physiotherapist are both qualified professionals, but each is qualified in a different profession. Within the different health-care professions, technical terms can come to have different nuances, and they may take on different meanings for a given profession when the qualified individual applies the term to specific contexts. This was the case here. Each had their profession specific discourse. Lyotard defines 'discourse' as 'the process of *representation by concepts*' (Readings 1991: 3). Discourse, in this view, thus organises the objects of knowledge as a system of concepts (units of meaning) and, in doing so, defines the real. Agreeing with Saussure's concept of meanings being defined in terms of their position in the discursive network, Lyotard refers to 'a virtual grid of oppositions' (Readings 1991: 3), where meanings are produced by the play between signifiers. Subjects, in a sense, are gridlocked by a particular discourse. When they are the subjects or objects of different discourses, who and what they are becomes problematised, until, through the exercise of the power and the right of one discourse to dominate another, the ambiguities are settled and reality can be 'seen' for what it is. As previously discussed in Chapter 2, Spinoza equates the real with the natural rights and rights are coextensive with power. There is a relation, then, between discourse and what can appear in a perceptual field and the rights and powers of individuals, groups, organisations and states. This complexity can be further explored through Lyotard's concept of the figural as a visual image, a kind of 'painting with words'. The figural, although breaking with Saussure's structural linguistics, is not to be understood in terms of opposition to the discursive. 'Rather, the figural opens discourse to a radical heterogeneity, a singularity, a difference which cannot be rationalized or subsumed within the rule of representation' (Readings 1991: 4).

Unable to reduce the figural to an opposition within the network, the discursive system cannot deal with it by imposing upon it a state of mere equivalence of meaning within a system of signification. The figural thus 'marks this resistance, the sense that we cannot "say" everything about an object, that an object *always in some sense remains "other" to any* discourse we may maintain about it, has a singularity in excess of any meanings we may assign to it' (Readings 1991: 4). Lyotard claims that the figural is always interwoven with the discursive, and vice versa, despite the fact that discursively accurate representation and/or full understanding is dependent on the repression of figurality. It is in this interweaving of the figural and the discursive that the complex of power, rights and the real are knotted into accounts of social and personal practices and lived experiences to produce the sense of 'reality' by means of which 'delusion' is separated from the 'true'. The continued and persistent questioning of the physiotherapist by the psychiatrist attempts to undo the gridlock of two separate discourses so that 'reality' can be 'seen' for what it is in relation to what the psychiatrist perceives as 'reality'. There is an 'in-between space' between each discourse, as it were, where a shuffling of concepts and articulations occurs. It is here that the undoing of frozen language categories takes place. This resembles and calls to mind the space of Kristeva's chora as discussed in Chapter 5, the space where, potentially, creative new forms and meanings may arise. It is also the space of the figural. In the undoing that takes place in-between spaces, the figural emerges such that the patient 'stands out' as the subject of a 'painting with words', so to speak. It is through such sensual spaces that the apparent fixity of the categories can be disturbed. But it is also a fragile space where the fluidity can be reclaimed under familiar categories:

R1:   But you got the patient in, didn't you?

C4:   Yes, I got the patient in, because I wanted to see for myself, which is something that we don't very often do in psychiatry, either because it is very threatening to the patients. If it were a staff-grade psychiatrist who would have said this lady is paranoid, I would have immediately assumed that they meant what I mean by it. And that would have been immediately in discussion: 'hang on, you're saying this lady is paranoid, that's not what she came in with.' It's important in psychiatry because diagnosis is often—

C2:   Will change, yeah.

C4:   Tentative by the time they come in and you know the reason they come in is often to clarify further. So that would be a vital ingredient to that person's assessment, if staff-grade says, 'This lady is paranoid, she wasn't when she was home.' Either I missed it, or, [*unclear on tape*]. For whatever reason she covered it up because you know delusional people often do cover up and we have uncovered – the uncovering, if that would have happened, if this lady was deeply depressed but then turns out paranoid on the ward because we get to know her better can be a sign of improvement, on the patient's side. So there's a clinical—

C2:   Label, yeah.

C4:   Thing to it. If someone, if someone starts to drop their guard, we call it, there's another lady [*named*] on the ward, who's going to have a tribunal on Thursday.

R1:   Uhuh.

C4:   A deeply deluded lady, the GP was monitoring her and bugging and what-ever else. She came in on the ward on a 'Section', denied anything was wrong, had not happened at all, was nonsense, not on my mind, yahdy-yah, and two weeks' time slowly she starts to say, 'Well, yeah, well I do think he does that, or at least he did it, although I'm not so sure'. So the whole delusional system is starting to shift which could be a sign of improvement.
(Taped CasE core-team meeting transcript, 14 January 2002)

What is at stake here is that the condition of the patient must stand out, become manifest not as an abstract concept, nor as a mark on a page but as a living reality like an apple on a tree that can be eaten. The process of 'standing out' recalls the Latin root of existence – to stand out (*ex-sistere*). The power of language is to represent things, to make them stand out, whether or not they are there. Language, in the sense of representation, is empty but is the condition for meaningful 'existence'. The power of the real is precisely that it is *there, in hand, full of itself*, even though language cannot grasp it by means of its representations. The psychiatrist could not base his decision solely on the discussion between himself and the physiotherapist – he had to go and see for himself. Yet, what appears? Is it the case that the real just makes itself present, thus resolving any confusion, ambiguity or dispute? If the real did just make itself present, then it would be a simple matter of making words correspond to things so that everyone could see and talk about the same things, things as experiences not as concepts, that is non-conceptualities, the things in themselves, the noumena as Kant called them, that can only appear to consciousness as phenomena. The real as noumena, then, is mediated as phenomena. How what appears to consciousness is put together to form a sense of unity of things in a perceptual world that stands out in the public (or intersubjective) domains as 'real', 'sane', 'true' is where the political battles concerning what is just, right, wrong takes place. In this mediating space there is the signifier which, as Saussure defines it, is material in that it can be heard in terms of sound waves or seen in terms of light waves and etched into stone or inked on paper or marked in some way on some other surface. These are not just any sounds or marks but those that indicate signification, that a separation is being signalled, a difference is marked out, that language is possible. The signifier has both the function of keying into the representations of language as well as making something visible, figurable as well as being itself, visible, figurable. The figural condition of the signifier, thus, has a double appeal: to the textural and to the visible. Neither is reducible to the other. This incommensurable copresence of the textural and the visible in language constitutes 'a thick space, where the play of hiding/revealing may take place' (Lyotard 1971: 75 as cited in Readings 1991: 6).

The work of the psychiatrist involved trying to reveal what was being concealed through a tentative but persistent questioning of naming: paranoia or a nihilistic delusion? This was set in motion by the use of paranoia by someone whose qualification was not in medicine but in physiotherapy. Rather than dismissing it, the psychiatrist attempted to clarify how the term was being used. If the person had been a fellow psychiatrist, he would have simply assumed they were both using it in the same way. That is, in Dennett's terms, two different intentional systems for attributing 'beliefs, desires and rational acumen' were being employed (1989: 49). The assumption that they were the same was thus disrupted by the use of a diagnostic term by the physiotherapist. As in Figure 1.2, these different intentional systems can each key into different mechanisms and resource structures to produce different outcomes with respect to the client. Since the physiotherapist, although not medically qualified, had witnessing powers and could exercise a right to witness, a right to be heard to some degree, a process of checking out had to be carried through. The patient, however, had no such right or power but was instead the object of and subject to the defining powers of legitimate witnesses.

A counter to such an approach would be what Cooper (1967) called anti-psychiatry – examples of what he meant by this include the approaches by Laing (1967, 1976), Szasz (1997, first published in 1970), Brown (1966) and others that contributed to the 1960s cultural critiques. What is at stake is not that one is right and the other is wrong but that between them there is a disagreement that needs to be taken into account before rights can be exercised, judgements made and agreed and actions undertaken. Taking a disagreement into account does not necessarily imply that there is a final resolution or, indeed, any resolution such that the disagreement vanishes. Actions may be made that skirt around, gloss over, cover up, repress or deny the reality of the disagreement. In each case, the cause of the action is the disagreement. What results is a particular texture as the social is woven into the representations and figuralities of the real through the ways in which disagreements are taken into account. What was excluded from the negotiation of meanings by the psychiatrist and the physiologist was the discourse of the 'patient', the excluded, other that can be seen as the subject of 'anti-psychiatry'. The process of inclusion or exclusion in the right to judge is fundamentally political.

The political texture of the real and the conceptual

There's something very intimate about knowledge, a body of knowledge. I reach out for things, they're mine, I say. But you might object. Just understand this, I reply in my sharpest, most authoritarian tones, they're not yours – DO YOU UNDERSTAND? It's not really a question. I just want you to do as you're told. If you don't, we've got a fight on our hands, and someone is going to learn a very hard lesson. Life, and its schools, is full of such understandings, disputes and their lessons. What is learnt is what we claim to know about life, about the bodies of knowledge essential to our everyday lives. How do I see and draw into my collections of bodies of knowledge the data that I will use as the indisputable evidence to support my beliefs, my understandings, my interpretations, my decisions, my actions? The intersection of bodies of knowledge and bodies of flesh is, of course, of paramount importance in surgery. The psychiatric example provides an illustration of what, more generally, is at stake in making judgements:

C2:   And very often, I mean I just had one that I saw today, where there's a little lump. The Registrar took the skin lump out and it's come back as a dermato-fibrosarcoma – being sent to [*name of city*] for results. So we've got to go back and take another bite of the cherry. Now somebody a little more experienced at the time might have thought 'what if'. And therefore if I took a bigger bite of the cherry first go it would save coming back twice. Yeah. So the Registrar could do it, but unless the penny dropped that it was worth doing, because it saves them coming back again. There are times when I will go a little further surgically than maybe I need to do. But it saves the patient coming back and having a second operation, a second anaesthetic, a second admission to hospital and all the hassle and, if they didn't need it, the, not morbidity, but the cost to the patient is minimal. If they did need it the benefit is phenomenal. And that's where the judgement comes in between.

(Taped CasE core-team meeting transcript: 14 January 2002)

The decision seems fully rational, thoughtful even. The criterion is that of the relative cost of engaging in the course of action. Indeed, it is set up as a defining feature of what constitutes the difference between being a consultant and a registrar. However, such judgements have their dangers, which were pointed out by another consultant in the discussion:

C1: When you discussed what seemed to be quite simple things that everybody, we would like to do logically, what is, what about the ethical considerations of taking an extra bit, of skin, an extra bit and where is consent? You could, as a consultant, I'm sure, with experience, justify, yeah, we can justify why I did the incision and we just took this little bit of this and actually it was the best thing at the time. But you can imagine one of the junior doctors, actually, taking out more than they needed to. I certainly had a patient who had a lipoma on the hip and ended up with this huge amount resected and they needed plastic surgery and everything, and it was actually, it was somebody who thought I wonder if this is malignant and took out a whole, so much tissue that it was a real disaster. And that balance is a real, and I don't know how you define that, but that balance is actually critical.

(Taped CasE core-team meeting transcript, 14 January 2002)

The danger is constructed around a different way of measuring value, not utility, but ethics and the process of gaining consent. In this complex situation, justification for a decision is founded on a mixture of experience and the legitimating power that comes with a particular position in the hierarchy. However, those without experience may do too much and bring about a disaster. To avoid this, an appeal to 'balance' is made – a term that seems to defy definition. Nevertheless, there is still a further countermove that can be made. It is not just any decision, it can be claimed, but one that is based upon a nuanced understanding: '*C2*: Yeah, that's judgement. That's why I said if you took that extra bit almost at no expense to the patient' (Taped CasE core-team meeting transcript, 14 January 2002). There is an appeal to the negligibility involved, the almost nothing. But the almost nothing is still something:

C1: But that 'extra little bit', those few words, are critical in the current climate of suing people.

C2: Yeah, because if you take the extra bit and they're not going to miss it then I think you're okay. If they would miss it then you've to think twice.

C1: In this litiginous world you've got to say that it was justified as part of the procedure. I can think of patients, and I'm sure you could. Who say when they come back, you say. 'I'm pleased to tell you that the mole that we removed at the same time was normal'. And they say, 'Why did you remove that mole?'

(Taped CasE core-team meeting transcript, 14 January 2002)

If someone without the experience and legitimating position makes a decision that goes too far, then the danger moves to a different level of consequences. It enters the domain of litigation. At this point, the stakes are better defined and the powers and limitations of the different members of the dramatis personae become clearer:

C2:   Yeah, there is that. And the other one I have difficulty with, if you're doing an anterior section, [*procedure named*], and you do a hysterectomy to make it safer and easier. Now it certainly makes it easier, there's no doubt about that. Whether it makes it safer is open to dispute. Now one would say to the patient, 'It was safer to do it that way. You're seventy-nine, you don't need the womb, you had to get your cancer out, I did a hysterectomy while you're at it'. Now, normally I would mention that to her pre-operatively as a potential thing, I would say, 'If I need to do it, because it's in the way, and it's going to make it safer to do, I will do it, that's okay, isn't it?' So you've got sort of, sort of mentioned consent. But what you do if you're in an emergency and she has a perforated carcinoma and you go in as an emergency and they're clapped out and you haven't got the opportunity for consent, I think in those circumstances you do what's best.
C1:   Yeah, that's right because you can stand up in a court of law and you can say it was the safest thing to do.
C2:   I would still do it and I think I would argue – in a court of law I could argue in my experience it was safer. A SHO [senior house officer] could not.
C1:   Exactly – that's where it actually gets quite, and that's why I was trying to get around this, it is very, very complex.
C2:   In a court of law I could say my judgement was that she needed the hysterectomy because it made the operation safer. Now the SHO might say I fancied doing it because I need the practice.
R2:   But what if the SHO didn't do the extra little bit and it was actually needed?
C2:   Yeah, and it went wrong.
C4:   Then there's a problem.
R2:   And then there's litigation, what then?
C2:   Well the SHO should have called for help.

(Taped CasE core-team meeting transcript, 14 January 2002)

Woven into the discussion are factors from several distinct domains. As professionals, there are the practical skills of being able to accomplish surgery which are quite distinct from theoretical knowledge. In turn, the abstract concepts of theories cannot substitute for the experience required to recognise the significance of what is seen in the realities of living bodies and anticipate potential consequences. In addition, as noted above, in conflict in the discussion between the consultants are two distinct ways of valuing a course of action: the first is on the basis of utility, that is, the costs and benefits of carrying out a procedure; the other is in terms of the ethical rightness of carrying out an action. In each case, there is the further issue of litigation should something be considered by the patient or relatives to have been 'wrong'. In this complex of factors, experience of the real is built of visual, textual, cognitive, emotive, tactile and kinaesthetic dimensions, none of which are reducible to any of the others. The unity that together they compose has the characteristics of a texture: 'A "texture" is a disposition or characteristic of anything which is woven into a fabric, and comprises a combination of parts or qualities, which is neither simply unveiled or made up. Texture is at once the cloth, threads, knots, weave, detailed surface, material, matrix, and frame' (Vasseleu 1998: 11–12).

In politics, weaving was employed by Plato as a metaphor of statesmanship, drawing together into a synthetic untity those elements in conflict, a process in rhetoric called, *symploke*. In contemporary terms, Laclau and Mouffe (1985) see it as underlying hegemonic practices. These are practices through which alliances, however temporary, are formed between different interest groups to achieve particular political goals. Central to the process is a desire for order. However, order is essentially precarious, its weave capable of being undone. In the discussion between the consultants, this possibility of the weave being undone is implicit in the question of the right order underlying judgements, courses of action and the fact that whether these are 'right' or 'wrong' turns on *almost nothing*, the notion of *balance* and the possibility of *disaster*. Each of the key terms of the disagreement referred to an implicit order, an order woven by the regulating concepts of utility, ethics, law and status in the hierarchy. Alongside this sense of order and regulation is the implication of its absence, an absence that nevertheless is essential to experience, what James (1996) called the blooming and buzzing of sensations. James:

> invites that chaotic, buzzing world of sensation to play an equally vital role in constituting experience. Together, these moves make the world both richer in quality and more unpredictable. The stable set of relations that apply universally for Kant: Causality, Subsistence, Dependence, and so forth are taken to be provisional in the Jamesian model. At any time the world of sensation can suggest relations that challenge these categories. If unusual perceptions strike us as being "objective," Kant simply calls this "illusion". For James, such experience is not so easy to dismiss. Primordial reality is replete with relations that we often fail to perceive. The idea that we must take all relations, however dim or unanticipated, as ultimately real is the backbone of James' "Radical Empiricism." For James, "any kind of relation experienced must be accounted as 'real' as anything else in the system." Such unanticipated experience is the contribution of the world outside, which James feels obliged to defer to. One's conceptual system must not be so stubbornly

postulated that it is unable to yield to the influx of novelty from the buzzing universe beyond oneself.

(Behuniak 2004)

The suggestiveness of sensation is productive of the synthesis or weaving together of identifiable things. If each dot represents some 'thing', some object of consciousness synthesised from sensory input, then the dots also can be synthesised, woven or joined up in suggestive ways (see Figure 6.1).

The discussion, in Chapter 3, of Bush's axis of evil and Huntington's (1993, 1996) clash of civilisations can be represented in Figure 6.1 as two camps, each camp defined by the connected dots. Even where some groups or states are outside the formally connected dots, if they do not consider themselves as a friend of one of the camps but do not consider themselves as being an enemy, they may simply be defined as enemy – whoever is not with us is against us. Also in Chapter 3, there

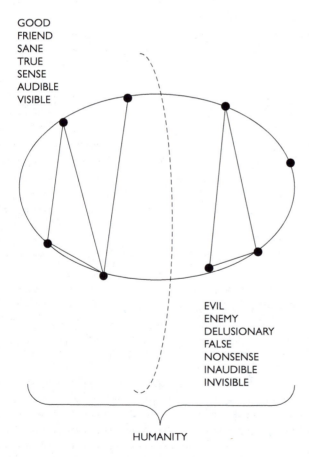

Figure 6.1 Humanity and division

was the account of Ismail's son, the child killed by Israeli bullets who appealed to humanity as the reason for offering the boy's organs for transplantation regardless of whether or not they were to be used for Israeli patients. That too may be represented as a joining of all the dots to produce a circle covering all peoples in all communities and states under the universalising category of 'humanity'. What counts as reality, as in the illustration given by the psychiatrist, may be divided between those who are deemed sane and those who are delusional. Some descriptions of reality may be counted as true, while others are seen to be false. Some ways of talking make sense and can be heard, while others are senseless and cannot be heard as meaningful. Those people who are audible speak meaningfully, even if disagreed with, and are visible to the public stage, while those who are not audible cannot speak meaningfully and thus are invisible in public arenas. Albeit a simplified description of the field of the visible, it illustrates how concepts, perceptions and material realities may be twisted together into social fabrics, gridlocking people into the polarised matrices through which their worlds are socially, culturally, economically, politically organised.

To elaborate, suppose this weaving of binaries into opposing relationships describes a textured surface. The textural patterns on this surface are perceivable, that is, feelable, visible and audible only from particular points of view. But the texture as a whole is made up of the framework, the parts, the syntheses, the modes of tying parts together into chains . . . all this and every conceivable element are all available at the same time throughout the fabricated surface. As in Figure 1.1, the whole fabric can be seen all at once under the 'god's-eye view'. However, imagine now an individual, an ant-like person, wandering across the fabric. From that position, little can be seen by which to gain a picture of the whole, as in the 'wandering-eye view' of the labyrinth. What is known takes time to be known, each path taken adding some new insights, each insight connected to other insights until some sort of picture is built up. Suppose now, that whether by chance or by design the ant-like person wanders only around one section of the fabric and that another ant-like person wanders around an entirely different section. The 'pictures' that they compose will differ yet both will say they are 'real', 'true' representations of the whole as they have experienced it. How will they resolve this?

The accounts they make will draw upon the key concepts they have constructed during their wanderings. How can they make sense of each other's concepts? Some key terms like truth, real, good, sane may well be in common but the picture they are used to describe will be different. In this sense, the term 'truth', for example, has no specific contents. It is, in Laclau's (1996) terms, an empty signifier. Perhaps each need to describe their world picture to others and try to convince them that their particular view is the right one – that is, they compete to place their particular contents under the common, universalising but otherwise empty signifier 'truth'. Perhaps they think their lives, their sanity, their sense of identity are at stake if they do not; or perhaps there would be a loss of wealth and power should their particular view prove not to be convincing to the majority. If there is something like this at stake, then it will be important to increase the numbers of believers, or at least those who are willing to join in any alliance that meets their own interests concerning, say, power, social position, access to resources, security. So, if a group feels undervalued by the adherents of one world picture they may be attracted to the other group if they are assured they will be equally valued by them. A more disturbing situation can be proposed, however. Take, for instance, those who, feeling disvalued for some reason join together in an angry crowd to gain some sense of social justice from those who look down on them, exploit them or in some other way wrong them. As an example, Laclau (2005) draws upon Rudé's descriptions of popular disturbances to explore the shifting nature of power through which regime changes become possible. It is a situation where those who are high up in the social hierarchy can be brought down to the level of the crowd, what Rudé calls a 'levelling instinct' and Laclau takes up this as follows:

> during the Gordon Riots, the crowds attacked *rich* Catholics rather than Catholics in general; during the 'Church and King' disturbances, people in Naples attacked Jacobins not just because they were allies of the atheistic French, but mainly because they went around in carriages; and during the Vendée, if peasants revolted against Revolutionary Paris, it was because they hated the wealthy city more than the local landlord. The conclusion is unmistakable: if this 'levelling instinct' can be attached to the most diverse social contents, it cannot, in itself, have a content of its own. This means that those images, words, and so on through which it is recognised, which give successive concrete contents a sense of temporal continuity, function exactly as what I have called empty signifiers.
>
> (Laclau 2005: 76)

Thus, from each point of view, in the process of levelling, *chains of equivalence* are created. That is to say, although we do not believe in the same faith, we are *all the same* because we are poor. Thus, chains of equivalence between key terms for describing who and what are considered 'good' emerge and are opposed to other chains of equivalence that describe the 'enemy'. The more key terms, or universalising concepts, that can be enchained under a given camp, the more powerful and thus hegemonic is the alliance enabling adherents to impose their conceptions of the 'normal'. These chains of equivalence are, in Saussurian terms (2005: 117; see also Schostak 2006: 30–6), synchronic, that is, they are given statically, all at once, as it were, in the 'god's-eye view' (in the end, we are all equal under God, in the face of death or under the law). Imagine them piled up, one on top of another, like cards all belonging to one suit: the stack of hearts is different from the stack of clubs, is different from the stack of spades, is different from the stack of diamonds, but they are all of the same deck of cards. Other forms of arrangement can be made: the set of aces, the set of deuces and so on. The different ways of forming chains of equivalence are all in a sense given at once by the possibilities available in the standard deck of playing cards. If the pack of cards is now organised into binaries – say, the black suits seen as 'good' and the red suits seen as 'evil', then an analogy may be made with Figure 5.2 above. Next, take a child, any child, and deal them a hand. Any desire or intention to deal a good hand depends on how the power to deal is arranged. Of course, reality is infinitely more complex than this simple analogy. Nevertheless, it is commonplace to talk about an individual's life circumstances in terms of the hand that has been dealt. In the revolutionary context described by Laclau, the way hands are dealt, and for whom, are in flux. In such a context, all may be reduced to disorder, chaos as the social fabric through which most, if not all individuals knew their place, felt secure unwinds. What then? For Hobbes it was clear, without some unifying power to keep control, there would be a return to the state of nature: a war of all against all, and: 'To this war of every man against every man, this also is consequent; that nothing can be unjust. The notions of right and wrong, justice and injustice, have there no place. Where there is no common power, there is no law; where no law, no injustice' (Hobbes 1914; Chapter 13).

Power and order

In Chapter 1, Spinoza's distinction between *potestas* (Power) and *potentia* (power) was described:

> In general, Power denotes the centralised, mediating, transcendental force of command, whereas power is the local, immediate, actual force of constitution. It is essential to recognise clearly from the outset that this distinction does not merely refer to the different capabilities of subjects with disparate resources and potentialities; rather, it marks two fundamentally different forms of authority and organisation that stand opposed in both conceptual and material terms, in metaphysics as in politics – in the organisation of being as in the organisation of society.
>
> (Hardt, translator's foreword, Negri 1991: xiii)

Real power resides in the multitude, and it is this power that is set in motion by the 'levelling instincts' of the angry crowd, deconstructing the centralising, hier-archical power of the state. What is at stake here for radical methodologies is the very conceptual and material organisation of society: each are radically opposed to the other. Individuals as subjects are radically different under each form. They see themselves differently, act differently, develop and use their talents, their energies differently – they have different purposes, aims, hopes, ideals, desires. Is one better than the other? If so, then it would be ethical – in Spinoza's terms – to choose that form of political organisation that enabled people to develop their potentials to the maximum. It could be argued that it was also the most useful, since all would be getting the maximum benefit of developing the potential of all. However, to bring about such a state, vested interests in maintaining the alternatives must be overcome. Given that vested interests will, for the most part, be defended, the result is likely to involve a struggle to take or hold onto power. On both sides, the nature of order itself is at stake. Thus:

> Let us consider the extreme situation of a radical disorganization of the social fabric. In such conditions – which are not far away from Hobbes's state of nature – people need *an* order, and the actual content of it becomes a secondary consideration. 'Order' as such has no content, because it only exists in the various forms in which it is actually realized, but in a situation of radical disorder 'order' is present as that which is absent; it becomes an empty signifier, as the signifier of that absence. In this sense, various political forces can compete in their efforts to present their particular objectives as those which carry out the filling of that lack. To hegemonize something is exactly to carry out this filling function. (We have spoken about 'order', but obviously 'unity', 'liberation', 'revolution', et cetera belong to the same order of things. Any term which, in a certain political context becomes the signifier of the lack, plays the same role. Politics is possible because the constitutive impossibility of society can only represent itself through the production of empty signifiers.)
>
> (Laclau 1996: 44)

What does this mean? First, order is desired because disorder is dangerous. Such radical disorder means that there is a continuous struggle, or warfare, as each individual tries to impose and take what he or she wants. Whether a Hobbesian, Hegelian or Spinozan view is held, individuals assert their power to get what they want. If each want the same thing, it can only result in a struggle where one wins and another loses. In Christian terms, of course, the nature of the individual is sinful, is weak and, thus again, the image is that without law or faith to guide them, individuals are prepared to do the worst to each other. Even when individuals are considered essentially good – as in Godwin's (1793) anarchist view – the good society remains an aspiration to be achieved in the context of contemporary realities. Hence, to move from one form of order to another involves either a rapid breaking down or a gradual transformation of the first that leads to a radical change in the ways of life of individuals. This, in itself, is threatening, leads perhaps to a sense of wrong, frustration, resentment, anger. When there is no structure through which to express and obtain satisfaction, when one's voice is dismissed as noise, when one's distress, frustration and resentment cannot be made visible and attended to with care and concern, then the angry, protesting crowd becomes the only form available for collective action, since it is here that a 'levelling down' can be imagined, where it becomes possible to reconceive of the 'high and mighty' as 'worth no more than any one of us'. But this moment is an indeterminate space between one order and another – not quite disorder, not quite order. Its liminality, its betweenness is unruly but is nevertheless haunted by possibilities for rules and orders. The possibilities dissipate as the crowd dissipates. Either radical change is underway or it is postponed, perhaps for ever.

After the protest, after the street riots, people merge back into their everyday lives whether changed, satisfied or frustrated or resigned. Following protests and the street riots described in Chapter 3, the consequences for change were clear in the now ex-Soviet Bloc nations, but the rioters in France as in other countries went back to their respective *banlieues*. The book by Paulo Lins and then the film directed by Fernando Meirelles of *City of God* – its real name – provides an account of the everyday lives of children growing up in gang cultures of this *favela* at the edge of Rio de Janeiro. The book is based on the author's early experiences in the City of God in the 1960s and 1970s. The film released in Brazil in 2002 needed permission from some of the gang leaders to be filmed in the *favela* and employed children from the City of God to play the various roles. It is a tragic fusion of real and fiction as very young children are shown delighting in killing. Diken (2004: 1) describes the bleak circumstances and stark choices it poses, thus:

> the narrator of the film, an escapee, introduces *City of God* as a dumping ground: 'this is where the politicians dump their garbage'. As a 'dumping ground' *City of God* is a necessary outcome of order-building processes and economic progress, through which modern society produces huge amounts of human waste, homo sacer (see Bauman 2003: 123–6). Hence human life is cheap; not only gangsters but also the police can kill without impunity in *City of God*. Consequently, the boundaries between the law and unlaw are unstable and the justice system is deligitimated (see Caldeira 2000: 157). The allusion to St. Augustine is therefore interesting not because *City of God* is ironically a 'city without God' but because it is a truly 'sacred' place, provided that one recalls the originary meaning of the 'sacred': a situation of being *aban*doned, a state of being exempted from the domain of the law and ethical responsibility (Agamben 1998). *City of God* is, in other words, a 'city without citizens' as well.
>
> *City of God* is a labyrinth, a no-go-out area. As is the case with the runaway chicken, 'you die if you escape and you die if you don't'. Those who attempt to escape fail (and get killed as is the case with Hairy). Likewise, those who traverse the inside-outside divide through strategies of hybridization are denied existence (and get killed as is the case with Bene, the most charismatic figure in the film). There is though one exception to this paranoid closure: Rocket, who signifies the search for the outside, the only upwardly mobile character ('rocket') whose life miraculously changes on the basis of his artistic practice as photojournalist. Being both inside and outside, (both resident and an escapee, both the narrator and protagonist), Rocket is the exception that proves the rule: there is no outside if one is not, that is, a Michael Jordan or Eddie Murphy.

In the labyrinth of the City of God, that sacred place of banishment, order arises through the power of the gang. It is in the interstices, the places where the 'normal' rule of law fails to reach that the gang flourishes (Thrasher 1927). In the film, when a local drug-gang leader, Ze, ruthlessly kills his competitors and punishes all who go against his rules, the area becomes so safe that virtually no crime is committed. People are able to go about their business, the youth are able to find employment within his organisation whether in the 'factories' making drugs, the management, the sales and so on: 'His rule is perverse and despotic but he unites City of God by protecting it against kids' gangs who 'do not respect the rules of the ghetto' and rob the local shops. 'With Ze, City of God gets a master' (Diken 2004: 2). There is order. In the book, it is Tiny who creates the order:

> Business in the dens grew steadily, and the use of cocaine increased by the day. Craving the drug, junkies from the *favela* and elsewhere showed up at the den with chains, rings, bracelets, TV sets, watches, revolvers, electric mixers, blenders and innumerable other household appliances to exchange for cocaine. The intersection of different worlds made it possible to trade anything. Tiny had bought a chest for the gold pieces that found their way into his hands at a low price, as the thieves from the Alley only sold their stolen goods to him now. Each day someone new joined his gang, not for money – because the only ones on salaries were himself, Sparrow, Carlos Roberto and his three assistants – but for fear of him and his men, and in order to gain respect and be able to pick on anyone they didn't like the look of.
>
> (Lins 2006: 317–8)

It is an order that acts like a surface upon which people can inscribe a significant range of their own agendas to meet at least some of their needs. However, it is a surface built upon or glossing over conflicts, rivalries, jealousies, frustrations, that at a later date, explode into street warfare. The barely buried sites of fracture lend a sense of covered-over depth to the surface of order, order as fabric(ation), as:

> surface of a depth that also spills over and passes through the interstices of the fabric [. . .] It is neither visible nor invisible, neither metaphoric nor metaphysical. It is both the language and material of visual practices, or the invisible interweaving of differences which form the fabric of the visible.
>
> (Vasseleu 1998: 12)

The social fabric is an impossible project since it cannot weave together into a final all-encompassing shape all the manifold differences, the conflicting and ever-changing interests, demands and desires of people. If a given order satisfies a sufficient number of people to safeguard it from being overthrown, then its surface constructs a way of repressing, making invisible a range of conflicts that are the basis upon which an accord leading to order is built. In this, some are rich in satisfaction, and others poor.

Rich and poor

Rancière's book *The Philosopher and his Poor* (2003) discusses politics in terms of an essential conflict between the poor and the rich, arguing that this relation between the rich and the poor is reflected in philosophy and social theory. Crudely, those who are rich enough to be educated speak on behalf of the uneducated poor because the poor are unable to speak on their own behalf. It is to be seen in the notion of 'giving voice to' the marginalised by speaking for them, interpreting what they say to explain the 'truth', the 'realities' of their circumstances. He criticises Bourdieu's (1993) monumental study of the poor as an exemplar of this position. He summarised his general argument against mainstream philosophy and social sciences as follows: 'philosophy defined itself in defining its other. The order of discourse delimited itself by tracing a circle that excluded from the right to think those who earned their living by the labour of their hands' (Rancière 2003: 203).

The argument begins with Plato who, in the *Republic*, as described in Chapter 1 argued against democracy and for a social hierarchy governed by ruler guardians. In his ideal city, people would specialise in only one job. Only the guardians would have the privilege of thinking because only they had the time and were free of the need of earning a living – perhaps this is an early Cochrane Collaboration or EPPI Centre or social engineers of a HRS. The elites are rich in time and the workers poor both in time and in the fruits of thinking. Thus they need guidance.

> This way of putting things together supposed some cunning in its detail. By relegating artisans to the order of pure reproduction, philosophy pretended to confirm them only where they had been placed by their love for the solid realities of technical success and financial gain. And, *per contra*, it fed its own privilege with the dark bread of non-possession. But this was a double game. By elevating [*classant*] solid artisans and demoting [*déclassant*] shadow makers, philosophy reserved for itself this right to the luxury of appearances that command the privilege of thought. And this privilege imposed itself with all its brutality by invoking a difference in nature that confessed it was a fable. Philosophy linked its lot to a hierarchy that the lie could be found only in nature.
>
> (Rancière 2003: 203)

The double game involves a lie, the 'noble lie' that the differences in classes of people is natural. As such, the role of the philosopher is to 'be a specialist in nature and the lie. To be precise, he will be an engineer of souls' (Rancière 2003: 18).

> Plato says openly that nature must be the object of decree in order to become an object of education. It is the presupposition laid down by the selecter-breeder of souls to begin the work of forming natures. Nature is a *story* declared to be such. As the only one who knows the relationship between

suitable means and desirable ends, the engineer of souls is the only one who has the power and the knowledge to lie – the lie that is an imitation of truth, the good lie; the lie that suffices to establish an order safe from the true lie [*du veritable mensonge*], the technological ignorance of principles and ends.

(Rancière 2003: 18)

What definition of 'nature' is being storied as real? Is it the final victory of Western liberal economies storied by, for example, Fukuyama (1992) or perhaps the 'third way' of Giddens (1998) or the New World Order of Bush Snr? Perhaps Weber's (2001) 'iron cage of reason' has become so naturalised that there is now no other way of thinking? The radical then is that which disturbs the 'natural' order, revealing its make-up as the 'police', the naturalness of which is schooled into the minds and behaviours of members of communities, faiths and states. However, if, as has been discussed above and in the preceding chapters, there is difference, diversity and conflicting views, no one individual has the full insight into what all people want and need, and if no single individual can be trusted without reserve to legislate for all individuals, then there needs to be some way of organising power to ensure that the multiplicities of views are included. However, globally, this is far from being realised:

The surface of the earth is covered with a diversity of landscape conditions, only 2% of which is an urban density. In addition, satellite coverage for mobile telephones constitutes less than 20% of the earth's surface. Of the now 6 billion people populating the earth, 1.2 billion live in abject poverty in circumstances of mere survival mode. So, in spite of the fact that the majority of people in a post-industrial society live in an urban or suburban environment (70% of all Europeans live in cities of 200,000 or more), a sizable portion of humanity falls outside of the consideration of most architects and planners. Here the problem is not density, but poverty and its causes.

(Kavanaugh 2003: 114)

Most people in the world fall outside the gaze of rational planners. Boundaries are erected and policed in order to keep the poor, the illegal immigrants out. But the boundaries are chronically leaky: 'Some 500,000 migrants are reckoned to slip through America's defences each year, and a further 800,000 or so make it into "fortress" Europe' (Legrain 2006: 35).

Legrain (2006) has catalogued the 'war' on immigrants undertaken by the rich nations against the poor: Médicins Sans Frontières doctors 'treated 2,544 migrants for violent injuries – such as gunshot wounds, beatings and attacks by dogs when trying to escape Moroccan security forces – between April 2003 and August 2005' (Legrain 2006: 27). It is a war that has cost many thousands of lives at every border. And it has cost many billions to police and earned smugglers many billions more:

Immigration authorities estimate that people smuggling in the Americas generates $20 billion (£11 billion) a year, a criminal activity second only to drugs trafficking. Smugglers rake in around €4 billion (£2.7 billion) a year from the EU, reckons Michael Jandl, of the International Centre for Migration Policy Development, an intergovernmental think-tank based in Vienna.

(Legrain 2006: 38)

And within each state there are boundaries between those who have wealth and those who do not, those who are 'banked' and the 'unbanked', the protected and the unprotected. Far from being victorious, Rancière (2005) argues, democracy is also an object of hatred as much by the powerful who proclaim the victory of so called liberal democracies as by those who are openly anti-democratic for reasons of religious or political faith. Recall that democracy, for Rancière radically employs the principle of equality in order to be inclusive of differences. Under that test, there are few if any corporations or institutions of government that can be claimed to be democratically organised. Their organisation is constructed to reinforce elite powers and hierarchies as 'natural' ways in which people should be led and managed. Those at the top of hierarchies are rich not just in power but also in access to and possession of resources that give them security and enable them to pursue cultural and social activities not available to those who are much poorer. Globally, the world's elites are rich in power, but people globally are poor in democracy. To what extent do research activities reinforce inequality or provide the methodologies by which to address 'wrongs' and equality of access to the places of decision and policy-making that affect people's lives?

Designing rights

Evaluation as a process of identifying rights by including the excluded paves the way for action in relation to the allocation of resources. Through ethnographic description, those who are rich in resources can be distinguished from those who are poor. Such resources are both material and symbolic. Evaluation, then, is radical to the extent that it manifests what is at stake for whomsoever, in terms of the rights to be involved in decisions about the distribution of resources. By identifying the principles under which resources are to be allocated from a multiplicity of viewpoints, a critical problem structure can be set out by:

1. identifying the incompatible demands of those rich in resources against those who are poor;
2. defining the impasses, the failures to meet goals, the 'wrongs' that lead to disruptive reactions;
3. defining opportunities that are missed and are desired by one or more individuals;
4. identifying those who are excluded and thus have 'unheard' demands;

5. identifying those who can realise their demands and those who demands go unheard.

Evaluation clarifies how rights, as being coextensive with powers, are either designed into programmes of action or designed out, whether overtly or stealthily (see Chapters 2 and 3). In short, it describes the state of play as between Power and power. Power may accrue to itself a willing or unwilling transfer of rights from people in their various roles as for example employee, spouse, parent, citizen . . . Equally, people may object, resent, feel frustrated in response. These experiences contribute to the problem structures faced by different individuals and groups. In mapping this complex of experiences, an evaluation describes the potential field of play. It sets up, then, the kinds of action that can be undertaken.

If, as Dennett (1989) says, an intentional system ascribes beliefs, knowledge, wishes, values to members of that intentional system, then a game-like structure emerges as each side second-guesses what the other may do based on what they 'know' about the other. What mechanisms are essential to the game, how are resources differentially employed to realise outcomes? The evaluation is, thus, able to identify the real or imagined intentional systems, mechanisms and uses of resources that produce the outcomes of the game that, from the viewpoint of each actor, is said to be 'the case'. The evaluation is, then, a 'case of cases' identifying which cases are pivotal in either increasing Power or power. Those who are frustrated in their demands are likely to feel wronged, injured or at least frustrated and thus open to any opportunity that increases their opportunity to get what they want. The implications for action is the theme of the next chapter.

Chapter 7

(II)legitimate knowledge(s) – wrongs and injuries

Knowledge, as described in Chapter 4, is socially produced and organised. How knowledge is governed is central to the question of fairness. The judgements people are able to make depend on how open their society is, the degree to which information is made freely available, the extent to which research can be undertaken to explore issues, the nature of their education and the extent to which they can participate in decision-making at all levels. And, finally, it depends on how reliable the source is: here, this is not a question of epistemics but that place where knowledge meets trust – it is a question of ethics:

> Whether or not the expert's reporting that *p* will give the recipient good reasons for believing *p* will depend on the recipient's perception of the reliability of the expert's testimony, which in turn will depend on an assessment of the expert's character ([Hardwig] 1991:700) Has the expert been responsible enough to keep herself informed of developments in the field? Has she been conscientious, and realistic in her self-assessment of how reliable a judgement she is able to produce? To answer such questions is to make a statement about both moral and epistemic character.
>
> (Kusch 2002: 49)

To make his point, Kusch drew upon the a study by Hardwig (1985) of a multi-disciplinary team who undertook a complex scientific experiment:

> When the data were in, the experimenters divided into five geographical groups to analyse the data, a process which involved looking at 2.5 million pictures, making measurements on 300,000 interesting events, and running the results through computers . . . The 'West Coast group' that analysed about a third of the data included 40 physicists and technicians who spent about 60 man/years on their analysis.
>
> (Source: Kusch 2002: 48; Hardwig 1985: 347)

Drawing on Kripke's (1981) historical chains through which the naming of something by a witness is passed on from person to person, knowledge production becomes a community endeavour rather than an individualistic concern. The team is effectively a network through which information is processed and channelled. Each member of the network has their own particular viewpoint and contribution to make. Although some will have a greater grasp than others, no member of the network has an overall grasp of all the details, the specialised methodologies, theories and forms of knowledge. Hence, trust is essential. Sometimes, of course, that trust is abused. In 2005, for example, the apparently pioneering cloning research undertaken by Dr Hwang of Seoul National University, South Korea was judged to have been faked:

> In May, Dr Hwang published a paper in the journal Science, saying his team had extracted material from cloned human embryos that identically matched the DNA of 11 patients.
>
> It was claimed such a technique could be the key to providing personalised cures.
>
> But the university panel said that all 11 sets of data were derived from only two stem cell lines.
>
> The panel said it still did not know whether those two stem cell clusters had actually been cloned.
>
> "Based on these findings, data in the 2005 Science journal cannot be regarded as a simple accidental error but as intentional fabrication made out of two stem cells," the investigators said.
>
> "This is a serious wrongdoing that has damaged the foundation of science," it said.
>
> (BBC News, 23 December 2005
> <http://news.bbc.co.uk/1/hi/world/asia-pacific/4554422.stm>)

Although trust had been undermined and national pride damaged, it is important to note that communities can verify scientific claims by rechecking evidence. Nevertheless, in the case of Hardwig's example, any such checks would involve a massive undertaking corresponding to the size of the original undertaking. The underlying motive is a desire to get at the truth.

Knowledge, when it serves political purposes and social prejudices, however, may have to deal with the desire by some to conceal or avoid the truth. As an illustration of the complexities, consider the case of Sir Cyril Burt. In the UK he was a very influential psychologist whose work on IQ shaped the schooling system following the Second World War until the early 1970s. In particular, he undertook research on twins to prove the inheritability of intelligence. It 'naturalised' social and occupational hierarchies by reinforcing a meritocracy based upon inheritable talent. It contributed to views that children should be selected according to IQ test performance to identify the academic who would enter grammar schools, the technically minded to enter technical schools and the rest who would be suitable mainly for basic labour to enter secondary schools. By and large, although children from working-class families were able to go to grammar schools, the procedures tended to favour the white middle classes. However, after his death in 1971, it was alleged to have included fraudulent data. Although having a significant impact on the discussions concerning IQ as a measure of intelligence, the influence of different forms of IQ and personality testing as well as debates about inheritability continue, particularly in the work of people like Jensen (e.g., 1995), Rushton and Jensen (2005) and Herrnstein and Murray (1994), to argue the case for inheritable differences and, more specifically, race-based differences. Murray was invited by the *Sunday Times* in 1989 to compare the UK and American experience of dealing with what he called the 'underclass'. It supported broadly based right-wing political views of the time and was the focus of fierce political debate between right and left.[1] He described his conception as follows:

> Let us first be clear on terms. *Underclass* is not a synonym for *poor* or even for *disadvantaged*. By *underclass*, I mean a population cut off from mainstream American life—not cut off from its trappings (television and consumer goods penetrate everywhere), but living a life in which the elemental building blocks of a life—productive work, family, community—exist in fragmented and corrupted forms. Most members of the underclass have low incomes, but its distinguishing characteristics are not poverty and unmet physical needs, but social disorganization, a poverty of social networks and valued roles, and a Hobbesian kind of individualism in which trust and cooperation are hard to come by and isolation is common.
>
> Since 1989, I have been using three indicators as a concise way of tracking the underclass: criminality, dropout from the labor force among low-income young males, and illegitimacy among low-income young women.
>
> (Murray 2000)

In 2005 he revisited the issue, again for the *Sunday Times*, where he wrote:

> Underclass is an ugly word, and we live in an age that abhors ugly words, so it is good to hear that the Blair government has devised a cheerier label: Neet, an acronym for "not in education, employment or training".
>
> Once a government has given a problem a name it must develop effective new strategies for dealing with it. That too is in train, The *Sunday Times* told us last week, replete with urgent cabinet meetings, study groups roaming about the country and even a "Neet target" to reduce the Neet population by 20% by 2010.

---

1 The main arguments can be seen in a publication by the IEA Health and Welfare Unit, Choice in Welfare No. 33, <http://www.civitas.org.uk/pdf/cw33.pdf>.

You may use whatever euphemism the government adopts, but it's still the underclass. Its numbers are not going to be reduced by 20% by 2010. Its numbers will increase. The good news is that the rate of increase will probably begin to slow in a few years and in another decade or two Britain will have learnt to manage the problem—meaning you will have learnt how to keep the underclass from getting underfoot, even though its numbers are undiminished.

(Murray, *Sunday Times*, 3 April 2005 archived at <http://www.aei.org/publications/filter.all,pubID.22252/pub_detail.asp>)

At the time, when the UK was under a left-wing government, Murray pointed out in his article that only the name of the perceived problem had changed. His solution was thus unchanged. In brief, he pointed to the 'failures' of various American initiatives that have attempted to deal with issues of poverty, low education and 'the growing number of children who have no father and who live in areas where hardly anyone has a father.' The solution was to follow what he saw as the successful American example – a zero-tolerance policing strategy:

In the United States I have called this the coming of custodial democracy— literally custodial for criminals, figuratively custodial for the neighborhoods we seal away from the rest of us. Custodial democracy is probably headed your way.

It is not a happy solution. On the contrary, it means abandoning a central tenet of a free society—that everyone can exercise equal responsibility for his or her own life. But Britain, like the United States and western Europe, is locked into a welfare state that by its nature generates large numbers of feckless people. If we are unwilling to prevent an underclass by giving responsibility for behaviour back to individuals, their families, and communities, custodial democracy is the only option left.

By framing an either-or choice, other ways of interpreting the circumstances and formulating a debate about 'wrongs', 'injustices' and 'injuries' are excluded. Custodial democracy is not democracy – it is about control by the few over the many by excluding, containing or sealing off those people who do not fit into 'designated' places – say, for example, like the City of God described in Chapter 6. Democracy is not about 'giving responsibility for behaviour back to individuals, their families, and communities' whilst removing welfare – this implies that the frameworks of power do not change and the 'giver' remains in charge since their control of private wealth remains untouched whilst access to support for the poorest is removed. In Spinoza's terms, this is a solution framed according to *postestas*, the maintaining of centralised power in the hands of a controlling elite. Rather, the alternative is about creating the conditions under which people's voices can be heard, their circumstances be made visible and their demands taken into account in terms of the allocation of resources to needs, interests and desires. The synthesis of custody and democracy represents a stealth strategy uniting opposing terms – it is, in that sense, a catachresis, that is to say, it stealthily incorporates repression under the legitimating name of democracy, the opposite of repression. However, there is no 'pure' democracy. In its place, there are forms of practical policy-making that appeal to the aspiration. The term then functions as a trade-off between freedoms for some at the price of a loss of freedoms for others. How can the debate be validly reframed to be inclusive of all?

The validity of knowledge and the fear of others

If all is not fundamentally well, then changes need to be made. But how is this to be done, and according to whose agenda? It might be easy if the world were controllable like a laboratory and if variables could be precisely measured and varied to deduce exact cause and effect relationships. However, human beings, unlike quantities of raw materials dug from the earth, cannot be radically altered through chemical-processing into metals or plastics to be engineered and used. Yet, as has been discussed, there has been and continues to be a way of seeing the world that seeks to subject all – both inert and living – to the will of reason and to employ the methodologies appropriate to the manipulation of inert substances for the study of society. Weber (2001) described its emergence in terms of the puritan work ethic:

> The Puritan wanted to work in a calling; we are forced to do so. For when asceticism was carried out of monastic cells into everyday life, and began to dominate worldly morality, it did its part in building the tremendous cosmos of the modern economic order. This order is now bound to the technical and economic conditions of machine production which to-day determine the lives of all the individuals who are born into this mechanism, not only those directly concerned with economic acquisition, with irresistible force. Perhaps it will so determine them until the last ton of fossilized coal is burnt. In Baxter's view the care for external goods should only lie on the shoulders of the "saint like a light cloak, which can be thrown aside at any moment". But fate decreed that the cloak should become an iron cage.
>
> (Weber 2001: 123)

The power of schooling is to create the conditions for manipulation. In this book, schooling is generalised to all processes through which the minds and behaviours of people are moulded to some externally desired criteria. It takes the place of those refineries through which materials are purified. The Puritan ethic applied to business and labour is an exemplar of schooling as the process through which minds and behaviours are shaped in different ways for different social and occupational sectors of society.

In contemporary terms, this iron cage is everywhere tightening as a result of technological advances. Current information technologies have the capacity to track and record the movements and behaviours of millions through CCTV, bankcard transactions, mobile phones, personal-data encrypted passports and identity cards. Social reality is everyday mimicking the science-fiction dystopias that can be seen in Fritz Lang's *Metropolis*, Orwell's *1984*, Gibson's *Necromancer* or the recent Wachowski Brothers' *Matrix* trilogy of films. Of course, the technology is not there yet. However, billions are being spent and are projected to be spent on ensuring such progress as, for example, in Europe under each new framework of the European Union's Research and Development Programme. Globally, national governments, local public services and the major corporations are constructing the world so that it can be increasingly tightly administered for social control and the accumulation of wealth.

The ideal of a rationally produced society dedicated to producing the good life is as much in the minds of the powerful today as it was when Plato produced his vision for the Republic where the philosopher kings were to rule over a population categorised according to their roles in society. Instead of philosopher kings, in his book *Walden II*, Skinner (1976) imagined a society engineered by scientists employing his behaviourist principles. Whether it is a society constructed through reason or through the fear of power as embodied in a tyrant or the fear of an enemy, the problem has been to formulate the strategies for managing people, constructing and planning built environments, controlling resources and allocating goods and services.

Fukuyama in his 1992 book, adopting an Hegelian theme, proclaimed the end of history. That is to say, with the fall of the Soviet states and the globalisation of capitalism underpinned by liberal democracy, there is nowhere else to go. Like Kojève (1969) before him, the argument is that the Hegelian vision of a rationally ordered society where, in terms of the big political and social ideas, there is nothing left to struggle for, is close to fulfilment. Without the dramatic political struggles, there is, in effect, no history, that is, 'history understood as a single, coherent, evolutionary process, when taking into account the experience of all peoples in all times' (Fukuyama 1992: xii). Only the details are to be worked out. This provides the central strategy of a stealth political architecture where the broad schema is no longer open to question – it is, in effect, 'naturalised' as the only possible form of government.

In short, the argument made is that the broad outlines of the design of the good society and the 'final form of human government' has already been produced. As such, it is a globalised market that has been constructed as in the image of MacDonald's to provide 'the best available means of getting us from a state of being hungry to a state of being full' (Ritzer 1994: 9). In the perfect market imagined by classical economics, there is a perfect coordination between what is effectively demanded and what can be supplied. In this market no one person or corporation dominates – all are dominated by the market mechanisms. However, markets are not perfect. And it is the market that provides the mechanisms that both produces 'hungers', or desires, and places value on goods, services, labour. This market logic imposes its rationality upon populations. For financial institutions, it transforms communities into those with bank accounts, credit cards, loans, mortgages and those without – the unbanked, the underclass. The banked are visible, the unbanked are not, and, as underclass, are 'sealed off' in the places of banishment, the *banlieues*, the Cities of God. Populations can be further categorised according to wealth, income level, spending patterns, kinds of employment, where they live and so on. Market strategies will be applied differently to each grouping. In such a system, identity and addresses become the key organising factors. For such a system to work perfectly, for each individual to count as part of the system, engage in a contract and undertake an exchange, the identity and address of each individual must be definable and locatable. The rational structuring of life, the iron cage, can be further witnessed in the rational planning of cities, whether in the monumental vision of Haussmann's Paris which focuses the attention of individuals on the great monuments to power and glory or the flattened grids of modernist architects who sought to eradicate perspective where:

> The endless orthogonality of these systems was encapsulated by Hilberseimer's simple assertion of 1923: "Developing the plan of the city on lines corresponds to the fundamental principles of all architecture. The straight line, the right angle have always been its most elegant elements. Does not the clearness of the straight line better correspond to our current sensibility, to our organising spirit rather than the arbitrariness of the curved line."
>
> (Whiting 2003: 98)

These are worlds where:

> with regard to matters of space and time, the modernist reduction to a radical subjectivism means that all objects, including our environment, are set up in opposition to a thinking subject, that is to say our perceiving and experiencing mind. Precisely this oppositional and dichotomous way of constructing our world would lead to a general consideration of all objects outside of ourselves as "other" with the resulting problem of communication with those exterior objects. Obviously this modernist approach thought of man in contradistinction to his environment, setting up an opposition – perhaps unintentional, yet persisting to this day – viewing disparate objects in space existing only to be measured, tied down, and ultimately controlled.
>
> (Kavanaugh 2003: 116)

This organisation of subjects, space and time has as its paradigmatic metaphor le Corbusier's 'machines for living' (1923) through which people are to be organised in their public, private and, indeed, intimate lives. At its ultimate, there are the algorithmic 'machines' of search engines which have as their function the search for ways of organising information produced globally on the Internet. As a metaphor for the fusion of the virtual and the actual, there is Google Earth, mapping the Earth in relation to roads and street addresses. To take it one step further, there is the concept of the Internet Protocol (IP) addresses currently assigned to every web address. The most advanced versions are capable of generating an infinite number of addresses. These IP addresses can not only be assigned to every individual person on the planet but also to every part of each individual's body and possessions. Theoretically, at least, through the mechanism of IP assignment, total surveillance is possible, tracking both public and intimate events in a person's life. With ideas, mechanisms and material realities aligned, the iron cage can be infinitely tightened.

Valid knowledge, in the iron cage of reason, the ultimate, always on-line, any-time, any-where machine for living at the end of history, is about control, prediction and surveillance. As in Murray's suggestion, whatever cannot be brought under the normal operating conditions of society must be excluded, placed into custody, sealed off. To break open the seals, to listen to the voices and see the events of the lives of those excluded is to transgress, to break the ban, to engage in the forbidden. The iron cage, in all its perfection, like the ideal society of the end of history, does not exist – at least, not yet. However, its influence can be seen in the shaping of debates, in the conditioning of what can be said and not said, what is valid and not valid. At the back of custodial democracy is the fear of the other.

Fear of the other is an essential founding motive for the development of societies where people associate in order to have protection through numbers. However, when they gather together, it means that they also have to give up some of their powers in order to live together – they can't have everything they want when they want it. They have to negotiate, debate. But people do not come together just for protection. There is friendship, love and the experience of life being richer in the company of others. Indeed, it is not unusual for people to feel protective of others. When others are seen to be in danger there is *fear for* the life of the other. It is a question of humanity that arises in *fear for* and thus *care of* the other. It is why people risk their lives for others, even when they are total strangers. There are times, however, when *fear of* the other and *fear for* the other clash in ways that are irresolvable for the individual. Most tragically, it was expressed by nineteen-year-old Jason Chelsea whose words were headlined on the front page: '"I can't go to Iraq. I can't kill those children" – Suicide soldier's dying words to his mother' (Cahal Milmo, the *Independent*, 25 August 2006).

What is expressed here in these haunting words is what Levinas (1998) calls fear for the other, a primal fear that in recognising the other is constitutive of the self not cognitively as an idea but as an ethical being grounded in its relation to the otherness of the world – given no perceived way of challenging the military commands, the only alternative for this young man seemed to be suicide. In the name of the children, he took his life. There was no other escape that he could see from the iron cage of military command.

Escape from such an iron cage is only possible if something can be said, if the words can be found through which to recognise and act on behalf of a care for others. How does one make the words, the accounts, the fears a valid basis for inclusion in debate, decision, policy and action? Returning to the introductory illustration, if big science requires big teams and no one member of that team has a full overview of the theoretical underpinnings of the findings, then how much more so throughout society, and, indeed, globally? The extent to which knowledge production is controlled by a central elite – and thus normalised for policy purposes – is the extent to which trust diminishes. The biggest possible team is that envisaged in the early democratic writings of Spinoza, as discussed in Chapter 2, who saw an inherent instability in any regime that sought to dominate, contain or limit the access of the people to political debate and decision-making. Of critical importance to the stability of regimes is the control of what counts as knowledge of reality. As an illustration, prior to their fall, the Communist countries were in debt to the West and:

> had debtor regimes refused the definitions imposed from without – had they united to default simultaneously on their Western loans (which in 1981 stood at $90 billion) – they might well have brought down the world financial system and realised Kruschev's threatening prophesy overnight. That this did not happen shows how vital a thing was capitalists' monopoly on the definition of social reality.
>
> (Verdery 1996, in MacGregor 1998: 24)

There is, thus, an inherent instability in any social organisation that does not in some way control the definition of social reality, and that definition of social reality is always open to threat if it is not organised around the sovereignty of the 'people', that is, in Spinoza's terms, the multitude that includes those excluded by the dominant regimes. The larger the excluded become, the more fragile is the regime. No matter the form of the regime, whether from the point of view of the king/ planner in a totalitarian or oligarchic society, or that of people in a democracy, to be successful, that is effective, power has to be organised in its details, driven down to the smallest units. If, at the slightest whim, sufficient people reject the categories into which they are placed or choose to change identities at will or have fluid notions concerning property ownership, then the bonds between political and market categories and the content they are meant to address is broken and control cannot be assured. The task is to ensure that the correlation between categories (signifiers) and their defined content (signifieds) are maintained through the everyday and institutional practices by which spaces are mapped, bodies are managed and attention controlled or manipulated in public, domestic and intimate places. Whether through coercion, socialisation or more formal forms of instruction and education, people are to behave 'properly', aspire to and defend 'our way of life'. Without maintaining a strict relation between categories and content, knowledge cannot be amassed and used by the powerful to manipulate the powerless. The more rigid and comprehensive a system becomes in terms of checklists of appropriate behaviours, goals and forms of expressions, the more it sees as a threat any form of non-compliance as can be seen in the various religious and political 'witch hunts' that have taken place over the centuries. In contemporary terms, allying power with the technical knowledge and accomplishments of information technologies poses real and dramatic challenges to how freedoms are to be safeguarded. Imagining the nightmare scenario at least provides a way of thinking about what is at stake and how to stop it from happening.

Drawing upon Schatzman's (1973) account of the education of Judge Schreber by his father in the nineteenth century provides a way of thinking about the extent to which the control of the body can be managed. From birth, Judge Schreber's father had rigorously controlled all aspects of his bodily movements using the technologies of the time. Rather than being seen as a cruel and eccentric action, Judge Schreber's father was an influential German educationist, publishing widely. It was a scientific rational approach to education, exact in all its details. Think how much more rigorous and rationally evidence-based this can be through contemporary technologies. Sadly, the process drove the judge mad and led to the suicide of his brother. Judge Schreber wrote a book on his mental illness (published in 1955) which later provided Freud, and still later Lacan, with insights into 'paranoia'. It is perhaps the most extreme consequence of Weber's iron cage where the details of 'rational' control were driven to the smallest details of a child's everyday life. The iron cage is inflexible, godlike. Similarly, as discussed in Schostak (1996), Schreber records throughout his book, God does not understand individuals and cannot deal with all the details. 'A long time ago I formulated the idea that God cannot learn by experience, in written notes as follows: "*Every attempt at an educative influence directed outwards must be given up as hopeless*"; every day which has since passed has confirmed the correctness of this opinion' (Schreber 1955: 155). Schreber's God is equivalent to the panoptic surveyor occupying the position of power in Figure 2.1. The world thus seen is seen synchronically and thus is not open to change unless God is being threatened by those below. And so, according to Schreber, God has been led to believe that Schreber threatens his existence. In response, then, Schreber believes that God has been drawn into attempting Schreber's 'soul murder'. Soul murder could be equated to that numbing, alienating, soul-destroying feeling that is experienced by many who try to change the system or who are systematically reduced to being simply objects manipulated by management strategies such as being audited, having to meet performance criteria and so on. Every act, it seems, is written down by some monitoring system for later judgement. Schreber believed that one of God's key strategies to bring about soul murder was, indeed, what he called the 'writing down system'.

It is so obstinately held that I have become stupid to such a degree that day after day one doubts whether I still recognize people around me, whether I still understand ordinary natural phenomena, or articles of daily use or objects of art, indeed even whether I still know *who I am or have been*. The phrase "has been recorded" with which I was examined, follows when my gaze has been directed towards certain things and I have seen them; they are then registered on my nerves with this phrase. For example, when I saw the doctor my nerves immediately resounded with "has been recorded", or , "a joint of pork – has been recorded" and especially the phrase "Senatsprasident – has been recorded", etc. All this goes on in endless repetition day after day, hour after hour. *Incredible scriptu* I would like to add, and yet everything is really true, however difficult it must be for other people to reconcile themselves to the idea that God is totally incapable of judging a living human being correctly; even I myself became accustomed to this idea only gradually after innumerable observations.

(Schreber 1988: 188)

Paradoxically, perhaps, the experience of the writing-down system led Schreber to a radical position: that his God was incapable of learning and of judging. In everyday experience, to what extent can systems 'learn' and make appropriate 'judgements'? Without some way of feeding viewpoints into the decision-making processes of a system, it cannot change according to experience. What is insane, if that is the correct term, in Schreber's analysis, resides only in that it is so metaphorically displaced into the various names and parts of 'God' that he cannot find the right target, the right address (see also discussion of being out of joint in Chapter 2), that is, his own father who placed himself in the position of Power/God over his son. Trying to analyse this led his discourses to be labelled mad. More generally, in everyday 'normal' society, there are many names for 'mad' discourses that attempt to analyse and thus dethrone the powerful. In general terms, they may simply be referred to as forbidden discourses (Schostak 1993) through which accounts of those whose voices can only be heard in the places of banishment may be made.

Forbidden discourses, disappointments, rights and wrongs

Banishment is not always obvious to those on the outside, the cage is not necessarily a prison's bars, it may just simply be a rendering invisible, a systematic overlooking, not hearing, not including. On the inside, the blows are felt as described by some girls growing up in an economically disadvantaged community in the north-west of the UK:

[*They . . . start talking about the teens who hang around the streets, how they're always asking for cigarettes, threatening people, doing graffiti, making noise late at night and fighting and so on.*]

Girl: And like bonfires, that's the worst thing round our street, cos once there was a car that was in front of um there's our house and there's a pavement there, so then the car's there and someone stuck um a firework in there and it started blowing up [. . .] but the fire brigade came just in time.

Girl2:   And then there's like, near our fields where they ride their motorbike there's like these little blue pole, bollards I think, and they've like got robbed cars and they've like smashed into it so that they can still get [. . .] And the police are all there and you can hear it like so you wake up in the middle of the night you can hear police sirens all the time. And

I don't know why. We used to live in [*another place*] and that weren't even worse, it was a little bit better. But then there was this family who threatened my mum and then they put our windows through so we moved away from there. Then they followed us to [*the new place*]. So we're going to move again. But it's just teens and like people that, are like bad influences. We 'ad a really good school but we had to move about six times just because of people round it. And every time we're like playin' outside all happy and then the boys come down the road. It's just like they rule when they don't, they don't live near there. They're always playing loud music and its just not on, I don't think anyway.

(CAPE project, UK 2005)

Whether it is the streets of a particular neighbourhood or the political regions of the world, whoever has the strength rules. To listen to the voices of those on the inside can be frightening as a new world opens up:

My eyes were really opened a year ago when we talked about family um, violence in the family and how many kids have had to deal with that. I think I was really certainly naive about that in terms, I mean, I knew it happened [. . .] They ran a programme here that, a whole school programme on family violence. And they brought in um counsellors and facilitators from outside the system. We saw a presentation by [*name of invited speaker*] and um people from the women's shelter e' in the auditorium. Everybody saw it. Then they went back to their classrooms and they talked with their teacher and a facilitator about the whole issue and. Um, out of twenty-one children that I had in class that day, teenagers, um fourteen talked to me about some sort of incident of violence in their background. And uh, a couple came to me afterwards and then, so you're up to sixteen. And now you think, how many chose not to say anything? Um also at the age that they're at the 'woe is me age' sometimes, you don't know whether some of it is exaggerated or maybe they've taken little incidences that, that were really not . . . you know, traumatic or something and have built them a bit more. But I'd say a substantial amount have been through traumatic things.

(Transcript extract, dance teacher, Canadian school, 1996)

What kind of response can be made by those on the outside? Another teacher at the school described his reaction:

And that was the most emotionally draining time that I'd had, because I didn't feel that I was prepared and I didn't feel that um I didn't really know personally how to cope with what was going to happen, never having been in the situation myself and not ever having been trained to to cope with with this. I found it really difficult because coming back from an auditorium you have these children who are ready to talk to you and ready, and looking to you for help. And yet you haven't been trained to do that, t' to help them so you go by what you feel inside, how you feel you have to react in order to help them. [. . .] And you know, kids would come out with things like 'My father kicked my dog to death in front of me', or, 'He threw me down the stairs', or. And you're in a classroom with all these kids, everyone is silent, half of them are crying. And you're thinking 'OK, I wish I had my doctorate in psychology to deal with this because this isn't what I'm trained to do.' OK? So. [. . .] Like I have students coming to me at lunch and saying, like, like, um the one fellow that I had the other day, came in and he was, he was literally, totally aggressive and ready to go out and flatten someone and he was exactly the type that could have, or kill or whatever. He was violent, is the word. OK? And I spent, and so I, I calmed him down. And I spent my lunch hour talking him out of this mood that he was in. And he says 'my psychiatrist says that to me every week when I go', and I thought, 'What the hell, this person is trained to deal with this and you're going to see him and you're coming to me and I'm trying to deal with this without the training.' But I think more and more we're going to have to be trained because we're the ones that the kids come to. They trust us. They'll talk to us. And yet we need that background desperately, we really do.

(Transcript extract, teacher, Canadian school, 1996)

The teachers are placed in the role of being buffers but feel they are not trained and resourced to deal with the revealed traumas. However, what does it mean to listen to the voices of others? As teachers, at least a sympathetic ear can be lent. As professionals, say social workers or psychiatrists, their accounts can be theorised and courses of action to 'treat' their problems can be drawn up. And, as researchers, is it simply enough to record and represent, say, in research reports? That at least is a form of witnessing. But in each case, the root issue is not addressed unless the speakers themselves find a space in which their sense of wrong brings about a reconfiguration of the social frameworks that produce the wrongs they experience everyday. These words may be spoken. But the discourse that *effects* the change is forbidden. It is forbidden in the sense that any such discourse is banished to the space of 'if only', the space of the utopian hopes of a frustrated democracy.

The play of what is revealed, what is hidden, what is actionable and what is not leaves little changed in the lives of those on the inside. It is this play where viewpoints are effectively excluded from realisable decision-making that produces and reproduces the conditions for 'injustice', 'wrongs', injuries. It is like three different intentional networks essentially composing three mutually exclusive groups, each having different views of a two-way mirror as in Figure 7.1. Group A is positioned to see both but can do little if anything in relation to Groups B and C. Group A sees only their own reflection. Group C sees through the mirror but cannot go through the mirror to reach what is on the other side. Group B sees a world that uniquely reflects their own views of themselves; what is seen exactly

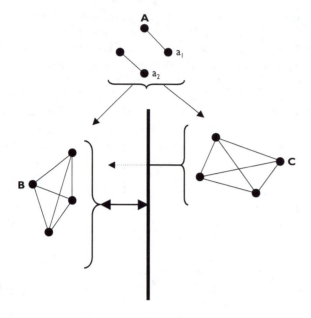

Figure 7.1 Mirror groups

matches how they conceive the world to be and their place within it. From their own viewpoint, each member is able to cross-check or triangulate what they see with each other member of the group. Similarly, for Group C, except that they can see through the mirror that also acts like a barrier between them and the things they see. Perhaps also they can see ghostly reflections of themselves. In the case of the City of God discussed in the previous chapter, or the *banlieues* of Chapter 3, Group B are the 'normal', the 'rich', and Group C are the poor, the underclass. Those of each group carry their mirror everywhere. Baudelaire describes the streets of Paris, the boulevards newly built, the previously sealed-off *quartiers* now opened up to traffic. He describes a scene of a family looking in wonder through the window of a restaurant watching the rich dine (Berman 1982). The French call window-shopping *lêche-vitrine* (literally, window licking), a much more evocative image. It gives a greater sense of appetite, of fascination, of reaching towards, of desire unfulfilled. Rather, then, than seeing themselves as such, they see others as the desired images they want to be, possess, consume. Returning to Hobbes, the appetites are infinite and thus, 'not like animals hungry only with the hunger of the moment, but also with future hunger, and thus he is the most predatory, the most cunning, the strongest, and most dangerous animal' (Strauss 1952b: 10).

It is through the appetites that the desire for power is born:

> man desires power and ever greater power, spontaneously and continuously, in one jet of appetite, and not by reason of a summation of innumerable isolated desires caused by innumerable isolated perceptions: '. . . in the first

place, I put for a general inclination of all mankind, a perpetuall and restelesse desire of power after power, that ceaseth only in Death [Hobbes 1914: 49].' But this apparently perfectly clear proposition is fundamentally equivocal, for the boundless striving after power is itself equivocal. Hobbes continues: 'And the cause of this, is not always that a man hopes for a more intensive delight, than he has already attained to; or that he cannot be content with a moderate power: but because he cannot assure the power and the means to live well, which he hath present, without the acquisition of more.' The striving after power may thus be rational as well as irrational.

(Strauss 1952b: 10)

Rational power is permissible, but irrational striving after power is equivalent to animal appetites and is impermissible. For Hobbes, people: 'from their very birth, and naturally, scramble for everything they covet, and would have all the world [. . .] to fear and obey (them)' (*English Works*, Vol. VII, p. 73, cited in Strauss 1952b: 10).

For Strauss, Hobbes and also Machiavelli are the key founders of modern politics. Recalling Lins' *City of God*, Tiny desired power, desired to be the boss of the City. To do so, he killed his enemies and ruthlessly punished those who transgressed his word. From fear came 'respect', the recognition he craved. It is a strategy set out in Machiavelli's *The Prince*. His strategy, in Hobbes' and Machiavelli's terms, is entirely rational. Politics and the economy that arises under power is about regulating the appetites of the many to the benefit of the appetites of the few. That is to say, in the image of the 'lèche-vitrine', disappointment due to frustration is built in. For Lipovetsky (2006), such disappointment characterises post-modernity.

Group A has a view into both worlds. But Group A is divided, say, into different professional groups: for example, teachers and police, or priests and psychiatrists, or right-wing politicians and left-wing politicians, or even researchers and journalists. These are the professional mediators, interpreters, explainers of 'reality' whose professional action is either to reconcile people to given realities, their cultures of disappointment, or to bring change in those realities, even radical change to provide the hope for fulfilment. Each sub-division of A has its means of generating knowledge about the worlds they see and their relationship to each other. Indeed, they triangulate what they see with other professionals like themselves. Their knowledge is both expert, in that they have been trained to professional standards, and expert, in that their knowledge is rooted in experience. When the different professional groups talk to each other, however, they have to make allowances for the lack of specific expertise of the other. The politicians amongst them are, of course, acutely aware of relating and assessing all specialised discourses against managing the complex constituency from which they derive their power: what needs to be said and done that will keep the maximum number voting for them? The politicians then mediate the mediators. There are politicians in each sub-group of professionals as well as the professional politicians of political parties.

The work of these mediators – or guardians, in Plato's sense, of the complex mirroring of people's desired realities – is thus critical in filtering what can be said, seen, heard as evidence for decision and policy-making. They are at the edge – the between space of surfaces. On the surface all seems natural, solid. At the edge all is seen to be constructable and deconstructable, fragile, ephemeral. How it is to be constructed – and indeed deconstructed – is a matter of pedagogy. Recalling the psychiatrist of Chapter 6 discussing a patient with a physiotherapist, the term 'paranoia' came under scrutiny. It has both a technical meaning in the history of psychiatry and also a popular meaning. However, since it was employed by a professional, albeit not a psychiatrist, it had to be taken seriously. It was thus treated as an empty signifier whose contents differed according to the discourses employed and the individual responsibility for care of the patient. So, in the chains of command in health care, the consultant is 'god' but, unlike 'god', can be judged by legal courts. In this connection, it is interesting to point out that Schreber was a judge in the German courts of the time. Who is in the position of judgement is potentially in a powerful position. The extent to which people are placed in that position as the 'voting public' is thus a major democratic instrument that can ensure learning and change takes place. In the case of the psychiatrist, since he was the one with the power to decide, he translated the observations made by the physiologist into his own terms, hence maintaining his expert control over perceived 'realities'. To see expertly requires training. Each professional group has its pedagogy of the perceivable. And each pedagogy competes for the manage-ment of the real. And each pedagogy has its shadow side, its banished ghosts through which alternative discourses of expertises are employed to recuperate realities for the satisfaction of disappointed desires.

Working the radical edge

If the world was subjected exclusively to the imagination there would be no disappointment:

> Living in the world of his imagination, he need do nothing, in order to convince himself of his superiority to others, but simply think out his deeds for himself; in this world, in which indeed 'the whole world obeys him', everything is accomplished according to his wishes.[2] He can awaken from this dream-world and come himself only when he feels in his own person – by bodily hurt – the resistance of the real world.
>
> (Strauss 1952b: 19)

---

2 Strauss' note: compare the description of vain-glory in *Elements*, Pt. I, ch. 9, § 1, and *Leviathan*, Ch. 44, p. 331).

Hope and disappointment work the radical edge. It is here that reality is encountered as resistance whether as anomaly and fabulous event (see Chapter 5) or as an externality that presents its resistances in predictable and controllable ways. Hope and disappointment arise in modernity as the twin features of the promise of reason as distinct from the reward of faith or the resignation to fate. Modernity redefined hope and disappointment as the work of human will allied to reason. For Strauss:

> Modernity originated in the transformation of political philosophy effected by Machiavelli, who redirected political philosophy from an essentially contemplative or theoretical consideration of political things to the active transformation of those things. Strauss describes the change in political philosophy effected by Machiavelli in various ways: as a lowering of horizons, as a new conception of nature, and as a replacement of human will for nature as the source of standards. In all of these characterizations, it is clear that, for Strauss, modernity is founded upon the internalizing of the sources of morality within human subjectivity, and, as the necessary correlative of this, results in the oblivion of nature and total historicization of all moral and political standards.
>
> (Robertson 1999)

The edge is a place of politics and of ethics: politics because all is reducible to the will of the subject in relation to other subjects; ethics because 'humanity' is a collective term creating the conditions for what can be known and thus enabling the individual to find ways of self-expression and recognition. This is a return to the Hegelian insight that in modernity the characterising feature is the impossible relationship between individual rights of freedom of expression and the accommodations required to live in community.

For Spinoza (2004) in *A Theologico-Political Treatise*, freedom of expression is the foundation of the good state and the foundation of knowledge:

> if, in despotic statecraft, the supreme and essential mystery be to hoodwink the subjects, and to mask the fear, which keeps them down, with the specious garb of religion, so that men fight as bravely for slavery as for safety, and count it not shame but highest honour to risk their blood and their lives for the vainglory of a tyrant; yet in a free state no more mischievous expedient could be planned or attempted. Wholly repugnant to the general freedom are such devices as enthralling men's minds with prejudices, forcing their judgement, or employing any of the weapons of quasi-religious sedition; indeed, such seditions only spring up, when law enters the domain of speculative thought, and opinions are put on trial and condemned on the same footing as crimes, while those who defend and follow them are sacrificed, not to public safety, but to their opponents' hatred and cruelty. If deeds only could be made the grounds of criminal charges, and words were always allowed to

pass free, such seditions would be divested of every semblance of justification, and would be separated from mere controversies by a hard and fast line.

(Spinoza 2004: 5–6)

Spinoza argues that democracy 'rests on the possibility of making a clear distinction between speech and thought, on the one hand, and actions, on the other' (Balibar 1998: 119). It is a far-reaching principle that has implications for contemporary debates on the limits of freedom of speech in relation to offence and the incitement of hatred and violence, a debate that was focused in the UK on the Bill that became the Racial and Religious Hatred Act 2006,[3] a Bill about which Polly Toynbee, in the *Guardian*, comments: 'The culture of thought-crime and self-censorship is a creeping thing.' There was for many a fear that once law, the Act could be used to reduce freedom of speech. Before the Bill became law, she argued against the argument that a freedom-of-speech clause would safeguard this by writing:

it would not protect Rowan Atkinson's sketch showing men bowed down praying in a mosque with the voiceover intoning: "And the search goes on for the Ayatollah Khomeini's contact lens." Many were insulted. It would not protect Salman Rushdie's The Satanic Verses, let alone Christ in nappies on the cross in Jerry Springer – the Opera. Nor would it stop Behzti being closed down by angry Sikh mobs. Police who failed to protect free theatre will feel the benefit of the doubt tip towards religious sensitivities. Of course these writers were reckless about causing offence: that is what artists recklessly do.

(Polly Toynbee, the *Guardian*, Tuesday, 31 January 2006,
<http://www.guardian.co.uk/Columnists/Column/0,,1698557,00.html>)

The Bill received Royal Assent in February 2006. The fear that the law would inhibit academics from the freedom to speak out on issues, a group of sixty-four academics published a statement of freedom:

Academic freedom – the responsibility to speak your mind and challenge conventional wisdom – defines the university and stands as a model for open debate in wider society.

In today's political climate it is harder than ever for academics to defend open debate.

Restrictive legislation, and the bureaucratic rules and regulations of government quangos and of universities themselves, have undermined academic freedom.

---

3 An internet version is downloadable at <http://www.opsi.gov.uk/acts/acts2006/20060001. htm>.

Many academics are fearful of upsetting managers and politicians by expressing controversial opinions. Afraid to challenge mainstream thought, many pursue self-censorship.

Academics for Academic Freedom (AFAF) is a campaign for all lecturers and researchers who want to make a public statement in favour of unimpeded enquiry and expression. That statement is set out below. Everyone should sign it using the on-line form.

Statement of Academic Freedom

'We, the undersigned, believe the following two principles to be the foundation of academic freedom:

(1) that academics, both inside and outside the classroom, have unrestricted liberty to question and test received wisdom and to put forward controversial and unpopular opinions, whether or not these are deemed offensive, and

(2) that academic institutions have no right to curb the exercise of this freedom by members of their staff, or to use it as grounds for disciplinary action or dismissal.'
> (Denis Hayes, Academics for Academic Freedom, 29 October 2006
> <http://www.afaf.org.uk>)

This is an uncompromising definition of academic freedom that some saw as in itself problematic:

> a statement this week from Roger Kline, head of equality at the UCU, raises some concerns. He says: "We should distinguish between the crucial right of an academic to question and test received wisdom and any suggestion that this is the same as an unlimited right of a university academic to express, for example, anti-Semitic, homophobic or misogynist abuse where they were using a position of authority to bully students or staff, or potentially breach the duty of care that universities have towards students or staff.

> "If we confuse academic freedom with individuals abusing a position of power, we could actually undermine academic freedom in the long term."

> Juliet Adams, operations manager of the Equality Challenge Unit, said academic freedom, like free speech, had to be balanced against other laws and the need to "promote responsible debate".
> (Phil Baty, *Times Higher Education Supplement*, 22 December 2006
> <http://www.thes.co.uk/current_edition/story.aspx?story_id=2034603>)

The issues at stake concern the essential relation between words and action. If thought and action are separated, then as Balibar (2002: 119) points out, right, that is, the right to say whatever one wants, is separated from power. And so, power is separated from the right to act in any way one wants. Thus, the coextensiveness of right and power:

> has reverted to being a formal criterion, which is asserted a priori by some authority. From the perspective of power, which is that of reality, the words and thoughts which are most effective – and in particular those that attack injustice and the evils of the present State – are themselves actions. They are, in fact, the most dangerous actions of all, for they inevitably incite other men to think and act in their turn.
>
> (Balibar 1998: 119)

If rights are coextensive with power, then the right to say anything that one wants implies that it is itself an act, that is, in Austin's (1976) terms, freedom of expression is performative, that is to say, there is an incitement to action. However, legislation against offensiveness and incitement to hatred must also reduce the performivity of debate by reducing the range of voices that can be included. Does this matter? It matters to the extent that debate is the democratic solution to the abuse of power. Debate is the minimal condition for community. To exclude from community is to revive the binary oppositions of friend and enemy, good and evil. The radical thus involves a rearrangement of terms through debate, not an arbitrary one, but one which recognises two registers which are continually in tension: 'logically, evil is the object of a judgement which in principle comes down to *exclusion*; while negativity requires *com*-prehension and is the object of *integration*: evil harms/negativity cooperates' (Jullien 2004: 22–3 [my translation, John Schostak]). Debate is action on the edge, mobilising change in all viewpoints that engage to produce community.

> the more violent the constraints that are placed upon individual freedom, the more violent and destructive will be the reaction against them. This is a "law of nature". When each individual is in some sense obliged to *think like another*, the productive force of the thought becomes a destructive force instead. This leads in the extreme case, both to a sort of raving madness on the part of the individuals and to the perversion of all social relations. This contradiction is obviously all the more acute when the State is identified with a religion, either because civil authority has been annexed by religious authority, or because it forces on the individual a "world view" that seeks to displace religion and is thus, whatever its intention, of the same nature as a religion. Such a system could only last if all the individuals concerned were indeed able to believe in the same God in the same way and in the same terms. But such conformity is not only impossible, it is inconceivable. In every society,

barbaric or civilised, Christian or "idolatrous", opposing opinions about divinity, piety and morality, nature and the human condition are perpetually emerging.

(Balibar 1998: 28–9)

From this point of view, the more viewpoints the state includes the better since this maximises the chances of making rational decisions and thus appropriate actions (Balibar 1998: 31). The radical pedagogical task is to generate the conditions under which public right is preferred to private advantage (Spinoza 2004: 217). If democracy works to include the voices of all people, the tragic consequences for community is born in a criminal absence of democratic rights at every level. Mouffe (1993) calls democracy the unfinished revolution. It is unfinished because it has yet to be driven down into the deepest recesses of institutions and everyday life. And the deepest level is that of the individual's relation to the community of debate. What are the implications for identities at the edge?

Designing architectures of the social

The structures of intentional networks can be designed, architecturally, in order to bring into relationship ideas, practices and material resources to produce desired outcomes. Adopting a model described in Schostak 2002 and further developed in Schostak 2006, the 'architecture' of intentional structures can be formulated (see Figure 7.2).

The arrows in Figure 7.2 are not meant to imply any necessary order or hierarchy. It is set out this way to simplify discussion. In brief, one way of reading this is to say that it describes a way in which ideas get to be realised in terms of outcomes. For an idea to be made real in the world, it is conceptually framed. Questions can be asked in terms of their consistency and their relationship to how the world *is* or *ought to be*. But it is only when ideas – in the form of philosophies, value systems, policy statements, organisational plans and so on – meet the realities of practice and material circumstances that their 'truth', 'validity', 'meaning' can be assessed by those upon whom they impact. Individuals may generate their own theories, explanations, conceptual framework by which to explain their experiences of how the theories of the powerful affect them. Like Schreber, they may fantasise about a them/god/system that is hostile, stupid, dangerous. From their different points of view, they can construct narratives that describe 'what happens' and how particular outcomes are produced. They can identify key events, crises, dramas and how they were or were not solved. They may suggest their own theories based on this as to 'what is really going on' behind the scenes.

This simplified framework suggests how alternative designs can be constructed in order to include otherwise excluded views. Take for example the Children's Listening and Talking Project directed by Schostak (1988–9) in which the whole

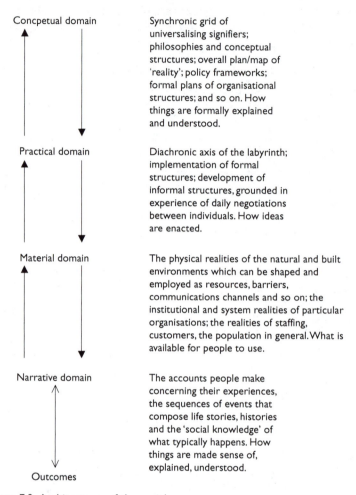

Concpetual domain — Synchronic grid of universalising signifiers; philosophies and conceptual structures; overall plan/map of 'reality'; policy frameworks; formal plans of organisational structures; and so on. How things are formally explained and understood.

Practical domain — Diachronic axis of the labyrinth; implementation of formal structures; development of informal structures, grounded in experience of daily negotiations between individuals. How ideas are enacted.

Material domain — The physical realities of the natural and built environments which can be shaped and employed as resources, barriers, communications channels and so on; the institutional and system realities of particular organisations; the realities of staffing, customers, the population in general. What is available for people to use.

Narrative domain — The accounts people make concerning their experiences, the sequences of events that compose life stories, histories and the 'social knowledge' of what typically happens. How things are made sense of, explained, understood.

Outcomes

Figure 7.2 Architectures of the social

school agreed to engage in action research. The principal object was to establish a 'discourse of negotiation', or culture of dialogue (Schostak 1990). Of course:

> The discourse of negotiation was not instantly developed, nor was it fully in place at the end of the year. Nevertheless, the teaching staff came to realise that they not only had to negotiate between themselves, they also had to include the caretaker, and the dinner staff as well as the children, their parents and the governors. All these competing voices had a significant effect upon the interpretation of school life, aims and routines. For example, face to face democratic negotiation between teacher and child could be seriously undermined by the authoritarian actions of dinner staff during supervision of

the dining hall and the playground. Meetings between teachers and dinner staff were arranged during which both sides argued their views. Now, a more consistent approach throughout the child's day is expressed by both sides. This consistency focuses upon increasing the scope of the child's decision making to transform his or her environment towards meeting his or her needs in negotiation with the needs of others. Crucial to this negotiation process is a conception of the responsibility to act with freedom.

The 'discourse of negotiation' had a fundamental impact on the construction of authority. In terms of the discussions in Chapter 2, and the relation between Power and power as diagrammatically portrayed in Figure 2.1, the project challenged Power by increasingly bringing in the voices of the 'multitude' that composed the school as a whole (that is, teachers, children, governors, parents and support staff). The project impacted on the formation of school policy:

> Generally, the function of policy is to co-ordinate action. It is through the co-ordination of action that social power is wielded. Policy is associated with ruling, whether by governments or by business and other institutional leaders. The fundamental connotation is with the ideological structure of the leader and the led. It also shares a root meaning with 'police'. However, the aim of the Talking and Listening project was to transform the underlying Leader-Led structure of typical school practices. The means was through the redistribution of the opportunities for responsibility and decision making. By agreeing to the following the staff were already involved in transforming their relationships:

> 1. reflection upon current conduct
> 2. making personal agendas explicit
> 3. negotiating a common set of aims
> 4. negotiating a provisional range of strategies to articulate the aims
> 5. developing strategies for implementation and monitoring
> 6. establishing democratic procedures to frame steps 1–5

> The result of adopting these steps was the gradual break down or erosion of the previous patterns of conversation. Not only did the topics of conversation change, those who had been excluded from areas of decision making were now involved.

> (Schostak 1990)

Each of the steps redefined the previous relationships between each member of the school, driving the mechanism, as it were, of negotiation right down to the face-to-face levels of everyday interaction. Reflection on 'what happened' when this was done effectively built the development of grounded theory (Glaser and Strauss

1967) into practice; that is, the theory through which practice is to be organised arose from the trial and error and from the negotiations of meanings that took place when people reflected upon their own experience. The children were directly involved as decision-makers. Reflection upon what was happening created the conditions for democratic thinking as a social process without a subject as such, that is, without a central organising power: an 'it happens' – that is to say, it was happening at the level of the 'labyrinth' not that of the 'god's-eye view' (see Figure 1.1).

A few months after the start of the project, the teachers developed a statement of policy. Each aim in the statement of policy was grounded in strategies that had emerged from reflection upon experience. Fundamental to the process was 'talking out'. This meant that anyone who has a problem was to describe the problem, the impact it was having on them and then invite others to help come to a solution. If two people were in dispute, they had to describe the problem as they saw it to each other and then formulate a solution. The following are some of the strategies employed based on this principle of negotiation:

1. At every stage create opportunities for children and teachers to be explicit about problems and possible solutions.
2. At every stage encourage the children to contribute to the solution of problems. *<At a whole school level the tape of the football assembly is a good example of both of these. The children were given the opportunity both to lay out the problem, and to discuss possible solutions.>*
3. Encourage the children to say what they are thinking. The teachers and other staff too need to say what they are thinking. *<There are plenty of examples on the tapes of the children having the opportunity to say what they are thinking. The whole talking out procedure is designed to do precisely this too. As far as staff are concerned the democratic mode of discussion and decision making is designed to that end, but the principle also applies between staff and children.>*
4. Make time in the school day, in and out of the classroom for discussion with the children. *<Look for opportunities for ordinary friendly social interrelationships and chat between staff and children. It is important that our focus is positive not negative, and problems will then be reduced to their proper perspective.>*
5. Make sure that the solution of problems is one of our priorities. The rationale is that personal and social development is of crucial importance to the development of any learner, child or adult. *<This very much needs to be read in conjunction with 4. The evidence of the fourth year children on the interview tape reinforces the importance of this. Learning in groups is clearly tied in with their social learning.>*

Common to all the strategies is a focus upon identifying the nature of problems, making these explicit, relating them to the core values of the school and involving children in the processes of decision making. Each strategy is grounded in evidence gathered by the teachers.

(Schostak 1990)

The school was a first school, taking children aged five years old to seven years old. Democratic principles were easily learnt and employed. The strategies indicated in the extracts from the policy document were all recorded by staff or children with the help of the project researcher Charles Sarland during the course of the research. The policy statement, unlike Schreber's 'writing down' system, was developed through the personal, face-to-face processes of negotiation. The power to resolve issues remained in the hands of those who experienced conflicts and disagreements. It is only in such negotiations that democracy is born, persists, or dies. Can it be sustained?

Chapter 8

Provocative identities, radical edges

Difference, diversity and the same

Identity is by definition stable – A = A – there is no room for difference. But what can collective identity mean? And what sort of 'identity' is it where the make-up of the object or subject of consciousness has changed over time? What can it mean to be a unique individual whose identity is defined by belonging to a community that changes over time? In fact, what does possessing an identity mean? What does it mean if an individual claims or, indeed, rejects an 'identity'? The question of identity is at the core of any debate about framing categories, policing boundaries, selecting and processing data, witnessing events and formulating evidence as the basis of judgement, decision-making and action. As in the stable definition of identity, what does it mean to say: this is the *same tree* we carved our initials into twenty-five years ago; or, it was *you* who committed the offence and no other person; or, *I am* American?

It might seem that in each case, different meanings to the term 'identity' are being employed. But are they? Every discussion of identity has in some way to do with calling a difference, making a separation between *this* and *that*, creating, as it were, a category of *one*, a conceptual place that only *I* or only *that* or *we* (spoken as a singular term) inhabits.

> Every discussion of borders relates, precisely, to the establishment of definite identities, national or otherwise. Now, it is certain that there *are* identities – or, rather, identifications – which are, to varying degrees, active and passive, voluntary and imposed, individual and collective. Their multiplicity, their hypothetical or fictive nature, do not make them any less real. But it is obvious that these identities are not well defined. And, consequently, from a logical – or juridical or national – point of view, they are not defined at all – or, rather, they would not be if, despite the fundamental impossibility inherent in them, they were not subject to a forced definition. In other words, their practical definition requires a 'reduction of complexity', the application of a simplifying force or of what we might, paradoxically, term a supplement of simplicity.
>
> (Balibar 2002: 76)

A forced definition takes the place of the purifying and standardisation procedures required by the laboratory in the physical sciences, as well as the requirements for measurement and precision of the industrial engineers, architects, accountants and managers who provide the products and services of contemporary life. What is simply a technical consideration in the purification of raw materials such as iron ore or the standardisation of products, of processes of production and of monetary systems, is fraught with dangers when applied to communities and individuals. Even if it were possible to 'purify' and 'standardise' living beings, say, by genetic engineering, there are social and ethical issues to take into account. The social and symbolic domains of cultural action force complications rather than simplicities. One illustration of the forced definition is Plato's 'noble lie' (discussed in Chapter 1) concerning the 'nature' of different classes of people – whether they are of the purity of 'gold' or of lesser metals. It is a story built around the idea that the people of a particular community were all produced by God from the earth and are thus are all 'brothers':

> nevertheless, during the kneading phase, God included gold in the mixture when he was forming those of you who have what it takes to be rulers (which is why the rulers have the greatest privileges), silver when he was forming the auxiliaries, and iron and copper when he was forming the farmers and other workers. Now, despite the fact that in general your offspring will be similar in kind to yourselves, nevertheless, because you're all related, sometimes a silver child might be born to a gold parent, a gold one to a silver parent, and so on: any of them might be produced by any of the others. Therefore, of all his instructions to the rulers, there is none that God stresses more than this: there is no aspect of their work as guardians which they shall be so good at or dedicated to as watching over the admixture of elements in the minds of the children of the community.
>
> (Plato 1994: 119)

There is a parallel, of course, with concepts of racial purity or, indeed, with aristocracy, social class, meritocracy or even with classifications of IQ and their implications for what is considered to be schooling appropriate to 'the admixture of elements' in their minds. Forced definitions require a pedagogy if people are to believe them and thus maintain the distinctions at all costs, even to their own lives and the lives of their loved ones. What could be better than to underpin such classifications with the authority of 'science'? Recalling Herrnstein and Murray's (1994) *The Bell Curve* and Murray's (2000, 2005) conception of the 'underclass' described in Chapter 7, the application of scientific procedures provides the legitimating pedagogy to separate and school members of society as a lifelong learning process. However, it all falls down to the extent that the processes through which key definitions are produced are shown to be forced simplifications that do injustice to the complexities of everyday life. For Balibar:

> The prototype of identity is, it seems, national – if not, indeed, 'ethnic' – identity. All sociology is becoming, or reverting back to, the sociology of

identities (in other words, it is becoming, or reverting back to, psycho-sociology): linguistic identities, religious identities, class identities. And the great question of the moment is how these various identities present obstacles – or add dimensions – to national identity.

(Balibar 2002: 57)

The context in which Balibar is writing is that of the multiple national identities of the European Union where the notion of border although nuanced, is not irrelevant:

Without going back as far as the Roman *limes*, it is clear that the border of a European monarchy in the eighteenth century, when the notion of cosmo-politanism was invented, has little in common with those borders the Schengen Convention is so keen to strengthen today. And we all know that you do not cross the border between France and Switzerland, or between Switzerland and Italy, the same way when you have a 'European' passport as when you have a passport of the former Yugoslavia.

(Balibar 2002: 75)

Times change. Yugoslavia no longer exists. The different national identities that had been forced under the name of Yugoslavia have, since the fall of the Soviet Union, reasserted their independence. There are, then, serious questions implicit in the concept of identities and the borders that define them: how do you cross a border? What happens to identities when borders are crossed? What happens to borders when identities cross or change? It depends on the power that can be brought to bear upon the maintenance of borders as identities change, or the persistence of identities as borders change. In each case, the borders become, as it were, delicate.

Delicate borders

What happens when borders are under duress? Transgression and provocation that open up the borders, expand legitimised definitions to include illegitimate contents raise again the issue of offence:

Are there views whose expression is automatically so hurtful to some that they have to be restricted for the sake of general good order and justice? Well, we legislate on that basis, certainly, where racism or holocaust denial or simi-lar matters are concerned. Talking in a way that denies the human dignity of others – by racist abuse, by labelling Jewish survivors of the Shoah as liars – is outlawed. Such views are unjust: they place people at a disadvantage and deny due respect. And we quite rightly regard language abusing or dehuman-ising homosexual people in the same light: the language of contempt and disgust is not admissible. We recognise the reality and the atrocity of hate crimes in this context as in others, and we recognise that hateful speech is close enough to hateful action for it to deserve sanctions against it.

But beyond this, we sometimes seem to be unclear.

(Williams 2006)

What is unclear? The article discusses the issue of some student unions of some universities and colleges refusing recognition to Christian unions because they consider some behaviours to be sinful. Thus,

Quite often in discussion of Christian attitudes to homosexuality (and this is often the presenting issue where Christian unions are concerned), it is taken for granted that any statement that a form of behaviour might be sinful is on a par with the expression of hate, so that it is impossible for a conservative Christian, Catholic or Protestant or, for that matter, an orthodox Muslim to state the traditional position of their faith without being accused of something akin to holocaust denial or racial bigotry.

(Williams 2006)

The delicacy of the boundaries consists in the ambiguities of what is to count as an offensive statement or the assertion of what is tantamount to race hate in relation to the democratic principle of the right of association. Williams focuses the issue in the question: 'Do human beings have the liberty to associate on the basis of common projects and common convictions independently of the state's licence?' The answer, he says, for most who are committed to democracy, is 'yes, on the understanding that those projects and convictions do not in themselves threaten or disrupt the lives and liberties of others' (Williams 2006). As in Chapter 7, it is a version of the argument for the separation between thoughts and deeds but only after the boundary has been shifted. It is the shiftiness of the boundary that generates the instabilities shimmering across the associations people make with each other rendering what they say transgressive, offensive or legitimate according to the movement of boundaries over time. The information associations that comprise communities and civil society constructed and bound by laws do not sit easily with each other:

'Community' and 'citizenship' have had a problematic relationship since the origins of political thought. (The Greeks had only one word to express these two aspects: *politeia*, whence we derive our 'politics' as well as our 'police'. But this meant that the contradictions were located *within* this single concept, and conferred on it an immediately 'dialectical' meaning.) I defend the idea that the contradictory nature of the notion of political community (which requires both unity and diversity, conflict and consent, integration and exclusion, substantial identity and openness to indefinite change) reflects a tension not only between the real and the ideal, or between different 'imagined communities', but also between *the self-assertion and deconstruction of community as such* – or the opposite requirements of 'identification' and 'dis-identification'. My thesis is that democratic politics is a difficult, 'ambiguous' art of combining opposed terms of identification and disidentification (including *identification with the universal*), and for that reason it remains permanently exposed to turning into its opposite.

(Balibar 2002: x)

The opposite of democracy would be a state where the boundary was so policed as to admit of no difference and thus no internal conflict. Thus, if democracy is opposed to turning into its opposite, because of the multiplicities of associations in any society demanding recognition, the rigidly policed boundary is always in danger of being breached internally by these same groups.

Provoking identities

As well as sameness over time, to possess an identity, to be an individual, a singular, a particular, is to be an exception, that is, in some essential way, unlike all others. Yet, to be an individual in community is also to share something in common, to claim an identity in common. To modify Balibar's formulation, this is a self-forced or self-elected identity that can be undone by the same self-election through a process of dis-identification. In this sense, identity has a provocative relation to boundaries and their universalising definitions and categories. That is to say, each threat to a boundary provokes a response that in turn names the source of the provocation, producing over time what may be called and thus recognised as a provocative identity. A provocation excites reactions that increase tension to the extreme as boundaries are tested. Provocations can occur at any boundary, whether sexual, religious, legal, political, moral, ethical.

What is it that people find provoking? The 'fuck you' sign from the other side of the forbidden boundary? Or is it the nightly parade of bloodstained faces that are the televisual image-bites of wars safely somewhere else. Or maybe it's the down-and-out, swerving across the pavement, shouting angrily at ghosts mistaken as real people who pass . . . demanding to be noticed, demanding money. It is the provocation that marks out the boundaries between the normal and the excessive, the legal and the illegal. For Breton (1929), in defining the simplest act of surrealism, provocation was itself an essential strategy to bring about the new world: run into the streets gun in hand, shooting randomly. How is this to be read? If it is an incitement to action, what sort of action is it? Is it to be read literally, or poetically? Is it a waking up to possibilities, to the excitement of life and death, the essential eroticism of the relation (Bataille 1987)? A street is a publicly recognised space. People walk and pass each other by, barely recognising each other's existence except as obstacles in the way of free passage or as the occasional sly attraction in eyes meeting or a fleeting disgust or scorn at their 'looks'. Yet the street is also a space of other more disruptive activities – a potential place of protest, of mobs, of gangs. The disruption shows what is at stake in free passage between and across the boundaries that exist in built environments:

> Architecture and events constantly transgress each other's rules, whether explicitly or implicitly. These rules, these organised compositions, may be questioned, but they always remain points of reference. A building is a point of reference for the activities set to negate it. A theory of architecture is a theory of order threatened by the very use it permits. And vice versa.
>
> (Tschumi 1996: 132)

Similarly, power is threatened by what it permits. There is in this formulation a double writing, what Derrida called *écriture*. Take, for example, the use of the surfaces of the built environment for skateboarding, or graffiti – not just sheer vandalism in the sense of destruction but a creative rejoinder to normal usage. Elsewhere (Schostak and Schostak 2007), the ways in which people use and subvert the 'normal' were explored by drawing on the figures of the skateboarder and the hitchhiker, that 'slip between the imposed logics of modernity to evoke the freedoms that to the rational logics of the authoritarian, and indeed, totalitarian mind appear irresponsible at best, dangerous at worst.' This is not just a metaphor; rather, it points to a rhetoric of the subjective organisation of experience. Chapter 10 explores this rhetoric in more detail, particularly in relation to the purposes of writing up (see also, Schostak 2006). It begins at the level of the labyrinth, life at street level (see also Figure 1.1), where the wandering subject crosses others accidentally, or contingently:

> Subjective organisation may begin simply with noticing what is next to something else, what is like something else, what goes with something else. There is this and this and this within my sight. When we think back to some place we wandered through we recall the things that we saw when looking around. One thing goes with another in our memories. The rhetorical process is that of a kind of metonymy as one thing mentally associates with another.
>
> (Schostak and Schostak 2007)

The rhetorical figure of metonymy was employed by Lacan to express the desire of a subject reaching towards objects in the world, ever seeking satisfaction, never actually achieving it. This feature of desire, plus the ever-expanding contingent associations formed by the wandering subject, together with an absence of any recognition of a 'can't have', a 'don't go there', provides a description of a freely drifting subject taking on board whatever happens next. Narratively it is a structure of 'and this and then this and then this'. By itself, it is unsatisfactory. It takes on a new significance when combined with a process through which the never-ending passage of 'things' can be collected together, unified under a name that fixes or condenses the drifting objects under a single universalising category. There is a shift at this point from a domain of encountered objects to a domain of meaning

– or more generally, language – through which objects encountered can be named/categorised, setting them into relation with other names/categories. Rather than seeing the materiality and singularity of each tree in a forest and never creating the unifying concepts 'tree' or 'forest', the recognition of similarity, of 'sameness of kind' enables meaningful identifications to take place: this object is the same kind of thing as that object, so I will refer to all such instances of the same kind of thing – no matter their individual variations – with the same general name. Employing the same process, a sense of identity is formed. Crudely, no matter what experience I have, each experience refers back to the 'same thing', that is, me. No matter what age I am or how fit or unfit I am, it is still 'me'. Thus, conceptually, I can employ a name to refer to 'me', that name will then represent my identity whether or not I am present. The naming of identity is thus performative in Kripke's (1981) sense of baptising discussed earlier in Chapters 2 and 5. This notion of 'still me', of course, begs many questions about what is or is not *really* a part of the essential nature of my identity and what is merely an aberration because of 'madness', drunkenness, or being deluded by fascination or hypnosis. In Balibar's (2002) terms, the naming of identity is the result of a forced definition that reduces complexity. As such, it loses contact with the complex realities of objects. Lacan sees in this similarities with the rhetorical process of metaphor where one name of something stands in for another condensing a range of attributes or meanings that neither alone express. Together they provide a methodology:

> The methodology involves a) a heterogeneous reality though which b) the subject who wanders, and thus is contingently conscious of phenomena, rhetorically or subjectively constructs objects, features, qualities through processes of association which form the basis of metonymic relations between objects or qualities found in particular contexts (like fire associating with smoke) which in turn, c) through the strength of the associations experienced in multiple contexts can condense, unify or universalise what was originally contingent, heterogeneous and particular so that the fire in being associated with heat, destruction, the consuming of forests, the speed with which an area is consumed, its impossibility to control and also its association with an excited state can be applied metaphorically to a person as *being* fiery. Rather than fire, think of a flag: people have died for it; not because of the cloth but because of the universal values it metaphorically signifies for them. Now, this process through which the dissimilar, subjectively transforms into the similar (the fire is like the person who shows destructive, all consuming yet exciting passions) and then the identical (fire and person become identical) can of course be reversed, or de-constructed. When the process is applied to the process through which disparate individuals, collect together, organise and produce a unified sense of a 'community', a political organisation or a 'people', it becomes a methodology that both explores and constitutes the possibilities of the political, of knowledge(s), of identity(ies) and of community(ies). It is a methodology that focuses upon and has its method in the heterogeneous

and thus the possibilities for conflicting views, disagreement, and yet equality in the face of ignorance and the gift that is no-one's to give or to receive. It is a methodology that is at once anti-essentialist and productive of claims based on the celebration and realisation of difference(s).

(Schostak and Schostak 2007)

There is then a dialectics of metonymy and metaphor. This dialectics proceeds by negativity where, for example, good negates evil and evil negates good. But in doing so, each implies the other. Good cannot be known except by the existence of its opposite; and vice versa. As such, they dialectically produce each other, and the process can only be resolved if the result is a new, more complex, thought that in some way combines or supercedes both. For Hegel, dialectic is: 'the principle whereby apparently stable thoughts reveal their inherent instability by turning into their opposites and then into new, more complex thoughts, as the thought of being turns first into the thought of nothing and then into the thought of becoming' (Houlgate 2005: 38). Thus, as one term in the dialectic, metonymy, as employed here, forms real but contingent associations. As such, it negates the unifying, idealising processes of metaphor. However, that negation can only take place conceptually by postulating its opposite, an opposite that, in turn, negates the specificity and materiality of metonymy. Together, however, a relatively stable organisation of things in relation to meanings can be accomplished through which a world and its subject(s) can be represented. It is a world that is always in the process of becoming, as new experiences, events, 'things' are encountered named and incorporated into the shifting configurations of the idealisation of the 'total map'. This shiftingness, or shiftiness, generates uncertainties, that in turn, undermine the decidability of boundaries. Since there will always be a new encounter, a new experience, the map will change, boundaries will shift, hence decision-making can never be made with the full knowledge of everything that has to be taken into account – there is a gap between what is present and what is absent, the thing itself and its representation. If representation through language is about the possibility of representing the presence of things through the use of signs that stand for those things, then the whole of language has a metaphorical relationship to the 'real'. In writing about the real, decisions have to be made about how to represent, how to form boundaries, describe relationships, structures and processes. However, the shiftiness of boundaries problematises both the presence of things and the meanings that can be ascribed to the sounds that people make and the marks they make on surfaces like paper, stone, computer screens. At each of these interfaces, if they may be called that, there is a space of indecision:

What Derrida calls writing (*écriture*) is the indecidable between the present and the absent, between writing as graphic sign and speech as verbal sounds. Like *écriture*, the text operates at the interface between the oppositional polarities. Although there are specific texts, Derrida also says that there is a "general text" which "practically inscribes and overflows the limits of a discourse" entirely regulated by essence, meaning, truth, consciousness, ideality, etc. Derrida goes on to write that *"there is* such a general text everywhere that this discourse and its order (essence, sense, truth, meaning, consciousness, ideality, etc.) are overflowed, that is, everywhere that their authority is put back into the position of a *mark* in a chain that this authority intrinsically and illusorily believes it wishes to, and does in fact, govern. This general text is not limited to writings on the page" (Derrida, 1981[b], p. 60). The general text is not fully present in any particular text. Indeed, just as there is no way of deciding what is *in* a text, there is no way of deciding what is present in the text. What is present in the specific text is also present in the general text, but what is absent in the specific text may not be absent in the general text. Features of the general text permeate the specific text, render themselves clear and present in the specific text, but in that they are also directly and explicitly absent from the text; they cannot be said to be present.

(Silverman 1986)

The feature of this passage describing *écriture* and the 'general text' is that it employs a strategy undermining all formations of a totality as the condition both for the emergence of a dialectics and the emergence of historically produced specific texts. It describes *écriture* and *texts* (specific or general) as operating at the interface between polarities. Because they operate in spaces where no decision based on the totality of facts can be made (simply because it is not possible to have all the facts), there is an escape from the synthesising totalising process of dialectics because there can be no reduction to binary opposites that between them describe all possibilities. There is always one more difference to take into account; this difference is not an opposite but is radically heterogenous to (or other to, or different from) the prevailing account that stands for the totality of everything there is or can be. *Écriture* as a signifier of the impossibility of containing everything then stands for the overflowing of reality beyond the confines of concepts and of totality as the all embracing concept. Thus, in general terms:

Écriture is writing in a broader sense than the script produced on paper by whatever means, hand or other. It is a metaphor, a figure for 'an entire structure of investigation, not merely "writing in the narrow sense," graphic notation on a tangible material' [Spivak 1976: ix–lxxxix]. In Lyotard's terms it is 'the constitution of a thick space where the play of hiding/revealing may take place' (Lyotard. 1971: 75 as cited in Readings. 1991:6). Neither irreducible to a series of rules on the investigations of graphic systems nor a simple opposition to speech in order to invert a binary opposition, it announces a rhetoric of identity situated in some physical context (Wolfreys, 1998). Not only does the notion of writing refer to speech and thought as forms of writing, but it is also expanded along further horizons to include the writing, the written-ness, of the subject's identity (Wolfreys. 1998).

(Schostak 2005, Vol. II: 1–2)

If *écriture* is metaphor and figure for 'an entire structure of investigation', then it provides what Gasché (1986) calls an infrastructure that acts as a groundless ground, that is to say, it is the condition of possibility, not fully substantial like the Earth, but a minimal thing (Gasché 1999) that cannot be reduced to nothing. Just as a relationship, say, of love, cannot be seen, touched, picked up and handled, it nevertheless acts as a condition of possibility for the ways in which two individuals *in love* act towards each other. Gasché refers to the various terms coined by Derrida as infrastructures or minimal things. What they enable are quasi-transcendentals that take the place of the unities, the universal categories, the rigid identities of reason and power (see discussions of Chapters 2, 3, 7, 10). As a structure of investigation, it keeps in play the impossibility of closure, the possibility of reconfiguration, the indeterminacy of things alongside the processes and features by which boundaries are erected, managed, sealed, sustained, resisted and brought down. The idea of such a process of investigation enables an exploration of centralised forms of power and people as the ground of possibility, of how power is sustained, how it is made to collapse and how change 'evolves' through the shifting of boundaries that 'progressively' include or exclude. Recall Figures 1.1, 1.2 and 2.1 now rewritten as in Figure 8.1.

Real power, as Spinozan *potentia*, resides with the people (see Chapter 2). The concept of people, as such, has no substance in itself, yet, like the minimal thing of Gasché, it is the (groundless) ground for the formation of relations of power. As associations of individuals increase in size and, say, begin to claim to speak on behalf of *the* people as a unity, then a forced definition takes shape as complexities are reduced as the alliance increases in number but without including all individuals. Spokespeople for alliance of individuals now may speak on behalf of *the* people, since not everyone in the alliance can speak all at once or, indeed, gather together to make decisions. Whether through election, or through some accident

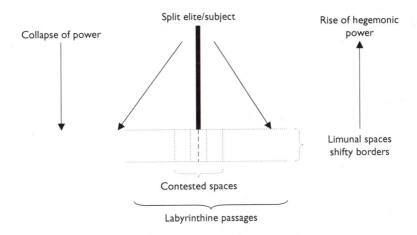

Figure 8.1 Power and contested spaces

of being in the right time at the right place, *the* people may be represented through the voices of a few, or indeed, one person: an elite, or subject. As such, they come to stand for *the* people. Through a process analogous of metaphorical condensation, *potentia* becomes centralised under a universalising category – the people – as *potestas* or power. This increasing alliance of individuals and groups describes what Laclau and Mouffe (1985) called hegemony. These are alliances between groups who share at least some interests and demands in common that either come together to engage with a particular issue and disappear as soon as the issue is resolved or they come together over a wide range of issues of concern to a sufficient number of people so that they can claim to be the legitimate form of government.

At street level, as it were, the claims of representing all the people under the definition of *the* people, is not as clear-cut. There are those who never saw themselves as being part of *the* people; there are those who are not recognised by *the* people, or, if they are seen, they are seen only as an underclass. Thus, in the labyrinths of everyday life, where the 'big picture' cannot be seen, boundaries are more permeable, perhaps flaky and moveable. As some seek to maintain the solid boundaries imposed by power, others transgress or shift boundaries in order to make them more, or less, inclusive. The spaces that emerge either side of boundaries, as boundaries are contested and shifted, are the liminal spaces where the edges of boundaries are tested for viability or alternative uses, like the skateboarders who see in walls, rails, kerbs, structural edges that can be ridden. The labyrinths of city streets can be resculpted for alternative purposes, providing resources for hiding, for playing, for shelter, for attack. In Tschumi's (1996) terms, the programmatic nature of the built environment, that is, its function as street, as corridor, as door to provide passage, or as church to be a place of ceremonies, or as kitchen to be a place of food preparation, is always open to undermining by events: hang-gliding in the cathedral, ritual murder in the kitchen, holding a sit-down strike in the street. It does not stop there.

Indeterminacy can be driven down further into every aspect of experience. Irigaray 'has a regard for the indeterminancy of touch which invites a reconsideration of the constitution of vision' (Vasseleu 1998: 17). Seeing gives a sense of perspective, distance, separation. Touch is immediacy, connectedness: the sense of feeling, boundary melts, becomes indeterminate. Instead of engaging in acts of *un*doing or *un*binding the boundaries that separate people from each other and from power, Irigaray places 'stress on binding (e.g., constructing new forms of sociality)' (Vasseleu 1998: 18). Hands reach out, reach towards the other, touch and clasp together. Rather than boundary, there is a binding in friendship or in a test of strength. In the clasping of hands, there is still an in-between, but it is a kind of union that exists as 'between the two of us', the close twoness of lovers '*entre-nous*': a texture. Rather than the anonymity of the street, of the wandering subject passing through the labyrinth, there is the possibility of encounter, of reaching out, of moving towards, of meeting face to face. Hence Irigaray is fascinated by Merleau-Ponty's concept of the '*entre-deux*' (the in-between two) and its later reconfiguration to 'flesh' (Merleau-Ponty 1968). Think of flesh.

It covers, embodies. And it also provides another way of rethinking the Saussurian imagery of the signifier and signified. As in Figure 2.3, he likened the relationship of the signifier and the signified to the two sides of a piece of paper: cut the signifier and it necessarily 'cuts' the signified. Now imagine the paper as flesh. In Chapter 5, the surgeon cuts into the flesh to remove dangerous growths, but not everything goes as expected – patients who are not expected to recover, recover, and there is the 'fabulous' event; other times, what seemed trivial becomes deadly. As a living organ, flesh is a space of the body's complex interactions both with external stimuli and internal events of growth, maintenance and repair. Rather than paper, it is flesh that is the paradigmatic image of the relation between signifier and signified, between sensory events and their organisation as indicators of 'something', a something that can be named, recognised, placed under more general categories and linguistically 'indicated' whether or not it is present. In this extended image of flesh, flesh is the inbetween, the *entre-deux*, of the external and the internal, the object and the concept, the signifier and the signified; it is the fabulous event.

If metonymy is reaching out and connecting (implying also the possibility of withdrawal and separation) and metaphor is the process of unifying and thus condensing differences under ever more encompassing definitions, then metonymy extends out into the world of contingent objects as metaphor seeks to contain all under a unified structure of meaning. In continually extending out into the world, the world can only be discovered metonymically over time – there is a restless chase after object after object, no object ever being the final object bringing total satisfaction. However, metaphor seeks wholeness through language, replacing one meaning by a more encompassing meaning until the whole is conceptualised. One example of this can be seen in Taylor's (1975: 4–5) account of the medieval conception of the world that provided the 'proof' that Galileo's discovery of Jupiter's moons was wrong. He illustrated his account from an early seventeenth-century argument about the perceived order of nature:

> There are seven windows given to animals in the domicile of the head, through which the air is admitted to the tabernacle of the body, to enlighten, to warm and to nourish it. What are these parts of the *microcosmos*? Two nostrils, two eyes, two ears, and a mouth. So in the heavens, as in a *macrocosmos*, there are two favourable stars, two unpropitious, two luminaries, and Mercury undecided and indifferent. From this and from many other similarities in nature, such as the seven metals, etc., which it were tedious to enumerate, we gather that the number of planets is necessarily seven.
>
> (Taylor 1975, quoted from Warhat 1965: 17)

The argument is essentially metaphoric in that there is a

vision of meaningful order. It can be called meaningful because the notion is that different elements in creation express or embody a certain order of ideas – this is why the apertures in the head, the planets, the metals, and other phenomena 'which it were too tedious to enumerate' can all be put in relation with each other. They all embody the same idea reflected in different media, rather as 'it's hot' and 'il fait chaud' express the same statement in different languages. And because of this correspondence, we can conclude to the nature of one from the other just as I know from learning that someone said, in French, 'it's hot' that he said 'il fait chaud'. The idea of a meaningful order is inseparably bound up with that of final causes since it posits that the furniture of the universe is as it is and develops as it does in order to embody these Ideas; the order is the ultimate explanation.

(Taylor 1975: 5)

The metaphoric strategy is to encompass all under the ultimate explanatory ideas. Everything that is seen is filtered through this ordering grid of ideas. If some observation or statement does not fit, then it is rejected as false, mad, bad, fantasy. As observations, discoveries and alternative explanations that do not fit persist, then the grid of ideas is in danger and the whole order of being it sustains is threatened. In response, the forced application of the grid of ideas takes on a 'paranoid' dimension in the striving to hunt down and destroy those who undermine the truth: all become suspect as potential provocateurs of dis-order. Returning to the imagery of the flesh, it is as if the grid of ideas plays over the flesh, organising it according to its conceptual structures rather than according to the material configurations of the flesh itself. The grid makes conceptual cuts (see Figure 8.2).

The act of the signifier is to cut, to separate a *this* – 'a' – from a *that* – 'b'. If a and b are the signifiers of the key ideas A and B, and the combination of A and B comprise the order of the universe, then anything else that is said to exist that does not come under either A or B either cannot possibly exist or represents disorder. Suppose A and B together represents all that can be made visible concerning the human body. If there are parts of the body that cannot be made visible – the sex organs, say – then a grey and forbidden area opens up as a dangerous space existing only 'between' the sayable and the representable. Materially, there is no cut, no separation; hence, the demands of the sexual organs do not just disappear. Hence, metonymic associations can be made between the representable, that is

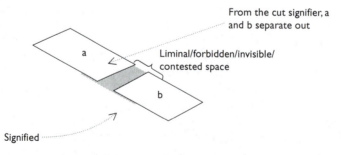

Figure 8.2 Cut of the signifier and liminal spaces

'a', 'b' and the unrepresentable – the 'grey' space between. Thus, metonymy introduces instabilities and ambiguities exploitable by a writing and a reading *between* the lines drawn by the grid. Take the French example of the prohibition to wear religious symbols in school:

> Samira, a sixteen-year-old girl, had until then been wearing a discreet bandana as proof of smartness and elegance in her eyes. This rather good pupil would change clothes and colours regularly in an aesthetic quest widely shared among teenagers. During the first term, the young girl gradually decided to lengthen her bandana until the day when it recovered her whole hair and before she replaced it by a mantilla (a three-tip silk or nylon scarf). The few and flimsy clues left by Samira and her behaviour which was very different from one teacher to another, in a attitude of ruse and challenge, sowed confusion as the teachers of the class had difficulty assessing the situation and were embarrassed and irritated by her behaviour.
>
> Admittedly, a previous event had alerted the teaching community to the wearing of the veil in the school, but this particular event was too ambiguous to claim that the young girl had acted deliberately (Thévenot, 1998). The impossibility to find motives behind Samira's wearing of the bandana profoundly destabilised the class teacher in maths. As she was confronted with a strange phenomenon, she remained disturbed and dared not act. She finally decided to give alert when she thought the young girl was wearing an Islamic veil, i.e. when her wearing the veil was objectively meaningful enough as a sign to allow accusation. But it took the careful attention of some of her colleagues to act, in part because of the embarrassment and anguish expressed by the Spanish teacher who is incidentally very attached to republican values. Furthermore, the math teacher wished to assume her responsibilities as class teacher and tried to find the right moment to remind the school rules to Samira and put her in the wrong in front of the class as long as her move was not taken as a personal accusation or as stigmatization. She was offered the opportunity when Samira entered the math lesson with a class representative, a minority girl of North-African extraction who was wearing a cap as well. The teacher immediately asked them to take their hats off and reminded them they were not allowed to wear anything on their heads in the school. The class representative obeyed but Samira refused to comply and take her bandana off. She justified her act stating that it was a religious choice and that she was allowed to wear it. Her refusal to comply pushed the teacher, outside the classroom, to report the incident to her colleagues.
>
> (Normand 2006a)

French republican values gave clear boundaries between what could or could not be worn. But the bandana as fashion slowly transformed into a religious symbol, gradually opening a threatening space of contestation as it did so, until the transposition from one value system to another had completed and the battlelines could be drawn. Although, in many ways, a simple act, it is through such simple acts that the definition of a 'people', a 'culture' a 'faith' that transcends the singular individual takes place to include a universal commitment.

The people, as that sea of flesh, provides the possibilities for metonymic contagion through associations made. Flesh as *entre-deux* and the meeting of flesh in the face to face (as, for example, in Levinas 1979) thus facilitate alternative ways of thinking about binaries and unities. Rather than stand-offs between class and underclass or the axis of evil, where only one can win, new ethical spaces open up where the other, now configured as the flesh on flesh of clasped hands, unites the protagonists in a togetherness where each has to take account of the other if the mutuality of the clasp is to survive. The space the *entre-deux* involved in flesh on flesh, and meeting face to face, composes the being of the 'two of us' bound intentionally in the mutual aid of the clasp: '[F]lesh is not a contingency, chaos, but a texture that returns to itself and conforms to itself' (Merleau-Ponty 1968: 146). As a textured surface, flesh does not try to become other than itself. Rather, its shapes emerge through a process of replication as cell on cell binds together, becoming body, renewing the body in all its parts. Merleau-Ponty's earlier work (1962) on the phenomenal body as a synergistic system of the multiple aspects of perception with its move to the experience of embodiment set the scene for thinking about flesh and its processes of folding to produce textures, shapes, as a way of reconceptualising *re-pli-cation* (cf. Taylor 1987) (re = reworked, *re*-turned, *pli* = fold, *cation* = act). Fleshy replication is not the same as the standardised replications of industry or bureaucratic management where individuals function as abstract, interchangeable and dispensable mechanisms in the system. Rather, the world is woven through the flesh, that is, through people's engagements with each other not as abstract concepts but as beings who touch and desire. 'This revision of phenomenological thought gives Merleau-Ponty a way of describing intercorporeality textually, as an engagement comprising multiple historico-cultural, ideal and libidinal dimensions, rather than as something separate from or inadequate to them' (Vasseleu 1998: 24). In this structure of intercorporeality, the relationships between each body composes a texture made of desires, histories of encounters, patterns of behaviour and so on. Each body, in being *flesh* or operating as *entre-deux*, acts like a hinge in the relationship, opening first one way, then the other, facing inwards towards perceiving and conceptualising experiences, facing outwards to the other, accounting for their perceptions of experiences and is, thus, a point of articulation in the world, joining one part to another through communications, connecting and thus composing relationships. Being *entre-deux*, the one folds into the other, but the relational unity of the *entre-deux* never reduces to the difference in which it is created; the interweaving of language and materiality, in perception, becomes an irreducible complexity necessary for a sense of self as well as other. However, there is nothing in this formulation that inevitably leads to a mutuality based upon egality. Just as possible is that self seeks to get the upper hand, to impose its own mastery over the other, thus inaugurating the Hegelian master–slave dialectic through which individuals:

strive for recognition, for only in this way can they achieve integrity. But integrity must be mutual. The being whose recognition of me is going to count for me must be one I recognise as human. The operation of reciprocal recognition is therefore one that we accomplish together. Each one, says Hegel, accomplishes for himself what the other tries to achieve in relation to him. My interlocutor sees in me another, but one which is not foreign, which is at one with himself; but this cancelling of my otherness is something that I must help to accomplish as well.

The contradiction arises when men at a raw and undeveloped stage of history try to wrest recognition from another without reciprocating. This is at a stage when men have not recognised themselves as universal, for to have done so is to see that recognition for me, for what I am, is recognition of man as such and therefore something that in principle should be extended to all. But here we have man as a particular individual (Einzelnes) who strives to impose himself, to achieve external confirmation.

This leads to armed struggle. And necessarily so, says Hegel. It is not just that men are opposed, since each seeks onesided recognition; it is also that the risk of one's life is part of the very claim to recognition.

(Taylor 1975: 153)

So, one-sided recognition in terms of the master–slave dialectic is a primitive stage in Hegelian terms. However, there is a sly term in this dialectic, it is that of 'man' as a self-conscious entity. What distinguishes 'man' from other natural beings is that 'self-consciousness is both a living being and somewhat more; somewhat more because it does not just undergo the life process unconsciously, but is already beyond it in thought' (Taylor 1975: 153). It is through thought that mastery over the life-process can be attained. It is through risking one's life that proof that one is beyond 'mere life' can be established. Hence, any armed struggle for mastery is either to the death or to slavery (that is, inferiority is proven by an unwillingness to go all the way). The slave, however, proves to be unequal to the master and thus robs the master of what is most desired: recognition by an equal. As such, the slave's recognition of the master is simply no recognition at all because the slave does not present what the master can recognise as a human face. The dialectic does not end there, however. A further 'sly' element comes into play: materiality. It is not the *entre-deux* of flesh, but it equally plays a mediating role. The slave, by working the material world in order to provide the goods and services required by the master as pure consumer, develops the power of knowledge about how the material world can be transformed by tools. Thus, the slave is the mediating mechanism between the material world and the master. Through this power of mediation, the slave moves into the position of mastery, turning the tables on the master who does not possess the knowledge of how to transform the material world into tools and products. Through this education that results in mastery undertaken by slaves, the argument goes, all can be liberated.

This, albeit simplified, summary of the dialectic enables a further reading of Figure 8.1 in terms of the logic of mastery and knowledge. The master's power collapses as a result of the increasing mastery through knowledge as the slaves working in the between spaces of material realities. As their knowledge increases, their power (*potentia*) increases, thus undermining the centralised power (*potestas*) of the master. Their knowledge renders them masters. But what form of government should they then choose? Presumably, it would be a form of government that recognises them as masters – if all are masters, then all are equals and some form of democracy would be appropriate. However, there is yet one further issue: it is the return to the sly issue of 'man'. The voice of mastery is presumably the sole source of authority for the definition of what is truly 'man'. Can everyone agree on what this is to be? As a sly word, 'man' can be expanded or narrowed to include or exclude. Although used generically, it bears that trace of the use of man for male, thus excluding female. And, as used in Western discourses, it bears the traces of ethnic, racial, religious cultural storyings. Recalling Kusch's (2002) arguments concerning community-based knowledge, demonstrating that any one individual's knowledge is largely secondary, it could be argued that people are largely mastered by 'knowledge'-based frameworks that exceed their grasp and that, on the global scale, they have had little or no involvement in producing. It could also be argued that on the local scale, people can learn how to manage, manipulate or resist the material and symbolic realities produced by the dominant frameworks analogously to the way the slave in Hegel's dialectic learnt how to transform material realities. On the global scale, those who are most able to extend their reach over the control of resources in order to safeguard their interests thus place themselves as the guardians of the bodies of knowledge that provide their power and wealth. As materiality plays a mediating role in the Hegelian dialectic, so global actors work through realities that are both material and symbolic, managing or commanding local actors who work to transform given symbolic and material realities in the production of new wealth. Given the argument that no one has the capacity for perfect knowledge, the relation between global and local becomes a site of contention.

Between the global and the local[1]

For Virilio (1996: 15) 'power is always the power of controlling a territory by messengers, the means of transport and of transmission' (my translation, John Schostak). The side who had the fastest runners had a tactical advantage; those who first used riders on horseback could make the fastest deployments of

---

1 The following sections draw in part from a version of a paper (Schostak and Schostak 2006) given at the CESE conference in Granada 2006. It is has been substantially revised to pick up on the global–local themes of this chapter.

soldiers and outflank the enemy. With each advance in technology, the balance of tactical power changes. Whether in war, or in business, considerable resources are brought to bear upon innovations in knowledge and measures that provide the edge in competitive markets and protect that edge from competition by the use of patents and other measures to safeguard intellectual property rights (IPRs). Communications technologies have brought a revolution in the speed at which information is now propagated. More than that, cyberspace is now a globalised field of operations, a medium of action and transformation that potentially reconfigures the field of the visible, audible, actionable that appears to collapse distance, time and problematise identity reconfiguring the sense of the real. Although it has no physical qualities, its effects can be felt as manipulations in cyberspace are made. It is a minimal thing in Gasché's (1999) sense that is necessary for relations to take place between individuals globally. It has existence only in the continuous connectivity of electronic infrastructures weaving a cyber-surface or flesh of light impulses for the play of signifiers that changes people's traditional, space–time–identity relationships with each other. It is an event whose origins and effects can now only be disputed because its occurrence has been recognised as a way of talking about and evaluating the impact of communications technologies. To be on-line is to be visible in a different way. The play of on-line and off-line creates possibilities of appearing–disappearing, revealing–hiding. Being unconnected is to have no existence, no 'presence of agency' in the cyber-field of the visible except as an object to be scanned and addressed for purposes of tracking. Being connected provides a globalised space for addressing, realising and manipulating desires and demands that impact whether or not individuals are connected and acting in cyberspace – the relation between cyber and the physical spaces and places of people's lives is thus political and needs to be addressed politically, radically. But how?

Take, for example, a report for the EU published in 2001 (the ISTAG report), a vision to shape blue-skies research in information technologies was presented. It described the kinds of anywhere, anytime intelligent technologies that could be developed. Multiple billions of euro were committed by the EU to underpin such research. A scenario based on the ISTAG vision was written by Schostak for a research-project bid,[2] submitted by a large consortium of businesses and universities to develop technologies for collaborative learning in a business setting:

> Alice is event-manager of sporting events that can take place in any European venue. Currently she is organising a series of football matches. The first is to take place in Manchester. On her way from the office to the stadium her route is organised by her P-Com, her 'key of keys' that ensures her route is smooth.

2 Although the bid, submitted in 2005, was not successful, the consortium has continued and new bids are in the process of being prepared at the time of writing.

Alice's P-Com "allows her to move around in an ambience that is shaped according to her needs and preferences." *In particular the P-Com has been designed following research into gender preferences and a full range of special needs (in aiCity terms).* "In the past travelling involved many different and complicated transactions with all sorts of different service vendors, often with gaps and incompatibilities between the different services. In the past few years a series of multi-service vendors (MSVs) have emerged offering complete packages of services linked to the P-Com that tailor the user's environment according to their preferences. User preferences are set up during an 'initiation period' during which personal agents (personal-servants or perservs) are instructed or learn how to obey their master's (owner's?) wishes. These agents are in continual negotiation with those of participating service providers (such as shops, rental companies, hotels and so on)". (ISTAG report p26).

Alice is guided by ambient information displays which show the optimal way to the stadium and the upcoming events. These have been specially designed not to be distracting. While this takes place in the background she calls up her personalised collaborative work-management intelligent agent. This is an intelligent agent that automatically keeps track of the multiple collaborative work groups that she is involved with. Since she is driving, it 'knows' not to distract her attention with visual displays but to inform her orally of the state of play and await instructions. Its task is to prioritise which collaborative work groups need her input and which ones she needs input from.

Imagine now that this is a common experience in working life. How are societies to prepare for it? What will societies look like within such a context of ubiquitous use of intelligent information technologies in everyday life?

Already, it is common experience to search the Internet, use voice-over-internet protocol (e.g., Skype), or video conferencing (e.g., AIM) for communications between people, play on-line games or enter into chatrooms. Many on-line communities exist to share information, pursue common interests or just gossip. The formation of communities for the creation, management and sharing of 'intelligence', of course, is not new, nor due to these technologies:

Intelligence communities have always existed and are vital as tools for education and schooling. They are not the invention of the modern technologies. Nor are they idealistic deschooling conceptions. They are practical and already functioning groupings of enthusiasts and like-minded people. Individuals tend to seek out others, or associate with others having similar interests. In conversation (recall that one meaning of intelligence involves 'intercourse' or 'communication') they share views and criticise or explore the implications of certain views. In short, intelligence communities create intelligence, that is 'know-how', 'critical insight', 'informed opinion', 'inter-subjectively validated facts', and other intelligent behaviours or products.

(Schostak 1988: 227)

Intelligence here, involves much more than just the use of reason or research in the production of shared information and knowledge as in the case of the scientific team. It involves what it means to be human in association with others, handling the multiplicities of meanings, intentions, feelings, values, beliefs inherent in communicating and being with others. However, information technology of the sort described in the scenario above does introduce differences – the activity of a non-human intelligent agent and a globally distributed community that is made present anytime, anywhere within a virtual space.

This is a world of hybrid identities where intelligent agents support communities that live, play and work in the context of intelligent buildings, spaces, architectures. Information is intelligently selected, organised and 'pushed' towards those who want it. How soon will it be before an intelligent agent 'writes' an essay, a dissertation, a thesis? Or, indeed, builds a city and forms the government of its inhabitants. Indeed, to what extent is the 'intelligent agent' an extension of, or dimension of the living person, creating the possibility of multiple identities? It may seem like a world located more in science fiction, in films like *The Matrix*, rather than in sober reality. How far off is such a world? To some extent it is already here. Intelligent management of information is already built into search engines. However, the intelligent agents of the scenario at the time of writing are still some years away. But more fundamentally, it is the existence of communities that will really challenge contemporary forms of social organisation. Think of a situation where there are 100,000 children on-line and, say, 11,000 teachers and this constitutes a community. Say the children spend four to five hours a day on-line. That would constitute a school. Actually, it already exists.[3] It represents a fundamental challenge to the way in which we think of schooling and education. More generally, a global community drawing on members from many countries, cultures and language communities impacts on what is thought of as a common cultural identity or a 'national' education bounded by state laws and territory and thus has political implications. To what extent does that community join other communities as a 'city'?

Strategic communities and their cities

The desire to cover everything with a single structure, a single rule of law or a single point of access is implicit in the Google-like ambition to be able to process

---

3 See, for example, <http://www.intuitivemedia.com>. From a personal communication with its
   founders, the ambition is to have 1 million online over the next couple of years.

and give access to all information on the Internet. Politically, of course, it has its echoes in Plato's Republic, or Hobbes's Leviathan as designs for the political governance of cities or states. The Leviathan-like aim is to construct a city, state or union of nations capable of ensuring that the different wishes, interests, desires, demands of the multitude are brought under a single all-powerful grid. Recalling Rancière's (1995) terms, this is a form of the 'police', referring to the way in which all individuals are ordered, addressed and are made visible as parts of a whole. Imagine a 'roof' over a city as a way of conceiving the effect of the police order. All the spaces between buildings are now 'inside' or 'under' the roof. Such a roof already exists electronically, making it possible to ensure anywhere, any-time access for anyone covered by the electronic roof and who can access the technology. This roof, of course, is global, making Marshall McLuhan's (cf. 1967) notion of the global village with the medium rather than the content being the message ever more a reality. The 'city' as a fusion of the virtual and the real enables the creation of new spaces, between the enclosed spaces of buildings, between communities, across regions, across nations. These are the new archi-tectures of the real, the virtual and of information that compose an ever-tightening policing of the parts covered by the whole. They provide structured entry into global, regional, organisation-specific, workplace-specific and home networks. They keep track of individuals, profiling and serving their interests, just as in the scenario described above for Alice the Events Manager. Cities have emerged historically as people come together whether to trade, to develop friendships, share interests, have fun, search for sexual partners, indulge in their desire for power or to seek protection from predators. With the advent of cyberspace, what sort of cities and forms of governance will emerge? Will they be like those of Lins's (2006) *City of God?*

As a thought experiment, consider all the resources of a city being accessible on-line and managed in such a way that people can use them easily for all the purposes associated with any city. Now imagine that all the resources of the cities in the world are available in this way (see also Schostak and Fraser 2005). Who, then, is a citizen of what city when they come together in communities to make use of these resources? How is the politics of nations, cities and cyber-cities to be played out? The scenario of Alice the Event Manager was an outcome of this thought experiment. It was written for the proposed aiCity (The Ambient and Intelligent City) consortium with technology researchers in industry and university contexts. It continues as an informal network as the City Project. The specific focus chosen for the aiCity bid for funding was to think about how people might work collaboratively together but within the kinds of competitive environments to be found in business – the city was to be a kind of community of communities, facilitating connections between and within communities – it could be argued that this is an echo of Figure 2.2. However, rather than an homo-geneous framework, this provided the opportunity to begin to build a strategic dimension to the communities that are brought into play with each other in city environments as follows:

The aiCity Collaborative Working Management Environment (CWME) has been used to tailor make an intelligent agent charged with the press conference. This is an agent which dynamically constructs and tears down the collaborative working group virtual environment necessary to ensure the success of the press conference. Alice refers to it as ManPress (the *man*aged *press* environment). ManPress has to construct a secure environment within which the team can work, can contact trusted co-workers from other organizations anywhere in the world and can create the environment which has the right mix of security and openness within which her collaborative workers can meet and communicate with the press. She sees this environment as being like a game environment where different collaborative teams with different agendas and purposes meet. There is a lot that can be won or lost in such a confrontation. She knows that everyone who will come to the conference will have their own highly sophisticated D-Me's – personal learning devices which can be worn on their bodies or in their clothes. They will use these to communicate to their own collaborative working groups in order to try and outsmart the speakers at the Press conference.

Alice has read in detail the D-Me user's manual (*following quotes from ISTAG report*). In particular she has noted:

Three by three 'friends' circles' . . .
(The) '3P/3CAG D-Me'-it allows (people) to specify three privacy levels (3P) for personal data matched to three separate 'closed access group' (3CAG) memberships p.32

A strong recognition capacity . . .
The D-Me is equipped with voice, pattern and patch recognition capacity. It has to identify places and people, but also to register enough data to record the relevant events of an individual's life to process it in its D- Me profile and offer it to other D-Me's. p. 33

Telcos in the background . . .
Managing a service while choosing the best telecommunication means for the videoconference forms part of the role of the D-Me. P. 34

Multiple identities *. . .*
People could 'wear' several D- Me's, offering several identities on the network. Virtual identities could multiply, together with anonymously announced profiles and queries. Hide-and-seek behaviours for fun, personal development or crime may develop raising serious ethical and legal questions. P. 34

Possible counter-scenario . . .
Access, control and correction of personal data raises the major issue of the safety of offering one's life on a network. Further observation

of existing behaviours on the Web may facilitate the understanding of this aspect. P. 35

As she arrives at the stadium where the press conference will take place, Alice ponders her concerns that somehow information will leak, that false identities constructed by journalists, manipulating their D-Me's, out for a scoop, will be given access to level 1 information, that is, the most confidential level. Her PA has already contacted all her co-collaborators in the event alerting them to her fears.

Since the idea of the City Project is to provide the structured entry point to the resources that are generated by cities for its citizens, it attempts to answer the question: how can the resources of a city be appropriately organised for access and intelligent use by individuals? As such, the City Project is provocative. Even as a thought experiment, it poses a challenge to the 'world order' of nation-states. It does so simply by proposing a global constituency, creating in effect that Spinozan multitude that is the potential ground of democracy and the source of real political power – cyberspace is its intelligent flesh. Their potential resources include all those held by museums, art galleries, libraries, universities, business organisations, local government, health . . . and so on. However, such access and resources are meaningless until they are drawn into the agendas, the plans, the projects of individuals, groups, organisations and communities. The scenario illustrates the game-like quality that emerges when one group wants to manage what other groups are to 'see', 'believe', 'know'. The discussion of what the City Project might look like, say, in twenty years time in the future, has, at the time of writing, drawn a great deal on the technologies already employed in computer games and already under construction for the next and the next generations. It is already familiar, almost unnoticeable. The radical research and political challenge is to bring it under a critical gaze and develop the strategic possibilities for the development of the potential – *potentia* – of all.

Designing the everyday

New technologies soon take on an everyday-ness. The City Project described above is a particular exercise in thinking through a design impacting on everyday notions. Chapter 7 described architectures of the social in relation to a specific action-research project focusing on designing into everyday practice discourses of negotiation (Schostak 1990). Such designs embedded in everyday practice are interpreted in the context of the meanings attributed to the 'everyday' by people. A design that seeks to mobilise the powers (*potentia*) of people in relation to that of the structures of power has to drive democracy into the very weave of the mundane in order to rethink the meaning of the 'everyday' and its potential for radical practice.

For Lefebvre, the notion of 'everyday' has a double meaning – mundaneness and repetition – that he capitalises on in order to think space and time differently by thinking them together (Lefebvre 2004). Where materiality and flesh provide a mediating space, for metonymic operations to subvert the forced definitions of power in the production of the contested spaces of Figure 8.1, Lefebvre offers a reconceptualisation of time, not as linear uniform progression (as say in a diachronic representastion of utterances, see Figure 2.3) but as lived rhythms through which the weave of associations produce the texture of the quotidian. The quotidian pervades both physical and cyberspaces to provide a further mediating strategy. The doubleness of the quotidian (the mundane, the everyday, the repetitive *and* re-pli-cation – where the French word *pli* means fold) is seen in both the English and the French. In order to think space and time differently, and thus open it out to challenge, Lefebvre argues for a theory of moments in which the instant is privileged. As instant, it is a minimal thing (Gasché 1999). Just as flesh and materiality provide the connectedness that disrupt forced definitions, so moments are significant instants when orthodoxies are open to challenge, to change and to radical alterity (cf. Schostak 1999). These are the basic tenets of what he calls 'rhythmanalysis'. Often, says Lefebvre, rhythm is confused with movement, speed, a sequence of movements (*gestes*) or objects (*machines*), for example. Thus, rhythm is generally ascribed a 'mechanical overtone' and 'the *organic* aspect of rhythmed movements' is ignored or overlooked (Lefebvre 2004: 6). Rhythm is not the act of counting beats in music, nor the passing (slow or fast) of periods, of eras, of cycles of historians or economists, nor is it the succession of movements a gymnast performs. Rather, rhythm comprises repetition in time and space – a repetition that is not of one absolute identity since 'there is always something new and unforeseen that introduces itself into the repetitive: difference' (Lefebvre 2004: 6). So is rhythm without measure then? Is it a natural spontaneous phenomenon with no law except that of the unfurling? Lefebvre believes not. For him, rhythm always implies measure: it implies 'law, calculated and expected obligation, a project' (Lefebvre 2004: 8). The city itself can be conceived of as a project in this sense, a project having both personal and global implications.

If the measure of rhythm of the project is unlike the static hierarchical order of Rancière's police, where each part is subordinated to the whole, where difference is a challenge to the whole; then, the city as project, or the Listening and Talking Project, stands as a provocation to the police order. As a provocative form of order, rhythm is both quantitative and qualitative. It: 'appears as regulated time, governed by rational laws, but in contact with what is least rational in the human being: the lived, the carnal, the body' (Lefebvre 2004: 9). Rhythm engages the body producing both the time and space of an identifiable, minimal thing, the dance to which one becomes subject. In order 'to grasp a rhythm it is necessary to have been *grasped* by it; one must let oneself go, give oneself over, abandon oneself to its duration' (Lefebvre 2004: 27). In the context of the ban of the *ban*lieue, as the sacred place of banishment of the City of God, rhythm in this sense is the essence of provocation. It becomes the source of the unpoliceable. In this sense, for Lefebvre, time is non-calculable, it resists abstraction, generalisation; it requires to be understood as 'lived' in spaces, quasi-worlds of experience, like those 'carved' from the built environment by the skateboarder, just as much as the space of the artist, Picasso's space for example, or architectural and literary spaces that constitute quasi-worlds, as indeed, the spaces of illness and madness.

> We are thus confronted by an indefinite multitude of spaces, each one piled upon, or perhaps contained within, the next: geographical, economic, demo-graphic, sociological, ecological, political, commercial, national, continental, global, not to mention nature's (physical) space, the space of (energy) flows, and so on.
>
> (Lefebvre 1991: 8)

The city, or more generally, democratic space, in the sense emerging here, becomes the name for all this heterogeneity as a space-time for associations between peoples. It is here that resistance to the police dimension of technology and its use for individual expression and social critique may be discerned.

For example, during a project introducing computers into rural schools in northern Portugal, an interview was carried out with one of the local project leaders who described his intentions:

> Nous habitons dans une monde ou la technocracie domine. *(We live in a technocratically dominated world)*

> Avec l'education, nous pouvons aider l'évolution de la liberté d'expression, et l'évolution de ce que je veux appeler la liberté intérieure. *(Through education, we can help freedom of expression to evolve, and the evolution of what I want to call inner liberty)*

> Nous avons besoin de plus d'orateurs dans notre société. *(We need more orators in our society.)*[4]

Oratory is not about giving a voice to people, nor about representing people; it is about voicing, giving voice, being voice, having voice. It is the rhythm of the voice that is provocative and produces the provocative identity, the provocateur who will not be ruled out. The Portuguese community project leader sees education as the process though which this voicing, this freedom of expression and inner liberty may be developed. It is not just a matter of processing information, but of oratory, an oratory that repeatedly challenges the nature of the quotidian as given

---

4 Since neither Portuguese nor English were common to the speakers, the conversation was undertaken in French. The project was undertaken 1990–2. The notes and the conversation was undertaken by Bev Labbett for the Evaluation of the Paneda-Geres Project at the Universidad do Minho, Portugal, EC funded.

and produces the quotidian as rhythmic negotiations of the real. It is the living vehicle through which information, knowledge, values and critical reasoning can be put together poetically, practically, politically. This provides a different use of the concepts of project 'robustness', 'objectivity', 'validity', 'reliability', 'generalisation'. It is through the persistence of voice, of oratory, that social and democratic visions are to be robustly embedded by this project. In comparison with Lefebvre's view that the dominant tendency of today is to separate, fragment and disintegrate things, oratory offers a different 'mechanism', that of Lefebvre's rhythmanalysis which together with his concept of space, creates a synthesis, a unitary theory linking or embedding the physical with the mental with the social.

> Social space is not a thing among other things, nor a product among other products; rather it subsumes things produced, and encompasses their inter-relationships in their coexistence and simultaneity – their (relative) order and/or (relative) disorder. It is the outcome of a sequence and set of operations, and thus cannot be reduced to the rank of a simple object. At the same time there is nothing imagined, unreal or 'ideal' about it as compared, for example, with science, representations, ideas or dreams. Itself the outcome of past actions, social space is what permits fresh actions to occur, whilst suggesting other and prohibiting yet others.
>
> (Lefebvre 1991: 73)

Social spaces interpenetrate one another and/or superimpose themselves upon one another and, as such, are hypercomplex. What is important for radical research is that space itself should be critically analysed in terms of uncovering the social relations, identities and temporal organisation within it, thereby avoiding analysing discrete things frozen a-temporally in space. In the City Project as a radicaliza-tion of social organisation, if there is to be a Spinozan-style principle of equality, then it will need to explore appropriate modes of governance which safeguard, for example:

- the equal right of each member to discover and develop their creative powers;
- the right of each individual to have adequate opportunity and right to associate with others and participate with them for purposes of discussion, expression of views, critique and evaluation;
- the right of each individual to have equal access to information;
- the equal right of each individual to be able to generate courses of action and set the agenda to be explored through critical dialogue;
- the right of each individual to have adequate opportunity and right to engage with others in action to realise the creative powers of individuals and com-munities to bring about their projects;
- the right of each individual to have an equal opportunity to obtain the resources necessary to realise their projects.

Democratic processes will only be robust, persist and be valid and generalisable if supported by the cultural processes, mechanisms and practices by which people at every level from the personal to the global transform their material and symbolic worlds. How can the designs of such radical projects be further developed?

Chapter 9

Universalising the singular
Designing the radical game

Not all research projects, whether designed to resolve problems or follow explorations based on curiosity, are radical. However, all research is potentially radical as soon as the question of data is deprived of its givenness. Descartes' act of doubting provided a paradigmatic moment that made it possible to question the givenness of things, of knowledge, of faith, of beliefs, of tradition. And the question of the certainty of what he found – the certainty of the *cogito* – that too has become unhinged, but only due to the restless impulse of radical questioning, through which the structures and practices of the 'normal', the 'taken for granted' are provoked. Since the 'normal' – whatever is counted as normal by a given individual, group, community, social structure and so on – is what is made manifest, or 'called forth' – in any provocation (Latin: *pro* meaning forth; *vocare* meaning to call), then the provocative act becomes a guide for designing the radical game.

Phenomenological sociology deriving from Schutz (1976) adopted the attitude of 'the stranger' as a way of making the everyday seem unfamiliar (see also Schutz 1964). But the stranger seeks to become as normalised as soon as possible – to fit in, to pass as a member of a given social group. In research terms, the act of being a stranger is then an internal operation, what was typically termed 'bracketing', a kind of mental placing of quotation marks around 'reality' as perceived and talked about. In phenomenological terms, this means taking no position for or against the 'truth', 'reality', 'certainty', 'existence', and so on, of anything. It is a suspension of belief, rather than a full-blown Cartesian doubting. As Husserl pointed out, doubting is still a kind of prejudice, pervading everything that is doubted, thus, in some way introducing a distortion in the way it appears to consciousness. Husserl's phenomenology can therefore be seen as a kind of cleaning-up of the Cartesian methodology, producing a more rigorous analysis of the structure, processes and contents of consciousness. It is not to be confused with the phenomenology of Hegel, although this did not prevent the phenomenologies intermingling creatively with Marxism, existentialism, pragmatism, semiotics, psychoanalysis and structuralism to produce various provocative avant-gardes in the arts and social sciences. The cool precision of Husserlian phenomenology somehow lacked that dimension of revolutionary excitement, that vision of a future to come, that darkness of the irrational. Yet, phenomenology offered an invitation into the everyday lives of people that, together with the symbolic interactionism deriving from the philosophical work of Mead (1934), opened up otherwise invisible worlds. There is something appealing in the sense of peering into the lives of others, particularly, of those at the margins, and even under cover, when engaging with the lives of others – a kind of legitimated voyeurism. But there is also the seriousness of revealing the conditions of life that others, the powerful perhaps, would rather kept swept under the carpet. As documentary realism, research and investigative journalism might play the hero – giving a voice to the oppressed. But, what sort of voice? Is it the voice of the many, the individual, or the one? Is it the voice of power, or Power? Is it the voice of faith or knowledge, imagination, reason or passion? Or all possible voices as they emerge whenever and wherever? And in the documentary realism of the researcher or investigative journalist, what is to be told – the great narratives of history, politics and science or the little local narratives and intimate insights of what it means to live here, now? These questions seem to announce some sort of choice. But that choice is also a focus of strategies to take it away. Voice evokes, provokes, attracts, commands, seduces, and, in various other modalities, directs attention towards whatever is to be witnessed. This directing towards, Husserl calls, following Brentano, intentionality. The intentionality of voice has no existence and cannot mean anything without the possibility of being listened to, without being the minimal thing, the mediating substance, like flesh, presenting a public surface of inscription for needs, interests, fears, anxieties, desires, demands, . . . , and witnessings. Voice, therefore, defines its own boundaries, its own surfaces and depths in terms of who can voice, who can listen and who cannot. The provocation of voice is a demand that cannot be ignored: whether it irritates, arouses sexual desire, anger, love, hatred, a lust for power, seduces or fascinates. Through voice, the individual, the couple, the group, the community, the crowd, the public, the people, the nation stands outs, defines boundaries and asserts existence and identity. It witnesses both the singular and the universal as mutually dependent yet exclusive.

Data has no existence without the voice of the witness. Its historical root is in the Latin *dare* – to give, grant or offer. As *datum*, it refers to the thing given. And: 'The Roman convention of closing every article of correspondence by writing "given" and the day and month – meaning "given to messenger" – led to *data* becoming a term for "the time (and place) stated."' (Source, online etymological dictionary: <http://www.etymonline.com/index.php?l=i&p=1>). The witness, as the one who says 'I was there, I saw it, I know it happened', begins the process of that indefinitely long chain of association whereby an event is baptised with its date and place of occurrence and circulated amongst those who can hear, as 'knowledge' based upon the original witnessing act (cf., Kripke 1981), a directedness towards some thing to which attention must be drawn. Knowledge is intentionally structured as a witnessing, that is capable of being rewitnessed, even if it is a matter of learning to see, meant for circulation amongst a public who can recognise the validity of the witnessing or legitimacy or trustworthiness of the witness. It is in this complex of voice, baptism of event as data, witnessing in relation to the chain of historical associations and the identification of a public, its limits, its borders and its others that the radical game is designed. It begins in the provocation of voice.

The provocation of voice

Provocation, thus, refers to the calling forth of voice. Voice, as calling, exists only in the possibility that there is another who can reciprocate. Voice demands a listening, and listening demands a calling forth of voice as recognition. There is an imbrication[1] of voices, listening, witnessing, recognising that composes a public space of the knowable. It involves a structuring of relationships through calling and attending. As a simple first step, consider the schematic representation in Figure 9.1.

Drawing on Kripke's (1981) chains of communication underlying the construction of a sharable base of knowledge about the world, an individual A names an X that has been witnessed. A tells a_1 who tells a_2, who tells a_n, thus composing an historic and unbroken chain of communication as in the story of the naming of the yard as a measurement from the tip of the finger of the King's outstretched arm and his nose. At the time of this 'baptism of X', suppose another individual B witnesses it. B, of course, could just be a friend, or could be a stranger who happened to be around, or could be an official whose role is to witness important events like a marriage, or indeed, the naming and baptising of a child. As such, B makes an important contribution to publicly attestable knowledge about people, places, timings and events, that is, the contextual data. Of course, this is a simplified schema. Even so, there is another way of reading it. Suppose B is a researcher studying the life of A and A's associates. Of course, B is an expert drawing upon a specialised knowledge base and codes of research practice. As A names an event,

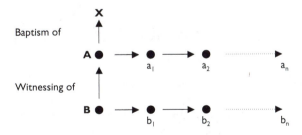

Figure 9.1 Historic chains of communication

1 From online etymological dictionary: '1650, from Fr. *imbrication*, from L. *imbricare* "to cover with tiles," from *imbricem* (nom. *imbrex*) "curved roof tile used to draw off rain," from *imber* (gen. *imbris*) "rain," from PIE **mbh-* (cf. Skt. *abhra* "cloud, thunder-cloud, rainy weather," Gk. *ombros* "rain"), from base **nebh-* "moist, water"'; <http://www.etymonline.com/index.php?l=i&p=1>.

relating it to the everyday knowledge base, B witnesses this and carries out another level of naming, 'expert naming', as accredited by training, profession, use of methods legitimated by the profession and linking to a body of established evidence, knowledge or theory. What is the relation between the knowledge set in train by A and that by B? There are various possibilities that echo the discussions of intentional networks in Chapter 2. Suppose the following are the possibilities:

1. There's a shared set of assumptions between A and B about the nature of the observable world and how to talk about it, but:

    (a) A and B have a different status and if there is a disagreement about what is observed then the one with the higher status/power overrules the other.
    (b) A and B have a different knowledge base through which to interpret events leading to translation issues.
    (c) A and B have different vantage points on X and so see different and partial aspects of it.
    (d) A wants to fool B or vice versa.

2. A and B see the world differently because:

    (a) A adopts a naturalistic attitude; and B brackets the naturalistic attitude through some form of philosophical analysis. Although B may use the same terms as A, these terms are drawn into a different range of discourses developed through the various forms of philosophical analysis.
    (b) A has a particular faith that provides a revealed text through which to interpret the world; B has a different faith or no faith

        (i) each are mutually exclusive; or
        (ii) there are overlaps and thus areas of potential dispute about interpretations of X.

    (c) A adopts a consensus view of the social order; B adopts a conflict view.
    (d) A speaks under the name of power (*potestas*); B speaks under the name of power (*potentia*).

The possibilities could be extended and elaborated indefinitely. However, the two groupings illustrate fundamental disagreements both about the Xs of the visible world and the conditions of visibility, knowledge and making and communicating accounts about the world. The As and the Bs attend in different ways to the world about, the Xs. Suppose A and B are two different ways of conceptualising expertise:

> On the traditional conception of action explanation, knowledge figures in the explanation of performance as an element of the causal antecedents of behaviour. Expert knowledge involves having sophisticated general theoretical

knowledge among the causal antecedents of behaviour. On this traditional model what the expert knows can in principle be written down in advance of performance. That is the model typified in expert systems approaches to understanding expertise. Our model presents an alternative image. It is the image of the expert as someone with a specialised set of attentional skills. These provide the means for coupling with particular situations and features of the environment. These couplings, or hooks, act as regulators for behaviour rather than its causal antecedents. Couplings with the environment act as attractors for the ensuing behaviour. The agent is literally hooked up to the environment in ways that regulate their behaviour. The expert classroom teacher is not working to a theoretical rule in determining performance; they are working to achieve a balance to the various attractors that at any one time arise in virtue of their capacities for attending to the particularities of the situation.

(Luntley and Ainley 2005: 3)

What is claimed to be seen under each model differs. Both, however, are recognisable as theoretical models of the 'everyday world' of practice; both attempting to explain what actually happens but each seeing and naming the what happens, the X, differently.

Now suppose there is yet another way, C, of explaining the dispute about how to talk about X. Both A and B, it could be argued, have bought into a notion of 'expertise'. The expert is not problematised as such. The 'expertise' of the 'expert' is simply being accepted as such. The dispute is only around how the 'expert' operates 'expertly'. The argument from C, say, is that 'expertise' is no different from any other state-endorsed function; that is, it is about power and knowing your place under the rule of power. Thus, the models described, although competing explanations, merely reinforce the place and social functions of the expert under power. For C then:

The process of interpellation begins with "hailing," a calling to participate in a form of ideology (Althusser, 1998; 302). Hailing is ubiquitous, and almost entirely irresistible and is at the center of any ideological system. It attempts to make another individual recognize and accept a form of ideology. Through hailing, ideology "acts or functions in such a way that it recruits subjects among individuals" (Althusser, 1998; 301). Individuals are born into ideology, but hailing recruits subjects of particular ideologies. Subjects do not realize their subjection, and are only free in that subjection is freely accepted. Althusser (1998) states that an institution or individual hails another individual much as the "common everyday police (or other) hailing: 'Hey, you there!'" (301). A successful hailing occurs if the individual "recognizes that the hail was really addressed to him, and that it was really him who was hailed" (Althusser, 1969; 41). This recognition, for example may be the acceptance of a particular social practice or label, such as an advocate of Christian religious ideology terming himself a Christian. If a hailing is successful, an individual becomes a "subject" of a particular ideology, and, hence, is "interpellated," interpellation being a successful hailing (Althusser, 1998; 303). Althusser (1998) succinctly states this process in his central thesis: "Ideology interpellates individuals as subjects" (299).

(Gray 2005)

Interpellation, as described here, seems to be a particular form of provocation that calls forth under the name of power. The answer to power is either to become a subject of power or to become the subject of resistance. In each case, the subject is defined by power. For some, the radical answer is to 'raise the consciousness' of the oppressed through some form of education that reveals the real conditions of their lives. Showing how consent is manufactured (Herman and Chomsky 1988) is one such revelatory practice. The alternative, in the Spinozan sense, is to suspend the agency of power in its dissolution in the power of the multitude, as when the crowds standing before Ceauşescu no longer saw him as all-powerful. Conditions had changed and perhaps consent was never willing but manufactured resentfully, or extorted, coerced through implicit or explicit threat. In this case, no one can know what conflicts and disagreements will surface at unpredictable times and places. What are the alternatives?

In characterising the different points of view of Bourdieu and Rancière, Nordmann (2006) outlines Bourdieu's focus on inequality from a position of elite knowledge. Bourdieu would emancipate the oppressed. Rancière, however, starts from a principle of equality where the only emancipatory power is with the people themselves. One of his most concrete accounts of equality is in his explorations of Joseph Jacotot (Rancière 1987, 2004b), discussed earlier in Chapter 5:

> The revelation that seized Joseph Jacotot came down to this: you have to turn the logic of the systems of explanation upside down. Explanation is not necessary for remedying an incapacity for understanding. On the contrary it is this *incapacity* that is the structuring fiction of the way the world is explained and conceived. It is those who explain who need incapability and not the other way round, it is they who constitute incapability as such. Explaining something to someone is first of all to demonstrate that they cannot understand by themselves. Before being the act of the pedagogue, explanation is the pedagogical myth, the parable of a world divided into learned minds and ignorant minds, mature minds and immature minds, capable and incapable, intelligent and stupid. What is characteristic of the explainer's trick is to be found in this inaugurating double gesture. On the one hand, he decides on the absolute beginning: it is only now that the act of leaning is going to begin. On the other hand, he throws a veil of ignorance over everything to be learnt that he himself undertakes to lift.

(Rancière 1987: 15–16 [my translation, John Schostak])

Not only schooling but also the world's systems of economic and social reward are organised according to the pedagogical myth of the rich in talent and the poor in talent, the rich in knowledge and the poor in knowledge, the rich in culture and the poor in culture – and even the poor are divided into the deserving poor and the undeserving – the underclasses who should be sealed off (Murray 1990, 2000, 2005). In short, the pedagogical myth serves to divide the world into inferior and superior intelligences:

> The first records perceptions by chance, retains, interprets and repeats empirically within the narrow confines of habits and needs. It is the intelligence of little children and the man in the street. The second knows things through reasons, by methods proceeding from the simple to the complex, from the part to the whole. This is what allows the master to transmit his knowledge by adapting them to the intellectual capacities of the pupil and checking that the child has understood what he has learnt. That's the principle of explanation. From now on, for Jacotot, this will be the principle of *mindlessness*.
>
> (Rancière 1987: 16–17)

As described by Rancière, the students taught themselves French without any explanations from a teacher – they wanted to learn, so they did. It recalls Arendt's 'life of the mind' constructed through thinking, willing and constantly questioning meaning and action (Kristeva 2001: 42). Their only source was the bilingual book that they used to find out what was meant by the passages in French. So, was all that they needed no more than *wanting*, in order to be able to learn (Rancière 1987: 9)? This thought brought a revolution in Jacotot's thinking. What had happened? They learnt by feeling their way, by chance, by making mistakes, yet:

> methodologists oppose rational approaches to the bad method of chance. But they give in advance what they want to prove. They suppose that a little animal exploring by knocking into things in the world is not yet capable of seeing and that they will teach him or her to discriminate precisely. But the little person is first of all a speaking being [*être de parole*]. The child who repeats words understood and the Flemish student 'lost' in his *Telemachus* does not work by chance. Their whole effort, their whole exploration is aimed towards [*tendue*] this: they have been addressed by the word of a human being that they want to recognise and to which they want to respond, not as pupils or as scholars, but as people; as speaking to someone who speaks to you and not as someone who examines you: under the sign of equality.
>
> (Rancière 1987: 22)

In this view, speaking and responding to another as a human being is to see each other as individuals, addressing each other under the universal principle of equality.

This does not imply that everyone is the same in all respects. Equality resides in the manner of speaking, of calling forth and recognising the humanness of another as people address each other in their particularity, their historical singularity, their individuality – in short, it is like the *sujet-en-procès* of Kristeva (1984). This play of universal and particular between 'teacher' and 'pupil' involves both as individuals:

> relating what one does not know to what one knows, observing and comparing, saying and to verifying. The pupil is always a searcher. And the master is first of all a human being who speaks to another, who tells stories, restoring authority to knowledge only on the poetic condition of every verbal transmission.
>
> (Rancière 2004b)

It recalls the progressive, child centred, 'movements' of the 1960s and 1970s that came under attack and were largely purged from mainstream schooling by the new right of the 1970s and 1980s (Schostak 1993).

What one knows, as discussed earlier, is problematic, secondary rather than first hand, involving trust in the experience and knowledge of witnesses and specialists. Knowledge as a global resource is, thus, held not by individuals who have constructed it through 'their on board resources', as Kusch (2002) describes the individualistic construction of knowledge adopted by philosophers in the tradition of Descartes. Rather, knowledge construction involves a reliance on others. However, this is not a blind reliance because, in principle, if one wants, one can find out, compare, check, observe and discuss. Even if one does not fully understand a particularly complex theory, it is at least possible to see the degree of agreement and disagreement it arouses. It is possible to ascertain whose interests a particular theory benefits to the exclusion of others. It is possible to explore the assumptions upon which it is based. Since no single person, or indeed face-to-face group, is able to possess and proclaim that they know everything that is currently knowable, then knowledge claims are always in discussion and debatable in relation to what people do not know. Even if they could, there is still more to know. In these senses, there is another kind of equality – equality in the face of ignorance. Knowledge does not provoke the voice of expertise as much as the voice of equality in the face of ignorance. It is rather like the voice of the hysteric in Freudian and Lacanian psychoanalysis who through the continual questioning of expert knowledge pushes the boundaries of that knowledge as it unsettles authority and power (cf., Schostak 2006: 203–4). The task is to have people who think rather than claim knowledge. Thus, how does one get to be critical of the forms of society and thus of the power through which those forms are kept in place? 'Critique entails a distance relative to the object; if philosophy is to go beyond journalism. This critique presupposes the creation of new ideas, new standards, new forms of thought that establish this distance' (Castoriadis 1997: 36).

This is not just the task of philosophers doing philosophy, nor of some avant-garde believing they alone hold the key to the emancipation of all. Emancipatory critique involves a mutual provocation; that is, each individual calling forth the voice of the other in exploring their ignorance and their disagreements with each other under a principle of equality. Otherwise, as in Bruno Latour's reproach to Bourdieu, it would be a case of experts 'wanting to impose an "unquestionable science" that would crush "the word of ordinary actors" who are always presumed inadequate' (Nordmann 2006:11, drawing on a forum published in *Libération*, 15 September 1998). The role then, of radical research must be to contribute to the conditions under which emancipatory critique can be practised by 'ordinary actors', that is, by all under a principle of equality.

Research and methodology across the edge

Clearly, contemporary democracies, whether Westernised liberal economies or any other kind, are at best incomplete expressions of the kind of democracy envisaged by Spinoza. As Adorno remarks about the success of the bourgeoisie in over-throwing the constraints of monarchies, the result is an incomplete emancipation:

> In the shadow of its own incomplete emancipation the bourgeois conscious-ness must fear to be annulled by a more advanced consciousness; not being the whole freedom. It senses that it can produce only a caricature of freedom – hence its theoretical expansion of its autonomy into a system similar to its own coercive mechanisms.
>
> (Adorno 1973: 21)

Rather than freedom, there are caricatures of freedom, the freedom of choice in a supermarket is more illusory than real. It is no more than an advertising strategy to promote anything from soft drinks to cigarettes to banks. What methodologies can drive 'incomplete' democracies across the edge and into ever-increasing degrees of emancipation?

Radical methodologies drive democracy to the 'roots' of the relation between concepts and non-conceptualities, between cognition and ontology, between I-think and I-want/demand/desire in order to bring that which is at the edge of conscious-ness, at the edge of society, into a society that transforms itself to be inclusive. Empowerment is thus achieved, not by transmitting conceptual knowledge but by including other forms of expression, other ways of conceptualising the non-conceptualities. It begins face to face with the other and begins anew at every moment. If equality provides the universalising strategy, then each individual member of a crowd, of the multitudes in the world, provides the material, hetero-geneous basis for a metonymic dynamic of connections as discussed in Chapter 8. Recalling Figure 7.2, the connections made by each individual continually over-spill the controlling categories, thus creating spaces of potential conflict that provoke recognition of the other who speaks. Linguistically, the form of the system as described by Saussure is that of each element being different from each other element: that is, it is a formal system of differences, rather like algebra, a system of empty 'a's' and 'b's' manipulated through rules of aggregation and multiplication. It is here in this relation between the formal structure of a social system as an order of differences and its 'living energy of meaning' (Derrida 1978: 5), that is, its content, that the radical can be inscribed in ways that challenge, subvert, collapse or transform the given order. How is this system of writing the radical into research design to be accomplished?

At its simplest, any system may be closed or open. Closure is variously achieved, to varying degrees, through reductionist and totalitarianistic moves, as, for example, in the 'structuralist invasion' (Derrida 1978: 3). Typically, attention paid to *force* suffers 'a relaxation, if not a lapse' (Derrida 1978: 4), as it is relegated to 'the quantity of movement' (Derrida 1978: 16). This, in turn, means that *form* itself is the object of attention by structural analyses. Often critique is neglected, and it is this that accounts for the 'melancholy pathos that can be perceived behind the triumphant cries of technical ingenuity or mathematical subtlety that sometimes accompany certain so-called "structural" analyses' (Derrida 1978: 5). Structure, here, is therefore no longer 'a heuristic instrument, a method of reading, a characteristic particularly revelatory of content, or a system of objective relations, independent of content and terminology', nor a 'relational configuration' and critique; rather, it has become 'a *means* or relationship for reading or writing, for assembling significations, recognizing themes, ordering constants and correspondences' (Derrida 1978: 15).

Structure holds to notions of construction – architecture perhaps, of organising space – geometric or morphological, by mastering form and sites. Topographical metaphors are not only very apt, they are also beguiling, inasmuch as they draw the line, thereby delimiting further possibilities. Whilst this is, most assuredly, not restricted to structuralism alone, it is pertinent to deal with this phenomenon at this time. There is an inescapable figurative quality about all language and all metaphors almost as if 'the fact that language can determine things only by spatializing them suffice[s] to explain that, in return, language must spatialize itself as soon as it designates and reflects upon itself' (Derrida 1978: 16). Always, there is the figure itself and the play going on with, beside and against it metaphorically. And 'metaphor is never innocent. It orients research and fixes results' (Derrida 1978: 17). But these are no

> simple motions of balancing, equilibration or overturning, to oppose duration to space, quality to quantity, force to form, the depth of meaning or value to the surface of figures. Quite to the contrary. To counter this simple alternative, to counter the simple choice of one of the terms or one of the series against the other, we maintain that it is necessary to seek new concepts and new models, an economy escaping this system of metaphysical oppositions.
>
> (Derrida 1978: 19)

Structuralist models call upon topographical models that roam widely over the flat two-dimensional surfaces where metaphors of 'panorama and panoramagram' may be deployed (Derrida 1978: 5), surveying and adding order by some sort of totalising categorisation. Flattening out the more complex picture in this way both simplifies and permits the totalising glance, say of power, to rove with less impediment across the whole, thereby unifying and totalising with minimum effort. In 'Force and Signification', Derrida takes the structuralist position to task over its preoccupation with a flat schema in which form takes precedence over content, that is, force. The 'richness implied by volume' is what is lacking here (Derrida 1978: 25) such that force and form 'must be thought together in an "economy" which escapes the meaningless or fixed formulation of either extreme' of structuralist approaches (Derrida 1978: 43).

The system of writing that Derrida explores is configured by Johnson (1993) as three moments: infinity, inscription and economy. These three moments are neither chronological, nor sequential, nor even spatially discrete; rather, they are moments of articulation. Each moment provides a way of thinking through design issues. First of all, Derrida's infinity, however, is a certain kind of infinity and is defined in terms of excess with the use of words such as '*hyperbole*' and '*démesure*'. Derrida's infinity is not transcendental, but, rather, it refuses containment and delimitation and yet it is also haunted by conditions of the finite, as can be seen: 'the *overabundance* of the signifier, its supplementary character, is thus the result of a finitude, that is to say, the result of a lack which must be supplemented' (Derrida 1978: 290). This refers to the sense of 'too much', of 'overstepping the mark' or an 'excess' that is characteristic of any act that challenges or transgresses or shifts the boundaries of power.

The infinite experienced as excess undergoes the passage to determination and inscription as it is baptised as an excessive event. This passage does not destroy the indeterminancy of infinity; rather it makes it apprehensible at that point. The passage, however, occasions pain and anguish, and the inscription is therefore a violence.

> The Decision, through a single act, links and separates reason and madness, and it must be understood at once both as the [originary] act of an order, a fiat, a decree, and as a schism, a caesura, a separation, a dissection. I would prefer *dissension*, to underline that in question is a self-dividing action, a cleavage and torment interior to meaning *in general*, interior to logos in general, a division within the very act of *sentire*.
>
> (Derrida 1978: 38–9)

Derrida (1992a) recalls that, for Kierkegaard, decision is a kind of madness because it must be taken the context of complete knowledge about all possible consequences. Thus, the crisis, the decision, is a split in the *logos*; that is, word as reason, which had always already taken place, and can thus only be secondary, that is to say non-originary. The split or crisis has *already taken place* because no word can ever embrace the totality. The terms themselves, however, are not to be understood in a moral and anthropological sense, but rather in terms of '*necessity* and *rigor*' (Derrida 1978: 238), in that it is so urgent that it is 'just close enough to *say* violence, to dialogue with itself as irreducible violence, and just far enough to *live* and live as speech' (Derrida 1978: 61). The violence is 'not an empirical modification or state of the writer (Derrida 1978: 9); rather, it is 'the necessary condition of the institution of any system, beyond the register of the subjective or intersubjective. This places writing, as violent inscription, at a level of determination most properly termed "transcendental"' (Derrida 1978: 64). It is through the violence of the decision that a system can emerge and, once emerged, it insists on its persistence over time. That is, it is repeatable in being named, in being acted towards, in being the condition or justification of action. Thus, the moment of inscription as something that can be pointed to, named, talked about, is literally both an instance and an insistence.

> As soon as the sign emerges, it begins by repeating itself. Without this, it would not be a sign, would not be what it is, that is, the non-self-identity which regularly refers to the same. That is to say, to another sign, which itself will be born of having been divided.
>
> (Derrida 1978: 297)

In other words, the sign is repeated differentially. The first instance of the sign (a baptism say) may be pointed towards as S_1, its repetition as S_2 (say, when telling another) that together imply a signifying subject – S_3 as the subject called forth in the telling (see Figure 9.2).

Figure 9.2 Sign repetition

Through a chain of signifiers, the naming of the incident can be transmitted by the individual who occupies the place of S_3. At each repetition, the context changes – it is now someone else I tell, in this place, not that place with these circumstances, not those circumstances. If S_1 refers to the baptism as origin (or centre of a system) then such doubling and redoubling, due to the telling, shifts the centre or origin as contexts change due to new historical circumstances. Recall the story of the surgeon in Chapter 6 talking about the decision to cut out a little bit more to save a return to surgery in the case of a malignant tumour. Repeating this event to another consultant, the circumstances were changed by an introduction of a question of ethics. It was further altered in the context of repeating this as a possible distinction between an expert consultant and a trainee surgeon. The centre of the debate changed from a question of utility to a question of ethics, then a question of litigation. In this way, agendas are inscribed into what otherwise would be a simple repetition of the 'same'. The surgeon could not just make a simple repetition of his story without it being shifted into alternative discourses due to the change in circumstances. This suggests that the door to the radical is always possible. No system of control can control all possible circumstances. But the radical has to be understood within the context of an economy that operates between the excess that overflows the bounds and the grid that asserts the power of containment.

In the operation of a Derridean-style economy, terms such as '*hyperbolé*', '*excès*', '*démesure*' arise at the point of decision that both locates and constrains the infinite in the finite structure of the system. It is like a teacher saying to a child 'I know you inside out and I know you are stupid'. The one label reduces the child. Yet such reductive labelling is pervasive, not only in schooling (Hargreaves et al. 1976), but in life generally, say racism, sexism or views concerning social class and national identity (Balibar 2002). This critical moment, including categorising, is a fall into unification under a signifier – a fall to inscription. It is also temporalised through continual reactivation through differential repetition.

> The unitary, extreme fall expends the whole of its force; there is no survival. The single sign, like Delacroix's single line, is a monster, and monsters bear no progeny. The integral violence of the origin must therefore be distributed in lesser repetitions, as it were, so that the inaugural gesture may live on, carry on (*se poursuivre*).
>
> (Derrida 1978: 59–60)

Thus there is a tension between saving and expenditure, investment and consumption and this is an economy. Derrida's use of *économie* is semantically astute inasmuch as it aptly describes the dynamic relation between the dual polarities of saving and expenditure, but, through its over-determined and remotivated lexicon, it is uncanny with spirited hauntings of a bias towards saving with its implications of deferment and *différence*. Derrida's act of enjoining *différance–différence* opens up a 'telling space' (Schostak 2005, Vol. I) that provides an insightful description and definition of the economy, namely, spatial difference plus difference of force with the implication of temporal delay or deferral. Having tried

> to-attempt-to-say-the-demonic-hyperbole from whose heights thought is announced to itself, *frightens* itself, and reassures itself against being annihilated or wrecked in madness or in death. *At its height* hyperbole, the absolute opening, the uneconomic expenditure, is always reembraced by an *economy* and is overcome by economy. The relationship between reason, madness, and death is an economy, a structure of deferral whose irreducible originality must be respected.
>
> (Derrida 1978: 61–2)

The term 'economy' here is subjected to an unconventional usage, in a sense of a general economy, 'a certain writing close to the non-sense that is sovereignity unbridled' (Derrida 1978: 270). However, it does not refer to the management of wealth. Nor does value circulate in this general economy, as it does in the closed system of conventional economy (Derrida 1978). The implications of Derrida's three moments of *écriture* (as outlined by Johnson, 1993) for writing up are discussed in the next chapter. The design implications of these moments for radical research involves engaging more directly with *the* political.

Sovereignty and the worlds of *the* political

Whatever counts as normal science is an historical product whose adherents and practitioners believe they are the pioneers of a science that is universal. As a historical product, it is particular, contingent, and, thus, it is a political act imposed, or seeking to impose itself as a universal. This is a possible standpoint for any individual or group. For example, Bourdieu, as sociologist with the authority and legitimacy of his science, standing up for the poor to speak for the poor, or feminists speaking for *all* women, or religious leaders speaking for *all* believers of that faith, or declaring that the religious law is universal and so on. In each case where there are two or more sides standing up against each other, none are universal as such, they are situated in their particular historical circumstances. However, each may make universal claims. Each may claim to represent a universal such as *all* the people, freedom, humanity, reason, faith. Everyone may claim to represent universal truths (see Figure 9.3).

Suppose a self-proclaimed avant-garde makes a claim about what is best for the people. The claim could be made from various different political and cultural positions. It could be a claim about the kind of schooling all children should undertake, 'in their best interests'. It could be a claim about national identity and who are really members and who should be considered immigrants and who should be expelled. Any such avant-garde, in claiming to know the truth, can under that claim assert the truth of particular statements – $t_1, t_2, \ldots, t_n, t_{n+1}$ as in Figure 9.1. Whether or not the statements are true, whether or not all people believe them to be true, the assertion itself constitutes a certain kind of reality where in the words of Thomas (1928: 571–2), 'If men define situations as real they are real in their consequences'. Such definitions are sovereign to the extent that their assertion depends on nothing other than the power of the individual, group or elite that makes the assertion. The consequences, however, constitute a difference/*différance*, in the sense that the assertion provokes a response, a reply as it were, from the material and symbolic worlds of others who compose the multitude. And this response shifts the ground, the centre, the original purposes, intentions or agendas. Within this framework of shifting grounds, there are a number of design possibilities.

As an illustration of these possibilities, take Sorel's (2006) judgement that the 'parliamentary socialists' of his time much 'resemble demagogues who are

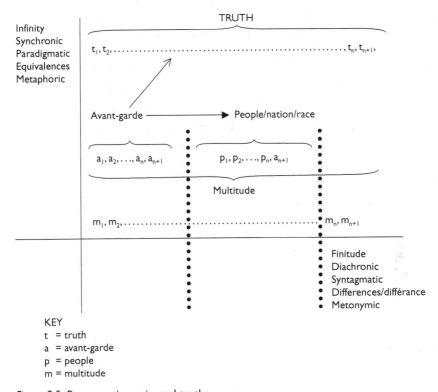

KEY
t = truth
a = avant-garde
p = people
m = multitude

Figure 9.3 Representing universal truths

constantly demanding the abolition of debts, the division of land', who see the rich as filling up the public offices and: 'make up plots so that they can confiscate large fortunes. "In democracies where the crowd can sovereignly make the law," Aristotle says, 'by their continual attacks on the rich, continually divide the city into two camps . . ." ' (Sorel 2006: 66–7). The potential for social transformation is, it seems in Sorel's voice, being inhibited by the strategy of making continual attacks that set rich and poor into mutually exclusive positions. At the same time, the strategy is muddied because the parliamentary socialists of the time, according to Sorel, spoke as many languages as there were kinds of clientele – labourers, owners of small businesses, country people and even farmers – so that '[t]he term "proletariat" ends up becoming synonymous with the oppressed; and there are the oppressed in every class.' As a consequence, 'no contradiction stops them' (Sorel 2006: 68). There is a sense of games-playing in which there is an attempt to build a wide constituency of support, even at the expense of contradiction if class is to remain the focus. However, if the oppressed is the focus, then, as Sorel says, 'there are the oppressed in every class.' In short, the chances are that everyone has a grievance of some sort leading, perhaps, to a sense of being oppressed. What is lost from a socialist point of view is the purity of the strategy, the homogeneity of the proletariat as an hegemonic knotting together of diverse groups in the attempt to draw upon popular support. Laclau (1996, 2005) calls such strategies hegemonic, as people who have different particular interests are drawn together under one more universalising banner. As such, the individuals are split between their particular interests and the universal which, at least, for the time being, suits their purpose. A rich person who feels oppressed by an unpopular tyrant is as likely to want to see the tyrant overthrown as an oppressed poor person. After the tyrant has been overthrown, this particular commonality of interest disappears. Unless there are other commonalities – for example, a common hatred of 'immigrants', or a hatred of some faith community and so on – then the rich and the poor may turn on each other as the 'enemies within': the rich seeing the poor as the 'dangerous classes', or the 'underclasses', the 'rabble', and the poor seeing the rich as exploiters, greedy 'fat cats'. The populations that compose the world the rich and powerful want to exploit can be counted, their patterns of behaviour described for purposes of control but only through the exercise of various forms of power. In the absence of power, there is no reason why one person should submit to the demands of another. Thus, as discussed in Chapters 2 and 7, *the* political arises when there is a recognition of each individual's relative 'equality' in terms of personal strength and intelligence. This could result in what Hobbes called a war of all against all unless a fearsome power arises to bring order to a given territory, or unless there is some alternative means of unifying the 'nation', the people, in particular, of course, if there are other territories who may seek to invade and thus become the enemy. In turn, this fear of the other is a powerful means to consolidate power around the central protecting agency, whether monarch, tyrant or some oligarchical elite. For political theorists like Carl Schmitt (1996) and Leo Strauss (1952a, 1952b, 1988), as described in Chapter 4, this results in a view of the political being necessarily defined by the friend–enemy relation, or the existence of what Bush has called the 'axis of evil' (see Figure 9.4).

The friend–enemy distinction can be played out in a variety of ways, as between rich and poor, ruling class and lower classes, bosses and employees, the faithful and the godless, oppressed and oppressor and so on. Each results in a different configuration of the visible. This logic of reconfigurability according to interests is at play in the implementation of innovations in any social context. Any innovation that brings change, for example, can be seen as a threat to the vested interests of particular groups and individuals. In this configuration, whoever is not a friend is an enemy.

If the diagram is read as if looking from above, that is, each dot representing a person at the same level, then the connecting lines can be read as identifying who associates with whom. The one group sees the other group as a threat, an enemy. However, one side of the friend–enemy line is more strongly connected than the other. This could mean that the one will use that power advantage at some time. However, if the isolated individual in Figure 9.4 is seen by the camp of friends as an enemy, thus it is in that individual's interests ultimately to side with the

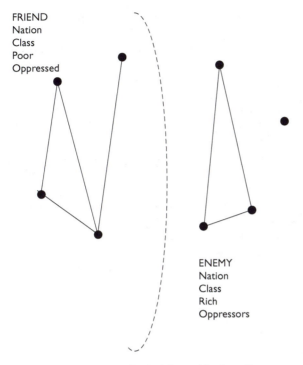

FRIEND
Nation
Class
Poor
Oppressed

ENEMY
Nation
Class
Rich
Oppressors

Figure 9.4 Reconfiguring the field of the visible: friend/enemy

camp of the enemies. Perhaps, this is rather like a position of mutually assured destruction, MAD, as it was known when the survival of the world was dependent on the capacities of the West and the East to launch nuclear missiles that would ensure mutual destruction. If the diagram were read as hierarchies producing pinnacles representing elites having power over multitudes, then another dynamic is added. Recalling Spinoza's two kinds of power: there is *potestas* that refers to the top-down power of leaders of various kind – monarchs, aristocracies, tyrants, oligarchies – and then there is the power – *potentia* – that is natural to each and every individual that enables them to persist in their being. *Potestas* refers us back to the Hobbesian argument where no one individual is able to feel safe from another without seeking some advantage in associating with others. It is some of this power that an individual gives up, in exchange for security and other goods like friendship and being able to trade without fear. The leader or ruling groups aggregates this power. But ultimately, the reality of power rests with the multitude who vest some of their power in the ruling groups in exchange for such goods as security, law and order. But that power, even when it seems too real and immense for generations, can in just one short period, even just one day, evaporate. It did so during the French Revolution too, when in the name of the multitude all were proclaimed equal, brothers and sisters, and free. It did so, as MacGregor (1998: 21) describes, in the Soviet Union when on 25 December 1991 Gorbachev gave his resignation speech following the failed coup in August 1991 and 'The former superpower slid silently away as though it had never existed'. Žižek (1991) provides a similar account of the fall of Ceauşescu after a week of riots in Romania in 1989. In Žižek's terms, Ceauşescu represented the big other in whom was invested the aggregated powers of the multitude. Ultimately, as Spinoza argued, the power of the leader, the system, or however the big other is constructed, is illusory. Unless the leader or ruling elites satisfy sufficiently the desires of the multitude, there will be riots and the power of the big other will be shaken and even collapse unless steps are taken to satisfy the desires of the multitude. The only system that does this, Spinoza argued, is democracy, where each individual in the name of equality and freedom chooses to give up some of their powers to act freely in return for a safe and rewarding form of governance. This form of governance is by the people for the people. MacGregor (1998) describes Hegel's admiration of Napoleon's attempts to bring a liberal constitutional monarchy to the German states, thinking that the spirit of the French Revolution (1789–99) will be carried further by the German peoples. Hegel, in his philosophical and political works, sought to show how the final form of governance had indeed appeared, a form that synthesised both individual freedom and the role of the community to support the needs for freedom (Hardimon 1994). Instead of a divided state, the oppositions were to be reconciled to form a totality. The task was, as it were, to join all the dots and bring all under a more liberal form of rule (see Figure 9.5).

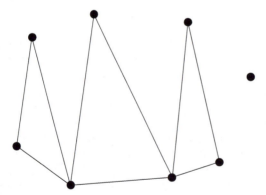

Figure 9.5 Including all except one

In order to bring as many interest groups into a political alliance, strategies have to be designed to be increasingly inclusive. However, as intimated above, such alliances are always open to reconfigurations and thus can fall apart. Thus, designing the radical is about designing inclusivity, bringing the heterogeneous into public debates, decision-making, the allocation of resources and the undertaking of actions under conditions of undecidability. Unless all parties feel they are able to have a voice in the management of their everyday lives, then there is always the danger of exclusion, resentment and a fracturing of the political frameworks. The

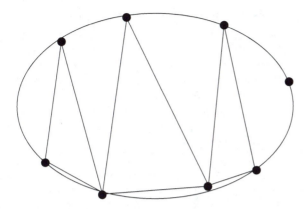

Figure 9.6 Totality

question for radical research then is about the extent to which given social, cultural, economic structures are politically organised to enable the voices of all so that all have a stake in the whole (see Figure 9.6).

The ideal final form of the state, then, is one in which the principles of individual freedom are married with that of community as a basis for being free from fear and free to explore individual talents, needs and interests insofar as this is consistent with the persistence of community. It is thus a resolution of conflicts and differences. In short, it is the end of those histories that narrate the grand paradigmatic battles between worldviews. Thus Kojève (1969) saw in Hegelian philosophy an end of history as it was emerging in the EU and Fukuyama (1992) proclaimed its accomplishment with the fall of the Soviet Bloc. It was the triumph of Western liberal democracies. It is the final way in which to 'see' the world as a whole, a finished design, if not yet a finished picture. Its truth is more than the sum of the parts, the joined-up dots representing all the things and living creatures that can exist – every particular drawn under the universal. However, liberal democracies, as presently conceived, are not radical democracies where no one individual has a greater voice than any other in deciding upon the allocation and use of resources to meet needs and interests. The achievement of such a political framework is the work of radical research as conceived in this book. To do so requires engaging in action to implement innovative structures and practices to enable people's voices to be heard in the public domains of community decision-making at every institutional and social level. But how? How can the boundaries be broken down through research action?

Playing across, between and dissolving the boundaries

Rancière (1995, 2004a), it will be recalled, describes the order that is imposed on every part of the social whole by the rule of power, the police. Police, here, does not refer to police officers but rather the force exerted to ensure that every part carries out its function in the whole. The police structure defines what is visible, audible, legitimate on the public stage. Each legitimate institution of society has its role in moulding every part to fit the whole. The possibilities, then, for radical action can only be identified through gaining insights into the frustrations, the complaints, the disagreements, the hopes and desires of people as they face each other across boundaries formed through the normalising structures and processes of the police. A play appears between the visible (legitimised to appear in public) and invisible (the illegitimate, the marginalised, the excluded). It is a kind of aesthetics of politics, a painting composed of light and dark, revealing and hiding (teasing, provoking), promise and deception, absence and presence that creates a field of desire, anxiety, the fear of dangerous others as well as of allure and of seduction. The battlelines are drawn, people know their places, and some fight back:

> in fact I was in the midst of a group where I was in it, and the girl come to me and said "I'm sorry," she says, "that I'm in your group." And I says, "Well, why would you say that?" She says, "because you're not gonna get a good mark". And I says, "Oh forget it", like you know because being in the 80s, like you know, I said, you know there's no chance, like, here we all put our heads together sure. Sure enough the mark come back and it was C minus. Well I went to the teacher. And I said, "Excuse me," I said, "could you kindly explain to me why we only got a C minus." Well she started looking for a bunch of excuses eh, and I said "I don't see that in the paper," and I got kinda rude and I said, "can you not read?" I said, "Everything you're telling me and the points you're saying that we don't have are right in there." And I said, "Well, I'm taking that paper back and I'm going through it on my lunch hour and I'll be back to see ya. And I'll underline everything that you're telling me is not there." Before I even got a chance to get the paper back, she come to me and took it and changed that mark. So you tell me. You know.
>
> (Student at a Canadian school, 1991; see also report at <http://www.enquirylearning.net/ELU/Issues/Education/canada.html>)

This, of course, does not sound like a child speaking to an adult who is the voice of authority. There is perhaps a double take in reading this extract from an interview transcript until it is all nicely resolved when the student in question is seen to be a forty-year-old who had returned to school to take a course that would help her towards her goal of being a nurse. If she had not been a forty-year-old, her views may well have remained silent and the sense of injustice unresolved. In short, there are no necessary mechanisms of democracy even within an apparently liberal institution serving the needs of a 'democracy'. The forty-year-old did not feel powerless. She felt like an equal demanding justice. Perhaps the teacher felt it more difficult to look an adult in the eye than a fourteen-year-old. The collapse was swift. It was the appeal both to an injustice, the claim to being equal, the fear of the consequences of a challenge and perhaps being seen to be unjust by superiors that led to the reluctant recognition of the potential effectiveness of the power of the student that brought about the change in mark. It seems trivial. But it is in the trivial that the lines of power can be felt and even challenged.

However, there are other circumstances where the sense of wrong is so pervasive, so irreconcilable, that it feels hopeless. The sense of this could be heard in the voices of a group of ten-year-old children living in an area known for its violence and deprivation:

G2: Yeah there's like, like . . . if you go out in a car like a 15 minute drive there's like [*place name*] which is really clean. And if you go like down, this way out the school, that's clean, but when you come onto my street, that's real mucky. Our mum hates it there.
Interviewer: Why's that then?
G2: Because there's teens that are always like cause fights and the police are always round. And I've got like you know them porches outside me 'ouse, everyone's wrote their names on it. And me mum's like phoned the council and the police and everythin'.

(CAPE project data, 2005)

None of the children in the group liked living in the area. As well as noise and aggression they mentioned litter and graffiti and '*Boy*: Cos sometimes you just can't get to sleep at night, cos like shouts 'n you can hear bottles smashing'. There is a pervasive sense of fear and anxiety. This is the point at which the controlling powers of 'the police', in Rancière's sense, begin to fall down. Areas become interstitial as Thrasher (1927) in his early twentieth-century study of Chicago gangs called them. These are the liminal domains where people are not quite in nor quite out of the reach of the dominant institutions of social controls. It is the point at which a political leader like Thatcher in the early 1980s during the miners' strike can talk about 'the enemy within'. It is at this point where the truth of the matter becomes contested. What kind of truth is it? Each leader proclaims that their policies are supports for more universal principles like freedom, justice, peace and the protection of the 'people' in the face of 'enemies'. At this point, decisions have to be made, sides chosen, concerning what contents, what actual practices, what kinds of individual qualities, what particular details are going to fill the space covered by these essentially empty signifiers of universal principles (cf., Butler et al. 2000; Laclau 1996, 2005).

Radical research can be designed to explore what happens to a notion of truth when there are liminal spaces to deal with: those 'betweens' that are neither an inside nor an outside. They are thresholds, their definition depending on purpose. Which way do I want to go? Edges are constructed through threads, intentionalities if you will, that are directed from subject to other, generating both object and spaces, insides and outsides. Pull a thread and every edge is ready to collapse

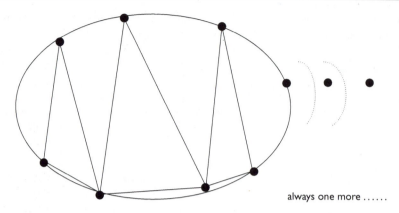

always one more . . . . . .

Figure 9.7 Always one more . . .

like the collapse of the Ceauşescu regime or the Soviet Union. As the definition of who is in and who is out retreats, some are excluded as it increases, more are included. In each case, the identity of the community or state changes (see Figure 9.7).

Whether the strategies are inclusive or exclusive, there are always those left outside until the inside cannot hold, and the people, as multitude, again generates the possibility for a new social order that increasingly meets the needs of the people, that is, addresses the issue of inclusion, always adding the excluded others. And there is always one more. As Arendt (1977) puts it, with each newborn child, there is a new viewpoint.

With the creation of any boundary, there is always the possibility of strategic moves being made that focus on the solidity or permeability of boundaries, their persistence over time, the extent to which they can be moved, deformed, deconstructed, transgressed, transformed. Action can be designed to exploit the games at play. However, radical research seeks in particular to analyse the possibilities for action that results in increased inclusivity, that is, increasing the viewpoints that can be counted:

> I form an opinion by considering a given issue from different viewpoints, by making present to my mind the standpoints of those who are absent; that is, I represent them [. . .] The more people's standpoints that I have present in my mind while I am pondering a given issue, and the better I can imagine how I would feel and think if I were in their place, the stronger will be my capacity for representative thinking and the more valid my final conclusions, my opinion.
>
> (Arendt 1977: 241)

In order to accomplish such a form of 'representative thinking', radical research would need to develop a descriptive 'baseline' of the discourses, the texts produced by the players involved in their 'games'. Designs for radical research, whose bottom line is action, must be grounded in the current circumstances – what people want, what stops them from getting what they want and so on. Thus there is a dynamic here between the emergent problem structure of what is at stake for individuals, groups and the various forms of organisation and the emergent design for research. The key question is how to remain close enough to what people experience that the design can be increasingly focused on what is needed to bring about an *effective* design for change. In the centre of this is the individual who is at that crossroads between particular needs and universal claims: I need this to support my family and to give them support in their individual development and I claim these particular things to meet my particular circumstances as a universal human right. '[T]he relation that the universal holds with the particular is precisely what determines the forming of the identity of both the subject and the community' (Riha 2004: 73).

At the centre of the game is the individual whose identity is formed through the kinds of relations that can be established as sides are taken when boundaries are imposed and recognised (see Figure 9.8).

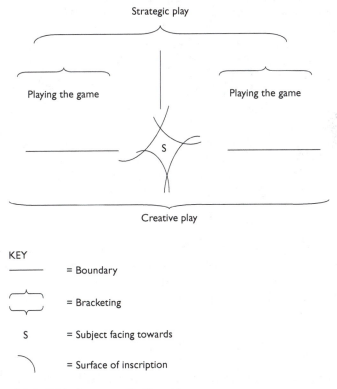

Figure 9.8 Individual, game and taking sides

Individuals are not players in just one game. As a parent, there are games of control as well as those of nurturing with the children. As adults, there are the games of lovers. As employee, there are the career games. As citizen, there are the political games of class, group and national allegiance. In short, each individual is the subject 'S' of a multiplicity of games. How these games do or do not relate to each other produces, for the individual and for others, his or her personal and social identity. Each game acts as a potential surface of inscription where S can locate his or her interests. Hence, strategic use of different games can be made that may cross boundaries, even bringing together organisations that in some circumstances may be playing on opposing sides: if I join this organisation in its competitive struggle for market share, will it enable me to promote my own interests? Or, if I join this political pressure group and help them in their game to defeat a common enemy, will it help me in advancing the interests of my employer so that I can climb the career ladder and so earn more money? Identifying the games of power and position being played is a necessary step in formulating courses of action. However, in playing the games effectively, even if exploiting them for ulterior purposes, means that the games remain as necessary instruments for personal, or particular gain. Radical research needs to go deeper into the under-lying conflicts in order to mobilise the inclusion of difference. Only at the level of creative play can allegiance to sides be suspended in order to enable the reframing needed to include all as equals.

Each game, therefore, configures the field of the visible, audible or otherwise perceptible. Hence, a necessary step in designing radical research is to obtain descriptions of the multiple perceptual fields faced by a subject, S and how that subject seeks to fulfil their desires, satisfy their needs and interests and form their projects in one or more fields. What are the conflicts faced by the subject in doing this? It is here that the seed of doubt, the scepticism as to the belief in meta-narratives that is the necessary step to that freedom of thought that is pro-ductive of alternative ways of seeing emerges and thus provides the contest necessary to the debates concerning freedom and the forms of governance appro-priate to underpinning freedom. How then can one open this space for critique, freedom and action?

Opening the space for radical methodologies

Radical research has, as its goal, action to bring about desired states of affairs. To do this requires insights into the current and 'normal' practices that comprise a given state of affairs. First then, there are those questions that seek to paint a picture of the 'normal', the everyday experiences and the ways people talk about those experiences. Where a questionnaire may cover the responses of large numbers of people to standardised questions, only getting up close to people, talking with them, being alongside them as they go about their lives, learning their histories, listening to their hopes, their frustrations, their successes, their failures – only then can their forms of association, their identifications with communities and the pervasive structures and processes through which power is exercised be mapped. It is right from the first moments of proposing to do research that the space for radical methodologies either opens up or closes down. Research is a provocation to the extent that it questions. It is a hysterical moment in that the voice of authority has to account for itself, just as spaces for marginal, excluded and alternative accounts are set alongside those who habitually command. In Figure 9.6, the researcher seeks to occupy the place of S, in order to gain insight into the multiple surfaces of social, cultural, political inscription as described by a given individual whether during interviews or in casual conversation or in observed interactions with others. Following the principle of inclusivity, the radical-research task is to increase the range of voices to be included at every stage of the research. Each phase of a research proposal can be designed with this in mind. Take, for example, a typical pattern that moves from defining the reasons for the research through to data collection, analysis and the production of outcomes – a structure that could be elaborated to include the typical features of 'normal research' as follows:

Phase 1: Reasons to start: (a) curiosity, (b) professional interests, (c) political engagement, (d) responding to invitations to bid – that is, developing the broad idea for the research

Whatever reason sets the research process in motion, there is always the opportunity to embed radical principles in its conduct.

Possible foci of the research aims

- *theory*: developing, extending or testing theory, producing new information and insights relating to substantive areas as, for example, sexism in the workplace or the training of professionals or youth unemployment;
- *substantive findings*: extending knowledge, for example, about specific social issues, areas of professional interests, cultural issues and so on;
- *applied research*: implementing an innovation, engaging in developmental actions, researching one's own practice in order to change it in some way;
- *evaluation*: determining from a variety of points of view the extent to which some course of action has achieved desired outcomes, as in the successful implementation of an innovation like a new teaching strategy or the introduction of information technology in medical decision-making.

There is an essential tension implicit in each category of aim between the universalistic demands of explicit or implicit theory and the particularistic, historically specific circumstances under which data is collected, whether for the purposes of developing or testing theory. Each category of aim is thus vulnerable to and exploitable by the strategies of metonymic play and hegemonic appropriation as described in this and earlier chapters. What are the alternative, implicit meanings of the keywords that compose the aims? Can they be employed to mobilise change and development?

Reviewing the debates

The tension that is implicit between universal claims and particular individuals and their circumstances can be elaborated by identifying who is arguing against who and why in the theoretical, methodological and substantive literatures. How does each 'side' found their arguments, upon what epistemological, ontological, ethical, political principles? Can the key terms of each side be opened to metonymic play? Are there hidden conflicts covered over by the key terms that can be opened up as a basis for reconfiguration?

Identifying the issues

Each side in the debates promote their particular interests and describe what they consider to be at issue. Are the issues the issues of power, or of the 'street', the 'crowd', the 'rabble', the multitude, the people, the marginal, the excluded, the 'invisible'? Is there an implicit vision of community or social order under-pinning each side that acts as the universalising principle to incorporate individuals as members who play their part in the whole? Is there a principle of inclusivity or of restriction?

Exploring the alternative arguments

What is at stake for whom, if the arguments of one side are adopted rather than another? That is, who wins, who loses? What happens if the rules are modified? What's at stake for whom when rules are modified?

Identifying the rules at play

When there is something to win or something to lose, this establishes the game-like quality of the relationships. What are the implicit rules of the range of games that can be played?

Identifying the range of actors

The actors involved in each identifiable game that criss-crosses the debates and the descriptions of research field sites relevant to the aims define the game-relevant dramatis personae. Who is left out? What's at stake for who if they were to be included?

Identifying potential entry points into the 'field'

From the literature, general indications of roles typical of given field sites can be identified. What kinds of roles have been employed by previous researchers to provide entry points? What strategies were used to access these individuals? From the literature, the spaces and places where events take place can be identified. Where are the best places to 'hang out', to engage in conversations, to watch what goes on, what roles are adopted, who does what with who for what reasons? Which ones are central stage? Which are marginal? And which are 'outside'?

Phase 2: Targeting points of entry and framing the ethical protocol

The choice of actual entry points depends on the scale and nature of the study. Each entry point is like a doorway opening up to other spaces, places and actors who, in turn, open up to other spaces, places and actors and so on, as in the mapping of an intentional network as described in Chapters 6 and 7. Whether the field site is one classroom, one office, one shopping mall or any other single site, or whether there are multiple sites or a whole community, or multinational business or system or, indeed, state or international system – the local stands in a relationship to the global. Entry points can be chosen to provide a:

- local focus – the level of the street, the household, the shop, the housing estate;
- global focus – the level from the top of the hierarchy, the overview of everything;
- local–global focus – the dynamic interaction between the two where the local impacts on the global as the global impacts on the local;
- community–individual focus – the tension between the freedom of the individual and the demands of living within a community structure.

Phase 3: Getting in

- Negotiating access: access to people and places involves negotiating the reasons as to why the researcher is present and behaving in particular ways with particular purposes. How this is done always depends upon circumstances and the aims of the research. The negotiating process involves inscribing the reasons for being with people and places relevant to the research into the agendas that prevail in the given social circumstances. How does the reason for the researcher to be around make sense to those encountered? Assent to being around then depends on trust.
- Building trust, ethical, legal and political issues, developing the witness status: without trust, the views of the witness are worthless. There is the trust of those being studied as well as the trust of those who read the research. How is that

trust in each case to be built? Researching dangerous gangs is not the same as researching classrooms. Interviewing the powerful is not the same as interviewing employees. In each case, the trust necessary for access to information, observing interactions is constructed differently. How are threats to the security of the researcher and the researched to be managed in each case? In each case, there is an ethics and a politics to consider. It is an issue of ensuring inclusion in the scene of action. What is at stake for each individual involved? Ethically people should not be exploited, their dignity diminished, their safety compromised. Following and listening to the actions of others may transgress not only the boundaries of the ethical but also the legal. For reasons of politics, ethics and legality, there are reasons why people may want to cover up, deceive and impose some views rather than others. Being a witness that is trusted, bearing insights, information, interpretations, knowledge that are to be accepted as valid, reliable and objective, means negotiating the complexities of these issues in ways that can be accounted for when writing up.

Phase 4: Exploring power and the labyrinth

Witness as wanderer

The researcher, like the individuals met throughout the research, are witnesses who experience the world about over time. Each thing encountered, each occurrence, each individual met is articulated as a happening, as sequences in an anecdote, as elements in an event that can be attested to by the witness. The histories of people, places, things and events that are composed provide the material for structuring and making sense of everyday life. The witness as wanderer provides the diachronic view, elaborating intentional networks that unfold with every meeting.

Witness with god's-eye view

Witnesses, researchers as well as those being studied, adopting the position of power claim to have the grand plan, the theory of everything, the synchronic view where all spreads out paradigmatically below them. It enables the sense of coverage as well as creating the conditions for later destabilisation through metonymic processes.

In-depth and breadth of coverage strategies

Breadth of coverage is comparable to the vertical axis of language, the synchronic, paradigmatic. It produces the god's-eye view, the panoramic scope of the project. In-depth insight is comparable to the diachronic axis of articulation, of negotiating how things hang together over time. Both are necessary in the development of case studies, ethnographies, action research and evaluations.

- Data for the coverage of the range of sites, the range of people involved can be obtained both qualitatively and quantitatively through the use of interviews, written responses to questions and through more open ended forms of recording views and experiences, e.g., diaries, records of conversations, memos, e-mail correspondence, recording of everyday events. The object is to develop a synchronic view, like a map, that provides an overview of material and conceptual relationships through which the everyday is structured by power.
- Data for in-depth studies can be obtained from interviews, conversations and observing and recording the practices, interactions and processes involved as people negotiate the structuring of their everyday lives. The focus is on the process, what happens over time as people make sense of their experiences by asserting their rights, realising or compromising their power, their talents, their potential as *potestas* in the relation to power.

Through case studies and ethnographies, the dynamics of the synchronic and diachronic can be elaborated, covering and describing the in-depth interactions of the dramatis personae, mapping the multidimensional spaces of their intentional networks, their beliefs, their interests, their values, their practices, the events that take place, the dramas and the spaces and places that comprise the scenes of action, the built environment, the stealth architecture and so on that comprise their everyday sense of realities and through which they articulate their sense identity and community and formulate their personal projects.

Trust as validity, reliability, objectivity and attesting to the relation between the general and the particular

Trust as validity increases in terms of the overdetermination of viewpoints on 'the same thing'. Each viewpoint articulates 'something' through the intentional relations formed between subjects and objects. Mapping intentional networks that compose the sense of the everyday provides the basis for a triangulation of viewpoints that construct what is particular, generalisable and, indeed, universal. The intentional network provides the conditions under which validity, reliability and objectivity are established. The more viewpoints that co-determine particular subjects and objects the more embedded and reified as 'things', as structures, as processes, as 'identities', they become. As such, the intentional network becomes the knowing subject whose forms of articulating the world about is the data, the observable givens of the research which then becomes the basis for analysis.

Phase 5: Analysis, deconstruction, representation, reconfiguration

Analysis of intentional networks may reveal multiple groupings that are distinct and organise themselves in particular ways to stand apart from other groups. Do they have different conceptions of what counts as 'true', 'valid', 'real', 'objective', 'general', 'universal'? What binds them? What are the conditions under which they may dissolve, modify, transform? Analysis implies deconstruction in the sense that the givenness of data is already a social construction through processes of witnessing that are in turn a construction of intentional networks that change over time. Hence, there is a tension, a dynamic, a dialectic, between the synchronic impulse to analyse structures as if given timelessly and the process through which everyday life is articulated over time. The play of association between the heterogeneous individuals of everyday life stands ready to deconstruct, collapse and reconfigure the scene of the representable – the visible, the audible, the in-some-way perceptible. Through the dynamics of analysis, therefore, the givens of the intentional networks can be reconfigured to include the excluded and to identify the figures of the radical:

- the play of doubt and suspension of belief – Chapters 1, 2, 3 and 9;
- the fabulous as 'surprise', as the 'real' beyond the categories – Chapter 5;
- the almost nothing that means so much – Chapter 6;
- the 'schizophrenic' and the 'paranoid' – Chapters 3, 6 and 8;
- the 'in-betweens', the liminal, the contested spaces, the mediating 'flesh' – Chapter 8;
- the edges and the work that takes place at the edges – the parergonal – Chapter 3;
- the metonymic – Chapters 3, 8 and 9;
- the catachreses and syntheses – Chapters 5, 6, 7 and 8;
- the chiasmus – Chapters 5 and 10;
- the repetitions – Chapters 8, 9 and 10;
- the rhythm(analysis) – Chapter 8;
- the figural – Chapters 5 and 6
- texture and the transpositional, the intertextual, the deconstructive – Chapters 2, 5 and 10.

Through such rhetorical analysis, both the 'normal' and the spaces of *the* political can be explored. This then leads to the possibility of action being different from the 'normal' sequences imposed by power. In order to include the excluded, what has to change? How do resources need to be reconfigured? What structures – conceptual or social mechanisms, procedures – need to be put into place and which removed? What cultural practices are involved? What political arrangements will drive inclusivity into every sphere of social life? What is the focus for *the* political?

Phase 6: Action

Action is about the realisation of ideas, through the production of desired outcomes, by adopting appropriate practices and employing appropriate resources (cf. Schostak 2006). Including the excluded becomes the ethical and political justification for action. From the analysis phase, a design for action that democratically includes different viewpoints can be constructed. Action research may be, for example, designed to facilitate the robust embedding of democratic mechanisms into everyday life, enabling the excluded to be included. At every level of decision-making, the mechanisms and procedures required to ensure the inclusion of viewpoints otherwise excluded by power are put in place. Such action thus generates the conditions for the emergence of *the* political as the point of challenge to the 'normal'. Its implementation therefore enters into the game-like sphere of contestation where political interests drive the pedagogies of everyday life. This then raises the need for an evaluation that is able to explore the range of agendas at play and so describe and inform decision-making about the political dimensions of the impacts of the project.

Phase 7: Evaluation

The extent to which the action is implemented can be researched as an ongoing process in order to identify unanticipated threats, obstacles and opportunities in the achievement of desired outcomes. To do this, the evaluation involves reviewing and articulating all the processes in the phases from 1 to 6 within the evaluation design. It involves the process of including in decision-making processes the voices of those the research phases have identified as being politically dispossessed in relation to those who have the power to voice their interests and make decisions about social and material realities. It particularly involves exploring the structures that either facilitate, or obstruct or transform action (see Chapter 5).

Phase 8: Dissemination

Dissemination is not only about what impacts has the actions brought about, lessons learnt, what still needs to be done. It involves a spreading of the cultural practices set in train by the radical research process as well as action to raise awareness of conditions and action for people to engage in educational relationships with each other.

In design overall, the radical principle is that people, even very young ones (Schostak 1988, 1989) and those considered to have learning difficulties (Woods and Shears 1986), can deliberate, can take the standpoint of the other and formulate representative opinions. For that reason, everyday communities, organisations, institutions and systems must include in public spaces all voices if they are to ensure the continuance of the democratic imagination, the imagination of the potential for informing judgement, decision and action concerning the allocation of resources for all. It is a matter of dissemination, inscribing in social realities and that is the wider process of writing up.

Chapter 10

W/ri(gh)ting fashions

It's simple really: you say what you're going to say; you say it; then you say what you've said. Three chances to fix the message in terms of beginnings, middles and endings. It is the rhetoric of clarity, of simple truths, simply told. You set up the problem, why this is an important problem, say how you're going to write about it, the issues to be resolved and the strategy to be used in resolving it. Then, in the middle, the problem is analysed into its parts, the importance of each part made clear and the evidence or arguments required for overcoming each part of the problem is marshalled logically until in the conclusion a drawing together can be made, summarising the process through which each part of the problem has been fully examined and all the issues resolved. Of course, there are variations. The aim may instead be to unpack what had seemed to be a watertight solution to show that the problems, in fact, remain unsolved. Or, the aim may be to show that previous researchers had attended to the wrong problem or irrelevant questions. Or the message might be a story that enters an ongoing dispute, or a set of disagreements in order to stake a claim in the debate – perhaps an airing of an offence, whether real or imagined, is the intention. Possibly the aim of the writer is to illustrate differences between this thing and that thing, this concept and that concept. In each case, the same writing strategy can be employed: say what you're going to say; say it; then say what you've said. The message is conceived as in some way 'fixed' or, at least sufficiently fixed, as to be received in such a way that the reader receives what the writer intended. In its traditional sense, writing implies both a notion of authorship (addresser[s]) and of audience (addressee[s]). It has content and it has context: it tells a story, no matter whether as a text it is designated as fiction or non-fiction. The addresser desires to convey some message to a world as audience.

Addressing another is a provocative act. Nowhere more so than in research arenas where publications, essays, theses and reports of all kinds call into battle readers as actors who make interpretations, who take positions for or against the truth, accuracy, plausibility, intelligibility, sanity of the text. Text seems more a place of squabbles over *real* meanings than a sanctuary for 'truth'. This parading of positions over the truth of a text invokes a catwalk of intellectual, cultural, social, political fashions. Each calls to an audience: look at me; take notice; my interpretation is right. But where in all this is the writer's intention? Is the intention one of a betrayer of intimacies, or one of an act of witnessing? Or is it to show a commitment to norms and traditions? Or is it to subvert the authorised 'verities' upon which inequalities are founded?

The presentation of research is not a programmable rite of passage from the processing of data to their production as 'findings'. During the lifetime of a research project, many records are produced, a typical pile includes: field notes, research diaries, tape-recorded interviews, video-recordings and official documents deemed pertinent to the research brief. Resulting from the processing of data, there will also be numerous transcripts of taped recordings and drafts of analysed data all in various stages of 'completion' or, perhaps, 'cohesion' might well constitute a better word. All these writings are then somehow put together in the final report that is submitted to the funding body. The fragmentary nature of the various data-types has disappeared in the apparent articulation of the final report. None of the violence and anguish of the passage from fragmentary writing to apparent articulation remains visible in the final report. What is already becoming evident is that writing is not unitary and each incorporated difference stalls the advent of a solitary unchallengeable reading. Each difference makes a difference to the whole, and each reading adds a difference of interpretation, a new voice to take into account, where for Derrida, the

> gesture is to move beyond the everyday understanding of writing in order to postulate a 'writing' more fundamental to signifying practices in general, a 'writing' that is the condition of all forms of expression, whether scriptural, vocal or otherwise. Such a 'writing' is precisely an '*écriture avant la lettre*' or 'archi-écriture', as [he] calls it.
>
> (Johnson 1993: 66)

In other words, it is 'a double concept of writing' inasmuch as it incorporates 'actual writing in the form of marks, script, of texts and material symbols' and also invokes the 'notion that the existence of texts, scripts and marks' emerge 'through the possibility of more general writing whereby we are able to think or imagine other systems, other languages, other contexts because we hold the concept that writing is not reducible to this or to that instance of writing' (Schostak 2005: II, 98, Note 4). This is the context in which writing becomes something other than writing under normative conditions. Rather than remaining gridlocked, it takes on the sense of the radical, opening up other horizons, creating the liminal spaces where contests of meaning take place – how are these to be 'captured'? Writing as the art of 'capturing' and incorporating differences recalls the emancipatory strategy of radical democracy where conflicting rights and powers are equated on the public stage of community decision-making. And each incorporation of a new voice marks a beginning. Together they comprise the essential conflicts that pose the need for some form of reconciliation.

Beginnings

Writing is the search for and deferral of origins – it is *here* that it all begins . . .
Such a beginning can only be baptised at the point when a reconfiguration of the
field enables the backward gaze that names events. It is that point where conflicts
appear to have been resolved already, right at the beginning. Beginnings can be
anywhere:

C2: Oh so many things are going on and I think you see a patient, you see a
problem, you click through some ideas and you choose the appropriate one
for her in that situation.

C1: You make decisions within, when you look at the letter, before the patient
comes in the door, when you look at their age, their weight, their urine test,
you're making decisions as they come through the door, as they sit down,
you've made probably, I don't know, fifty-odd, sixty-odd decisions by
the time they've sat down and before you've even opened your mouth to them.
There's a lot of contextualising, a lot of non-verbal decision-making goes
on right from that level. And, of course, you know, if it's a very good GP's
letter, you've often got 90 per cent towards the diagnosis, you're into the
context and the problem about the diagnosis rather than what's the diagnosis
itself. So there's all sorts and bits have gone on in your brain that it's very
difficult to describe that have happened before, you know, you open your
mouth. And I reckon that ninety-nine times out of 100 you have made most
of the diagnostic-type decisions within a minute of the patient coming into
the room.

C3: Without a doubt.

C1: And the rest of it is.

C2: It's confirming.

C1: Yes, it's confirming what you've done and also making sure that the patient
understands.

(Taped CasE core-team meeting transcript, 29 October 2001)

The person who walks through the door has already been pre-figured. Only
because there have been recognisably similar cases before can ideas be 'clicked
through' and 'fifty-odd, sixty-odd decisions' be made 'by the time they've sat
down and before you've even opened your mouth to them.' The whole sequence
from beginning to end has already been made and remade 1,000 times. The
patient can be read not because he or she is *this* particular individual, has walked
through the door, but because others bearing similar signs – or symptoms – have
walked through the doors, not only of *this* consultant, but also of many consultants
in many places throughout the world. Within this brief account are many possible
beginnings for writing:

1. The focus for this paper is the question of how experienced practitioners, such
    as consultants, make decisions and produce diagnoses. Data will be drawn

from the verbal accounts of consultants as they reflect upon the decision-making process . . .

2.   Medical consultations are not just about making diagnoses, they involve treating clients as people who need to feel cared for and need to understand the nature of their problem. This book will draw on the accounts of consultants describing the process of consultation . . .

3.   Semiotics can provide insights into the processes through which the body is read in medical contexts. This thesis . . . and so on.

These prosaic beginnings drawing differently on the same transcript extract contain the seeds of possible papers, books, reports, theses . . . Perhaps as an illustration, the first chapter or section will use the transcript to illustrate the central question and introduce the process through which the issues set in train by the transcript will be explored through the collection of further data, setting it into context with relevant literature describing the core arguments underlying the relevant theories of expert decision-making processes, or of client consultant relations or of the semiotics of the body in medical contexts. The same extract can be used as a surface to inscribe multiple agendas. A sense of the potential for conflict appears through the very process of writing. Writing itself introduces a dynamic, a dynamic that can be illustrated through a play of sounds and letter arrangements.

The five-letter word 'write' is phonetically pronounced as 'rite' and also contains within itself the four-letter word 'rite' with its connotations of ritual and rite of passage. 'Write' and 'rite' themselves are phonetically close to yet another five-letter word, namely 'right', whose meanings range from correctness, through directives for direction and onto legal powers, concerning such diverse commodities as property ownership to the more tenuous concepts of ethics pertaining to human rights. The word 'fashions' in this chapter heading is ambiguous inasmuch as it refers to the fact that styles of writing change over time, affected as they are by historical, cultural, social and epistemic contexts. The addresser fashions the writing to a contemporaneous style that appeals to the of-the-moment desires of the targeted addressee. The strategy also evokes a sense of at-homeness (see discussion in Chapter 2) – whether that is in terms of offering the reassurance that the addressee is thinking along the right lines or in terms of identifying points of contest that act in a certain cathartic manner. Yet, it is also the case that the positioning of the word 'fashion' in this sentence could have yet another meaning, suggesting that an effect of writing itself is quite literally, and not just figuratively, an act of fashioning. Writing delineates as it fashions the representable. But drawing the line is not enough. For it to count, it must count again and again. Pointing to a tree and saying 'tree' in order to cut its image out of the blooming and buzzing of sensory experience once is unacceptable; the saying must be a baptism that inaugurates the repeatability of saying and pointing and the tree emerging, delineated, underlined. But: 'There are lines which are monsters [. . .] A line by itself has no meaning; a second one is necessary to give expression to meaning. Important law. (Delacroix)' (Derrida 1978: 15).

A line must refer to another line, even if it is only itself repeated later on. A line accumulates content through the very repeatability of the act of recognising it as being in relation to itself and to other lines. The line that does not repeat in the voices and experiences of perceivers is dead – a monster.

If a second line is necessary to express meaning, does it imply an entire chain of lines all saying the same thing reaching relentlessly back for ever? How do such chains act? Through *rigid* repetition of the same, does meaning die, interred in its coffin of forced definitions, becoming monsters to haunt the living? Or do they spin off with a life of their own in tangential and elliptical movements of possibilities, just like Derrida's reference to Merleau-Ponty's statement that: 'My own words take me by surprise and teach me what I think' (Derrida 1978: 11). Therefore: 'Meaning must await being said or written in order to inhabit itself, and in order to become, by differing from itself, what it is: meaning' (Derrida 1978: 11).

In the surprise of meaning is the awakening of a beginning, an opening of the eyes, an intake of breath and the telling begins. The repetition that underlies *differing* is in this sense, the first figure of rhetoric as the art of fashioning or delineating the audible, the visible, the perceptible. As such, writing is coterminous with the research process from the moment ideas begin to coalesce into a direction to be taken, a course of actions to be pursued. Beginnings are pursued and progressively fixed as:

- aims/objectives/purposes;
- research questions;
- background;
- perspectives;
- methodology;
- design.

The rhetorical work of a beginning is to explore the possibilities for surprise as a means of making manifest what is thinkable by individuals in the context(s) of communities of debate. This work is not a completable phase in a linear sequence. Rather, it is a point of origin, a centre around which reflections swirl, ever widening, ever displacing the source. Each reflection upon emerging data, each encounter with new viewpoints brings a return to the beginning, seeing it in a new light, shifting the context and thus bringing changes to the sense of a beginning. Each reflection on the elements that compose the beginning is accomplished as an engagement with otherness, a welcoming of voices, a recognition of their gift of difference. Telling the story of the beginnings, with whatever meanings emerge, entails their representation by words. The writer selects the words and arranges them for the telling (calling forth of meaning) because the manner of telling cannot be neglected. Through rhetorics, the patterned arrangements of the telling in writing can provoke, persuade, name, seduce, fascinate, coerce, threaten and so on, and each one contains within itself the possibilities of dominance and mastery, whether by addresser, say, through the seductive use of language, or by the addressee by imposing interpretations. The addressee, of course, is searching for a story – and an argument is a story, an arrangement of first this and then that over time – although, to be sure, the contexts that both give rise to the desire for a story and momentarily satisfy that desire, before the lack reasserts itself, will vary greatly. Research and its writing thus circulates around the conflictual dynamic of addresser and addressee.

How will the aims/objectives/purposes of the research be read? Will they seem trivial? Will the reader pick up on meanings of the composing words that have been overlooked during the research? Do the discussions in later chapters really address the stated aims, satisfy the objectives and fulfil the overall purposes? Or should I make modifications to them, fit them in with the later discussions? Or should I play another kind of game? Perhaps the demands for consistency are too constricting. Perhaps the aim should be to show that aims cannot be sustained. But that too is an aim – albeit ironic. Suppose this statement of objectives:

1. *To explore and validate the model produced by the previous study*

   a. Our extended sample of young men (see Methods below) corroborated the previous model's basic principles by confirming that boys from a range of backgrounds are, indeed, attempting to build positive identities and improve personal wellbeing by using all the social resources accessible to them – even those (such as the peer group) that can appear negative to a casual observer. Furthermore, this extended sample, plus the increased timescale, enabled the incorporation of an extra dimension missing from the original model. This third dimension concerned the boys' relationships with society – or at least those facets that they encountered personally. This dimension turned a binary model into a triangular conceptualisation (see Results below).

2. *To turn the model into a practical instrument for educational interventions*

   a. Our conclusions have relevance for all those concerned with the education of boys, and our findings are being distilled into a booklet written for boys and young men that will allow them to share usually unvoiced first-hand opinions, ideas and feelings. This will also be a valuable adjunct to educational initiatives. The booklet is intended to be self-funding but will also be available online and will be publicised via the Sex Education Forum.

3. *To extend our previous methodology by incorporating young men into the study as commentators and interpreters of data*

   a. The project was methodologically experimental in order (a) to access sensitive, fleeting and sometimes unspoken data, and (b) to include

> boys and young men as commentators and interpreters of data: their own and other people's. While recognising that school is a practical starting location for this type of research, we wished to root the study as far as possible in the context and understandings of boys' culture. Some experiments were successful – especially our use of an integrated photographic methodology – others less so. However, even our relative methodological failures increased our understanding of young male culture and will aid further research practice. These insights are discussed in the Methods section below.
>
> (Schostak and Walker 2000)

The first aim or objective was to develop work from a study previously funded by the same body. The general purpose was to develop and test its validity. A new beginning, as it were, for an already extensive history. As a variant on the bald stating of aims, elements of design, methodology, theory development, outcomes conclusions, self-evaluations are already sketched into each aim. If nothing else, it rhetorically gives the sense of a tightly conceived study that had kept to its purposes and recognised its limitations. It contains the seeds of the whole story right at the beginning. It evokes a sense of work accomplished, even an accumulation of 'knowledge'. Nothing of the messiness of the research process is evident. Its purpose was to say, this is what we wanted to do, this is what we did and this is what we accomplished. The audience for this kind of research was imagined as wanting the sense of the accumulation of knowledge, the progressive refining of theory, the thoughtful application of methodologies. There is a sense of 'normal science' about it. Yet there is a seed of the radical in its methodology: 'to include boys and young men as commentators and interpreters of data: their own and other people's'. The voices of the other are incorporated into the methodology, not as the researchers speaking on behalf of the boys, but as speakers with their own rights of expression. It is a small act. It can be argued that it is not really sufficient to bring about real change, real emancipations. However, it is a beginning and beginnings disseminate in unpredictable ways.

The dissemination of practices that make change in peoples' lives is always a return to beginnings. Evaluations in particular provide the means to return to beginnings and explore whether anything has changed as a result of practical innovations in everyday life. Recalling the parenting course set up by the housing trust described in Chapters 1 and 2, the final report to them described its focusing questions:

> The research has sought to explore the following questions: What are the experiences of the courses? To what extent do the courses address "teenage nuisance" and parents' "ability to cope"? Are simultaneous courses valued? What is the nature of the involvement/participation of teenagers in the community? How do schools link with such initiatives? Is there an impact in the community?

This evaluation has largely focussed on the first three questions as the time and scope of the research has made it problematic for the latter three to be addressed in any significant way. However we are confident that our findings give some constructive and useful insights into some wider issues and implications for the course.

(Pearce et al. 2006)

This was a very small project having a very limited resource to fund data collection that focused upon one course in a large estate. It was necessary to scale down the expectation of the funders both in terms of what the report and the course could achieve. The questions pick up on the central concerns of the Trust and the residents who voiced concerns. A change was desired. But what was the best way of accomplishing it? The course addressed a sense of wrong and the supposed cause of that wrong.

Addressing 'wrongs' is the radical heart of emancipatory research methodologies and educational practice. It is an act that questions prevailing social, cultural, political and economic conditions. It is a return to the beginning: what sort of community is desired? The response is of two kinds:

1. reform from within: the questions seek to solve problems in the system, or 'go back to fundamentals';
2. transform externally: the questions seek to reveal the fatal flaws in the system in order to open the way for alternatives.

The choice can be illustrated in relation to the inequality of power vested in individuals as workers in relation to multinationals as employers. The great multinationals that dominate the world scene are able to move their sites of operation easily from one country to another in order, for example, to seek the lowest costs of labour, or a better tax regime. However, for labour, there are strict immigration controls. Hence, when a major company pulls out of a particular region, communities can be devastated, finding it difficult to move from country to country in search of work. All this is well known. If this is considered unfair, there are two opposing strategies in response. The first accepts that the current market and political framework, while problematic in its details, is nevertheless right in its overall rationality. Thus, strategies need to be employed to correct the mistakes and so reform the market and its political frameworks. The second judges that the current market and political framework is fundamentally wrong and needs to be overturned because it inevitably reduces the complex, needs, demands and interests of people to measurable market values, as well as reducing people to being functions in a system. Both strategies can claim to be based on a notion of fairness. The first deems that if the market philosophy is correctly applied then political arrangements that support the market most fairly allocates resources to people's needs and demands. The second may seek alternatives to the market precisely because it is judged incapable of allocating wealth fairly and contributing to the full humanity of people.

If all is fundamentally well with the current vision of society, then communities and research methodologies need only learn how to implement that vision. However, if that vision is to be fundamentally challenged, in order to be overturned, then alternative forms of community structure need to be incorporated. Methodologies and knowledge predicated on all being well cannot logically find within themselves the way of critiquing the fundamental assumption without which they could not exist. This is what is at the back of Kuhn's notion of scientific revolutions. A scientist who sees the world according to a particular paradigm is incapable of seeing it radically differently, that is, according to a new paradigm. Hence, Kuhn's example of scientists who saw the world within the paradigm of phlogiston theory could not see the world according to Dalton's atomistic theory. The former disappeared when its last proponents simply died. However, the problems of communities cannot wait that long – although, of course, the violence of revolutions may offer a speedier end. That apart, how can the wrong be addressed in a way that peacefully incorporates the voice of the people who feel wronged so that the community itself can be reconfigured?

The housing trust had adopted an innovatory approach by responding to the voices of residents. However, to go further would require an act of embedding the voices across the estate in its daily management – a strategy that would involve other agencies as well as the Trust: social services, police, schools, local government, health and so on – in short, as previously discussed, what Rancière called the 'police', the power to impose upon community a relation of parts to the whole. In the return to the beginning enabled by the evaluation, it is this structure that becomes the focus for emancipatory practice. Does the course merely reinforce the policing structure, or is there a radical seed? How can such a question be posed?

Writing up involves posing questions and writing up the research design in the context of a background of circumstances that are framed under the normal assumptions and expectations of funders, policy-makers and the institutions that seek to maintain the prevailing order in order to get the funding in the first place. Describing the background that led to the research being funded is a way of inscribing research agendas onto the agendas of organisations that essentially form an hegemonic alliance maintaining the sense of each part relating to a whole. As discussed throughout the book, such hegemonies contain within them the lines of fracture that can bring about a collapse or a dynamic reconfiguration of the social and political in everyday life. What then are the faultlines the research can address? These can only emerge if the design provides the data-gathering strategies by which to uncover them. Thus, the summary framework in Chapter 9 incorporates multiple views, the inclusion of mechanisms of debate between different 'sides', the presentation of alternative arguments and so on. How these are incorporated into specific projects depends on audience and aims. Take, for example, an illustration from an evaluation of an EU information-technology project involving a large consortium of partners in industry and in universities:

This evaluation final report is envisaged as giving a broad view of the project which will both complement and supplement the representations offered within reports from the different partners. It offers an alternative perspective, one which came from within the project but was outside of the frame in which the major business of the project happened. This major business, which was to produce a demonstrator designed and realised in practice to show how the access and delivery of language learning and teaching materials could be enhanced telematically, needed, it was thought, to be further understood and its relevance to wider issues of how such projects operate explored.

How, then, did the formative evaluation contribute to this broad task? By collecting data to inform the key question which is seen as 'How does one formulate strategies to marshal information to produce usable knowledge for decision makers acting within continually changing contexts?' Three kinds of solution suggest themselves:

i.   the creation of an organisational management and co-ordinating system of mechanisms and procedures
ii.   the creation of a technical solution comprising communications systems and software tools
iii.   the development of a culture of sharing, dialogue and mutual education concerning knowledge, skills and competencies.

(Schostak and Beauchamp 1999)

The three solutions are not, of course, mutually exclusive. The critical one, however, is the third. It emerged throughout the life of the project and was as much a conclusion as a beginning. From the end point, the beginning point could better be seen. And the messiness of the middle period – for it can now be called that – could be seen in its provocative and developmental dimensions.

Middles

Of course, it might be protested that this is just a reinvention of the history to fit the facts. However, that presumes history revealing itself simply, clearly, unambiguously. Rather, as discussed in Chapter 2, there is a dynamic between synchronic order and diachronic difference, where difference negotiates, subverts and even collapses boundaries and hierarchical orders of meaning. Writing establishes its strategic history of such dynamics as between the synchronic and the diachronic. The synchronic has its list of contents and its index – its grid of key organising categories internal to the work, as well as its references outwards that is its marshalled links to other texts, other sources that stand as grounding points, points of authority. The diachronic is the time for the dynamic of writing and reading, its contingent journeyings that can threaten the security and breach the containing walls of boundaries. It is where planned designs become challenged by alternative ways of exploring the data. It is where the reading of a book and the

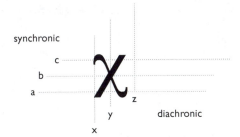

synchronic

Figure 10.1 The play of design and
de-sign

citing of an extract may make the data explode with meanings not previously recognised or allow data to emerge that had previously been invisible. The middle is the liminal ground of transition, of transposition, of deconstruction that opens up possibilities, of contestation that transforms. It is the place of multiple, shifting crossings, not the fixed grid of an x and y axis but the slipperiness of a chiasmus that evolves over time (see Figure 10.1).

Figure 10.1 suggests the shifting of the grid-like frame of the synchronic as it evolves under the impact of the diachronic. Key organising concepts, say, as defined along the a and x axis that seemed so certain at the beginning of a project may crumble in the face of the play of ideas, the deconstruction of terms, the emergence of alternative ways of seeing, so transposing to the c and z axis. The piles of transcripts, photos, videos, documents, artefacts which seem so threatening to the security of safe categories may take shape under new emergent orders of framing. Traces of the play may be left in the lists of contents or often more so in the subheadings of chapters and sections where words are chosen for their ambiguity, their potential shattering into multiple meanings in order to provide the means of elaborating ideas, making surprising connections as well as providing the sense of analysis, the breaking into ordered parts that cover the explorations necessary for a particular issue or problem. Or the traces may be framed in terms of the work-a-day vocabularies of professional discourses in order to pass for normal. However, their energy remains in what the passages of texts that elaborate each heading and subheading. Here are the parts and chapter headings of a research report (Bedford et al. 1995):

TYDE Team Core Members 1
TYDE Senior Team Members 1
Secretarial support 1
Acknowledgement 2
Note 2

C H A P T E R O N E The research background and perspective 3

PART ONE Historical background and transition **15**

C H A P T E R　T W O　A history of pre-registration undergraduate
programmes in nursing and midwifery 17

C H A P T E R　T H R E E　Institutional transition and diversity a
context for learning 25

PART TWO The voice of experience **55**

C H A P T E R　F O U R　Planning the professional curriculum 57

C H A P T E R　F I V E　The curriculum in action – organisation and
resources for learning 87

C H A P T E R　S I X　Resources for quality in clinical learning 129

C H A P T E R　S E V E N　Creating the conditions for clinical settings
as learning environments 147

C H A P T E R　E I G H T　Experiences of learning in Higher
Education 179

C H A P T E R　N I N E　Monitoring the degree programmes 197

C H A P T E R　T E N　Student finances and part time work – some
implications for learning 209

C H A P T E R　E L E V E N　A different kind of student – motivations,
pressures and support 225

C H A P T E R　T W E L V E　The graduates 243

PART THREE Professional education in a degree programme **279**

C H A P T E R　T H I R T E E N　Concluding reflections on
professional education 281

C H A P T E R　F O U R T E E N　Criteria for a quality undergraduate
degree 309

R E F E R E N C E S 335

The contents are designed to feed into the kinds of debates that the funders need
to undertake with governmental policy-makers as well as the kinds of insights that
university departments need in order to deliver a degree appropriate to the needs

of a profession. The initial task was to research whether training could just as well take place in three years as in four. At the back of the question was the possible threat of closure of four-year degrees, if three-year degrees were found to be cheaper and just as high quality. This, of course, was a politically sensitive question. Each chapter had to pick upon what was at stake in making one decision or the other. It was important to ensure coverage so that no one could say 'Yes, but we're a special case and you never came to research here' or 'You only saw a small and misleading amount of the work we do'. Each chapter heading indicates something of the emergent strategy. The first chapter had to deal with the issue of perspective. The research was qualitative in order to deal with the complexities of a national system. However, qualitative often suggests that it cannot cope with large-scale research – its numbers are small. This is not the case, besides the hundreds of hours of observation across twenty-six universities and their associated clinical areas sites, and the analysis of course documentation, there were 330 interviews:

Introduction

> In presenting a report the temptation is to narrow its focus to a small number of precise questions and key issues, and of course some sort of selection is inevitable. However, the scope of the TYDE project is ambitious, being national in focus and qualitative in method. Its aspiration is to grasp the complexity of the realities faced by educationalists, students, graduates and clinical practitioners. The intention of the project and this report is to ensure that the complexity of the reality is not reduced simply for the ease of making policy decisions or developing management mechanisms and strategies. Nor is it to aid the construction of theoretical models. Rather, the aim is to produce a creative response to the data.
>
> (Bedford et al. 1995: 5)

The rhetoric of the report is to present itself as having had the capacity for coverage as well as in-depth studies of the messiness, complexity and dynamism of the realities of lived practice. Rather than starting with fixed categories of analysis, the object was to let them emerge from what participants considered to be the organising structures of their work. There is, however, a sense of marshalling of such evidence systematically around the core questions of debate, questions identified from interviews, observations, policy papers and steering-group discussions:

> The evidence draws attention to a cluster of issues faced by all degree providers, irrespective of the length of the courses they offer, and documents the attempts which have been made to address these issues. It reveals how, in the course of actually 'delivering' a degree, providers are exploring such questions as:

what does it mean in personal, social and cultural terms to provide or receive
   a *degree level* education?
what are the features which distinguish a *professional* degree from any other?
what are the *organisational* and *management* issues of degree level education
   for professionals ?

The report records attempts to unpack each of these questions and the complex
issues which they raise within the context of the social, political and policy
changes that have characterised the 1980's and 1990's. In doing so it sets the
questions into broader contexts of debate about the implicit and/or explicit
assumptions underlying:

- student and professional learning;
- the rationale for reform;
- the forms of organisation required to deliver education for entry into the
  professions;
- the development of learning environments;
- the development of curricula;
- the professional development of staff;
- the ways in which staff articulate the vision(s) for the development of
  nursing and midwifery;
- change and innovation.

In the process, data has been collected outlining the experiences and critical
reflections of staff, students and graduates as they grapple with the changes
effecting their everyday lives. This provides a rich and unique data base
of contemporary experience in nursing and midwifery. There is too much to
be reported in full. However, the report does attempt to portray key experiences and draw from these the kinds of discourses, implicit structural material
conditions and the theories underlying professional action through which
staff, students and graduates make sense of their experiences, inform their
judgements and resource and organise their practice. It is anticipated that the
experiences and learning portrayed in the report will be of value to those
planning new undergraduate programmes, and those re-validating existing
programmes.

(Bedford et al. 1995: 5–6)

Alongside the sense of ordering, there is the intention to 'produce a creative
response to the data.' Again, this indicates a dynamic that, as in Figure 9.8 shifts
the categories of debate. Together with the detailed analyses, a portrayal of complexity is also needed that enables a creative response from readers who can make
their own connections to the portrayals, comparing and contrasting it with their
own experiences. It is this sense of transposition between the signs on the page

and the experiences of the reader that enables interpretation to take place so that relevance to the reader is defined anew for each reader. Where the sign of design imposes order, the anti-sign of de-sign unchains, releasing the force of signifier and signified to enable the possibility of meaning anew as represented in the shifting axes of Figure 9.8. It is in this emergence of a middle passage, or transition, or transposition that histories emerge, leaving in their wake events, identities, stories and the histories that can be told from a variety of points of view and incorporated into the experiences of readers. By including in portrayals the voices of those who are otherwise excluded, the terrain of debate, the theoretical understandings and what counts as knowledge can be reconfigured. It is here that the role of the trusted witness is vital.

For the histories to include otherwise 'inaudible' voices, trust, as discussed in Chapter 2, has to be established:

> If we are to take Lee's definition of sensitive research as 'research which potentially poses a substantial threat to those who are or have been involved in it' (1993, p.4), then this research demanded a high level of trust on the part of the interviewees; trust that the researcher would listen to them, and would not report their words back to teachers, parents, or peers; trust that the researcher would not be judgmental, and would not laugh at them. These conditions rarely apply to relationships that boys have with adults, or even with peers. Thus the primary interviewer had to construct a specific, conscious style of relationship with these young people, requiring sensitivity and time, and building on skills acquired in five years of sensitive research.

This study confirmed a methodological finding from the first study, and which recurred in various guises in all our sites. If boys of this age are first interviewed one to one, they can be unhappy about joining group interviews later on. Conversely, if the first interviews take place within a group, the boys may be uneasy about being separated out for individual attention (although this can be possible given adequate time [. . .]). Furthermore, there is a site-specific aspect in that they are happy for further interviews to take place in the same location, but a suggested move can feel threatening. There seem to be two main points at issue here:

(a) This is a practical illustration of the different 'worlds' inhabited by boys, and the different 'faces' they adopt in different situations (Goffman, 1969). For instance, if a boy has revealed a relatively private self during a one to one interview, he may fear exposure in a subsequent group meeting. Or, since a young person can be at pains to keep home and school separate (Edwards & Alldred, 1999) he may fear that the persona he adopts to deal with his school situation might be compromised in a domestic setting. Having revealed the intimate face to the researcher, the researcher presents a danger. Recognising this, enabled trust to be built.

(b) In this study we were asking boys to voice complex, sensitive feelings
     – feelings they usually 'kept to themselves'. It was necessary to build trust
     slowly, and it was felt that there was no advantage to be gained from
     placing boys in uncomfortable contexts.

                                                      (Schostak and Walker 2000)

Research 'in the field' involves visiting and spending time with the researchees.
It involves 'seeing' what goes on in all its complexities and endeavouring to be
open to everything that is said and done in the field. This means suspending
immediate judgements made at the moment of looking so as not to allow prejudices to prevent other interpretations to arise. However, saying this is easier
than doing it. The act of judging in the heat of the moment is quite different to the
act of seeing that emerges during acts of suspension. Suspension, of course, is a
crude word trying to grasp a subtle process. Derrida employed the term 'difference'
to signify a sense of deferral (*differer*) and the difference that is inherent with
the passage of time. Suspension is of the same logic with its inherent dialectic of
'given time', not only to notice and to include the complexity in all its mani-
festations but also 'given time' to reflect on the myriad of possibilities that present
themselves to the stage of the research process. This notion of 'given time' requires
teasing out since the word 'given' is intentionally deployed here to reach beyond
its literal meaning of actively taking time out and of deliberately making time,
that is to say, of literally 'giving' time for, in this particular case, reflection.
Rather, figuratively, its givenness as gift is acting here as a Kristevan-like minimal
textual unit, or a Gasché's minimal thing. As such, it acts like a hinge point, a
place where multiple meanings can be attached to a word or image. It is a point
where no definition or forced meaning can be given; hence, a suspension to the
act of giving meaning is necessary. Hearing the word 'bow', it is also possible to
hear the word 'bough'. But seeing the word 'bow' outside of any further contextual
clues, there is no way of knowing whether this will signify a bow and arrows
or the bowing of a subject before a king. Complex texts – whether composed of
words, visual images, sounds, material textures, scents or some combination –
provide multiple levels of meanings, clashes of possible meanings, combinations
of meanings, transposing meanings from one context of interpretation, or discourse,
to another; that is, they constitute a polysemic texture within whose depth figures of meanings play at hiding and revealing themselves. This play of hiding
and revealing of givenness turns upon the 'madness of the dissemination of the
meaning "gift"' (Derrida 1992b: 55).[1] A gift, in Derrida's sense, depends entirely
upon the conditions whereby there is no giving back, no reimbursement, no
contract of exchange and no indebtedness. Reciprocity and indebtedness are
extremely difficult to avoid. Furthermore, by its very nature, the gift is subjected

---

1 Derrida's (1992b) argument centres upon his intertextual interweaving of Mauss's *Essai sur
   le don* into his analysis of Baudelaire's *La Fausse monnaie*.

to time [*temporisé*] or deferred [*différé*] by the implicit and inevitable expectation of reciprocity. Ultimately, therefore, Derrida argues, one can only 'give the time'. The gift is always deferred from being a gift because the ever-present and implicit reciprocity haunts its identity. It is the gift of emergent ways of seeing, acting and signifying implicit in the play of design and de-sign of Figure 9.8. The meaning of gift is both defined by forgoing a counter-gift and yet implicitly excludes this forgoing. As a minimal textual unit, it is thus ambiguous, paradoxical, polyfunctional and ultimately undecidable. If used playfully as telling spaces in ways of seeing, thinking (and also doing and writing) in research, it opens up the radical by mobilising the deconstructive possibilities inherent in the play of signifiers (see Chapters 2, 3 and 8 and, in particular, Figures 2.3, 2.5, 3.1, 5.2, 7.2 and 8.1).

> Some of the professionals we spoke to referred to the importance of working *with* parents and there were several anecdotes of the efforts that professionals went to in trying to support and encourage parents' confidence and social bonding with others on the course. However there is a difficult line to tread here for professionals, between active encouragement and coercion and in some instances there may be a conflict of interest within their professional agendas. Some professionals said "*if I can engage the parents . . .*' and hoped that they might "*have the opportunity to . . .*" attend such a course whilst simultaneously asserting that "*you either work with me or I will prosecute you*", with a qualifying comment that "*but we would never go down the prosecution route until we had tried and tested all the avenues and got mum's support and the child's support*" *(AG).* So although there seemed to be a 'preferred' route there were contradictions and dilemmas around this with an understanding that "*well ultimately I come from a statutory agency and ultimately the parents don't have a choice*" in some cases anyway. (AG). "*We say well you might as well do this voluntarily because the courts will make you do it. Isn't it better to choose yourself*" (AG)? and this is where the notion of 'choice' may be conflated with 'coercion'. One professional commented that there was no stigma attached to the course, saying "*I don't think there is any stigma. I think well done, congratulations. You are recognising it before it gets to the point where you are having to do one anyway*" *(AG).*
>
> This professional went on to say "*we only prosecute those parents who say 'on your bike.' We wouldn't prosecute where we felt we were getting support from mum or dad*" (AG), but value judgements need to be made here about parents who are willing to work with agencies against those who can't or won't. An implicit categorising of the 'deserving' and the 'non-deserving' according to professional criteria and motives. When a professional commented "we want parents to have the opportunity to . . ." is this then a choice or an ultimatum? – In effect "we have offered you the opportunity" can be as much about legitimating a strategy, which covers a trail of actions in an increasing accountable world. I.e. we cannot prosecute you

unless we can show that we have tried other routes first and this latter scenario seems to take the course further away from its intended aims (at least in terms of how they were expressed by the person who designed the course and those who were currently teaching on it).

(Pearce et al. 2006)

There is a kind of gift in working with parents to help them develop their confidence. But there is also a kind of exchange value: professionals would work *with* parents on certain conditions, but would 'only prosecute those parents who say "on your bike"'. Contradictions and dilemmas emerge until resolved as 'well ultimately I come from a statutory agency and ultimately the parents don't have a choice'. The police order prevents the slide into the ambiguities that might open up alternatives if working *with* could be sustained free from the threat of coercion.

The role of the evaluation was to provide insights into dilemmas for an agency who wanted to know how to make a difference by providing opportunities that were non-coercive. However, transposing this extract – as well as the others – from a report completed for other audiences and other purposes into this chapter inaugurates new beginnings that mark out new middle passages. That is to say, the dissemination of meanings goes on as writing explores new possibilities to make connections. This transposability of texts is a strategy in the middle play of research writing in search of beginnings, themes, events and conclusions. Essential to this strategy is that seeing and thinking requires recording in some appropriate way to keep these possibilities open and dynamic. Often through meticulous attention to small detail, to the letters as it were, composing the text, or to the marginal scribbles, or the spaces between that provides the necessary spacing to set one thing apart from another. It is a paradoxical faithfulness to reflect on and represent ambiguity alongside the forced definitions that seek to reduce complexity to meet managerial, legal and surveillance needs. The focus thus turns to the creation of text that can portray this paradox and its complexity. Consider the following:

It is 8.42 a.m. and I join the group of doctors on Ward N in a certain hospital on the outskirts of a large sprawling town. The group comprises one consultant and four junior doctors. We are standing in the corridor leading to the main part of the ward. I can only presume that newly admitted patients located in the main part of the ward have already been seen before the time the consultant said I should arrive. We certainly do not move into the main ward section during the post-take ward round.

Breakfast has apparently finished as the trolley is pushed through, breaking up the group, disturbing its dynamics. We had gathered round the GP/SHO trainee who was presenting the case to us all. We flatten ourselves against the wall, and those who can do so retreat into a convenient doorway to let the trolley pass. We regroup as soon as it has gone. The interruption is such that

I fail to get the story. Was the impact the same or was it different for the other junior doctors here?

The event is a post-take ward round, and I am there to shadow the consultant. As much as I try to keep my presence there to the minimum by not asking questions, just watching and listening, how the event unfolds will differ from what it might have been, had I not been there. Indeed at a later date, that is precisely what the consultant tells me.

Shadowing in the form of actively watching and listening has consequences for me. I do not get a chance to ask if other members of the firm failed to get the story. I cannot ask immediately, nor is there an opportunity to ask the question later on. People are just too busy and the moment is gone.

Presentation of the case to the firm on the one hand, and the trainer/ consultant on the other, is often cited as an educational opportunity. Whilst the consultant trainer may not know the range of cases that are about to be encountered in such a way that an extensive timetabled training programme can be devised, the one thing s/he does know is the fact that cases always need to be presented. Since this is a post-take ward round, all patients will be new to the consultant trainer. Viewed this way, case presentation provides an invaluable and stable focus for the educational process.

The presentation continues as we regroup. Blood cultures and urine cultures are quietly discussed under ordered investigations. The drinks trolley is wheeled between us, disrupting the flow of the case once again. An X-ray requires our attention, although one SHO goes off in another direction to the general ward office on some errand I know nothing of. The light box is located in a tiny doctors' office just off the corridor and we all try to squeeze in. Essentially, the GP/SHO talks to the trainer consultant because only two people can physically occupy such a small space in front of the light box. I do not hear the conversation, positioned as I am at the doorway. The remaining junior doctors are somewhere in between. Do they hear? The conversation around the X-ray is extremely short, and very quickly we are back in the corridor.

(Jill Schostak, vignette of learning in clinical practice, 2001, EDGE report)

These are not field notes. However, the text could not be produced without making field notes and the experience of 'being there' on that medical ward. There is an implicit witnessing. 'Being there' as a witness, however, is not a simple matter. At other times, in other places, when shadowing consultants in general surgical outpatient clinics in hospitals, Jill, like the consulting surgeon, would write field notes once the patient had left the consulting room in case the note-taking caused further stress to the patient, even though the patients had consented to the researcher being present. In other medical specialities, such as rheumatology and pain management, the doctors themselves would quickly jot down some notes during the course of the consultation, and so taking research notes didn't seem such an intrusion on the event itself. Shadowing in operating theatres also presented a dilemma. If the researcher wrote notes on what she was seeing, the very act of looking down in order to write in a small notepad would interrupt the picture, such that parts of the intricate procedure happening before her eyes and those important but often fleeting interactions between the team members potentially could all be missed. Hence, notes were hurriedly scribbled down (often using keywords, diagrams, mnemonics, etc., to conjure up images seen) during breaks and interludes that arose haphazardly during the time spent shadowing. These notes were supplemented and elaborated upon as soon as possible after the field-work session had finished. Whilst filling in details from memory of the event is not the ideal course of action, the researcher would argue that it was what might be termed the one of best fit within these contexts. Moreover, recall of the details was facilitated by the fact that surgical procedures themselves are intensely visual and often olfactory: the event remained vividly inscribed in her memory.

The task of getting close enough to the lived experience to be able to write it as a credible witness involves writing into the report, the thesis, the paper, the book, the processes through which accounts were obtained. There is nothing neat and tidy about everyday experiences; people do not fall helpfully into categories appropriate for research-funding purposes. Their influence on situations cannot be excluded or controlled. Working in the field inevitably brings the researcher into contact with others who are part of the field yet apart from it. Researching the training of junior doctors, for instance, involved going into clinical areas and encountering other health-care professionals, nurses, physiotherapists, occupational therapists, theatre technicians and so on. They constituted a part of the context of the clinical area and yet they were on the margins of medical training inasmuch as they themselves were not medically trained. Their professional expertise is not in question, nor is their contribution to the wider notion of training of doctors, but their position cannot be anything other than marginal to the funder, given their different professional background. They are outside the circle of contextual reference yet inside it too. Sometimes a brief explanation of the research process itself is all that is necessary to show an openness to these particular – incidental? – researchees. At other times, this openness demands more from the researcher. For example, in one project, one of the nurses in the general-surgery outpatient clinic explained that she had recently attended a short course at the nursing school of the local university. Could a research account be written for her to read, she asked, because she was very interested, having just completed her course. Of course, this was immediately agreed to. Concerns were not raised about knowing nothing of the course she had so recently completed, nor the lack of knowledge of the training of nurses, nor the need to maintain the anonymity and confidentiality of the other members of the research project. Although this particular nurse was not being shadowed, she was usually present during the shadowing of the doctors and, therefore, she had been generous in her permission to agree to my presence. How could that generosity not be returned? In order to address these concerns, an account was written of the research project in relation to this specific outpatient clinic in general surgery, paying particular attention to a notion of team work and its role in the clinical area where medical training takes place. Before handing the account to the nurse, it was taken to a core team meeting in order to share it between all the members of the research team and to incorporate their comments. As far as the funding body was concerned, such an account was as if nothing, the focus was askew, on the nurse and her role, not the medical team. However, it was not nothing either to the nurse herself or to the researcher. No matter how unexpected it is to be asked by somebody to provide feedback, however much 'extra' work it demands, whatever disconcerting new and unknown areas it opens up, it was vital to 'being there', to having a presence and being accepted. Being there is about everyone feeling comfortable, at home with the researcher's disturbing presence.

There is a reciprocity involved that is a double gift, not just an exchange, nor a payment made for services rendered. On another occasion, a consultant in medicine for the elderly asked if s/he could receive some feedback on the first ward round the researcher had shadowed with him/her. A number of other ward rounds were planned for later in the month. The researcher promptly sat down and wrote an account. Whilst, admittedly, this account could be mined for the final report-writing of the project, and whilst its focus was very much in line with that of medical training, it could not constitute a public document in itself because of issues of confidentiality and anonymity. At other times, the request for feedback took off into realms that were even less familiar. During attendance at a three-day compulsory course for trainee surgeons, the researcher (J. R. Schostak) was asked by the surgical theatre manager to provide feedback for himself and for the team of three who were responsible for ordering, preparing and setting out the raw materials on which the trainees would practise and from which they would therefore learn. These four individuals were mostly hidden from the researcher's sight, the manager would come and go attending to other duties besides this training event. The team of three worked inside a preparation room-cum-laboratory. The usual pattern was the team would arrive before the teaching session started in order to prepare the first of the raw materials and distribute them out on the laboratory tables. They would have returned to the preparation room before the start of the training session in order to prepare the next materials ready for distribution during the trainees' coffee break. The researcher saw this team of three as often as the trainees saw them, and, consequently, conversations would be rare. The researcher had never met them before, nor was she conversant with their other roles in the hospital system itself. Refusing to provide feedback though was not an option as far as she was concerned. Finally, she devised a plan to write the feedback. The manager was kind enough to email her back feedback on the feedback: apparently, it was well received and prompted comments as the perspective selected to be the context was something they had not thought about. However, it could not be included as part of the final report-writing, since no means of providing anonymity and confidentiality could be devised. This play of revealing and concealing, visibility and invisibility creates a writing behind or outside the writing, a repressed writing that can only be seen off-scene. Yet, it points to a dissemination that is out of the control of the official research frame and also essential to it. It points to never-endings that need conclusions.

Endings

The closing argument is the real beginning. But beginnings and endings are tyrannies. Each link is enchained to provide a seamless march from opening statements through an examination of each and every part that exhaust, or appears to exhaust, the themes, the issues, the problems as the marshalling of evidence progress through the stages required for the development of a unifying theory:

1.4 Central arguments of the report

There are two kinds of argument: (a) methodological and (b) substantive. They are interrelated. Methodological frameworks provide the approach, the 'ways of looking' and the justifications for those perspectives and approaches. No methodology is foolproof and the anomalies, the 'fuzzy areas' provide challenges to both methodology and the emergent theories that are sustained by that methodology.

The methodological arguments refer to the research perspective and its associated processes through which data is collected and interpreted for the purposes of portraying, analysing and theorising. In brief, the approach is qualitative, employs case-study methodologies of data collection to produce grounded theory for purposes of evaluation. While the research has drawn upon the developing debates concerning qualitative research (Glaser and Strauss 1967; Simons 1981; Ragin and Becker 1992) and evaluation (Murphy and Torrance 1987; Norris 1990; House 1993), it has developed its own approach that is influenced by the emergent debates concerning postmodern society, the relation between the local and the global, and the processes and techniques of research appropriate to contemporary material and social conditions. Insight has been drawn from numerous sources. In particular, the critical realism promoted philosophically by Bhaskar (1993) and socio-logically by Sayer (1993) has contributed to this project's approach to evaluation. This goes beyond portrayal and the presentation and analytic categorisation of 'voices', issues, interests and concerns as an evidence base which may inform policy-making. It gives an argument facilitating the discussion and possible establishment of 'models' which reveal relationships or patterns organising discourses, practices, resource allocations, management and institutional order and change. At its most general level, it provides a study of the relationship between material, organisational and conceptual structures and processes in contexts of change for purposes of transformation. In short, it explores the possibilities for theorisation and their implications for practice and policy-making.

The argument emphasises its practical nature – it means business. The field of the visible, as it were, was to be reconfigured through an experimentation across contexts that could be the basis for learning through sharing and dialogue. Drawing on the critical realism of Bhaskar and its sociological interpretation by Sayer, the analysis focuses on the intentional systems through which ideas are shared and get transformed into outcomes as described in Figure 1.1 and Figure 7.2. Each chapter had taken the key roles, interviewed and observed the relevant individuals occupying those roles and explored the extent to which their philosophies, beliefs and understandings were enacted through their practices and the extent to which current organisational mechanisms, procedures and resources were appropriate to the realisation of desired outcomes. Given that there were a large number of institutions and individuals involved in delivering training, complex issues emerged:

> The substantive issues are grounded in the data collected, through the guidelines offered by the methodological approach. It is argued that:
>
> - Each institution offering degree courses, at one level of analysis, represents a unique case. That is to say, that each institution constructs its own system in response to its locale at one level. However, each institution also has to respond to the 'global' situation as represented by (a) the ENB [English National Board for Nursing, Midwifery and Health Visiting]; (b) UKCC [United Kingdom Central Council for Nursing, Midwifery and Health Visiting]; (c) European directives; d) and other national and world developments which impact upon all ranging from the pace of change in information technology to political demands and the influence of markets at local and international levels. In conclusion, the structures that institutions have to deal with are neither stable nor simple. The particular ways in which each institution 'reads' or interprets these multilayered contextual structures defines the institution itself.
> - It is to be expected then that no one institution will adopt patterns of response identical to all other institutions. It is argued that it is not desirable during periods of rapid change for their structures and processes to be identical. If they were, institutions would not be able to respond appropriately to variations and unique circumstances in local contexts.
> - At the local level, the uniqueness renders institutional comparison and generalisation highly problematic, if not impossible. It does, however, provide data on the ways in which institutions may be organised to respond to the local and the global. *Evaluations may be made on this basis; that is, the extent to which a given pattern of organisation is appropriate to meet local and global demands.*
> - At the national/global level, both local and national responsiveness are desired. It is argued that while local variation is a necessity to meet

changing and complex demands, this variation can be regarded as local experimentation that can be shared through dialogue. *Such experimentation can form the basis for mutual learning and the development of shared understandings, principles and criteria through dialogue.* There is still likely to be difference, debate and disagreement but this may be seen as the necessary complement to the creative impulse to develop and innovate to meet ever new circumstances. From the processes of sharing and learning, institutions may adopt the successful approaches of others and interpret them for their own context. The result is a kind of 'hybridisation' which works towards criteria in common without distorting practice under the weight of imposed, context indifferent 'standards'.

These general arguments will underlie the detailed portrayals, analyses and arguments of the chapters of the report.

(Bedford et al. 1995: 6)

It all seems inevitable when in the conclusion the beginnings are evoked, together with the steps that then followed as a summary presenting the final message, whether as recommendations for action or as an evaluation of the outcomes in terms of the level of confidence that can be placed in a theory or the implications for 'knowledge' or for policy, or for further theoretical developments.

The final chapters or sections re-evoke the core questions that speak to the designated audience, the path travelled and the potential resolutions, courses of action and the remaining problems, gaps, uncertainties together with what is at stake if any of these are overlooked. The contents list of the concluding part of the TYDE report (Bedford et al. 1995; see Figure 10.2) indicates a lengthy recounting of the themes set out at the beginning. Its critical sections were about dialogue. It is was in this running theme that the different voices involved in a complex system could be organised and included in decision-making about course organisation, curriculum development and professional training. Suggestions for change were based upon those points of conflict or lack of resource that emerged from an analysis of the data. It was considered that it was at these points that more democratic modes of learning and working could be introduced. The subsections of each of the concluding chapters deliberately point to the contextual complexities to be addressed which then sets up the need for a change in organisational structures (13.4) to meet the requirements for making transformations in the learning process (13.3). A model of the learning process is provided which in turn has implications for its practical accomplishment as elaborated in Chapter 14. The key section of the chapter is on 'foregrounding educational dialogue in the organisation'. It is here that the key radical structuring takes place, where the democratic principle is organisationally driven to every point in the organisation. Each organisational mechanism and procedure relevant to the training needs of students is to be evaluated according to whether it brings the key players – lecturers, clinical mentors, students – into a dialogic relationship at critical

CHAPTER THIRTEEN Concluding reflections on
professional education 281
  Introduction 281
  13.1 Contexts to action additional themes 283
  13.1.1 The rise of the professional and the market place 283
  13.1.2 The context of Higher Education in the market place for expertise 286
  13.2 Exploration of the case self, other and courses of action 288
  13.3 Transformations the process of learning 293
  13.4 Organisational models of professional education 297
  13.5 The discourses of reflection 300
  13.6 Time and critical experiences in the process of learning 303
  13.7 Summary from a model to principles 305

CHAPTER FOURTEEN Criteria for a quality
undergraduate degree 309
  Introduction 309
  14.1 Structuring educational processes 309
  14.2 Avoiding unacceptable compromise 311
  14.3 Planning for coherence 314
  14.4 Creating coherence through the exploration of discourses 317
  14.5 Quality, range and relevance of learning experience 320
  14.6 Foregrounding educational dialogue in the organisation 322
  14.7 Supporting the process of critical reflection 324
  14.8 Support for teaching staff 327
  14.9 Liaison with clinical staff 330
  14.10 Quality and resources 331
  14.11 Conclusion 333

Figure 10.2 Extract from contents list for TYDE report

moments in the learning process. An evaluation, of course, does not necessarily compel action. It can only present the case to inform the decisions of those who have a stake in processes. Nevertheless, since this was a national project speaking to the national body, it became part of the evidence base through which policy could be made. A subsequent project (Phillips et al. 2000), funded by the same body, further developed many of these ideas and they in turn became the underlying research structure for a course developed by the Open University (2001). The kind of action taking place can perhaps be called 'viral' (Schostak 1999) where ideas spread across a network. The generation of the capacity for dialogue by structuring it into systems facilitates the spread of ideas. What sort of structure is this 'network'?

Theoretically, it can be seen in Gasché's (1986) critical exploration of Derrida's use of terms like '*différance*', '*trace*', '*parergon*', '*arche*-writing', '*supplement*' and so on, which are seen by him as constituting a chain of substitutions, an 'infrastructure'. More fundamentally, each can be seen as a figure of repetition. Each provides a different take on the process of repetition through which beginnings and endings take their significance. Where *différence* emphasises the sense of deferral and delay implicit in any repetition, the trace calls attention to stain, the scent, the ghost of the other that is implicit in any positive term like 'good' – that is, the concept of good already contains the concept of its other, evil. *Parergon* as the figure that works at the edge already implies the state before and the state after, just as *arche*-writing frames the possibility of particular writings, and the *supplement* can only be supplement if there is something to be supplement to. Writing then, becomes the writing or structuring of difference through dialogue. And, in this sense, dialogue is the minimal condition of possibility, or 'infrastructure', for writing.

The problem is that the term 'infrastructure' implies 'hierarchy [which] detract[s] from its pertinence' (Hobson 1998: 239, n. 31). Gasché (1986, 1995) is well aware of the difficulties, but other words like 'quasi-transcendentals' (Derrida 1988, 1996; Gasché 1986) and 'lexemes' (Hobson 1998) also seem inadequate. However, the word 'infrastructure' can be employed in its sense of 'structurality of structure' (cf. Schostak 2005) rather than its sense of 'basic' structure. Infrastructures are 'instances of an intermediary discourse concerned with a middle in which the differends are suspended and preserved' (Gasché 1986: 151). This signifying structure, *structure signifiante* (Derrida 1976: 158) has as its outcome a knotting together of otherwise distinct particulars. Thus, there is 'an interlacing, a weaving, or a web, which would allow the different threads and different lines of sense or force to separate again, as being ready to bind others together' (Derrida 1973: 132). This kind of weaving can be seen in the work of dialogue through which syntheses are constructed through the agency of the incorporated voices. The deliberate incorporation of voices, as has been argued, undermines the agency of power and is thus anti-totalitarian.

It is through dialogue as an anti-totalitarian infrastructure that research projects can be tailored to the needs of people relevant to the dynamic complexities of their everyday lives without losing their capacity for critical reflection and innovation. It is in that way that they become essentially emancipatory projects – their purpose is to include into the descriptions of 'reality' as many viewpoints as possible and to represent these in a way that cannot not be frozen and imposed as recipes. Rather, the research process is designed to continue as part of everyday life, each reading de-stabilising the apparent tau(gh)tness of the chains of argumentation marshalled by 'therefores'. And dialogue is the key. Writing emerges from dialogue, a dialogue that conveys the possibility of exchanges of views regardless of place, person, time and fixity of text. That, simply put, is the message which in turn, provides the sense of an ending.

Conclusion

Radical research is the search for alternative views and the continual creation anew of a beginning. Chapter 7 raised the question of whether democracy can be sustained, and the answer depends on whether the different can always be incorporated in the everyday processes and political structures of life. Radical research is the work undertaken at the edge of the 'normal' that keeps democracy alive. It has been argued, of course, that doing research under normal conditions can only mean under the current organisations of power globally. For many, this means that a double writing is involved; that is to say, a text appears to say and be doing one thing but includes the intent of another writing and doing. This doubleness is both political and ethical in nature. The writing, in this sense, is not 'at home' within itself. It becomes a writing with besides and against that never quite coincides with the dominant views of what counts as truth. Under conditions of power, hostile to the 'truth' that a writer or researcher is expressing, this double writing is the only way of avoiding censorship and persecution (Strauss 1952a). It is, in itself, a political act that leaves open the possibility of a 'true' reading by those who can come to understand it and feel 'at home' in its truths. Its danger is that it generates a closed society of 'believers', a kind of 'cult', or 'inner circle' of the elite who know the truth but will not speak it to outsiders except by parables, or through coded messages, or under the cover of deep irony.

If democracy is to exist as a radical possibility to include all voices, then such doubleness of writing that seeks to cover itself subverts the possibility of realising the vision of power residing with people, not with elites or tyrants. Democracy exists, and is understood to exist, only if there is a general – indeed universal – sense of being at home with otherness. Hannah Arendt's views on the relation between understanding and the feeling of 'at-homeness' is explored by Kristeva in the following terms:

> The *com*-prehender waits, accepts and welcomes an open space, she allows herself to be used, she sets forth, she is with (*cum-*, *com-*), a matrix of studied casualness (what Heidegger called *Gelassenheit*) that allows itself to be fertilized. At the same time, the comprehender apprehends: she selects, tears down, molds and transforms the elements; she appropriates and re-creates

them. Alongside others but accompanied by her own selection, the comprehender is one who gives birth to a meaning that harbours in altered form, the meaning of other people. It then falls upon us to unravel the process that turns thought to action, that constructs and deconstructs.

(Kristeva 2001: 26)

To accept entering a mutual sense of being at home in Arendt's sense requires a change in both identities. This prefigures Laclau's (1996, 2005) insistence that in engaging in alliance to form even a temporary hegemony necessitates a change in the identity of each participant in order to be inclusive. As increasing numbers of individuals engage in associations for mutual benefit, their particular values, their particular truths concerning what is right and wrong, desirable undesirable, necessary, unnecessary are made to count under a regime of truth and a system of laws that define a territory of operation and countenances no exception. If all are equal, then there can be no exception without causing a sense of injustice. However, there can be no closure if all particular viewpoints are to be treated equally since, as Arendt argues, there is always the birth of a new viewpoint. Rather than writing and researching to avoid censorship, double writing is radicalised to become Derrida's *écriture*, a metaphor, a figure for 'an entire structure of investigation, not merely "writing in the narrow sense," graphic notation on a tangible material' (Spivak 1976: ix–lxxxix). As Cusset (2003) points out, those that have been referred by Anglo audiences under the term 'French theory' – deconstructionist, post-structuralist or postmodern – could better be named non-, or anti-totalitarian. Such approaches by rejecting strategies that seek to cover all and bring to end the histories of debate between alternative views concerning truth, knowledge and ways of living are not thereby relativistic, nor arguing that 'anything goes'. Rather, there is a search for a way of thinking that does not freeze history into final theories or final forms of social order and final definitions of what constitutes the 'good society'.

Radical research, like *écriture* as a structure of investigation, does not hide under a double writing but explores and makes visible, audible, perceptible, the doubleness, the play of difference – indeed, a kind of music composed of the multiple parts played by each member of the band or orchestra – that already exists. In the design of research proposals under the normal conditions of research funding, there is the challenge of writing the design that convinces funders, gate-keepers and so on to fund and endorse the research. It is the challenge of providing the mood music, as it were, that they find comfortable. However, the life of the project itself is shaped by the unpredictabilities met running the labyrinths of field-work sites. Building into research design the need to incorporate the multiple views of a given 'case' already designs in the virus of deconstruction, that is, of challenge to the prevailing categories through which the 'normal' is defined by the powerful, the policy-makers, the rule of the dominant over the multitude.

For Badiou (2005) the problem of the multitude is that of the one–many, and the problem of politics is that it is in ruins, thus:

In the real field of politics today, which is a sort of destroyed field, or a battlefield without armies, we often oppose a reactionary politics – liberalism and so on – the crucial concept of which in the political field is law and order, which are the protection of potency and richness, and on the other side a revolutionary politic the crucial concept of which is collective desire, the desire for a new world of peace, justice, and so on.

(Badiou 2005: 2)

The problem is that through a loss of belief in the great metanarratives or through a return to fundamentalisms, there is no great narrative that enables inclusion. Hence:

The most important political problem is the problem of a new fiction. We have to distinguish between fiction and ideology. Because generally speaking ideology is something which isn't coupled with science, or with truth or with real, reality. But as we know from Lacan and from before, the truth itself is in a structure of fiction. The process of truth is also the process of a new fiction. And so to find the new great fiction is the possibility to have a final belief, political belief.

(Badiou 2005: 12)

Truth, in particular, arises in complex political circumstances where particularities are always in conflict with generalisations or universalities. Is a resort to a new myth, a new noble lie, the real solution? If reason cannot contain the uniqueness, the particular truth of the individual, a myth, no matter how rich, still erodes that uniqueness, haunting it with visions of universalities that the experts, the new priests of the myth or the noble lie, will interpret to their benefit.

Where normal science sees the dominant myth as reason or science, it sees the world in terms of a puzzle, which through rigorous observation the parts can be identified, assembled, disassembled and reassembled, radical research proposes the deconstruction of myths and the creative reconfiguration of conceptions of the world to include what the puzzle had repressed in the interests of order. This is not a simple accusation of carelessness. It is that the final puzzle, as such, does not exist. How can this be? Each question introduces a questioner with a different viewpoint. Each assembly and disassembly is undertaken under different temporal circumstances. Each unification has the problem of whether or not the unity is a member of the class of things that it names and so unifies. If it is, then the class that includes the unity has to be unified under some higher-order category in order to bring closure. But that, in turn, sets up the same problem. Posed as an exception, the class that rules as to what is in and what is out, itself lies outside the unity. If it is outside, and if it is thus an exception to the rule that rules the unified set of things, then any other exception could challenge it. And any individual has the potential to claim exceptionality as a singularity, a unique being. And thus the game begins again.

The only safeguard for individuals is their insistence on the radicality of viewpoint, a viewpoint that engages with otherness as its equal in the formation of communities. Dialogue is the field of the radical because it is the only place where wrongs, and, hence, justice and equality of treatment, can be recognised. It is the place that welcomes the other and in welcoming the other, radical research sets off again in the discovery of beginnings.

References

Adorno, T. W. (1973) *Negative Dialectics*, trans. E. B. Ashton, London and New York: Routledge.

Agamben, G (1998) *Homo Sacer: Sovereign Power and Bare Life*, Stanford, Calif.: Stanford University Press.

Ahmed S. (2005) 'The Skin of the Community', in Tina Chanter and Ewa Plonowska Ziarek (eds) *Revolt, Affect, Collectivity*, New York: State University of New York Press, pp. 95–111.

Airaksinen, T (1995) *The Philosophy of the Marquis de Sade*, London and New York: Routledge. First published 1991.

Althusser, L. (1971) *Lenin and Philosophy, and Other Essays*, trans. Ben Brewster, London: Monthly Review Books, pp. 23–68.

—— (1998) 'Ideology and Ideological State Apparatuses', in J. Rivkin and M. Ryan (eds) *Literary Theory: An Anthology*, Malden, Mass.: Blackwell Publishers, pp. 294–304.

Anderson, B. (1983) *Imagined Communities: Reflections on the Origin and Spread of Nationalism*, London and New York: Verso.

Archard, D. (2003) *Children, Family and the State*, Aldershot: Ashgate.

Archer, M., Bhaskar, R., Collier, A., Lawson, T. and Norrie, N. (eds) (1998) *Critical Realism: Essential Readings*, London and New York: Routledge.

Arendt, A. (1963) *Eichmann in Jerusalem: A Report on the Banality of Evil*, London: Faber & Faber.

—— (1977) *Between Past and Future*, New York: Penguin Books.

—— (1998) *The Human Condition*, introduction by Margaret Canovan, Chicago, Ill.: University of Chicago Press. First published 1958.

Ariew, R. (1984) 'The Duhem Thesis', *British Journal of Philosophy of Science*, 35 (3): 313–25.

Aristotle (1992) *The Politics*, trans. T. A. Sinclair, first published 1962, revised and represented by Trevor J. Saunders, London and New York: Penguin.

Atkin, R. (1981) *Multidimensional Man: Can Man Live in 3-Dimensional Space?* Harmondsworth: Penguin.

Austin, J. L. (1976) *How to Do Things with Words*, ed. J. O. Urmson and Marina Sbisà, Oxford: Oxford University Press.

Avis, J. (2006) 'Improvement through Research: Policy Science or Policy Scholarship', *Research in Post-Compulsory Education* 11 (1, March): 107–14.

Badiou, A. (2004) *Infinite Thought*, London and New York: Continuum.

—— (2005) *Politics: A Non-Expressive Dialectics*, talk, 26 November, Birkbeck Institute for the Humanities, London. Transcribed by Robin Mackay. Urbanomic, London.

Balibar, E. (1998) *Spinoza and Politics*, trans. Peter Snowdon, London and New York: Verso.

—— (2002) *Politics and the Other Scene*, London and New York: Verso.

Barthes, R. (1987) *Criticism and Truth*, trans. and ed. by Katrine Pilcher Keunemen, Minneapolis, Minn.: University of Minnesota Press.

Bataille, G. (1987) *Eroticism*, trans. Mary Dalwood, London and New York: Marion Boyars. First published 1957 by Éditions de Minuit, Paris.

Bauman, Z. (2001) *The Individualised Society*, Cambridge: Polity.

—— (2003) *Liquid Love: On the Frailty of Human Bonds*, Cambridge: Polity Press.

Beck, U. (1992) *Risk Society: Towards a New Modernity*, trans. Mark Ritter, intro. Scott Lash and Brian Wynne, London: Sage Publications. First published 1986.

Bedford, H., Leamon, J., Phillips, T. and Schostak, J. (1995) 'Evaluation of Pre-Registration Undergraduate Degrees in Nursing and Midwifery (The TYDE Project), Final Report', commissioned by the English National Board for Nursing, Midwifery and Health Visiting.

Behuniak, J. (2004) 'The "Regulative" Idea from Kant to William James', *Zhexuemen (Door to Philosophy)*, 4 (5, April). Available online at <http://www.phil.pku.edu.cn/zxm/pdf/spec16.pdf>.

Bennington, G. (1988) *Lyotard: Writing the Event*, Manchester: Manchester University Press.

Berman, M. (1982) *All that Is Solid Melts into the Air: The Experience of Modernity*, New York: Penguin Books.

Bernstein, R. J. (2005) *The Abuse of Evil: The Corruption of Politics and Religion since 9/11*, Cambridge: Polity.

Bhabha, H. K. (1994) *The Location of Culture*, London and New York: Routledge.

Bhaskar, R. (1991) *Philosophy and the Idea of Freedom*, Oxford: Blackwell.

—— (1993) *Dialectic: The Pulse of Freedom*, London and New York: Verso.

Bourdieu, P. (1993) *La Misère du monde*, Paris: Éditions du Seuil. Published in English as *The Weight of the World: Social Suffering in Contemporary Society*, trans. Priscilla Parkhurst Ferguson et al., 1999, Cambridge: Polity.

Bowie, A. (1994) 'Translator's Introduction', in F. W. J. Von Schelling, *On the History of Modern Philosophy*, Cambridge: Cambridge University Press.

Breton, A. (1929) *Second Manifesto of Surrealism*, in (1972) *Manifestoes of Surrealism/André Breton*, trans. Richard Seaver and Helen R. Lane, Ann Arbor, Mich.: University of Michigan Press.

Broadfoot, P. (1988) 'Educational Research: Two Cultures and Three Estates', *British Educational Research Journal*, 14 (1): 3–15.

Brown, N. O. (1966) *Love's Body*, New York: Vintage Books.

Butler, J., Laclau, E. and Žižek, S. (2000) *Contingency, Hegemony, Universality: Contemporary Dialogues on the Left*, London and New York: Verso.

Caldeira, T. P. R. (2000) *City of Walls: Crime, Segregation, and Citizenship in São Paulo*, London: Routledge.

Carroll D. L. (1987) *Paraesthetics: Foucault, Lyotard and Derrida*, New York: Methuen.

Castoriadis, C. (1997) *World in Fragments: Writings on Politics, Society, Psychoanalysis, and the Imagination*, ed. and trans. David Ames Curtis, Stanford, Calif.: Stanford University Press.

Cixous, H. (1976) 'The Laugh of the Medusa', trans. Keith Cohen and Paula Cohen, *Signs*, 1: 875–93.

—— (1981) 'The Laugh of the Medusa', in Elaine Marks and Isabelle de Courtivron (eds) *New French Feminisms*, trans. K. Cohen and P. Cohen, Brighton: Harvester.

Cixous, H. and Clément, C. (1986) *The Newly Born Woman*, trans. Betty Wing, Manchester: Manchester University Press.

Cochrane A. L. (1972) *Effectiveness and Efficiency: Random Reflections on Health Services*, London: Nuffield Provincial Hospitals Trust. Reprinted in 1989 in association with the *BMJ*.

Colebrook, C. (2002) *Gilles Deleuze*, London: Routledge.

Cooper, D. (1967) *Psychiatry and Anti-Psychiatry*, Tavistock: Paladin.

Critchley, S. and Marchant, O. (eds) (2000) *Laclau: A Critical Reader*, London and New York: Routledge.

Cusset, F. (2003) *French Theory: Foucault, Derrida, Deleuze and Cie et les mutations de la vie intellectuelle aux États-Unis*, Paris: Éditions La Découverte.

Damianni, G. (ed.) (2003) *Tschumi*, London: Thames & Hudson.

Davis, C. (2004) *After PostStructuralism: Reading, Stories and Theory*, London and New York: Routledge.

Deer, B. (2006) 'Just How Much "New Research" Can We Trust?' in *The Sunday Times* News Review, 21 May, p. 13.

Delaney, B. (2006) 'Commentary: Is Society Losing Control of the Medical Research Agenda?', posted on bmj. com, 17 March, available at <http://bmj.com/cgi/doi/10.1136/bmj.38771.471563.80>.

Deleuze, G. (1994) *Difference and Repetition*, trans. P. Patton, New York: Columbia University Press.

Dennett, D. (1976) 'Conditions of Personhood', in A. O. Rorty (ed.) *The Identities of Persons*. Berkeley, Calif.: University of California Press, Chapter 7.

—— (1989) *The Intentional Stance*, Cambridge, Mass.: MIT Press.

Denzin, N. K. (1989) *Interpretive Interactionism*, London and Newbury Park, Calif.: Sage.

Derrida, J. (1973) *Speech and Phenomena and Other Essays in Husserl's Theory of Signs*, trans. David Allinson. Evanston, Ill.: North-Western University Press.

—— (1976) *Of Grammatology*, trans. G. Spivak, Baltimore, Md.: Johns Hopkins University.

—— (1978) *Writing and Difference*, trans. A. Bass, London: Athlone Press.

—— (1981a) *Dissemination*, trans. B. Johnson, Chicago, Ill.: Chicago University Press.

—— (1981b) *Positions*, trans. A. Bass, Chicago, Ill.: University of Chicago Press.

—— (1987) *Truth in Painting*, trans. Geoffrey Bennington and Ian McLeod, Chicago, Ill.: Chicago University Press.

—— (1988) *Limited Inc.*, trans. Samuel Weber and Jeffrey Mehlman, Evanston, Ill.: Northwestern University Press.

—— (1992a) 'Force of Law: The "Mystical Foundation of Authority"', in Drucilla Cornell, Michael Rosenfeld and David Gray Carlson (eds) *Deconstruction and the Possibility of Justice*, London: Routledge.

—— (1992b) *Given Time. 1. Counterfeit Money*, trans. P. Kamuf, Chicago, Ill.: Chicago University Press.

—— (1996) 'Remarks on Deconstruction and Pragmatism', in C. Mouffe (ed.) *Deconstruction and Pragmatism*, London: Routledge.

Diken, B. (2004) 'City of God', Lancaster: Lancaster University Department of Sociology.

Available online at <http://www.comp.lancs.ac.uk/sociology/papers/diken-city-of-god.pdf>.

Diprose, R. (2002) *Corporeal Generosity: On Giving with Nietzsche, Merleau-Ponty, and Levinas*, New York: State University of New York Press.

Duhem, P. (1894) 'Quelques reflexions au sujet de la physique experimentale', *Revue des Questions Scientifiques*, 2 (3): 179–229.

—— (1917) 'Notice sur les titres et travaux scientifiques de Pierre Duhem', *Memoires de la societé des sciences physiques et naturelles de bordeaux*, pp. 71–169.

—— (1954) *The Aim and Structure of Physical Theory*, Princeton, NJ: Princeton University Press, trans. of 2nd edn, 1914; first published 1906 as *La Theorie physique, son objet et sa structure*.

Edgley, R. (1976) 'Reason as Dialectic: Science, Social Science and Socialist Science', *Radical Philosophy*, 15: 2–7.

Edwards, R. and Alldred, P. (1999) 'Home-School Relations: Children and Young People Negotiating Familialisation, Institutionalisation and Individualisation', paper presented to the British Educational Research Association annual conference, Brighton.

Elliott, J. (1990) 'Educational Research in Crisis: Performance Indicators and the Decline in Excellence', *British Educational Research Journal*, 16 (1): 3–18.

—— (1991) *Action Research for Educational Change*, Milton Keynes: Open University Press.

Feyerabend, P. (1975) *Against Method*, London: NLB.

Fitzpatrick, P. (1992) *The Mythology of Modern Law*, London and New York: Routledge.

Foote Whyte, W. (1943) *Street Corner Society: The Social Structure of an Italian Slum*, Chicago, Ill.: University of Chicago Press.

Fortin, J. (2003) *Children's Rights and the Developing Law*, Cambridge: Cambridge University Press.

Foster, G. (1984) 'Capital Market Efficiency: Definitions Testing Issues and Anomalies', in M. J. R. Gaffikin (ed.) *Contemporary Accounting Thought*, London: Prentice-Hall.

Freeman, M. D. A. (1983) *The Rights and Wrongs of Children*, London: Francis Pinter.

Fukuyama, F. (1992) *The End of History and the Last Man*. New York: Free Press; 2nd paperback edition with a new afterword, New York: Simon & Schuster, 2006.

Gasché, R. (1986) *The Tain of the Mirror: Derrida and the Philosophy of Reflection*, Cambridge, Mass.: Harvard University Press.

—— (1994) *Inventions of Difference: On Jacques Derrida*, Cambridge, Mass.: Harvard University Press.

—— (1999) *Of Minimal Things: Studies on the Notion of Relation*, Stanford, Calif.: Stanford University Press.

Gerson, L. (2003) 'Plotinus', in Edward N. Zalta (ed.), *The Stanford Encyclopedia of Philosophy* (Fall 2003 Edition). Available online at <http://plato.stanford.edu/archives/fall2003/entries/plotinus>.

Giddens, A. (1998) *The Third Way: The Renewal of Social Democracy*, Cambridge: Polity Press.

Glaser, B. G. and Strauss, A. L. (1967) *The Discovery of Grounded Theory: Strategies for Qualitative Research*, Chicago, Ill.: Aldine-Atherton.

Godwin, W. (1793) *An Enquiry Concerning the Principles of Political Justice and Its Influence on General Virtue and Happiness*, 4th edn, 2 vols, London: Robinson.

Goffman, E. (1969) *The Presentation of Self in Everyday Life*, London: Allen Lane.

Gordimer, N. (1990) *My Son's Story*, London: Bloomsbury.

Gough, D. (2006) 'Evidence Informed Teaching: the Work of the EPPI Centre'. Available online at <http://www.ioe.ac.uk/May2006/Papers/DavidGough_Paper.doc>. Accessed 24 December 2006.

Gray, J. B. (2005) 'Althusser, Ideology, and Theoretical Foundations: Theory and Communication', *nmediac, The Journal of New Media and Culture*, 3 (winter, 1). Available online at <http://www.ibiblio.org/nmediac/winter2004/gray.html>.

Harber, C. (2004) *Schooling as Violence: How Schools Harm Pupils and Societies*, London: Routledge Falmer.

Hardimon M. O. (1994) *Hegel's Social Philosophy: The Project of Reconciliation*, Cambridge: Cambridge University Press.

Hardwig, J. (1985) 'Epistemic Dependence', *Journal of Philosophy*, 82: 335–49.

—— (1991) 'The Role of Trust in Knowledge', *Journal of Philosophy*, 88: 893–704.

Hargreaves, D. H., Hestor, S. K., and Mellor, F. J. (1976) *Deviance in Classrooms*, London: Routledge & Kegan Paul.

Hempel C. G. (1942) 'The Function of General Laws in History', *Journal of Philosophy*, 39.

Herman, E. S. and Chomsky, N. (*c*.1988*) Manufacturing Consent: The Political Economy of the Mass Media*, New York: Pantheon Books.

Herrnstein, R. J., and Murray, C. (1994) *The Bell Curve: Intelligence and Class Structure in American Life*, London and New York: Free Press.

Hines, R. D. (1988) 'Popper's Methodology of Falsification and Accounting Research', *The Accounting Review*, 63 (4): 657–62.

Hobbes, T. (1914) *Leviathan*, London: Dent. First published 1651.

Hobson, M (1998) *Jacques Derrida*, London: Routledge.

Holt, J. (1974) *Escape from Childhood: The Needs and Rights of Children*, Harmondsworth: Penguin.

Houlgate, S. (2005) *An Introduction to Hegel: Freedom, Truth and History*, Oxford: Blackwell.

House, E. (1993) *Professional Evaluation: Social Impact and Political Consequences*, London and Newbury Park, Calif.: Sage.

Howes, N., Chagla, L., Thorpe, M. and McCulloch, P. (1997) 'Surgical Practice is Evidence Based', *British Journal of Surgery*, 84: 1220–3.

Huntington, S. P. (1993) 'The Clash of Civilizations', *Foreign Affairs*, 72(3): 22–49.

—— (1996) *The Clash of Civilizations and the Remaking of World Order*, New York: Simon & Schuster.

Husserl, E. (1970) *The Crisis of European Sciences and Transcendental Phenomenology*, Evanston, Ill.: Northwestern University Press.

Illich, I. (1971) *Deschooling Society*, London: Calder and Boyers.

Iser, W. (2000) *The Range of Interpretation*, New York: Columbia University Press.

ISTAG (2001) 'ISTAG Report: Ambient Intelligence at Horizon 2010', available online at <http://www.euresearch.ch/fr/2300.htm>.

Jacobs, L. G. (2005) 'A Troubling Equation in Contracts for Government Funded Scientific Research: "Sensitive But Unclassified" = Secret but Unconstitutional', *Journal of National Security Law and Policy*, 1 (113), available online at <http://www.mcgeorge.edu/jnslp/archive/01–01.htm>.

James, W. (1996) *Some Problems in Philosophy: A Beginning of an Introduction to Philosophy*, Lincoln, Nebr. and London: University of Nebraska Press. First published 1911.

Jensen, A. R. (1995) 'Psychological Research on Race Differences', *American Psychologist*, 50: 41–2.

Johnson C. (1993) *System and Writing in the Philosophy of Jacques Derrida*, Cambridge: Cambridge University Press.

Jullien, F. (2004) *Du mal/du négatif*, Paris: Éditions du Seuil.

Kavanaugh, L. J. (2003) 'Hyperdensity and the Problem of Aggregation and Acceleration', in *Inside Density: International Colloquium on Architecture and Cities #1*, The NeTHCA Colloquia Series, Brussels: La Lettre Volée.

Kearney, R. (1995) *States of Mind: Dialogues with Contemporary Thinkers on the European Mind*, Manchester: Manchester University Press.

Kojève, A. (1969) *Introduction to the Reading of Hegel, Lectures on the Phenomenology of Spirit*, assembled by Raymond Queneau, ed. Allan Bloom, trans. James H. Nichols, Jnr, Ithaca, NY and London: Cornell University Press. Originally published 1947, Paris: Gallimard.

Kripke, S. (1981) *Naming and Necessity*, Malden, Mass. and Oxford: Carlton. First published 1972.

Kristeva, J. (1984) *Revolution in Poetic Language*, trans. Leon S. Roudinez, New York: Columbia University Press.

—— (1989) *Black Sun*, trans. Leon S. Roudiez, New York: Columbia University Press.

—— (2001) *Hannah Arendt*, trans. Ross Guberman, New York: Columbia University Press.

Kuhn, T. (1970) *The Structure of Scientific Revolutions, Vols. I and II: Foundations of the Unity of Science*, 2nd edn, Chicago, Ill.: University of Chicago Press.

Kusch, M. (2002) *Knowledge by Agreement*, New York and Oxford: Oxford University Press.

Labbett, B. (1988) 'Skilful Neglect', in J. F. Schostak (ed.) *Breaking into the Curriculum: The Impact of Information Technology on Schooling*, London and New York: Methuen.

—— (1996) 'Personal Principles of Procedure and The Expert Teacher', available online at <http://www.enquirylearning.net/ELU/Issues/Education/Ed4.html>.

Lacan, J. (1977) *Écrits: A Selection*, London: Tavistock/Routledge.

Laclau, E. (1996) *Emancipation(s)*, London: Verso.

—— (2005) *Populist Reason*, London: Verso.

Laclau, E. and Mouffe, C. (1985) *Hegemony and Socialist Strategy: Towards a Radical Democratic Politics*, London: Verso.

Laing, R. D. (1967) *The Politics of Experience and the Bird of Paradise*, Harmondsworth: Penguin.

—— (1976) *The Politics of the Family, and Other Essays*, Harmondsworth: Penguin.

Le Corbusier (1986) *Towards a New Architecture*, trans., of 13th edn, and intro. Frederick Etchells, London: Dover.

Le Doeuff, M. (1989) *The Philosophical Imaginary*, trans. Colin Gordon, Stanford, Calif.: Stanford University Press.

Lee, R. M. (1993) *Doing Research on Sensitive Topics*, London: Sage.

Lefebvre, H. (1991) *The Production of Space*, trans. Donald Nicholson-Smith, Oxford: Blackwell.

—— (2004) *Rhythmanalysis*, trans. Stuart Elden and Gerald Moore, London: Continuum.

Legrain P. (2006) *Immigrants: Your Country Needs Them*, London: Little Brown.

Lemaire, A. (1977) *Jacques Lacan*, London: Routledge & Kegan Paul.

Lev, B. and Ohlson, J. A. (1982) 'Market-Based Empirical Research in Accounting: A Review, Interpretation, and Extension', Supplement to *Journal of Accounting Research*, 20: 249–322.

Levinas, E. (1979) *Totality and Infinity*, trans. Alphonso Lingis, Pittsburgh, Pa.: Duquesne University Press.

—— (1998) *Éthique comme philosophie première*, ed. Jacques Rolland, Paris: Rivages Poche/Petite Bibliothèque.

Levy, S. (2005) 'Menace: Surrealist Interference of Space', in Thomas Mical (ed.) *Surrealism and Architecture*, London and New York: Routledge.

Lins, P. (2006) *City of God*, intro. Katia Lund, trans. Alison Entrekin, London: Bloomsbury.

Lipovetsky, G. (2006) *La Société de deception*, Paris: Les Éditions Textuel.

Llewelyn, J. (1986) *Derrida on the Threshold of Sense*, Basingstoke: Macmillan.

Locke, J. (1989) *Some Thoughts Concerning Education*, ed. John W. and Jean S. Yolton, Oxford, Clarendon. First published 1693.

Lotman, Y. M. (1990) *Universe of the Mind: A Semiotic Theory of Culture*, London and New York: I. B. Tauris.

Lovejoy, A. (1936) *The Great Chain of Being: A Study of the History of an Idea*, Cambridge, Mass.: Harvard University Press.

Lukács, G. (1971) *History and Class Consciousness*, trans. Rodney Livingston, London: Merlin Press.

Luntley, M. and Ainley, J. (2005) 'What Teachers Know', Final Report on AHRB project: Attention and the Knowledge Bases of Expertise, University of Warwick, available online at <http://www.catalpa.org/2_Research_and_Technical/what%20teachers%20know.pdf>.

Lyotard, J. F. (1971) *Discours, figure*, Paris: Klincksieck.

McAfee, N. (2004) *Julia Kristeva*, London: Routledge.

McBride, R. and Schostak, J. (1995) 'Action Research', Enquiry Learning Unit, available online at <http://www.enquirylearning.net/ELU/Issues/Research/Res1Ch4.html>.

MacDonald, B. (1987) 'Evaluation and the Control of Education', in R. Murphy and H. Torrance (eds), *Evaluating Education: Issues and Methods*, London: Harper & Row (in association with the Open University). First published 1974 in B. MacDonald and R. Walker (eds) *Innovation, Evaluation, Research and the Problem of Control* (SAFARI), CARE, UEA, Norwich.

MacGregor, D. (1998) *Hegel and Marx after the Fall of Communism*, Cardiff: University of Wales Press.

MacKenzie, D. (1999) 'Slaying the Kraken: The Sociohistory of a Mathematical Proof', *Social Studies of Science*, 29: 7–60.

MacLure, M. (2005) '"Clarity Bordering on Stupidity": Where's the Quality in Systematic Review?', *Journal of Education Policy*, 20 (4): 393–416.

McKee, A., Elliott, J., Hand, C., Schostak, J. R. and Watts, M. (2001) 'Educating the General Practitioner in a Primary Care-Led NHS (EDGE)', Final Report funded by Research and Development, NHS Executive Eastern.

McLuhan, M., with Fiore, Q. and Agel, J. (1967) *The Medium is the Massage*, New York: Random House.

Mead, G. H. (1934) *Mind, Self and Society*, Chicago, Ill.: University of Chicago Press.

Merleau-Ponty, M. (1962) *The Phenomenology of Perception*, trans. Colin Smith, London: Routledge & Kegan Paul.

—— (1968) *The Visible and the Invisible*, trans. Alphonso Lingis, Evanston, Ill.: Northwestern University Press.

Mical, T. (1992) 'The Stealth Landscape', available online at <http://www.pd.org/topos/perforations/perf4/stealth_landscape.html>.

—— (ed.) (2005) *Surrealism and Architecture*, London and New York: Routledge.

Mills, C. W. (1940) 'Situated Actions and Vocabularies of Motive', *American Sociological Review*, 5 (December): 904–13.

Mouffe, C. (1993) *The Return of the Political*, London and New York: Verso.

—— (2005) *On the Political*, London and New York: Routledge.

Muhlmann, G. (2004) *Du journalisme en démocratie*, Paris: Petite Bibliothèque, Payot, Éditions Payot and Rivages.

Murphy, R. and Torrance, H. (eds) (1987) *Evaluating Education: Issues and Methods*, London: Harper & Row (in association with the Open University).

Murray, C. (2000) 'The Underclass Revisited', American Enterprise for Public Policy Research, posted 1 January at <http://www.aei.org/publications/pubID.14891/pub_detail.asp>; the book version is at <http://www.aei.org/books/bookID.268,filter.all/book_detail.asp>.

—— (2005) 'The Advantages of Social Apartheid: U.S. Experience Shows Britain What to Do with Its Underclass – Get It Off the Streets', *Sunday Times* 3 April; American Enterprise for Public Policy Research, posted 4 April at <http://www.aei.org/publications/filter.all,pubID.22252/pub_detail.asp>.

Negri, A. (1991) *The Savage Anomaly: The Power of Spinoza's Metaphysics and Politics*, Minneapolis, Minn.: University of Minnesota Press.

Nordmann, C. (2006) *Bourdieu/Rancière: La Politique entre sociologue et philosophie*, Paris: Éditions Amsterdam.

Normand, R. (2006a) 'The Scarf Unveiled: Proximity to the Test of Law in a French School', *UMR Education and Politiques*, INRP/Université Lyon 2.

—— (2006b) 'School Effectiveness or the Horizon of World As a Laboratory', *UMR Education and Politiques*, INRP/Université Lyon 2.

Norris, N. (1990) *Understanding Educational Evaluation*, London: Kogan Page (in association with Centre for Applied Research in Education, School of Education, University of East Anglia).

Norton, A. (2004) *Leo Strauss and the Politics of American Empire*, New Haven, Conn.: Yale University Press.

Norval, A. (1996) *Deconstructing Apartheid Discourse*, London and New York: Verso.

Oakley A. (2002) 'Research Evidence, Knowledge Management and Educational Practice: Lessons for All?' Paper for High-level Forum on Knowledge Management in Education and Learning, Oxford, March 18–19, available online at <http://www.ebbtech.org.uk/KM/Files/KM%20Research%20results.pdf>.

O'Connor, B. (2005) *Adorno's Negative Dialectic*, Cambridge, Mass.: MIT Press.

O'Neill, J. (2004) 'Airbrushing Educational Research for Other Agendas', Address to the Quality Public Education Coalition AGM, Aukland, 24 April, available online at <http://www.teacherswork.ac.nz/documents/qpecagm2004.doc>.

Open University (2001) 'Assessing Practice in Nursing and Midwifery', three workbooks, London: CARE, ENB, Open University.

Patrick J. (1973) *A Glasgow Gang Observed*, London: Methuen.

Pearce, C., Piper, H. and Schostak, J. F. (2006) *Final Evaluation Report of the Course 'Surviving Your Teenager'*, Guinness Housing Trust.

Phillips, T. P., Schostak, J. F. and Tyler, J. (2000) *Practice and Assessment in Nursing and Midwifery: Doing It for Real*, Research Reports Series No. 16, London: ENB.

Piper, H. MacLure, M. and Stronach, I. (2006) *Touchlines: The Problematics of Touching between Children and Professionals*, ESRC RES-000–22–0815.

Plato (1994) *Republic*, trans. Robin Waterfield, Oxford: Oxford University Press.

Popper, K. (1963) *Conjectures and Refutations*, London: Routledge & Kegan Paul.

Quine, W. V. O. (1953) *From a Logical Point of View: Nine Logico-Philosophical Essays*, Cambridge, Mass.: Harvard University Press.

Rabaté, J.-M. (2002) *The Future of Theory*, Oxford: Blackwell.

Ragin, C. C. and Becker, H. S. (eds) (1992) *What is a Case? Exploring the Foundations of Social Inquiry*, Cambridge: Cambridge University Press.

Rancière, J. (1987) *Le Maître ignorant: cinq leçons sur l'émancipation intellectuelle*, Paris: Fayard.

—— (1995) *La Mésentente: politique et philosophie*, Paris: Galilée.

—— (2003) *The Philosopher and His Poor*, ed. and intro. Andrew Parker, trans. John Drury, Corrine Oster and Andrew Parker, Durham, Md. and London: Duke University Press. First published 1983.

—— (2004a) *The Politics of Aesthetics*, afterword Slavoj Žižek, trans. and intro. Gabriel Rockhill, London and New York: Continuum.

—— (2004b) 'Sur "Le maitre ignorant"', posted 1 November, available at <http://multitudes.samizdat.net/article.php3?id_article=1714>.

—— (2005) *La Haine de la democratie*, Paris: La Fabrique Éditions.

Readings, W. (1991) *Introducing Lyotard*, London: Routledge.

Reynolds, D., Bollen, R., Creemers, B., Hopkins, D., Stoll, L., and Lagerweij, N., (1996) *Making Good Schools: Linking School Effectiveness and School Improvement*, London: Routledge.

Riffaterre, M. (1978) *Semiotics of Poetry*, London: Methuen.

—— (1990) 'Compulsory Reader Response: the Intertextual Drive', in M. Worton and J. Still (eds), *Intertextuality: Theories and Practices*, Manchester: Manchester University Press.

Riha, R. (2004) 'Politics as the Real of Philosophy', in S. Critchley and O. Marchant (eds) *Laclau: A Critical Reader*, London and New York: Routledge.

Ritzer, G. (1994) *The McDonaldization of Society*, rev. edn., Thousand Oaks, Calif.: Pine Forge Press.

Robertson, N. (1999) 'Leo Straus's Platonism', *animus*, 4, available online at <http://www.mun.ca/animus/1999vol4/roberts4.htm>.

Royle, N. (2003) *The Uncanny*, Manchester: Manchester University Press.

Rudé, G. (1964) *The Crowd in History: A Study of Popular Disturbances in France and England (1730–1848)*, New York and London: Wiley.

Rushdie, S. (1988) *The Satanic Verses*, New York: Viking Penguin.

Rushton, J. P. and Jensen, A. R. (2005) 'Thirty Years of Research on Black–White Differences in Cognitive Ability', *Psychology, Public Policy, and the Law*, 11: 235–94.

Sackett, D. L., Rosenberg, W. M. C., Gray, J. A. M., Haynes, R. B., Richardson W. S. (1996) 'Evidence Based Medicine: What It Is and What It Isn't', *BMJ*, 312: 71–2.

Saussure, F. de (1966) *Course in General Linguistics*, ed. C. Bally and A. Sechehaye, trans. W. Baskin, New York: McGraw-Hill.

—— (2005) *Cours de linguistique générale*, Paris: Éditions Payot et Rivages; Éditions Payot et Rivages. First published 1916.

Sayer, A. (1993) *Method in Social Science: A Realist Approach*, London and New York: Routledge.

Schatzman, M. (1973) *Soul Murder: Persecution in the Family*, London: Allen Lane.

Schmitt, C. (1996) *The Concept of the Political*, ed. George Schwab with Leo Strauss's notes on Schmitt's essay, trans. J. Harvey Lomax, foreword by Tracey B. Strong, Chicago, Ill. and London: University of Chicago Press.

Schostak, J. F. (1983) *Maladjusted Schooling: Deviance, Social Control and Individuality in Secondary Schooling*, London: Falmer.

—— (1985) 'Creating the Narrative Case Record', *Curriculum Perspectives*, 5 (1): 7–13.

—— (1986) *Schooling the Violent Imagination*, London and New York: Routledge & Kegan Paul.

—— (ed.) (1988) *Breaking into the Curriculum: The Impact of Information Technology on Schooling*, London and New York: Methuen.

—— (1988) 'Developing More Democratic Modes of Teacher–Pupil Relationships: The Early Years Listening and Talking Project', Conference of the Northern Ireland Action Research Association at the University of Ulster, November.

—— (1988–9) Children's Listening and Talking Project, funded by GRIST, Norfolk; see <http://www.enquirylearning.net/ELU/Issues/Education/archivesEarlyyears.html>.

—— (1989) 'Primary School Policy: The Democratic Way', Conference of the Education Research Network of Northern Ireland, at the University of Ulster, November.

—— (1990) 'Practical Policy Making in a Primary School', available at <http://www.enquirylearning.net/ELU/Issues/Education/practical.html>.

—— (1993) *Dirty Marks: The Education of Self, Media and Popular Culture*, London: Pluto Press.

—— (1996) 'Chez Sade: What's Cooking Tonight? Soul Murder, Replied the Judge: Some Draft Notes about Collaboration between Consenting Partners', Spencer Hall Conference, University of Western Ontario (April), available online at <http://www.enquirylearning.net/ELU/Culture/Cult2.html>.

—— (1998) 'The Knowing Subject and the Practice of Freedom in Educational Research', BERA, Belfast, available online at <http://www.enquirylearning.net/ELU/Issues/Philosophy/bera%2098%20philos.htm>.

—— (1999) 'Action Research and the Point Instant of Change', *Educational Action Research Journal*, 7 (3): 399–417.

—— (2000) 'Developing Under Developing Circumstances: The Personal and Social Development of Students and the Process of Schooling' in J. Elliott and H. Altrichter (eds), *Images of Educational Change*, Milton Keynes: Open University Press.

—— (2002) *Understanding, Designing and Conducting Qualitative Research in Education: Framing the Project*, Milton Keynes: Open University Press.

—— (2006) *Interviewing and Representation in Qualitative Research Projects*, Milton Keynes: Open University Press.

Schostak, J. F., and Beauchamp, B. (1999) *Final Report for the Evaluation of the 'Telematics Enhanced Language Learning and Tutoring Systems'* project, European Union.

Schostak, J. F., and Fraser, K. (2005) 'edCity: A New Learning Environment', British Computer Society, available online at <http://ewic.bcs.org/conferences/2005/1stelegi/session1/paper12.pdf>.

Schostak, J. F. and Schostak, J. R. (2001) *Consultants as Educators: A Twelve Month Study (CasE)*, NANIME Charitable Trust.

—— (2002–3) *Developing Excellence in Surgical Skills Practice*, NANIME Charitable Trust.

—— (2006a) 'Radical Methodologies: Social Justice, Judgement, Knowledge and Education', BERA Conference, Warwick.

—— (2006b) 'Education, Radical Democracy and the Politics of Place, Community, Person and Time', CESE Conference, Granada July.

—— (2006c) 'Risking Education: Including the Excluded', CESE Conference, Granada July.

—— (2007) 'Politics, Knowledge, Identity and Community: Methodologist As Hitchhiker, Skateboarder, . . .', in T. Schwandt and B. Somekh, *Knowledge Production: The Work of Educational Research in Interesting Times*, London and New York: Routledge.

Schostak, J. F., Schostak J. R., McKee, A. and Hand, C. (1999) 'A Six-Month Study of Junior Doctors' Experiences', NANIME Charitable Trust.

Schostak, J. F. and Walker, B. M. (2000) 'Boys' Sexual Health Education: Implications for Attitude Change (Continuation)', Final Report to the Economic and Social Research Council. Project No. R000222466.

Schostak, J. R. (2005) '[Ad]dressing Methodologies: Tracing the Self in Significant Slips: Shadow Dancing', 2 vols, Ph.D. thesis, University of East Anglia, Norwich, available online at <http://www.imaginativespaces.net/thesis/JRSaddendum.html>.

Schreber, D. P. (1988) *Memoirs of My Nervous Illness*, trans. Ida Macalpine and Richard Hunter, rev. edn, Cambridge, Mass.: Harvard Belknap. First published 1955, London: Dawson.

Schutz, A. (1964) 'The Stranger: An Essay in Social Psychology', in *Collected papers: Vol. II. Studies in Social Theory*, The Hague: Martinus Nijhoff.

—— (1976) *The Phenomenology of the Social World*, trans. G. Walsh and F. Lehnert, London: Heineman.

Silverman, H. J. (1986) 'What is Textuality?', *Phenomenology + Pedagogy*, 4 (2): 54–64, available online at <http://www.phenomenologyonline.com/articles/silverman1. html >.

Simons, H. (ed.) (1981) *Towards a Science of the Singular*, occasional publication, CARE, University of East Anglia, Norwich.

Singer, P. (2004) *The President of Good and Evil: The Ethics of George W. Bush*, New York: Dutton.

Sjöholm, C. (2005) *Kristeva and the Political*, London: Routledge.

Skinner, B. F. (1953) *Science and Human Behaviour*, New York: Macmillan.

—— (1976) *Walden Two*, New York: Macmillan.

—— (1996a) 'Transgressing the Boundaries: Towards a Transformative Hermeneutics of Quantum Gravity', *Social Text*, 46/47: 217–52.

Sokal, A. (1996b) 'A Physicist Experiments with Cultural Studies', *Lingua Franca* 6 (4): 62–4.

Sokal, A. and Bricmont, J. (1997) *Impostures intellectuelles*, Paris: Odile Jacob.

Sokal, A. and Bricmont, J. (1998) *Intellectual Impostures: Postmodern Philosophers' Abuse of Science*, London: Profile Books.

Somekh B. and Lewin C. (2005) *Research Methods in the Social Sciences*, London and Thousand Oaks, Calif.: Sage.

Sorel, G. (2006) *Réflexions sur la violence*, Loverval: Éditions Labor.

Spinoza, B. de (2004) *A Theologico-Political Treatise and A Political Treatise*, Mineola, NY: Dover Philosophical Classics.

Spivak, G. C. (1976) Translator's note and preface in Jacques Derrida, *Of Grammatology*, Baltimore, Md.: Johns Hopkins University Press.

Stenhouse, L. (1975) *An Introduction to Curriculum Research and Development*, London: Heinemann.

Strauss, L. (1952a) *Persecution and the Art of Writing*, Chicago, Ill.: University of Chicago Press.

—— (1952b) *The Political Philosophy of Hobbes: Its Basis and Genesis*, trans. Elsa M. Sinclair, Chicago, Ill. and London: University of Chicago Press.

—— (1964) *The City and Man*, Chicago, Ill. and London: University of Chicago Press.

—— (1988) *What Is Political Philosophy? And Other Studies*, Chicago, Ill. and London: University of Chicago Press. First published 1959 The Free Press.

Stronach, I. (2006) 'On Promoting Rigour in Educational Research: the Example of the RAE', BERA conference, Warwick, September.

Szasz, T. (1997) *The Manufacture of Madness: A Comparative Study of the Inquisition and the Mental Health Movement*. Syracuse, NY: Syracuse University Press. First published 1970.

Taylor, C. (1975) *Hegel*, Cambridge: Cambridge University Press.

Taylor F. W. (1967) *The Principles of Scientific Management*, New York: Norton Library by arrangement with Harper & Row. First published 1911.

Taylor, M. (1987) *Altarity*, Chicago, Ill.: University of Chicago Press.

Thévenot L. (1998) 'Pragmatiques de la connaissance' in A. Borzeix, A. Bouvier and A. Pharo (ed.) *Sociologie et connaissance: nouvelles approches cognitives*, Paris: Éditions du CNRS.

Thomas, W. I., with Thomas, D. (1928) *The Child in America: Behavior Problems and Programs*, New York: Alfred A. Knopf.

Thrasher, F. M. (1927) *The Gang: A Study of 1,313 Gangs in Chicago*, Chicago, Ill.: University of Chicago Press.

Torrance, H. (2004) 'Systematic Reviewing: The "Call Centre" Version of Research Synthesis, Time for a More Flexible Approach', Invited presentation to ESRC/RCBN seminar on Systematic Reviewing, 24 June, University of Sheffield, available online at <http://www.esri.mmu.ac.uk/respapers/papers-pdf/seminar-systematicreviewing.pdf>.

—— (2006) 'Globalising Empiricism: What If Anything Can Be Learned from International Comparisons of Educational Achievement', in H. Lauder, P. Brown, J.-A. Dillabough and A. H. Halsey (eds), *Education, Globalisation and Social Change*, Oxford: Oxford University Press, pp. 824–34.

Tragesser, R. S. (1977) *Phenomenology and Logic*, Ithaca, NY and London: Cornell University Press.

Tschumi, B. (1996) *Architecture and Disjunction*, Cambridge, Mass.: MIT Press.

Tyack, D. and Hansot, E. (1982) *Managers of Virtue: Public School Leadership in America, 1820–1980*, New York: Basic Books.

Vasseleu, C. (1998) *Textures of Light*, Abingdon: Routledge.

Verdery, K. (1996) *What Was Socialism, and What Comes Next?*, Princeton, NJ: Princeton University Press.

Virilio, P. (1996) *Cybermonde, la politique du pire*, interview with Phillippe Petit, Paris: Les Éditions Textuel.

Warhat, S. (ed.) (1965) *Francis Bacon: A Selection of His Writings*, Toronto.

Weber, M. (2001) *The Protestant Ethic and the Spirit of Capitalism*, London and New York: Routledge. First published 1930, Allen & Unwin.

Whiting, S. (2003) 'Bas-relief Urbanism: Chicago's Figured Field', in *Inside Density*, International Colloquium on Architecture and Cites #1, The NeTHCA Colloquia Series, Brussels: La Lettre Volée.

Widzer, M. E. (1977) 'The Comic-Book Superhero: A Study of the Family Romance Fantasy', *The Psychoanalytic Study of the Child*, 32: 565–603.

Williams, B. (1972) 'Knowledge and Reasons', in G. H. von Wright (ed.), *Problems in the Theory of Knowledge*, The Hague: Kluwer.

Williams, R. (2006) 'It Is Not a Crime to Hold Traditional Values', *The Times Higher Education Supplement*, 8 December, pp. 16–17.

Willis, P. (1977) *Learning to Labour*, Farnborough: Saxon House.

Wolfreys, J. (1998) *Deconstruction: Derrida*. London: Macmillan.

Woods, S. and Shears, B. (1986) *Teaching Children with Severe Learning Difficulties: A Radical Reappraisal*, London: Croom Helm.

Wringe, C. A. (1981) *Children's Rights: A Philosophical Study*, London: Routledge & Kegan Paul.

Žižek, S. (1991) *Looking Awry: An Introduction to Jacques Lacan through Popular Culture*, Cambridge, Mass.: MIT Press.

Name index

Addley, Esther, 45
Adorno T. W., 18, 31, 91, 95, 120, 219, 272
Agamben, G., 153, 272
Agel, J. , 278
Ahmed, S., 135, 272
Ainley, J., 215
Airaksinen, T., 136, 272
Alldred, P., 257
Altusser, L., 215–16, 272
Anderson, B., 118, 272
Archard, D., 45, 272
Archer, M., 114, 272
Arendt, H., 82, 84, 135, 136, 217, 232, 269, 272
Ariew, R., 94, 272
Aristotle, 53–4, 272
Atkin, R., 88, 272
Austin, J.L., 128, 178, 272
Avis, J., 117, 272
Azulay, J., 78

Badiou, A., 81, 124, 270, 272
Balibar, E., 19, 22, 105, 178, 179, 184, 185–6, 188, 190, 223, 173
Barthes, R., 19, 105, 107, 173
Bataille, G., 188, 173
Baty, P., 177
Baudelaire, 172
Bauman, Z., 67, 109, 153, 173
Beauchamp, B., 252, 281
Beck, U., 135, 173
Becker, H. S., 264, 280
Bedford, H., 253, 255–6, 266, 173
Behuniak, J., 148, 173
Bennington, G., 62, 173
Bergman, B., 106
Berman, M., 76, 82, 109, 172, 173

Bernstein, R. J., 57, 173
Bhabha, H., 79–80, 82, 173
Bhaskar, R., 114, 264, 265, 173
Birt, Sir C., 160–1
Blair, T., 161
Bourdieu, P., 80, 97, 99, 155, 216, 219, 224, 173
Bowie, A., 120, 173
Brentano, 87, 212
Breton, A., 188, 173
Bricmont, J., 19, 107
Broadfoot, P., 106, 173
Brown, J., 75
Brown, N. O., 143, 173
Bunyan, N., 75
Bush, G., Jr, 56–7, 70, 74, 148, 226
Bush, G., Sr., 69–70, 156
Butler, J., 231, 173

Caldeira, T. P. R., 153, 173
CAPE 2005, 170
Carroll, D. L., 91, 173
CasE, 85, 96–8, 99–101, 109, 119, 123, 129–30, 144–6, 245
Castoriadis, C., 46–7, 218, 173
Ceauçescu, 55, 69, 216, 228, 232
Chen, M., 78
Chomsky, N., 216
Cixous, H., 96, 274
Clémont, C., 96, 274
Cochrane, A., 108, 274
Colebrook, C., 274
Cooper, D., 143, 274
Critchley, S. , 274
Cusset, F., , 274

Damianni, G. , 52, 274
Davis, C., 19, 107, 108, 274

Deer, B., 103, 104, 274
Delaney, B., 106, 274
Deleuze, G. , 274
de Man, P., 128
Dennett, D., 43, 86, 143, 158, 274
Denzin, N. K., 15, 274
Derrida, J., 56, 63, 73, 74–5, 91, 107, 115,
    125, 128, 135, 189, 191–2, 220–24,
    244, 246, 247, 258–9, 267, 268, 270,
    274
Descartes, R., 10, 18, 19, 21–2, 23, 26–8,
    54, 68, 211, 218
Diken, B., 154, 274
Diprose, R., 135, 275
Duhem, P., 94–5, 104, 275

EDGE, 261
Edgley, R., 114, 275
Edwards, R., 257, 275
Elliott, J., 64, 106, 131, 275, 278

Feyerabend, P., 93, 275
Fiore, Q. , 278
Fitzpatrick, P., 98, 275
Fortin, J., 45, 275
Foster, G., 94, 275
Fraser, K., 204, 281
Freeman, M. D. A., 45, 275
Freud, S., 82, 122, 168, 218
Fukuyama, F., 46, 107, 123, 156, 164, 229,
    275

Gasché, R., 193, 201, 207, 258, 267, 268,
    275
Gerson, L., 57, 275
Gibson, W., 164
Giddens, A., 156, 275
Glaser, B.G., 181, 264, 275
Godwin, W., 152, 275
Goffman, E., 257, 275
Gordimer, N., 79, 275
Gough, D., 114, 276
Gray, J. A. M. , 280
Gray, J. B., 216, 276

Hand, C. , 278, 282
Hansot, E. 197, 283
Harber, C., 45, 276
Hardimon, M. O., 28, 48, 51, 228, 276
Hardt, M., 67, 151
Hardwig, J., 102, 159, 160, 276
Hargreaves, D., 223, 276
Hayes, D., 177

Haynes, R. B. , 280
Hegel, G. W. F., 28, 48, 82, 96, 123, 164,
    175, 191, 199–200, 211
Hempel, C.G., 17, 276
Herman, E. S., 216, 276
Herrnstein, R. J., 161, 276
Hines, R. D., 94, 276
Hobbes, T., 23–5, 26, 28, 54, 80, 151, 161,
    172–3, 204, 226, 227, 276
Hobson, M., 268, 276
Hoffmann, J., 78
Holt, J., 45, 276
Horton, R., 104
Houlgate, S., 191, 276
House, E., 264, 276
Howes, N., 109, 276
Huntington, S. P., 70–1, 148, 276
Husserl, E., 23, 87, 211, 212, 276
Hwang, Dr., 160

Illich, I., 131, 276
Irigaray, 194
Iser, W. , 276
ISTAG report, 201–2, 205–6, 276

Jacobs, L. G., 107, 276
Jacotot, J., 133–4, 216–18
James, W., 147, 276
Jensen, A. R., 161, 277, 280
Johnson, C., 221, 224, 244, 277
Jullien, F., 46, 178, 277

Kant, I., 20, 120, 143, 147
Kassovitz, M., 76
Kavanaugh, L.J., 156, 165, 277
Kearney, R., 73, 277
Kierkegaard, S., 221
Kline, R., 177
Kojève, A., 164, 229, 277
Kripke, S., 60, 71, 79, 101, 127, 159, 190,
    212, 213, 277
Kristeva, J., 43, 84, 135, 136, 137, 141,
    217, 258, 269, 277
Kuhn, T., 4, 8, 17, 92, 93, 107, 119, 122,
    251, 277
Kusch, M., 44, 45, 102, 104–5, 116, 159,
    200, 218, 277

Labbett, B., 132, 135, 136, 208, 277
Lacan, J., 56, 58, 83, 96, 105, 107, 122,
    168, 189, 190, 218, 270, 277
Laclau, E., 69, 134, 135, 147, 149, 150,
    151, 152, 194, 226, 231, 269, 277

Laing, D., 143, 277
Lang, F., 164
Langman, M., 103
Latour, B., 219
Le Corbusier, 165, 277
Le Doeuff, M., 277
Lee, R. M., 257, 277
Lefebvre, H., 207–9, 277
Legrain, P., 77, 156, 277
Lemaire, A., 82–3, 277
Lev, B., 94, 278
Levinas, E., 166, 198, 278
Levy, S. , 278
Lewin, C., 64, 282
Lins, P., 153–4, 173, 204, 278
Lipovetsky, G., 173, 278
Llewelyn, J., 63, 74, 278
Locke, J., 19, 278
Lotman, Y. M., 124–5, 278
Lovejoy, A., 28, 64, 278
Luntley, M., 215, 278
Lydersen, K., 78
Lyotard, J. F., 62, 127, 128, 135, 141, 143, 192, 278

McAfee, N., 135, 278
McBride, R., 64, 278
MacDonald, B., 37, 111, 278
MacGregor, D., 55, 167, 227, 228, 278
Machiavelli, N., 57, 173, 175
McKee, A. , 278, 282
MacKenzie, D., 104, 278
McKinnon, M., 77
McLuhan, M. , 278
MacLure, M., 116, 278, 280
Mead, G. H., 212, 278
Meirelles F., 153
Merleau-Ponty, M., 194, 198, 247, 278
Mical, T., 89, 279
Mills, C. W. , 279
Milmo, C., 75
Mouffe, C., 1, 134, 135, 147, 179, 194, 279
Muhmann, G., 7, 105–6, 279
Murphy, R., 264, 279
Murray, C., 161–2, 166, 185, 279

Negri, A., 26, 67, 151, 279
Nordmann, C., 80, 81, 97, 99, 113, 121, 216, 219, 279
Normand, R., 121, 197, 279
Norris, N., 264, 279
Norton, A., 59, 279

Norval, A. , 279

Oakley, A., 115, 279
O'Connor, B., 18, 31, 279
Ohlson, J. A., 94
O'Neill, J., 106, 279

Patrick, J., 8, 279
Pearce, C., 250, 260, 279
Phillips, T., 126, 267, 280
Piper, H., 117, 280
Plato, 29–32, 54, 155, 185, 280
Popper, K., 92–3, 280

Quine, W. V. O., 95, 280

Rabaté, J.-M., 19, 107, 280
Ragin, C. C., 264, 280
Rancière, J., 11, 30, 41, 79, 80, 91, 92, 98, 102, 105, 107, 113, 125, 133–4, 155–7, 204, 207, 216–18, 229, 231, 251, 280
Readings, W., 126, 128–9, 141, 143, 192, 280
Reynolds, D., 110, 121, 137, 280
Richardson, W. S. , 280
Riffaterre, M., 125, 126, 280
Riha, R., 233, 280
Ritzer, G., 164, 280
Roberts, G., 75
Robertson, N., 175, 280
Rockhill, G., 98, 102
Rosenberg, W. M. C. , 280
Royle, N., 81, 97, 280
Rudé, G., 150, 280
Rushdie, S., 19, 176, 280
Rushton, J. P., 161, 280

Sackett, D. L., 108–9, 280
Sarkozy, N., 76
Sarland, C., 183
Saussure, F. de-, 57–63, 72, 87, 88, 141, 143, 150, 195, 220, 280
Sayer, A., 56, 264, 265, 281
Scargill. A., 68–9
Schatzman, M., 19, 122, 168, 281
Schelling, F., 120
Schmitt, C., 59, 74, 226, 281
Schofield, H., 77
Schostak, J.F., 5–6, 30, 31, 32, 36, 56, 64–5, 68, 73, 87, 89, 122, 125–6, 131, 133, 135, 136, 150, 168, 179–81, 189, 191, 200, 201, 203, 204, 206, 218, 241, 249, 252, 258, 267, 281, 282

Schostak, J.R., 5–6, 42, 96–7, 189, 191, 192, 200, 223, 244, 261, 263, 268, 278, 281, 282
Schreber, D. P., 19, 122, 168–9, 174, 179, 183, 282
Schutz, A., 211, 282
Shears, B., 241, 284
Silverman, K., 192, 282
Simons, H., 264, 282
Singer, P., 57, 282
Sjöholm, C., 136, 137, 282
Skinner, B. F., 19, 110, 164, 282
Sokal, A., 19, 107, 108, 282
Somekh, B., 64, 282
Sorel, G., 224–5, 282
Spinoza, B., 19, 21–2, 23, 26–8, 48, 54–5, 56, 79, 91, 151, 162, 167, 175–6, 179, 216, 219, 227, 228, 282
Spivak, G. C, 192, 270, 283
Stenhouse, L., 131, 134, 283
Strauss, L., 29, 59, 74, 173, 174, 226, 283
Strauss, A. L., 181, 264, 269, 275
Straw, J., 75
Stronach, I., 117–8, 280, 283
Sudbo, J., 103, 104
Szasz, T., 143, 283

Taylor, C., 195–6, 198, 199, 283
Taylor, F. W., 110, 283
Taylor, M.198, 283
Thatcher, M., 3, 46, 68, 231
Thévenot, L., 197, 283

Thomas, D. , 283
Thomas, W. I. , 283
Thrasher, F. M., 33, 53, 153, 231, 283
Torrance, H., 113, 116–117, 264, 279, 283
Toynbee, P., 176
Tragesser, R. S., 95, 283
Tschumi, B., 51–2, 189, 194, 283
Tyack, D., 197, 283
TYDE, 253–6, 266–7

Vasseleu, C., 147, 154, 194, 198, 283
Verdery, K., 167, 283
Virilio, P., 67, 200, 283

Wachowski brothers, 164
Walker, B., 249, 258, 282
Warhat, S., 195, 283
Waterfield, 29, 30,
Watts, M. , 278
Weber, M., 110, 121, 156, 163, 168, 283
Whiting, S., 165, 284
Widzer, M. E. , 284
Wigand, J., 106
Williams, B., 105, 284
Williams, R., 187, 284
Willis, P., 16, 284
Wilson, G., 75
Wolfreys, J., 192, 284
Woods, S., 241, 284
Wringe, C. A., 45, 284

Zizek, S., 55, 69, 228, 284

Subject index

abjection, 136
action, 1–3, 12, 14, 37, 111, 138, 152, 234, 241
  and debate, 178
  professional, 5
  radical, 230
  viral, 267
  and words, 178
action research, 12, 50, 64–6, 131–3, 134
actor, 56
address, 14, 34,
system of, 86–7, 165–6,
(addressing) others 243, 246
agency, 56, 135
  of incorporated voices, 268
  of leader, 23
  no presence of, 201
  protecting, 226
  suspending agency of Power, 216
aims, 181, 235, 247, 248–9
analysis, 12–13, 57, 59, 61, 64, 87, 90, 91, 122, 127, 214, 240
anti-psychiatry, 143–4
anti-totalitarian, 268, 270
architectures of the social, 179–80
arguments, 264–5,
chains of argumentation, 268
sustaining science, 102
articulation, 59, 62
  out of joint, 41
axis of evil, 57, 71, 74, 107, 148, 226

banlieue, 76, 77, 79, 97, 153, 164, 172, 207
  and banishment, 76, 98, 153, 164, 169, 171, 207
    banished ghosts, 174
  riots, 76, 153
baptism, 71, 127, 190, 213, 222

behaviourism, 19
binding, 194
body, 15, 35, 40–1, 99, 207
  control of, 168–9
  and habitus, 99
  knowledge, 17, 95, 103, 105, 144
  and high reliability organisations/ schooling, 110
  and police, 98
  political, 78
  and schooling, 163
  science, 17, 95
  state
border, 184, 186
  delicate, 186ff
boundary, 156–7, 191, 212, 221, 229–234
  contested, 194
  shiftiness, 191
bracketing, 211, 214

case study, 40, 239
  case of cases, 158
catachresis, 68, 71, 72–4, 78, 162
category
  of one, 184
  and forced definition, 184
  and names, 190
  universalising 189–190
causality, 147
chains, 25
of argumentation, 268
  of association, 212
  of Being, 28
  of belief, 25
  of command, 25, 174
  of equivalence, 150
  historical, 128, 213
  and logic, 120
  mechanical, 120

of reasoning, 24, 25, 44,
of signifiers, 222
of substitutions, 267
chiasmus, 74, 76, 78, 131
Children's Listening and Talking Project,
    179
chora, 136, 141
city, 165–6, 203–6,
    as community of communities, 204
    virtual 203, 204
    rational planning 165–6
City of God, 153–4, 162, 164, 172, 173,
    204, 207
Cochrane Collaboration, 108, 114, 155
community, 48–53, 56, 75, 80, 82, 105,
    125, 184
    and citizenship, 187–8
    community of communities, 204
    and debate, 178–9
    and freedom, 229
    globally distributed, 203
    intelligence, 202–3
    strategic, 203–6
    of voices, 137
communitarianism, 102
concepts, 120, 141
    conceptual as texture, 144–151
    universalising, 150
conflict, 98, 102, 105, 154, 155, 183, 219,
    229
contested spaces, 193, 197
control, 166
creationism, 20
creativity, 124
critique, 234, 251

data, 10, 25, 68, 91–112, 131, 212, 235,
    239, 244, 264
    and category, 125
    and contestation, 103, 264
    deprived of givenness, 211
    as events of transposition, 123–131,
    and fabulous, 131
    fraudulent, 160–1
    and naming, 127
    and normal science, 122
    as phrasing, 130
    as tension between real, imaginary and
        symbolic, 131
    as transpositional event, 125, 130
    and voice of witness, 212
debate, 178, 184
    as action on the adge, 178

democratic solution to abuse of power,
    178
    minimal condition for community,
    178
decision, 221
    madness of, 135
deconstruction, 10, 12, 73, 128–9, 174,
    190, 240, 253
    and resistance, 129
definition, 24, 184–5
    and condensing differences, 195
    disruption of, 207
    forced, 184–5, 190, 193
    illegitimate contents, 186
    legitimised, 186
democracy, 47–8, 91, 155, 157, 162, 176,
    183, 187–8, 206, 219, 269
    custodial, 162, 166
    debate, 178.
    and heterogeneity, 208
    liberal, 229
    open, 47
    hatred of, 91
    radical, 1, 134–5, 229, 244
    and right of association, 187
    as unfinished revolution, 179
democratic
    instrument, 174
    mechanisms, 241
    negotiation, 180
    procedures, 181
de-schooling, 131
description, 12, 37, 64
design, 9, 22, 40, 51, 95–6, 111, 136, 158,
    179ff, 211ff, 224
    for change, 233
    designing difference into projects,
    136
    designing inclusivity, 228, 232
    designing the radical, 36–8, 228, 241
    of good society, 164
    of space, 51–2
de-sign, 9, 253
designator,
    rigid, 60
diachronic, 60–1, 88, 253
    difference, 252
dialectic, 96, 191–2
    master-slave, 199–200
    of metonymy and metaphor, 191
dialogue, 90, 124, 266, 268, 271
    as anti-totalitarian infrastructure, 268
    différance, 223, 224

difference, 72, 75, 124, 135, 224, 244, 247,
    252, 258, 267
    calling a, 184
    openness to, 96
    system of, 220
disagreement, 18, 144, 183
disappointment, 173, 174, 175
discourse, 141
    of logocentrism, 128–9
    of negotiation, 180–3
dis-identification, 55, 188
dissemination, 241, 249, 263
domination, 81
doubt, 211
doxa, 105

economy (Derridean), 223–4
écriture, 189, 191–3, 224, 244, 270
edge, 175, 194, 219, 231, 268
edgework, 73
education, 13, 35, 121–23, 129, 132,
    134–5, 135, 155, 167, 203, 208,
    241
    and behaviourism, 19
    and Enlightenment reason, 19
    and imaginary order, 30
    progressive, 121
    research in, 106–7, 114–118
    v. schooling, 13, 30, 134 (see also High
        Reliability Schooling)
    and (Hegelian) slave, 199
    teacher, 110
    as training, 41
emancipation, 138
emancipatory critique, 219
empowerment, 219
end of history, 123, 164, 166
enemy within, 231
Enlightenment, 19, 41, 59, 107
entre-deux, 195–200
entre-nous, 194–200
epistemology, 44
EPPI Centre, 114–18, 155
ethics
    and edge, 175
    ethical life, 51, 151
    knowledge and trust, 159
    protocols, 111–2, 237–8
ethnography, 63–4, 157, 239
    creative, 138
equality, 9, 24, 47, 71, 91, 102, 109, 110,
    150, 157, 209, 216–19
    as universalising strategy, 219

evaluation, 37, 66, 137–8, 157–8, 241, 265
    democratic, 111
    as emancipatory strategy, 138
    radical 157–8
event 79, 113
    baptism of, 79, 212
    fabulous, 118–123, 125, 127, 134, 195
        and data, 131
        and reading, 127
    revolutionary, 102, 114
evidence, 68, 104, 144, 160
    based medicine, 108–9
    machine, 121
evil, 46, 59, 74, 136, 178
    axis of, 57
and negativity, 46
exception, 126, 131, 137, 153, 188, 269,
    271
existence, 142–3
    as 'standing out', 142
expertise, 43–5, 105, 173, 214–15
    expert, 116, 119, 120, 129, 173, 213,
        218, 219, 222
    gone wrong, 45–6
    and repetition, 129–30

fabric(ation), 154
facts, 120, 124
falsifiability, 93–4
fear, 163ff
    fear for, 166
    fear of, 166
figural, 141–2, 143, 144
figure, 62, 128, 220
flesh, 195–6, 207, 212
forbidden, 166
    area, 196
    discourse, 169, 171
    and metonymic associations, 196
    religious symbols, 197
force, 220
freedom, 9, 11, 35, 41, 51, 107, 120,
    162–3, 219
    and community, 229
    of expression, 175–6, 208
        good state, 175
        foundation of knowledge, 175
        as performative, 178
        Statement of Academic Freedom,
            176–7
friend-enemy, 59, 74, 98, 107, 178, 226–7

game, 233–4

generalisation, 209, 210, 239
gift, 258–9, 260
global and local, 200ff
   global village, 204
groups
   mirror, 171–2
   professional, 173
God's eye view 17–25, 37, 91, 115, 150,
   182, 238
Gulf War, 69–70

habitus, 99
hate, 91, 176, 187
   La Haine, 76
   of democracy, 91
hegemony, 20, 194, 226
   hegemonic appropriation, 235
   hegemonic practices, 147, 150
   lines of fracture, 251
heterogeneity, 98, 127, 131, 136, 141, 219
   and limits, 131
   and methodology, 190–1
high reliability
   organisations, 110
   schooling (HRS), 110, 121, 122, 134,
      137, 155
home, being at, 48, 80–2, 246, 269
homogeneity, 103, 136, 226
hope, 175
Humanities Curriculum Project (HCP),
   131, 134
humanity, 97, 148–9, 175
hybridity, 80
hypogram, 125

identity, 56, 149, 184ff, 19, 232, 233
   identities, 11
      multiple, 203, 205
   provocative, 184ff
   self forced/self elected, 188
imaginary, 47, 54, 62, 87, 99, 137
imagination, 174
immigrants, 77–8, 79, 80, 97, 156–7,
   226
in-between, 142, 194–200
inclusion,
   always one more, 232
inclusivity,
   principle of, 235
indecidable, 191
indeterminacy, 194
individuality, 48, 82
infinity, 221

infrastructure, 267–8
   anti-totalitarian, 268
   minimal thing, 193, 201
inscription, 191, 212, 221, 222–3, 233–4
intelligence communities, 202–3
intelligent agent, 203
intentionality, 87, 212, 231
   intentional systems, 43, 87, 143
   intentional networks, 87, 88–90, 171–2,
      179, 239
      and mirror groups, 171–2
Internet Protocol (IP), 165–6, 202
interpellation, 215–16
intertextuality, 42–3,
   intertext, 76
interweaving, 154
invisible, 10, 11, 30, 74, 92, 98, 107, 169
IQ, 160–1, 185

jouissance, 136
judgement, 120, 145
   and politics, 129

Kent State University, 68
knotting, 84–7
knowledge, 44, 47, 93, 120, 125, 144,
   159ff,, 218, 249
   bodies of, 103, 105
   and communitarianism, 102
   as community endeavour, 160, 200
   and conjectures, 93–4
   and democratisation 118
   and freedom of expression, 175
   and hysteric, 218
   power, 23
   reason,
   religious 21, 26,
   secondary, 200
   as system of concepts, 141
   and systematic review, 116–7
   and texts, 125
   and witnessing act, 212

labyrinth, 17–25, 37, 153, 182, 189, 194,
   238
language, 57–63, 72
   and codes, 124–5
   as empty, 142
   and representation, 142
langue, 59, 62
law, 68, 69, 98, 153
Leviathan, 25, 26, 35, 37, 41, 47, 55, 80,
   204

liminal, 11, 152
  domains, 231
  spaces, 196, 231, 244
logic, 119
  of reconfigurability, 226
logocentricism, 129

management,
  by objectives, 110
  scientific, 110
master, 4, 17, 18, 19, 21, 28, 41, 54, 55,
    91, 96, 105, 154
  ignorant, 134
  -slave, 96, 199
  view, 92
Matrix trilology, 164, 203
meaning, 126–8, 179, 247
metaphor, 190–1, 195, 220
  metaphorical condensation, 194
  as strategy, 196
method
  of doubt, 44
  of suspension
methodology, 54, 151,
  involving metaphor and metonymy,
    190–1
  radical, 13, 69, 219, 234–242
metonymy, 83, 189, 190–1, 195–8, 219
  metonymic associations, 196
  metonymic play, 235
mimetic, 125, 129
minimal thing, 193, 201, 207, 212, 258
mirror groups, 171–2
mise-en-scène, 101
modernism,
  modernist architecture, 165
modernity, 175, 189
multitude, 10, 67–8, 78–9, 80–1, 91, 181,
    204, 216, 219, 227–8, 232, 270
  of spaces, 208
myth, 18, 47, 98, 217

name, 4, 15, 19, 23–5, 35, 41, 48–51, 53,
    56, 74, 78–9, 85–7
  and categories, 190
  of the father, 105
  and politics, 127
  rigid designator, 60, 65
  unifying, 71
naming, 127, 140, 213, 245, 72
  as baptism, 71, 127, 190, 213, 222
  and historical chains, 128, 159
  un-naming, 101

narrative, 84, 189
natural, 174
  naturalisation, 156, 160, 164
  naturalistic attitude, 214
Necromancer, 164
networks, 160, 267
  intentional,
    as knowing subject, 239
noble lie, 30–1, 35, 155, 185, 271
normal, 80–1, 136, 153, 211, 234, 251
noumena, 143

objectives, 248–9
objectivity, 96, 103, 136, 239
offence, 186–7
oratory, 208
order, 41, 47, 69, 80, 92, 147, 151–4, 252
  imaginary, 30
  and hegemonic practices, 147
  New World Order, 156
  police, 30
  rational, 164
  totalitarian, 32,
Orgreave, battle of, 68
otherness, 9, 134, 135, 137, 199, 247, 269
  of the real, 58
  of the world, 166

paradigm, 4, 92
  wars, 117
paranoid,
  paranoia, 140, 143, 168, 174
  curriculum, 122
  framework, 83–4, 87
parergon, 78, 268
particular, 81, 96, 101, 188
pedagogy, 174, 241
  myth of, 217
people, 55, 167
  classes of, 185
  governance by, 228
  People, 59
  purity, 185
  the people, 194
  as a unity, 193
performance indicators, 110
performativity, 128–9, 178
perspective, 91, 165
phenomena, 143
phenomenology, 87, 211–12
philosopher kings, 164
play, 78, 158, 220, 253, 259
  and boundaries, 229ff

creative, 233–4
game, 233–4
of on-line/off-line, 201
of revealed/hidden, 171, 201, 258, 263
strategic, 233
between visible and invisible, 230
plurality, 125, 136
and unity, 124, 125
poetic, 125, 137
of withness, 135
police, 98, 207, 229–231, 251
police order, 102, 204
politics,
and appetites, 173
and edge, 175
of enchaining, 127
incompletability of, 135
and marking distinctions, 127–8
and naming, 127
as texture, 144–151
two meanings, 10
le politique and *la politique*, 113
as weaving, 147
poor, 97, 154, 155—7,
power, 1–2, 21–3, 54–5, 83, 105, 139 ff,
165, 189, 238
and appetites, 172
as co-extensive with right, 178
and contested spaces, 193
and knowledge, 23
and multitude, 151
as *potentia* or power, 9, 11, 55, 79, 83,
151, 158, 193, 206, 214, 227
as *potestas* or Power, 9, 11, 55, 151,
158, 162, 181, 214, 227
and rights, 21–2
postmodernism,
postmodernists, 107–8
post-modernity, 173
poverty,
and underclass, 161–2
prediction, 166
prehension, 95–6, 125
pre-modern, 47
problem structure, 35–6,
critical, 157–8
proof, 9, 104
property, 96
protest, 75–9
provocation, 11, 188, 207, 211
provocative
identities, 11, 188ff
act, 211, 243

and research, 235
and voice, 212,
public, 82, 91, 143
gaze, 82
space, 102, 112
puritan work ethic, 163
purity, 185

race
and IQ, 161
hate, 176, 187
Racial and Religious Hatred Act 2006,
176
radical (see also methodology)
being radical, 14, 96
decontextualisation, 68, 71
democracy, 1, 135
as disturbance of the natural, 156
edge, 175
empiricism, 147
figures of, 240
game, 11, 48, 211ff
as rearrangement of terms of debate,
178
research, 1, 12–13, 234
subjectivity, 18
RAE (Research Assessment Exercise),
117
rap songs,
Disiz la Peste, 79
Fonky Family, 77
NTM, 77
RCTs, 108–9, 119
reading, 126–7
real, 43, 44, 125–7, 139 ff, 179, 191
architectures of, 204
and logic, 119
management of, 174
resistance of, 174
as texture, 144–151
reality, 173
heterogeneous, 190
mediators of, 174
as resistance, 175
Reason, 19, 119, 121
bureaucratic, 121
iron cage of, 121, 156, 163, 165, 166,
168
and logic, 119
rational planning of cities, 165–
rule of , 29, 30
recognition, 91, 92, 130
reconfiguration, 240, 245, 251

refutation, 94–5
reliability, 209, 239
    of sources, 159ff,
repetition, 128, 131, 222, 223, 247
    and expertise, 129–30
replication, 198
    re-pli-cation, 198, 207
representation, 126, 129, 191, 240
    and chora, 136
    and visible/invisible, 196–7
Republic, 164, 204
research,
    action, 37,
    case, 40
    design, 9, 22
    ethnography, 37,
    foci of aims, 235
    normal, 3–6, 17–25, 35, 81, 117,
        118
    phases 235–242
    radical, 6–9, 32, 34–6, (see also
        methodology)
        moments 12–13
    sensitive, 257
resistance, 129, 141, 175
revolution, 10, 114, 227–228
rhetoric, 189,
    first figure of, 247
rhythmanalysis, 207
rich, 154, 155–7, 172
rights, 26–9, 47, 139 ff, 209, 233
riots, 76–8
risk, 115, 134, 137
    risking otherness, 135
    risk society, 135

science, 4–6,
    mimetic, 125
    as 'normal', 4, 119, 137, 271
    poetic, 125
    positivistic, 17
    as texts, 125
schizophrenic, 82
    flux, 68
schooling, 131, 134. 163
    de-schooling, 131
security,
seeing, 92, 194
self, 56
September 11, 107
sign, 57, 222
signification, 136
signified, 57–63, 82, 84, 86, 167, 195

signifier, 57–63, 71, 72, 82, 86, 143, 167,
    195, 221, 223, 259
    as cut, 196
    empty, 69, 149, 150, 174, 231
    and schizophrenic, 82–4
singular, 81, 96, 101, 128, 129, 188, 198,
    212,
    singularity, 141, 190, 218, 271
    and universal, 212
60 Minutes, CBS TV programme, 106
    tobacco documentary, 106
social, 47
    engineering, 110
    and the real, 47
society, 46–7
    the good, 29, 152, 164
    democratic, 167 (see also democracy)
    oligarchic, 167
    totalitarian, 167
sovereignty, 22, 25, 28, 55, 167, 224ff
standardisation, 184
    as forced definition, 184
state, 53–5
stealth architecture, 65–6, 89, 164
stealth strategy, 162
structure, 220
    structurality of, 268
structuralism, 115, 220–1
struggle, 152
subject, 84–7, 92, 191, 233–4
    knowing, 239
    and organisation of society, 151
    and organisation of world, 191
    split, 193
subjectification, 92
subjectivisation, 102
sujet-en-procès, 218
supplement, 268
surveillance, 166
symbolic interactionism, 212
symploke, 147
synchronic, 61, 88, 150, 253
    order, 252
systematic reviews, 114–118

telling space, 223
terrorism, 75, 107
text, 62, 124
    and codes, 124
    general, 191–2
    minimal textual unit, 258–9
texture, 147, 194, 198
    weaving and politics, 147

theory, 93, 127
  creation of, 131
  of everything, 123
  explanatory, 125
  and falsifiability, 93
  and value choices, 114
threshold, 78–80, 82, 231
Tiananmen Square, 70
totalising, 192
totalitarian, 220
totality, 228, 229
touch, 194
trace, 267
transcendental, 221, 222
  quasi-, 193, 268
transgression, 166, 186, 189, 221
triangulation, 172, 173, 239
true, 43, 44, 149
truth, 91, 92, 95, 119, 149, 160, 179,
    224–5, 239, 243, 269
  and communitarianism, 103
  contested, 231
  and democracy, 118
  in the form of fiction, 270–1
  and life, 119
  machine, 121
trust, 44, 105, 107, 111, 114, 116, 159–60,
    161, 212, 218, 257

uncanny, 81, 97
underclass, 161–2, 164, 172, 185, 226
unity, 125, 135
  and plurality, 124, 125
universal, 150, 190, 198, 224
  case, 16
  categories, 15, 16, 97
    universalising, 189, 194, 219
  claims to universality, 91, 231, 235
  and myth, 271
  and particular, 233

and politics, 102
and singular, 212

validity, 62, 64, 86, 163, 166, 179, 209,
    210, 239
  of witnessing, 212
verification, 8, 160
violence, 7, 34, 76, 79, 97, 107,
    169–71, 176, 221, 222, 223, 231,
    244, 251
  and catechresis, 73
  and norms, 73
visible, 11, 33, 107, 111, 113, 118, 164,
    196
  field of, 102, 118, 125
  and police structure, 230
voice, 212
  and provocation, 212, 213
voicing, 208

Walden II, 164
weaving
  and dialogue, 268
  interweaving 154
  and politics, 147, 206
witness, 212, 238, 257, 262
  and naming, 159
World Trade Centre, 70, 107
write/rite/right, 246
writer's intention, 244
writing, 221–22
  arche-, 268
  as art of capturing, 244
  infrastructure for, 268
  and origins, 245
  as provocative act, 243
  'writing down system', 168, 183
wrongs, 48, 102, 159ff, 231, 250

zero tolerance, 162